BURT FRANKLIN: BIBLIOGRAPHY & REFERENCE SERIES 32

A

BIOGRAPHICAL CHRONICLE

OF THE

ENGLISH DRAMA

T.

A

BIOGRAPHICAL CHRONICLE

OF THE

ENGLISH DRAMA

1559-1642

BY

FREDERICK GARD FLEAY

IN TWO VOLUMES

VOLUME II.

BURT FRANKLIN
New York, N. Y.

Published by LENOX HILL Pub. & Dist. Co. (Burt Franklin)
235 East 44th St., New York, N.Y. 10017
Reprinted: 1973
Printed in the U.S.A.

Burt Franklin: Bibliography and Reference Series 32

**The Library of Congress cataloged the original printing of this title
as follows.**

Fleay, Frederick Gard, 1831-1909.
A biographical chronicle of the English drama, 1559-1642. New
York, B. Franklin 1969.

2 v. 24 cm. (Burt Franklin bibliography and reference series no. 32)
Reprint of the 1891 London ed.
CONTENTS.—v. 1. Excursus on the Mirror for magistrates. Biographies
of the playwrights: 1557-1642. Jonson (continued)—Zouch. Plays by anonymous authors. Masks by anonymous authors. University plays in English.
University plays in Latin. Translations. Addenda. Additions on Middleton
from Mr. A.H. Bullen.
1. English drama—Early modern and Elizabethan—History and criticism.
I. Title.

PR651.F5 1969   822'.3'09   75-6464
ISBN 0-8337-1151-2

A BIOGRAPHICAL CHRONICLE

OF

THE ENGLISH DRAMA.

CONTENTS OF VOL. II.

—⊷—

A BIOGRAPHICAL CHRONICLE

OF

THE ENGLISH DRAMA.

1559–1642.

——⋈——

THE BIOGRAPHIES OF THE PLAYWRIGHTS.

———

JONSON, BENJAMIN—(*continued*).

MASKS AND ENTERTAINMENTS.

28. 1603, June, 25, 27. *Entertainment of the Queen and Prince at Althorpe, at the Lord Spencer's* [Sir Robert Spencer's, created Baron July 21], *as they came first into the Kingdom.* Called *The Satyr* by Gifford; but it is much better not to introduce new names for these performances. I have found such in several instances in the present volume very misleading. A two days' show; in that of the 27th Nobody is a character. Compare *Nobody and Somebody.* Published S. R. 1604, Mar. 19.

29. 1604, Mar. 15. *Entertainment (Part of the) to King James in London in passing to his Coronation:* arches i., v. Dekker (*q.v.*) wrote arches ii., iii., iv. Note the four-headed Janus and the allusion to the truchman of the puppets. Published with the preceding and *the Panegyre* on opening Parliament, Mar. 19.

30. 1604, May 1. *Entertainment of the King and Queen at Highgate, at Sir William Cornwallis'*. Called by Gifford *The Penates*. The chief character, Maia, "the delicate May," was probably performed by Dorothy Cornwallis, who married Archibald Earl of Argyle. This lady is said to have borne a child to Nat. Field. See *Athenæum* 1882, Jan 21. She was "his mistress, the Lady May," on whom the lines quoted in Collier's *Actors*, p. 217, were written. Why she is called the Lady May will now be manifest. Possibly Field played Mercury in this entertainment.

30.* 1605, Jan 6. *Blackness*, the first of Queen Anne's masks, was presented at Whitehall. Published 1608, April 21, S. R., as "invented by Ben Jonson." The Duke of Holstein, the Queen's brother, was present. It cost £3000. The presentation copy to the Queen, with Jonson's autograph Latin inscription, is in the British Museum. The names of the personators are printed at the end. "The bodily part was Master Ynigo Jones, his design and act."

31. 1606, Jan. 5, 6. *Hymenæi*: "masks and barriers on the eleventh and twelfth nights from Christmas at Court on the marriage between Robert Devereux, Earl of Essex, and Frances Howard, second daughter of the Earl of Suffolk." Published 1606 with a full title. Jonson suppressed the names in the 1616 Folio. This mask cost the Court £400. The names of the maskers are given. The Epithalamion is from Catullus. In the Quarto the design and habits are attributed to Inigo Jones, the music to Ferrabosco, and the dances to Thomas Giles. This notice was suppressed in the 1616 Folio. The women maskers' names not having been given in my *History of the Stage*, p. 184, I here append them:—1. Countess of Montgomery; 2. Lady Knolles; 3. Mrs. A. Sackvile; 4. Lady Berkely;

5. Lady Dorothy Hastings; 6. Lady Blanche Somerset; 7. Countess of Bedford; 8. Countess of Rutland. According to Pory's letter to Cotton (Collier, *Annals* i., 365, first edition), "Before the sacrifice could be performed Ben Jonson burned the globe of earth standing behind the altar." Jonson acted in the mask, then; but what part did he take? I suppose he must have been Hymen. In the *Barriers* (Jan. 6) there is more from Catullus. The Quarto gives the names of the combatants, which concern us here only because they, as well as those of the maskers, were suppressed in the 1616 Folio.

32. 1606, July 24. *The Entertainment at Theobalds* (Robert Cecil, Earl of Salisbury's) *of the Kings of Great Britain and Denmark.* Partly in Latin.

33. 1607, May 22. *Entertainment at Theobalds to the King and Queen,* "when the Earl delivered the house to the Queen (in exchange for the Manor of Hatfield), the Prince of Joinville, brother to the Duke of Guise, being present."

34. 1607, July 16, Thursday. At the entertainment of the King at Merchant Taylors' Hall, a speech of eighteen verses (not extant) by Jonson was pronounced, and pleased His Majesty. See Nichols, ii. 137, and Stow, p. 890*.

35. 1608, Jan. 10, Sunday after Twelfth Night. *Beauty,* the Queen's second mask, was presented at White-hall. Published with *Blackness,* S. R. 1608, July 21. According to Gifford and his faithful follower, F. Cunning-ham, this was not presented till 1609. I shall not further encumber my pages with the intolerably careless blunders in the dates assigned to the masks by these editors. I think the reader will trust me without that, and be spared much tedium. T. Giles made the dances; Portington the King's master-carpenter, (not I. Jones), the scene. A list of the lady personators is given. The other rites at Twelfth-

tide 1606, 1607 alluded to were the marriages of Earl Essex and Lord Hay.

36. 1608, Feb. 9. *The mask at the marriage of John Lord Ramsay, Viscount Haddington, with Lady Elizabeth Radcliffe, daughter to Robert Earl of Sussex* (called by Gifford *The Hue and Cry after Cupid*), was presented at Court. Published 1608. The dances were by T. Giles and Jerome Herne, who performed the Cyclopes; the tunes were Ferrabosco's; the device of the scene and trophies Master Inigo Jones'. In it the first of Jonson's Anti- or Antic-masks, that of Sports, is introduced. The description of Love's chariot drawn by swans and doves is noteworthy as explaining allusions in other masks and poems: in this mask Venus, not Cupid, rode in it. A list of the men maskers is given; the women were probably twelve of the sixteen who presented *Beauty*.

37. 1609, Feb. 2. *Queens celebrated from the House of Fame* was presented by the Queen at Whitehall. Published S. R. Feb. 12, with Dedication to Prince Henry. This was the Queen's third mask. Jonson was "careful to decline" (*i.e.*, afraid of declining) from "his own steps . . . since the last year he had an anti-mask of boys," and as the Queen wished for another, introduced an anti-mask of witches. To Gifford's monstrous perversion of these words to his own controversial purpose the reader may, if he cares to, refer; enough here to say that Jonson is speaking of anti-masks in general, not of any previous use of witches by himself or others. Jones devised the attire and the "architecture of the whole scene," John Allen sang, and Ferrabosco made the tunes. In a note Jonson refers to wax pictures of the late Queen found in a dunghill near Islington; he remembers the rumour of it, being then very young, and refers to Bodinus for a relation of the story by

a French ambassador. This must have afforded the plot to *The Witch of Islington*, a play written before 1592, and revived at the Rose 1597, June 14. A list of the Queen-actors is given.

38. 1610, Jan. 6. The speeches at Prince Henry's *Barriers* were delivered (Nichols, ii. 269). All the Royal Family were present. Jonson's fondness for anagrams, which he abuses when made by other men, shows in the "claims Arthur's seat" here, as in the "Unie" of the *Hymenæi*. A list of the Tilters is given. The mere fact that Henry was "in his sixteenth year" should have spared us the farrago of nonsense written by Gifford and F. Cunningham on the date of these *Barriers*. Henry was sixteen on 19th Feb. 1610.

39. 1611, Jan. 1. *Oberon the Fairy Prince*, Prince Henry's mask, was presented at Whitehall (*Stow*, p. 999). This was not published in quarto; Jonson was evidently preparing his Folio edition. The lady actors were the same as those in *Tethys' Festival* (see my *History of the Stage*, p. 184), except that Anne L. Winter was replaced by Mary L. Wintoun. In the list there given "Anne Rivet," taken from Nichols, ii. 174, ought to read "Katherine Somerset" (*ibid.*, ii. 349). This mask has a children's dance of "lesser fays" round the infant duke Charles, and refers to the praise of Prince Henry in the Althorpe entertainment 1603. The anti-mask is of Satyrs. I find no mention of Jones or other "architect" in connexion with this mask. No list of men actors is given, but they consisted of two Earls, three Barons, five Knights, two Esquires (Nichols, ii. 375).

40. 1611. *Love freed from Ignorance and Folly*, "a mask of her majesty's," was no doubt one of the two which she intended to give in the 1610—11 festivities, and which

would cost her only £600. Sir John More to Sir Ralph
Winwood, 1600, Dec. 15 (Nichols, ii. 372). The other
was probably not by Jonson. On 1611, Nov. 20, the
Queen was "practising for a new mask," which had perhaps been put off from Shrovetide; but this mask of
Jonson's was, I think, produced in January, for all indications point to his ceasing to supervise the Folio at p.
989, earlier than November; and the "new world in the
moon," his first allusion to Galileo's 1610 discoveries, must,
I think, have come on the heels of his hearing of them.
There is no mention of Inigo Jones or other carpenter, and
this was Jonson's last mask for Queen Anne. The anti-
mask was of She Fools.

No mask is known at Court for 1611–12 Christmas, and
Jonson had no share in those for the Princess Elizabeth's
marriage, 1613 Feb., in which Inigo Jones took a prominent part.

41. 1613, Dec. 27. *A challenge at Tilt at a Marriage*
was pronounced the day after the wedding of Carr Earl
of Somerset and Lady Frances Howard, divorced from the
Earl of Essex.

42. 1613, Dec. 29. *The Irish mask*, by Gentlemen the
King's servants (the Prince's gentlemen, *Stow*, p. 1005),
was performed. "Thy man Robin" (Robert Carr) and
"thy man Thomas of Suffolk his daughter" (Frances
Howard) are mentioned; yet Gifford and F. Cunningham
could not see the occasion of the mask. It was a "medley
mask" of " 5 English and 5 Scotch, called the high dancers,
among whom Serjeant Boyd, one Abercrombie, and Auch-
mouty, that was at Padua and Venice, are esteemed the
most principal and lofty." They were so well liked that
they were "appointed to perform it again on Monday,"
1611, Jan. 3 [not Jan. 10, as Nichols, ii. 718, 733, sup-

poses : *Stow* (Howes) expressly says " the Monday following," and the Christmas festivities ended on Jan. 6 ; for
" are appointed " in Chamberlain's letter of Jan. 5 read
" were appointed "] ; yet this " mimical imitation of the
Irish " displeased many, who thought its ridicule might
exasperate that nation.

43. 1614, Jan. 4. The Mayor entertained the married
pair with the nobility at Merchant Taylors' Hall with " a
play and a mask " (*Birch. MSS.* 4173). They had only four
days' warning, so the play was, of course, an old one. On
Jan. 18 (*City Records*) Middleton was paid for " disburse-
ments and pains taken by him and others " in " the last
Mask of Cupids and other shows lately made at the afore-
said Hall by the said Mr. Middleton." Howes (*Stow*) says
there were two masks and a play. All this is hard to re-
concile. I think Howes' " two several masks " mean simply
anti-mask and mask ; that Middleton, who this year was the
pageant poet and acting " city chronologer " (cf. *Triumphs
of Truth*), was, of course, the principal arranger and pay-
master ; that the play was one of his abridged for the purpose, and that " others " means Jonson, the mask being
Love Restored. Plutus (acted by a play-boy) says, " I am
neither player nor masker ; " and " the next shows " in the
last song seem, from the context, to refer to the mask of
Flowers forthcoming on Jan. 6. But however this may be,
this mask was not presented then for the first time, but
was written for a Court performance, and performed at
Whitehall (note the mention of the Terrace) by " Gentlemen the King's servants " (*i.e.*, I suppose, by the Prince's
servants, as in the case of *The Irish mask*). But when ?
Not in 1610–11, for the only Prince's mask in that year
is accounted for, and this is certainly not a Queen's mask ;
and Coryat is mentioned, whose *Crudities* did not appear

till 1611, June 7, S. R.   Had it been in 1613–14, at
Carr's marriage, or in 1612–13, at Lady Elizabeth's, it
would surely have been mentioned in the detailed notices,
of which there are several.   Again, had it been before
Prince Henry's death it would have been called a mask
of Prince Henry's.   The inscription, "by Gentlemen the
King's servants," indicates a Prince Charles' mask.   I
think that Plutus is introduced because Plutus was a
principal character in Chapman's 1613 mask, and that
"his brother, anti-Cupid," implies anteriority to the An-
teros, a preferable name, so fully explained in *The Tilt*
1614, Jan. 1.   On the whole, I think it may have been
written for Court performance at Lady Elizabeth's marriage,
or, more likely, just after the tilting 1614, Jan. 1, but that
it was put off and acted on some later occasion at Court;
and was also performed with necessary alterations at Merchant Taylors' Hall.   But I acknowledge greater doubt
than for any other mask.   Compare for a slightly different
hypothesis my *History of the Stage*, p. 182.   In this mask
(which in all the latter part bears evident marks of abridg-
ment) Cupid enters in his chariot without description; but
in the Tilt the "swans and doves borrowed of his mother"
are mentioned.   I think Lady Purbeck was the Cupid, her
mother having been the Venus of 1608, and that Lady
Hatton was one of the Graces who danced.   But Jonson
has purposely obscured everything in this mask   He did
not even mention Carr's marriage to Drummond when
speaking of his mask for the Earl of Essex; but that one
had been published with Essex' name on the title; the occasion of this one was always kept concealed.   He has even
omitted to give the dances (whether with ladies, &c., or
not).   It may, therefore, be worth while to mention that
in a full mask there were usually five dances: 1. The

Entry; 2. The Main; 3. With the Ladies; 4. The Revels (Galliards and Corantos); 5. The going out. 1, 5 are omitted in this mask, and there is no anti-mask. Robin Goodfellow may have been acted by Jonson; cf. the allusion to "invention and translation." The very unusual number of 10 maskers (8, 12, 16 were nearly always introduced) agrees with that of the knights in the Tilt. The "fighting bear of last year" and the ceasing of "the motions" will, when ascertained, clear up all difficulties; but the bear was certainly at Court, not the 1609 one baited at the Tower. The "Christmas cutpurse," who took a purse at Court in Christmas, cf. *Bartholomew Fair*, iii. 1 (1614, Oct. 31), probably performed this feat 1612–13.

44. [1615, Jan. 6.] *Mercury vindicated from the Alchemists* was presented at Court by Gentlemen the King's servants. A Prince Charles' mask, I suppose. There are two anti-masks—1. Alchemists; 2. Imperfect creatures. The song before the main dance is evidently imperfect, not being in stanzas, like the others. The "secretary to the stars" is evidently S. Forman; the "master of the duel," with his "business," I have not recognised. The conjectural date (Nichols') depends on the position of the mask in the 1616 Folio. "Excellent dancing, English and Scots," says Chamberlain of the 1615 mask. It was repeated Jan. 8 (Nichols, iii. 38).

45. 1616, Jan. 1. *The Golden Age restored*, 1615[–6; not of Jonson's but the printer's dating], by the Lords and Gentlemen the King's servants. A King's mask, I presume. Repeated Jan. 6. The Anti-mask of 12 Evils; 10 would seem to be Prince Charles' number.

46. 1616, Dec. 25. *Christmas his Mask*, at Court 1616. A show by the King's players, not a mask proper. See the allusions to Burbadge, Hemings, the play-boy, &c.

47. 1617, Jan. 6, 19. A mask was presented Jan. 6, in which Buckingham and Montgomery danced with the Queen, and at which Pocahontas was present. It was repeated Jan. 19. Nichols says this was the mask of *Christmas*, but does not say whether the Queen took the part of Minced Pie or Wassail. The true mask was *The Vision of Delight*, presented before King James (by the Queen, I suppose) Christmas 1617; *i.e.*, 1616–7, Jonson's usual notation. *Stylo recitativo* [Query Lanier. See next mask]. Two anti-masks: 1. Burretines and Pantaloons; 2. Phantasms.

48. 1617, Feb. 22. *Lovers made men* [Jonson's title, from the Quarto; the mask of *Lethe* is only Gifford's title], at Lord Hay's, to entertain Baron de Tour, the French Ambassador. "The whole mask was sung after the Italian manner, *stylo recitativo*, by Master Nicholas Lanier, who ordered and made both the scene and the music." A line near the end is from *The Vigil of Venus*.

49. 1618, Jan. 6. "On Twelfth Night was the Prince's mask" (Chamberlain, *apud* Nichols, iii. 457), "wherein the Prince was a principal actor, and that his first exercise in that kind" (*Finetti Philoxenis*, p, 48); Nichols, iii. 456, "dull." [Isabel] Edmonds [Lord De la Ware's wife], the comptroller's daughter, bore away the bell for delicate dancing. "On Shrove Tuesday [Feb. 17] the Prince's mask was represented again with some few alterations and additions, but little bettered" (Chamberlain, *apud* Nichols, iii. 468).

Pleasure Reconciled to Virtue was a Prince's mask, performed a second time with alterations and additions. *For the Honor of Wales*, in which the Prince of Wales performed "on Twelfth Night, the first time he ever play dance," and is, of course, the mask of 1618, though misdated 1619 (when Jonson was in Scotland, and wrote no mask) by all

the editors.   The anti-masks were, 1. Bottles ; 2. Pigmies ;
but these were exchanged for, 1. Men ; 2. Goats, when Atlas
on Feb. 17 became Craig Eriri ; only the mask proper being
the same in the two presentations.   For the maskers see my
History of the Stage, p. 262.   " When you were in your
own countries last two summers," Jenkins' blunder, who
reckons like an Oriental, has misled the editors.   If taken
literally, it would give the impossible 1619 date.   Evan the
Welsh attorney's " business " in duelling matters is the same
as the " business " of the master of the duel in *Mercury
Vindicated*.   He is also " Rector Chori."   Note Jenkins
calling the Bottle Anti-mask a tale of a tub, and Jonson's
anagram " Calls true hearts."   Probably this is *The Goats'
Mask* of Halliwell's *Dictionary*.

1620, Jan.   There were plays and revels at Court, but no
mask recorded, although the Courtiers intended one to the
French Ambassador.

50. 1621, Jan. 6, Feb. 11.   *News from the New World
discovered in the Moon* was presented to the King.   See
Nichols, iii. 635, 653.   A Prince's mask, in which the
maskers were " led by that excellent likeness of yourself, the
Truth."   The other chief maskers represented Harmony,
Knowledge, and Fame.   The Chronicler is A. Monday, who
was still at work on additions to Stow's *Survey of London*,
the continuation of which to 1618 he had already published.
The printer is, of course, Nat. Butter, and the factor with
his Staple of News is the foundation of the 1625 play.   The
anti-mask is of Volatees. The journey of Jonson, the " great "
[fat] poet, to Edinburgh on foot is mentioned, and Drayton's
Mooncalf alluded to.   The " woman's poet " is Campion, who,
in his mask at Lord Hay's marriage 1607, had " said of
himself " that " a lady's praise shall content my proudest
hope," and " soft ears one ought to pierce But with

smooth and gentle verse." I have little doubt that he wrote the 1619 mask for the Queen, and that Jonson's quotation to the same effect as the foregoing is taken verbally therefrom.

1620, May 20. On this day Charles, second son of William Cavendish, first Earl of Devonshire, was born, to whom Prince Charles soon after stood godfather. To this christening must be referred,

51. *The Entertainment at the Earl of Newcastle's, Black-friars* (in the *Cavendish MS.*). This Earl was Charles Cavendish, brother to William. See Anon. 24.

52. 1621, Aug.–Sept. A mask of *The Metamorphosed Gipsies* at Burley on the Hill (Aug. 3, the Duke of Buckingham's), at Belvoir (Aug. 5, Francis Earl of Rutland's), and at Windsor (Sept. c. 9). Published in 12mo 1640. The alterations for Belvoir were slight, but at Windsor the men's fortunes were introduced, viz., those of—1. William Herbert, Earl Pembroke; 2. Bishop John Williams; 3. Henry Montagu, Viscount Mandeville; 4. Henry Somerset, Earl Worcester; 5. Thomas Howard, Earl Arundel; 6. Lodowic Stuart, Duke of Lennox; 7. Marquis James Hamilton; 8. Walter Scott, Earl Buccleuch. The original fortunes were those of—1. The King; 2. Prince Charles; and of Buckingham's connexions, 3. Catherine Manners, his wife; 4. Cecily Tufton, Countess Rutland, her stepmother; 5. Frances Bruges, Countess Exeter, Lady Hatton's stepmother; 6. Mary Beaumont, Countess of Buckingham, his mother; 7. Frances Coke, Lady Purbeck, his sister-in-law; 8. Elizabeth Cecil, Lady Hatton, her mother. Buckingham (George Villiers) was the Captain, and Purbeck (John Villiers) a gipsy. The fortune of Lady Purbeck in connexion with *Charis* has already been noticed. Master Wolf in the Windsor Epilogue is John Wolfgango Rumlero (or John

Wolf Rumla, Nichols, iii. 330), the King's principal apothecary in 1617. He appears as John Vulp, the last of the
apothecaries, in the New Year's Gift list, 1606, Jan 1. See
Volpone.

53. 1622, Jan. 6, repeated May 6 as "acted the Christmas before by the Prince." *The mask of Augurs* with the
several anti-masks (viz., 1. Urson and his bears; 2. Stray-
ing and deformed Pilgrims). Note the form "antic-mask"
in the text, and "Disguise, the old English word for a
mask." The way in which Notch mentions "the King's
poet nor his architect" looks as if Inigo had made the
scenes, but there is no positive evidence. Prince Charles
led the Augurs. The prototype of Vangoose, the Britain
born, who speaks all languages in ill English, is a projector
of masks, and uses the "ars van de Catropricks," ought to
be discoverable, but I cannot discover him; Bretnor (Nor-
bret) in *Rollo,* iv. i., is great in optical devices; but Vangoose is a mask-projector.

54. 1623, Jan. 19. "The Prince's mask appointed for
Twelfth Day was performed." The speeches and songs by
Mr. Ben Johnson, and the scene by Mr. Inigo Jones, three
times changed—1. Whitehall with the Banqueting House;
2. A Cloud; 3. A Forest. The French Ambassador was
present. The Prince led the measures with the Ambassador's
wife. After the galliards two country dances, The Soldiers'
March and Huff Hamukin, when the Ambassador's wife and
Mdlle. St. Luke did dance.

The [second] Anti-mask of Tumblers and Jugglers, MS.
Herbert ("in Dulwich College," Nichols, iii. 785), *Variorum,*
iii. 147. But the first anti-mask was of the Curious. *More
dissemblers besides Women* was played in place of the mask
on Jan. 6. This mask was—

Time Vindicated to himself and to his Honors. "The

Curious must have had double masks, like a double Janus, as "four eyes" (not numerous eyes, as Gifford says) are mentioned. Chronomastix is George Wither, whose *Juvenilia* were collected in 1622, including *Abuses Stript and Whipt* of 1613, in which he mentions "the deep conceits of the now flourishing Jonson," and whose motto, *Nec habeo, nec careo, nec curo*, had appeared in 1621, June 16, S. R. The printer who "keeps his press in a hollow tree" is, I suppose, the printer of *The Scholar's Purgatory*, n.d., and *The Hymns and Songs of the Church*, 1623, "for G. Wither," but with no printer's name. I have found no S. R. entry of the *Juvenilia* printed for J. Budge. But I have not made a special study of Wither. Inigo Jones is not mentioned in the printed copy, which shows that he may also have made the scenes in the preceding masks from 1619 onwards.

55. 1623, June 19. *Pan's Anniversary*, or *The Shepherds' Holiday*, was evidently a sheep-shearing mask, an "increase of anniversary rites" for King James' birthday, with an anti-mask of Bœotians. The bearded politician, maker of mousetraps, who catches the ladies' favours in the dance with cringes, and is now a great inginer, is probably Sir John Maynard, author of masks 1623, Nov. 18, and 1624. He bore away the bell for dancing in the mask of 1619, when Jonson was in Scotland. The Tinker Epam, master of music, I do not recognise. For the designs made by Inigo Jones, whose name appears before Jonson's in the title here, and here only, see under Jones. This mask was performed before James in 1625, according to the title, which is impossible, James being then dead. Nichols gives the year as 1624. I think 1623 much more likely. *The Owls* and *The Fortunate Isles* are each misdated by two years, and Jonson and Inigo had parted in 1624. The whole anti-mask seems to me an anticipatory criticism of "young

Maynard's" mask, then in preparation. Pam, his musician, is "a-coming" with his kettledrums, and he "is to catch" the ladies' favours by his dancing.

56. 1624, Jan. 6. The Prince was practising a mask for this date (Nichols, iii. 947), but it was "put off altogether" (iii. 1027). This was

The Fortunate Isles and their Union, "designed for the Court on the Twelfth Night 1624" [Geo. III. collection copy, Brit. Mus.; wrongly altered to 1626 in later editions], but not performed. Jonson, not liking the non-performance of this mask, had it performed by the Palsgrave's company at the Fortune, for whom Herbert licensed it, as well as for the Press, Dec 29. Jonson alludes to the treatment he had received, "paid for't, regarded and rewarded, which few poets are nowadays." This procedure produced the result he desired.

57. 1625, Jan. 9. *Neptune's Triumph for the Return of Albion* was presented, after being put off from Twelfth Night. This was *The Fortunate Isles* with a different anti-mask; the Cook's pot instead of Howleglass, &c., to Dr. Rat[cliff]. But I think, from the nature of the differences, that, of the two, *Neptune's Triumph* is nearer the original mask intended for 1624. The alterations in *The Fortunate Isles* eliminate some scenery, and are more suitable for the public stage. Nevertheless, this is the earliest instance of any set scenes at all at a theatre. The Cook, whose "room and region too" is the Banqueting House, who is "poet no less than cook," who makes a "metaphorical" anti-mask ("had there been mask or no mask I had made it"), is Inigo Jones. Note especially the "business" of the posts, as well as—

> "And, brother poet, though the serious part
> Be yours, yet envy not the cook his art."

Thence I infer that Jones did not make the scenery for this

mask. Cartwright's military dinner in *The Ordinary* and the Cook's speech in *Rollo* (*q.v.*) should be closely compared with the anti-mask in considering the authorship of *Rollo*. For Antler and Buz compare *The Staple of News*, 1625. Archy is alluded to, and the non-presentment of 1624 is cunningly glossed over: —

> "*Cook.* But why not this till now ?
> *Poet.*   It was not time
> To mix this music with the vulgar's chime," &c.

Middleton's *Game at Chess* had been acted 1624 Aug.; hence the allusion in—

> "Receive thy dear and precious *pawn* again."

But Hippius-Haliclyon-Buckingham in Middleton's play was a knight, not a pawn. Proteus is Sir Francis Cottington, Portunus the Warden of the Cinq Ports, and Saron the Lord High Admiral. The omission of the lines—

> "The present prophecy that goes
> Of joining the bright Lily with the Rose" (*Fortunate Isles*),

is conclusive as to date. This was prophesied in 1624 Dec.; the marriage had been agreed on in Nov. In 1625 Jan. the difficulty about dispensation had arisen, and the lines were omitted; in 1626 Jan. (the date according to Gifford, &c.) the marriage had been solemnised and consummated. The "sea monster" seems to be a name given to Archy Armstrong for his dolphin-like "blowing and blustering" (Howell), but he may have appeared in the character of Arion in a pageant; cf. "Amphibion Archy." As to the Corrantos, compare *News from the Moon* and the nugatory Proclamation 1621, July 26, against their freedom of discourse in State affairs (Nichols, iii. 672). Of course Young Albion was to be acted by the Prince, and I suspect Inigo's in-

fluence with him caused all the pother about the putting off
of this mask.

58. 1624, Aug. 19. The mask of *Owls,* at Kenilworth, was
presented by the ghost of Captain Cox on his hobby-horse
[to Prince Charles, whose "three feathers" are alluded
to]. Dated 1626 in the 1641 Folio most absurdly.

59. 1631 [Jan. 6]. *Love's Triumph through Callipolis,*
a King's mask, was presented to the Queen and published
1630[−1]. The inventors, Ben Jonson, Inigo Jones. The
anti-mask and mask both of lovers. List of Maskers given.
This is a laureate mask. Jonson's pension was granted
1630, Mar. 26. The date is fixed to 1631, not 1630, by
Pory's letter of 1632, Jan. 12, referring to the Jonson
before Jones in the title as "this time twelvemonth."

60. 1631, Shrovetide [Feb. 20–22]. *Chloridia: Rites
to Chloris and her Nymphs.* A Queen's mask, presented in
return for the preceding to His Majesty. With eight meteoric
entries in the anti-mask, and (like the preceding) with fifteen
chief maskers. Published n.d. [but in 1631, after the quarrel
had burst out], without mention of Inigo Jones. The 1641
Folio inserts his name in the same order as in *Love's Triumph.*
This publication, like all those in Jonson's lifetime, was undoubtedly made with his authority, though he did not in one
instance (the end of the 1616 Folio) oversee the proofs.
Note that in the *Expostulation* it is this mask, not *Love's
Triumph,* that is referred to. Juno and Iris, the ascent of
Lady Fame, &c., are the "mighty shows" specially men-
tioned.

ENTERTAINMENTS.

61. 1633, May. *Love's Welcome,* the King's Entertainment at Welbeck, the Earl of Newcastle's (William Cavendish), before and after dinner, "at his going into Scotland."

VOL. II.   B

62. 1634, July 30. *Love's Welcome*, the King and Queen's Entertainment at Bolsover, the Earl of Newcastle's, at banquet on their progress. Coronel Iniquo Vitruvius, the surveyor and busy man, is Inigo Jones. Compare Father Fitzale, the "man of business," in 61.

JONSON, BENJAMIN, Junior. (Play.)

1. 1623. *A Fault in Friendship.* See Brome.

Born ? 1610, April 6; died 20th Nov. 1635. "Not on good terms with his father" (Dr. Andersen). The date of birth is P. Cunningham's, but I cannot believe in a playwright *ætatis* 13. See Jonson. The true date is probably 1603, after the death of the first Benjamin; and this Benjamin was no doubt the one married to Hester Hopkins 1623, July 27.

JORDAN, THOMAS. (Actor: Plays.)

2. *The Walks of Islington and Hogsdon*, with the Humours of Wood Street Compter, C., 1657.

4. *Fancy's Festivals*, Mask. Privately presented by persons of quality 1657.

3. *Money is an Ass*, C., 1668.

Jordan, when a boy, acted Lepida in Richards' *Messalina*, which was played by His Majesty's Revels company; (*Biog. Dram.* and Halliwell say at the Red Bull, but give no authority.)

1. *Love hath found out his eyes* was entered S. R. 1660, June 29. The MS. was destroyed by Warburton's cook.

2. *The Walks of Islington* was licensed by Herbert 1641, Aug. 2.

3. *Money is an Ass.* Jordan performed the part of Captain Penniless himself.

He also published *Poetical Varieties* 1637. His numerous *Pageants* and other writings after my limit of date will be found in Hazlitt's *Handbook*.

KEMPE, WILLIAM. (Actor and Jigmaker.)

Perhaps the son of William Kemp, servant with William Holliday, who was buried at St. Giles, Cripplegate, 15th April 1589. He is first heard of as the Jesting Will who went abroad with the Earl of Leicester 24th Mar. 1586. This company of players visited the Netherlands, Denmark, and Saxony. In Sept. 1588 Tarleton died, and Kempe was at once recognised as his successor as a clown-actor.

In *Theses Martinianæ*, 22nd July 1589, he is mentioned with "Dick," *i.e.*, Tarleton, as having assailed the Martinists. In 1590 he was addressed as "Cavalier" in the dedicatory epistle of *An Almond for a Parrat* (by Lyly); one phrase in which, "the Curtain of your countenance," would seem to imply that Kempe's company (Lord Strange's) had been acting at the Curtain: they certainly acted afterwards at the Cross Keys. In 1591, Dec. 28, S. R., the third and last part of *Kempe's Jig* was entered for Thomas Gosson. In 1592, June 10, he wrote and acted in "*The merriments of the men of Gotham,*" a scene in *A Knack how to Know a Knave*, as one of L. Strange's company at the Rose. In the precept 6th May 1595 we still find him in this company. In 1595, May 2, his *New Jig of the Kitchen Stuff Woman* was entered S. R. for William Blackwall; and 1595, Oct. 21, *A New Jig betwixt a Soldier and a Miser and Sym the Clown*, for Thomas Gosson. In 1597–8 he played Peter in *Romeo and Juliet* (Q 2), Dogberry in *Much Ado about Nothing*, and some part in *Every man in his Humor* for the Chamberlain's men at the Curtain. See Marston's *Scourge*, iii. 11. He does not appear in any play acted at the Globe, and therefore probably left the company, for which he had acted up to this time, on their leaving the Curtain in 1599. Shakespeare, who had hitherto introduced Clowns, acted by Kempe, into his plays, henceforward only has

Fool characters in their place; and the remarks of Hamlet against extemporising clowns, iii. 2, are undoubtedly directed against Kempe. In 1600, Feb. 11–Mar. 11, he danced his *Morris to Norwich*, having put out money at three to one that he would accomplish this feat. On 22nd April he published his pamphlet describing it (S. R. for N. Ling). In it he refers to certain ballad-writers—Thomas Deloney, recently dead, who had written ballads on *The Six Yeomen of the West*, *The Gentle Craft*, *John for the King*, &c.; Antony Monday, "Lord of little wit, one whose employment for the Pageant was utterly spent . . . Elderton's immediate heir; the author of a ballad on Macbeth, a miserable stolen story," whose name seems to have been Hart; and Richard Jonson, who had balladised the Morris, and to whom he recommends the *Prince of the Burning Crown* (a play containing the earlier part of the story of Chettle's *Hoffman*) as a good subject for a ballad. This play was probably the *Roderick* acted by Pembroke's men at the Rose in Oct. 1600, *Like unto like* (a forged title) being the second part, an earlier version of the extant *Hoffman*: one of many small indications of Kempe, with Duke, Beeston, and Pallant, having joined Pembroke's men on leaving the Chamberlain's. Between April 1600 and 2nd Sept. 1601 (when he was again in England) he visited France, Germany, Venice, and Rome, where he met Sir Anthony Shirley: "Then into France he took pains to skip it" (Weelkes' *Ayres*, 1608). "*Perigrinationem quandam in Germaniam et Italiam instituerat. . . . Ant. Shirley. . . . Romæ convenerat*" (MS. *Sloane*, 392, fol. 401, quoted by Collier). "When Kempe returns from Rome" (ballad, "A new medley;" cf. Collier). "The travel to Rome, with the return in certain days" (*Search for Money*, by W. Rowley, 1609). This last reference is the most important, as it shows that this journey, like the Norwich

Morris, was undertaken in order to raise money on the "putting out" system.

In *The Return from Parnassus* (acted Christmas 1602, but written Christmas 1601) Kempe is introduced as joint-manager of the Chamberlain's men with R. Burbadge. The University author seems not to have been aware that Kempe was acting with Worcester's men at the Rose 22nd Aug.–4th Sept. 1602. After this date I find no certain notice of him as alive. A William Kemp was buried at St. Saviour's, Southwark, 2nd Nov. 1603. In *The Travels of Three English Brothers*, written June 1607, he is introduced as meeting Shirley at Rome after the production of *England's Joy*, 6th Nov. 1602; but this we know to be a mistake, for Kempe had returned and joined Worcester's men before this. *The Honest Whore*, 1604, is alluded to in the same scene. As this play was acted by Queen Anne's men, who had been Worcester's, I cannot suppose that had he not been dead some time this error could have arisen. His extemporary additions are also alluded to. His name does not appear in the Queen's men's lists of 1603, 1604. He is mentioned between Tarleton (who died 1588) and Singer (last mentioned 13th Jan. 1603) in Dekker's *Gull's Hornbook*, 1609. I believe he left playing Sept. 1602, and died Nov. 1603.

But against this Collier quotes from the "civic archives" (a very vague reference) a positive statement that "Kempe, Armyn, and others, players at the Blackfriars" had brought on "their stage" aldermen of the City, when Lenard Haliday was Mayor, 1605; *i.e.*, between 31st Oct. 1605 and 25th March 1606, the very time when the Revels children, who occupied Blackfriars, had got into their trouble about *Eastward Ho*. On 4th May 1605 Armin was a King's man and fellow with Phillips (see Phillips' will); in

1607–8 he *wrote* for the King's Revels children; in 1610 he was still acting with the King's men in *The Alchemist.* Moreover, his name and Kempe's never occur elsewhere in connexion with the Queen's Revels, not even in the *Eastward Ho* business; and it is so improbable that the two most noted clown-actors of the time should have been performing together for a boy company that eschewed men performances, that I prefer to attach no importance to a document of which nothing is known beyond Collier's assertion, until further evidence is adduced. Nor can any stress be laid on the occupation of tenements in Langley's Rents, &c. The name William Kempe was just then a common one, as Collier himself has proved. My assertion that I have corrected 2000 errors in Collier has been disputed: there are over 100 corrections in this one short life.

KILLIGREW, HENRY. (Play.)

    1. 1638, Mar. 13, for Andrew Crooke. *The Conspiracy*, T., 1638, 1653.

Henry was fifth and youngest son of Sir Robert Killigrew. He was born at Hanworth, Middlesex, 11th Feb. 1612[–3]. He was educated under Mr. Thomas Farnaby. Commoner of Christ Church 1628; student, B.A., and a quadragesimal collector. Before he travelled, he was created M.A. July 1638; he then took orders, and became chaplain to the King's army. D.D. 1st Nov. 1642.

    1. *The Conspiracy* was written for the marriage of the eldest son of the Earl of Pembroke, Lord Charles Herbert, with the Duke of Buckingham's only daughter, Lady Mary Villiers. She was born in Mar. 1622. Her husband died in Florence 1636, the marriage never having been consummated. I think the date of the marriage, and therefore of the play, was in 1634, in spite of the statement in the printer's Address in the 1653 edition that the author

was only seventeen. The statement in the same Address
that the original MS. at the time of publication (March
1638) was in Italy is not true. Killigrew did not leave
England till after July; and such an anecdote as that about
Falkland's reply to an objector that Clearchus in the play
being seventeen might well speak as if he were thirty, seeing
that the author who made him speak thus was no older, must,
in any case, be taken *cum grano salis.* The second edition,
however, was much enlarged, and was called *Pallantus* and
Eudora. *The Conspiracy* was acted by the King's men at
Blackfriars, and had scenes fitted to it throughout, being
the first English *play* publicly acted with scenery. See
Jonson, 56. The next one was Heywood's *Love's Mistress,*
1634 Autumn, by the Queen's men at the Phœnix, in
which occurs an allusion (I think) to Herbert's marriage
to the immature Mary Villiers :—

> " Fine little rattle-babies, scarce thus high,
> Are now called wives. If long this hot world stand,
> We shall have all the earth turn Pigmy-land."

Killigrew, Thomas. (Plays.)

1. 1640, April 4, for Andrew Crooke. *The Prisoners,*
   T. C., 1641.
2. 1640, Aug. 4, for Andrew Crooke. *Claricilla,*
   T. C., 1641.
3. Written in Naples. *The Princess,* or *Love at First
   Sight,* T. C., 1664.
4. Written at Basil. *The Parson's Wedding,* C.,
   1664.
5. Written in Paris. *The Pilgrim,* T., 1664.

Written at, 1. Turin; 2. Florence. 1, 2 *Cecilia and
   Clorinda,* or *Love in arms,* T. C., 1663.

Written in Madrid. 1, 2 *Thomaso,* or *The Wanderer,*
   C., 1664.

Written in Venice. 1, 2 *Bellamira her dream*, or
The Love of Shadows, T. C., 1664.

Thomas, brother to Henry Killigrew, was born Feb.
1611[-12]. Educated for the Court. Travelled in 1635
in France, and wrote a sheet on the exorcising of the
Nuns of Tours. He was Page of Honour to Charles I., and
married Cecilia Crofts, one of his Queen's Maids of Honour.
Thomas Carew versified a dispute between this lady and
her lover on jealousy, and introduced it by way of Chorus
with three other songs (not into his *Cœlum Britannicum*,
but) into a play at an entertainment of the King and
Queen by the Lord Chamberlain. It appears from two
songs also introduced into the body of the play by Carew
that one of the characters was a lover in the disguise of
an Amazon, and another a Knight, who rescues a lady from
death, and in the instant leaves her. See further under
Shirley, James; *Arcadia*.

Killigrew was at Paris, and there obtained from Prince
Charles license to travel 23rd April 1647. 5. *The
Pilgrim* was probably written at that time. From 1649
to 1652 he was diplomatising at Vienna, Florence, &c.
During this period he made his last six plays, of which
Denham wrote :—

> " But who says he was not
>   A man of much *plot*
> May repent the false accusation,
>   Having plotted and penned
>   Six *plays* to attend
> The *Farce* of his negotiation."

These seven plays lie without our purview.

1. *The Prisoners* was acted at the Phœnix [by the
Queen's men before 1637].

2. *Claricilla* was also acted at the Phœnix [by the

Queen's men c. 1636]. The date, and therefore the company, is shown by a mention of the play in the Dublin Prologue to Shirley's *Rosania*, 1637.

3. *The Princess.* I know not whether this play was acted at the Phœnix or Blackfriars, but the arrangement of the plays in the Folio was evidently chronological.

4. *The Parson's Wedding* was written at Basil, probably in his 1635 travels, but not acted till c. Oct. 1640 at Blackfriars by the King's men, during a time when the plague was subsiding; cf. "The bill decreased 20 last week," iii. 1 ; and in iv. 4, "Let the whore alone till she wears out : nor is it safe to vamp them, as you shall find," fixes the date closely. *The Whore* new vamped (*q.v.*) was acted Sept. 1639, which gives the anterior limit ; and there was no decreasing plague till Oct. 1640. The company and theatre are known from the allusion to the play as " a new play at the Friars," v. 1, and the mention of Stephen [Hamerton] as the actor of Master Wild in the quasi-Epilogue.

A third brother, Sir William Killigrew, wrote plays, but after the Restoration.

KINWELMARSH, FRANCIS. See Gascoigne.

KIRKE, JOHN. (Plays.)

1. 1638, July 13, for John Oakes. *The seven champions of Christendom, with the life and death of Jack Straw and Wat Tyler,* 1638.

This play was acted at the Cockpit and the Red Bull ; *i.e.*, by Queen Henrietta's men before 1636 at the Cockpit, and by the Prince's men (who acquired it when the Queen's men removed to Salisbury Court) in 1637-8.

2. A play of Kirke's was burned by Herbert "for the offence that was in it," 1642, c. May ; and another new play of his, 3. *The Irish Rebellion,* was allowed 8th June 1642.

Kirke dedicated H. Shirley's *Martyred Soldier* (*q.v.*).

KNEVET, RALPH.   (Private Pastoral.)

1. *Rhodon and Iris*, P., presented at the Florists' Feast at Norwich 3rd May 1631.   The scene is in Thessaly; the subject the Loves of the Flowers.

For his other works see Hazlitt's *Handbook*.

KYD, THOMAS.   (Plays.)

 1. *The Rare triumphs of Love and Fortune* (by E. A[llde] for Edward White), 1589.

 4. 1592, April 3, for E. White.   *Arden of Feversham*, T., 1592, 1599, 1633.

 5. 1592, Oct. 6, for Abel Jeffes.   *The Spanish Tragedy of Don Horatio and Bell Imperia*, T., 1594 (for E. White), 1599, 1602 (with the additions), 1610.

 2. 1592, Nov. 20, for Edward White, *Soliman and Perseda*, 1599.

 8. 1594, Jan. 26, for N. Ling and J. Busbie.   *Cornelia*, trans. 1594.

 6. 1594, May 2, for Peter Short.   *The Taming of a Shrew*, 1594, 1596, 1607.

 3. 1 *Jeronymo* (with Don Andrea), for T. Pavier, 1605.

1. *A History of Love and Fortune* was shown on the Sunday before the New Year (Dec. 30) 1582, before Her Majesty at Windsor, by the Earl of Derby's men.   This is *The Rare Triumphs of Love and Fortune*, published by Ed. White in 1589.   The extreme similarity of plot between this play and *Solyman and Perseda* makes it probable that they were written by the same author.   Mr. Collier thinks it a remarkable play because it contains specimens of early blank verse.   It is indeed remarkable that not one blank verse, properly so called, occurs in it, the only blank lines being trimeters.

2. The Tragedy of *Solyman and Perseda* (entered by Ed.

White 20th Nov. 1592 S. R.), " wherein is laid open Love's constancy, Fortune's inconstancy, and Death's Triumphs," is partly written in blank verse. This play is clearly subsequent to *Love and Fortune*, and appears, from the last lines, to have been also a Court play. The introduction of the same story in the " play within the play " in the *Spanish Tragedy* suggests Kyd as the author. The phrase " the braggin'st knave in Christendom," and other similarities with Kyd's diction, point in the same direction ; while the coincidences, such as the following, with *The Taming of a Shrew* are abundant :—

"Neck whiter than the snowy Apennines" (*S. and P.*, iv. 1).
"Whiter than are the snowy Apennines" (*T. of a S.*, Sc. 2).

I date this play conjecturally c. 1583.

3. The First Part of *Jeronymo*, " with the Wars of Portugal and the life and death of Don Andrea," was acted soon after R. Wilson's *Three Ladies of London*. The line at the end,

" I hope there's never a Jew among you all,"

alludes to Gerontus in that play (acted 1583), not to Barabbas in Marlow's *Jew of Malta* (1589), which is of too late a date by some years to fit in with the plays yet to be mentioned, which must have been acted earlier than 1589. This play was acted at a public theatre. Jeronymo in it is of short stature. We only possess it now in a version printed for T. Pavier in 1605, and as it had been acted by the children of the Queen's Chapel in 1599–1600 ; see the allusion to it in Jonson's *Cynthia's Revels*, Indn., where Jonson mentions " the old *Hieronimo* as it was first acted," which implies alterations. I may caution the reader against Gifford's absurd interpretation of these words as necessarily referring to *The Spanish Tragedy*, for that play belonged to the Admiral's

men, and Jonson's alterations in it were made in September
1601 and June 1602, whereas *Cynthia's Revels* was performed in 1600. This first *Jeronymo* was the play acted by
Lord Strange's men at the Rose twenty-two times in the
year 1592, and in retaliation for the malappropriation of
which by the Chapel children they, then called the King's
men, produced *The Malcontent* of Marston, with Webster's
additions, in 1604.

4. The tragedy of *Arden of Feversham* was acted publicly.
In it a principal murderer has for name Black Will. This
name is historic, being taken from the chronicle account of
the murder in 1551. But an allusion to this Black Will in
the old *Richard* 3 shows that *Arden* was previously on the
stage, acted by the Queen's men, and that the part of Black
Will was taken by an actor called William Slaughter or
Slater; possibly the father of the Martin Slaughter, actor,
who sold old plays (Query plays that had belonged to the
Queen's men) to Henslow, and has therefore been elevated
by Collier and his follower Halliwell to the dignity of authorship. The passage runs thus:—"*Forest*. One of their names
is Will Sluter, yet the most part calls him Black Will; the
other is Jack Denten." Now, Forest and Deighton were the
names of the "murderers," according to the chronicles. No
Will Slaughter is found in them. He is introduced here as
a bit of "gag" addressed to the groundlings for the sake of
the wretched pun. For the same reason Deighton is changed
to Denten, which was a variant spelling of Dounton, known
as an actor. This *Richard* 3 was almost certainly acted
early in 1586 or late in 1585, before the theatres were
closed for the plague. The ballad founded on it was entered
S. R. Aug. 15, and I feel justified in dating *Arden* in 1585.
The name Arden was just then unpopular. Edward Arden
had been executed 20th December 1583 for treason. As to

the authorship, I think there is some ground for attributing it to Kyd.

"What dismal outcry calls me from my rest?" (iii. 1).

Compare—

"What outcry calls me from my naked bed?" (*Hieronymo*, ii. 5).

"Lime well your twigs to catch this wary bird" (iv. 2).

Compare—

"He breaks the worthless twigs,
And sees not that therewith the bird was limed" (*Hieronymo*, iii. 4).

"The railing'st knave in Christendom" (iv. 5).

Compare line quoted *supra*.

5. *The Spanish Tragedy.* When the theatres were re-opened after the plague-year of 1586, the Admiral's company became, for the time, the chief competitors with the Queen's men for public favour. Peele, Kyd, Dekker, and Lodge wrote plays for them; and Marlow, who at that time, in 1587, came up from Cambridge, added his then unequalled strength to a group of play-writers already far stronger than any other in London. Peele, in his *Farewell* (early in 1589), gives us a list of plays lately produced on the stage, viz., *Mahomet's pow* (Greene's *Alphonso*), *Tamburlaine* (by Marlow), *King Charlemain* (perhaps the play called by Mr. Buller *The Distracted Emperor* in his reprint, written, I think, by Dekker), *Tom Stukeley* (his own *Battle of Alcazar*), and the rest (Kyd's *Spanish Tragedy*, Marlow's *Doctor Faustus*, &c.). The majority of these were acted by the Admiral's men; and one, *The Spanish Tragedy*, not mentioned by name by Peele, is the only play which we know by external evidence to have been written by Kyd. It is expressly assigned to him by Heywood in his *Apology for actors*, 1612, but, like all his other acted plays, was published anonymously. It therefore forms the starting-point for all investigations respecting him.

Fortunately we have it in two forms, one as published by Abel Jeffes (S. R. 6th Oct. 1592), the other as altered by Jonson, who made additions to it on 25th Sept. 1601 and 24th June 1602. This play never passed out of the possession of the Admiral's men, although the Chapel boys did, I think, appropriate it c. 1599. The statements to the contrary by Collier and his followers are founded on confusion of it with the first part of *Jeronymo*, or *The Spanish Comedy*, as Henslow calls it. It would be convenient to adopt for this altered play the name *Hieronymo* (Jonson's spelling of *Jeronymo*). In the *Spanish Tragedy* the hero is not alluded to as of low stature, and this of itself indicates a different actor from the one in the " Comedy," and confirms my conclusion on other grounds, that the First *Jeronymo* was originally acted not by the Admiral's but the Queen's men. It was in this First *Jeronymo* that Jonson acted at the Curtain in 1598 as one of the Chamberlain's men. Aubrey's statement is accurate on this point, whatever Collier or Gifford allege to the contrary. By Jonson it was probably taken to the Chapel children, and I have no doubt (from internal evidence) by him revised for them. His revision, however, included no " additions ; " it rather consisted of " omissions " of Latin quotations, &c. The success of this revival by him in 1600 probably led to Henslow's revival of the Second Part in 1601 and 1602, and to his employing the same hand for the alterations in that play.

The extreme similarity of passages in this play to others in *Love and Fortune*, *Soliman and Perseda*, *Arden*, *The Taming of a Shrew*, and *The Spanish Comedy* is palpable on merely a cursory reading. To give them adequately would require an essay of double the length of this notice. An indication of their existence must now suffice. As a salient example, compare Balthazar's speech, ii. 1 —

"First in his hand he brandished a sword," &c.,

with *Soliman and Perseda,* iv. 1, Erastus' speech—

"And Rhodes itself is lost, or else destroyed," &c.

But I must not pass unnoticed the fact that in Shakespeare's *Hamlet,* founded on the old *Hamlet,* which, as we shall see, was written by Kyd, there still remain echoes of the earlier dramatists, such as, in diction—

"And if the world like not this Tragedy" (v. 1);
"For if the King like not the Comedy" (*Hamlet,* iii. 2);

in incident, the swearing on the cross of the sword-hilt, which occurs in both plays; and in general plot, the revenge of a son for a father in *Hamlet* with the revenge of a father for a son in the *Spanish Tragedy.*

Of the ridicule cast on this play by subsequent authors enough has been written by others; and yet I do not know if any one has noted the curious fact that Jonson, the chief parodist of the more obnoxious lines, was also the principal instrument in recalling them to the stage.

6. *The Taming of a Shrew.* On 29th March 1588 Green's *Perimedes* was entered S. R. In the often-quoted Address he complains that two gentlemen poets had it in derision that he could not make his verses jet it on the stage in tragical buskins, daring God out of heaven with the Atheist Tamburlain, or blaspheming with the mad priest of "the sonne" [*sic*]. No Priest of the Sun is known to the stage except in *The Looking-glass for London* (1591) and *The Sun's Darling* (founded on a play of Dekker's). These are too late, and the priests are not mad. Without falling back on the imbecile resource of supposing a lost play, I venture a conjecture which at first sight may seem absurd. A comparison of the passage from *Perimedes* with one in Nash's Address to *Menaphon* (quoted below) shows that

Marlow and Kyd are in both instances alluded to. The
"frequenting the hot-house" in one passage, and the
"turning over French dowdy" in the other, leaves no
doubt that the persons satirised are the same. But in
Kyd's play Hieronymo is "priest of his son:"—

> "Viceroy, I will not trust thee with my life,
> Which I this day have offered to my son" (v. 3).

Taking into account the peculiar use of "priest" in this
play—

> "Who first lays hands on me, I'll be his priest" (iii. 3),

and the excessive tendency of Greene to quibbling in these
"dark enigmas or strange conceits," as he calls his satirical
writings, and the spelling of "sonne" with an *o*, I incline to
believe that this play is the one aimed at, as it falls just
in accordance with the date. Of Greene's other allusion to
these gentlemen, that they made two madmen of Rome
beat his motto, *Omne tulit punctum*, out of their paper
bucklers, I can offer no explanation.

In 1589, on 23rd August, was entered S. R. Greene's
Menaphon. In the Address by Nash prefixed to this is a
vehement attack on Kyd. He is classed with trivial translators; shifting companions, that could scarcely Latinise
their neck verse; copyists of English Seneca, who can
afford you whole *Hamlets* of tragical speeches. These
followers of Seneca are like the Kid in Æsop, enamoured
of the Fox's new fangles. Sufficeth them to bodge up a
blank verse with if's and and's, while for recreation they
turn over French Dowdy in the city. They outbrave better
pens with the swelling bombast of a bragging blank verse,
a drumming decasyllabon. Brought up in a serving-man's
idleness, leaving the trade of *Noverint*, whereto they were
born, they take on them to be ironical censurers of all.

The actors of these men's plays fare no better at Nash's hands than the poets. They are vainglorious tragedians, who care not to excel in action, but think to share poets' immortality "if they but once get Boreas by the beard, and the heavenly Bull by the dewlap." The Kid and Hamlet in Nash's Address are personal enough, but in the book itself Greene improves on him. Doron, the representative of these idiot art-masters, says, "We had a Ewe among our Rams, whose fleece was as white as the hairs that grow on father Boreas' chin, or as the dangling dewlap of the Silver Bull; her front curled like to the Erimanthian Boar, and spangled like to the worsted stockings of Saturn; her face like Mars treading upon the milk-white clouds; her eyes were like the fiery torches tilting against the moon." Mr. R. Simpson pointed out, rightly, that this Doron was the author of *The Taming of a Shrew*, wherein the line occurs :—

> "Or icy hair that grows on Boreas' chin ; "

yet his guess that Doron is Shakespeare is worse than idle. Doron's speech, indeed, contains much in common with *Hamlet*, iii. 4 :—

> "Hyperion's *curls*, the *front* of Jove himself,
>   An eye *like Mars*," &c. ;

but this only shows that Shakespeare had retained hints from Kyd's play, on which he founded his own some dozen years after. There is nothing left for ridicule in Shakespeare's version, nor is there any doubt that Doron is Kyd.

7. *Hamlet*. The players for whom *The Taming of a Shrew* was written were Pembroke's company; it follows that Kyd's *Hamlet*, the Corambis *Hamlet*, was also acted by them. Accordingly, we find that both these plays,

along with *Titus Andronicus* (also known to have belonged
to Pembroke's company) and *Hester and Ahasuerus*, passed
into the possession of the Lord Strange's (Earl of Derby's)
men in 1594, and were acted by them at Newington Butts
in June, when, at his death, their patronage was transferred
to the Lord Chamberlain.   Nash describes Pembroke's men
as "a company of taffata fools, whose beauty, if our poets"
(*i.e.*, the poets who had written for the Queen's company—
Marlow and Kyd) "had not pieced[1] with the supply of
their periwigs, they might have antickt it until this time up
and down the country with *The King of Fairies*, and dined
every day at the pease-porridge ordinary with *Delphrigus*."
I have shown elsewhere that these plays were old moralities
written by R. Wilson for the Queen's men; and although
Nash here compliments him as a player with "the deserved
reputation of a Roscius," he cannot refrain from sneering
at him as an author.   Wilson, Kyd, Marlow, and perhaps
Dekker, were then, in 1589, attached to the company of
the Earl of Pembroke.

The date of both plays here considered, *The Taming of a
Shrew* and the Corambis *Hamlet*, must lie between 29th
Mar. 1588 and 23rd Aug. 1589.   It may be noticed, in
reading *Menaphon*, how Doron grows more and more clownish
towards the end, as if his identification were an afterthought,
the story not having originally any satirical bearing.   As it
now stands, Menaphon (the name of a character in *Tamburlain*) is Marlow, and Melicert most likely Greene
himself.

It will no doubt seem improbable that so many plays
should have been written by Kyd, and no definite attribution
of any, except the *The Spanish Tragedy*, to him by his con-

---

[1] Mr. Simpson absurdly alters this to deckt.   Mr. Arber follows him.   The
reading is quite plain "peecte."

temporaries have reached us; but if the student will start from that play as a sure standing-point, and read the others in chronological sequence (ascending and descending), he will, I am convinced, find so many parallelisms in them as to leave little doubt in his mind that they are here rightly attributed. No acted play of Kyd's was published with his name to it, and had it not been for Heywood's casual notice of him, we should have been entirely (as we are, indeed, now in great measure) dependent on inductions from writings made purposely obscure. Yet the works of the "Sporting Kyd" of Jonson, one of "the best for tragedy" of Meres, must have been well known in his own time. Ridiculed they often were, but some of them were popular, and two were used as foundations for higher superstructures by one known for all time.

8. *Cornelia.* I have only to add that Kyd's translation of *Cornelia* from the French of Garnier, which savours even more of Seneca than his own plays do, was entered 26th Jan. 1593–4, for Ling and Busby, S. R. It was dedicated to the Countess of Sussex. As he did not publish the *Portia* promised in this Dedication for "the next summer," I think it likely that he died in 1594. This is noteworthy in consideration of his problematic claim to the authorship of *Titus Andronicus*, which is, I think, much more likely to have been written by Marlow. I do not know if any one has noticed the frequent references to Dido and Æneas in that play. They strongly confirm Marlow's authorship.

KYNDER, PHILIP. (Latin.)

1. In MS. Ashmole, 788, is a Latin epistle "prefixt before my *Silvia*, a Latin comedy or pastoral translated from the *Archadia*, written at 18 years of age" by Philip Kynder; *temp.* Charles I.

LACEY, HENRY. (Latin.)

1. *Ricardus* 3. Acted at Trinity, Cambridge, 1586. Lacey was Fellow of Trinity.

LEGGE, THOMAS. (University: English and Latin.)

Born at Norwich 1535; member of Trinity and Jesus, Cambridge; second master of Caius; doctor in the Court of Arches; master in Chancery; the King's law professor; twice Vice-Chancellor of Cambridge. Died July 1607.

1. *The Destruction of Jerusalem*, T. Acted at Coventry 1577. Mentioned in Kirkman's Catalogue 1661.

2. *Richardus Tertius*, T. Acted at St. John's in three evenings 1579. There are some five MSS. of this play, of which that at Emmanuel College gives the names of the actors. It is alluded to in Harrington's *Apology of Poetry*, 1591, and Nash's *Have with you to Saffron Walden*, 1596. It has been reprinted, but most inaccurately.

For Legge's connexion with University performances in 1592 see my *History of the Stage*, under that date.

LE GRYS, Sir ROBERT. (Play.)

1. 1660, June 29, for H. Moseley. *Nothing impossible to Love*, T. C. MS. destroyed by Warburton's servant. As Le Grys translated Barclay's *Argennis* 1629 by the King's command, this play was probably not far from that date.

LILLY, or LYLY, JOHN. (Plays.)

1. *Alexander Campaspe and Diogenes*, C., 1584 (for Thomas Cadman), 1584 *bis*, 1591.

2. 1534, April 6, for Thomas Cadman. *Sappho*, C., 1584, 1591.

3. 1585, April 1, for Gabriel Cawood. *Tityrus and Galatea*, C.

1591. Oct. 4, for widow of W. Broome.
{ 4. *Endimion*, C., 1591.
  3. *Galatea*, C., 1592.
  7. *Midas*, C., 1592.

6. 1594, June 18, for Cuthbert Burbye. *Mother Bomby*,
C., 1594, 1598.

8. 1595, Sept. 22, for Robert Fynche. *A Woman
in the Moon*, C. 1597.

5. 1600, Nov. 25, for William Wood, *Love's Metamorphosis*, C., 1601.

1–6. *Six Court Comedies*, for Edward Blount (the first
six named above), 1632.

Lyly was born in the Weald of Kent c. 1553 ; a student
of Magdalen, Oxford, in the beginning of 1569, aged sixteen
or thereabouts ; matriculated as *plebis filius* 8th Oct. 1571 ;
B.A. 27th April 1573.   On 16th May 1574 he, a scholar,
wrote a Latin letter to Lord Burghley for the Queen's letters
to admit him Fellow.   This petition was not granted.   He
took his M.A. 1st June 1575, and then came to the Court.
Euphues, The Anatomy of Wit, was entered S. R. for Gabriel
Cawood 2nd Dec. 1578 ; Lyly was then at Court.   He had
entered the Queen's service by her "favour, strengthened with
conditions that I should aim all my courses at the Revels,
I dare not say with a promise, but with a hopeful *item* to
the Reversion."   Benger, the Master of the Revels, died in
March 1577, and Lyly expected the reversion of his office ;
but Blagrave was appointed "chief officer" 13th Dec. 1578,
and Tylney Master 24th July 1579.   On that same day
G. Cawood entered S. R. the Second Part of *Euphues*
(*Euphues and his England*).   Lyly had evidently meant this
book, in case of getting the Revels Mastership, to have a
Dedication to Burleigh or the Queen.   He did not, however,
issue it till the spring of 1580, and in the interim altered
it, especially in the dates, so as to conceal his disappointment.   One date, that of Philautus' last letter (Feb.
1579–80), could not be arranged so as to accord with the
others without being made July 1580 or Feb. 1580–1,

and the date of issue would not permit this; so it stands discordant and reveals the story.. In his Epistle Dedicatory to the Scholars of Oxford, when he says " not daring to bud till the cold be past," it is the Queen's favour more than the winter that he alludes to. In this year, 1579, he was incorporated M.A. of Cambridge. In 1581 he began his play-writing. ,

In Watson's *Hecatompathia* (S. R. 31st March 1582) we find a letter of Lyly's to the author; in July he wrote to Lord Burleigh defending himself from having maligned My Lady (the Queen, in whose service he then was; not Lady Burleigh, as usually supposed); his thoughts of her have been reverent, almost religious; devises, treachery, and faction are others' faults, not his. In 1585, when he had been " 10 years " waiting for the Reversion of the Revels, he petitioned the Queen for dismissal to " write prayers instead of plays." In Sept. 1589 he published *Pap with a Hatchet* against the Martinists. The allusions in Harvey's *Pierce's Supererogation,* Nov. 1589, leave no possible doubt as to his authorship: " would God Lilly had always been Euphues, and never Pap Hatchet." Just before this, in 1588, he petitioned the Queen a second time, three years after his first petition, for fines and forfeitures from the Rebels, " seeing nothing will come by the Revels." These Rebels were, I think, the fifteen executed 28th Aug. 1588; see S. R. under that date. In 1590 the Paul's boys, for whom he had been writing, were inhibited. The most important dates in Lyly's career hinge on this " Rebels " identification; and, unfortunately, the only thing definitely certain is that the years assigned by Oldys, Arber, and others are wrong. On 30th June 1596 *Lillie's light* was entered S. R. for E. Dawson. On 10th Sept. John Lyly, son of John Lillye, gent., was baptized at St. Bartholomew's;

on 20th Aug. 1597 he was buried at St. Botolph's, Bishops-gate.   Also in 1597 Lyly prefixed Latin verses to the Queen to Locke's *Ecclesiastes.*   On 3rd July 1600 another John Lillye was baptized at St. Bartholomew's; on 21st May 1603 Frances Lilly (Query named after her mother) was baptized, and on 30th Nov. 1606 John Lyly was there buried.   From Harvey's *Pierce's Supererogation,* 1593, and Nash's *Have with you,* &c., we learn that Lyly was of short stature, immoderate in tobacco-smoking, and at one time Vice-Master of Paul's.

In *Pap with a Hatchet,* 1589 [Sept.], I note the following allusions:—First, to Gabriel Harvey, p. 17 (Petheram's reprint): his *Epistle on Earthquakes* is accused of libel; his " Latin ends" are scoffed at; he writes without wit, as Martin does without honesty; they are coach companions; he is the son of a "Tyburn wright," *alias* a ropemaker. Note that this was anterior to R. Harvey's *Plain Percival,* and that the origin of the quarrel lies at the door of Greene and Lyly.   Then on stage matters, besides passages quoted in other parts of my book, in p. 32 we find, "Would those Comedies [against Martin] might be allowed to be played that are penned!"   No doubt they were played, and were those of L. Strange's and the Admiral's companies prohibited 1589, Nov. 6.   See my *History of the Stage,* p. 92.

1. *Alexander Campaspe and Diogenes,* or *Campaspe,* was played before the Queen on Twelfth Day at night (Q. 1, 1584); on New Year's Day at night (Q. 2, 1584); on Twelfth Day (Q. 3, 1591; printed from Q. 1.).   The nearest date to be found in the Court payments is New Year's Eve 1581, and this was no doubt the real date.   Apelles and Campaspe seem to shadow forth Leicester and the Countess of Essex, married 20th Sept. 1578.   Alexander, of course, means the Queen, and Hephæstion, I think, Burleigh.   The performers were

the Chapel children; but the Paul's boys acted it publicly at Blackfriars in 1581. A song in the 1632 edition of this play occurs also in *The Sun's Darling* (*q.v*). Diogenes, I think, means Lyly himself. The siege of Thebes, referred to at the end of the play, had been acted at Court 1574, Feb. 2, by the Merchant Taylors' boys, as *Timoclea at the siege of Thebes by Alexander*.

2. *Sappho and Phao*, or *Sappho*, was acted on Shrove Tuesday, *i.e.*, 27th Feb. 1582 (the only available date in the payment-lists), by the Chapel children, and publicly by the Paul's boys at Blackfriars. In this play the Queen is Sappho; Phao is Monsieur, who left England 6th Feb. 1582; Lyly is Pandion. That these two plays, when understood, gave offence is clear, for the Paul's boys were inhibited forthwith, and Lyly in July was in disgrace with the Queen for want of respect to her. There are allusions to flatterers and false accusers in the Pandion part of the play; and as the Chapel children were not inhibited till 1583, when all children's performances were stopped and the Queen's men set up, I think that it was the Paul's stage that gave the offence, and that the Chapel presentations were by command, that the Queen might judge the plays for herself. The S. R. entry of this play in 1584 was subject to Cadman's getting lawful allowance for it, and *Campaspe* does not appear in S. R. at all. In 1635 the Blackfriars Prologue was printed as belonging to *The Knight of the Burning Pestle*. Note the " parenthesis," meaning horns, in iii. 2.

3. *Gallathea* was entered as *Tityrus and Galathea* S. R. on 1st April 1585, but not published nor performed until the Paul's boys were reinstated in 1587. It was acted before the Queen at Greenwich on New Year's Day. The only such date at this place in the payment-list is 1st Jan. 1588. Performances in subsequent years were at Hampton

or Richmond. The internal evidence agrees. In iii. 3, v. 1, *octogesimus octavus mirabilis annus* is mentioned; also the conjunction of Saturn and Jupiter. The prophecies of the wonderful year were current at this time. See, for instance, T. Tymme's *A new year's gift*, comprehending a preparation against the prognosticated dangers of this year, S. R. 14th Dec. 1587. The characters satirised in the play are the astrologer (Dr. Dee), the alchemist (Sir. T. Smith, late Secretary of State), and the augur (T. Rogers), who collected these prophecies. See *Stow*, p. 709. I think the play was originally written 1582; thrown aside when the children were inhibited; taken up again and recomposed 1587. That it followed *Sappho* in chronological order is clear from v. 3, "always taken first by Sappho, now by Diana."

4. *Endymion* was performed by the Paul's boys before the Queen at Candlemas at Greenwich, therefore on 1st Feb. 1588. Mr. Halpin explained, though not completely, the allegory of this play. Endymion is Leicester; Eumenides, Sussex; Cynthia, the Queen; Tellus, the Countess of Sheffield; Floscula, the Countess of Essex; Dipsas, the Countess of Shrewsbury. Diana's nymphs (in *Galathea*) are alluded to in ii. 2.

5. *Love's Metamorphosis* was acted at Court by the children of Paul's, no doubt in 1588–9. It followed *Endymion* and *Galathea*. In v. 1 Diana hath felt some motions of love (*Galathea*); Vesta doth (*Endymion*, ii. 2); Ceres shall (*Love's Metamorphosis*). This play was revived by the Chapel children, probably c. 1599, before the Paul's boys recommenced in 1600. It was still acted by them at the date of publication, 25th Nov. 1600, S. R.

6. *Mother Bombie* also dates either in this year or possibly in 1589–90. In it and the following plays Euphuistic similes derived from fabulous natural history are very rare;

they are abundant in the precedent plays. "Pap with a hatchet" occurs i. 3, but not in such a way as to determine whether before or after the tract so named. The song in iii. 2 is clearly a later addition, not being assigned to the right characters; but this does not aid us in assigning the authorship of these songs. The scene is, strangely, placed at Rochester, just as that of *Galatea* is in Lincolnshire.

7. *Midas* was performed at Court on Twelfth Day. As it was clearly written after the Armada, iv. 4, this must have been on 6th Jan. 1590. Compare my *History of the Stage*, p. 80, for the dates of all these plays. But it was also publicly presented at Paul's (see Prologue). We do not know if the 1588-9 plays were acted in public. This is the most palpably satirical of all Lyly's plays. Philip of Spain is certainly represented in Midas of Phrygia; Lesbos, as usual, is England. The topical allusions are too numerous to quote, nor will it be needful to point them out to any one familiar with Elizabethan history.

8. *The Woman in the Moon* was probably acted on Jan. 1 or 4 this same year. It was Lyly's first verse-play—

"A poet's dream,
The first he had in Phœbus' holy bower;"

but not his first play. The blank verse is too easy in flow for 1579. There are no Euphuistic similes, and there is no payment date so early with which it can be connected. It is a satire on women's fickleness, and indirectly on the Queen's not keeping her promises to Lyly. Of course, she could not notice this personally with any dignity; but she could, and no doubt did, notice the meddling with State matters in *Midas*; Lyly was virtually dismissed, and the Paul's boys again suppressed. "Anger makes men witty, but it keeps them poor." This play was entered S. R. 1595, but evidently "stayed" till 1597.

For the question whether Lyly wrote any plays after this
date see under *The Maid's Metamorphosis*, noting previously
that Lyly, "the vice-master of Paul's," wrote for those boys
only; although, as already noticed, several of his plays got
into the hands of the Chapel children.

LODGE, THOMAS.   (Plays.)

 7, 8. *The Reign of King John*, in two parts, H., 1591
   (for Sampson Clarke), 1611, 1622.

 9. 1594, Mar. 5, for Thomas Creede. *The Looking-
   glass for London*, T. C., 1594.

 6. 1594, May 14, for Edward White. *Leir*, H., 1605.

 1. 1594, May 24, for John Danter. *Marius and
   Sylla*, T., 1594.

 2. *Mucedorus*, C., 1598 (for W. Jones), 1606, 1610,
   1613, 1615, 1619, 1629, 1634, 1639, n.d.,
   1668.

 10. 1599, Nov. 17, for William Aspley. *A Warning for Fair Women*, T., 1599.

 11. 1600, May 29, for James Roberts. *The Alarum
   for London*, 1602, for W. Ferbrand.

Thomas, son of Sir Thomas Lodge, grocer, who was Lord
Mayor in 1563, and of Anne, daughter of Sir William
Laxton, who was Lord Mayor in 1542 and 1556, was born
c. 1558.   His mother died in 1579, his father in 1583.   A
brother of his, born in 1563, had William Earl of Pembroke
for his godfather.   On 23rd March 1571 Lodge was admitted at Merchant Taylors' School (*Athenæum*, 21st Oct.
1882).   In 1573 he entered at Trinity, Oxford; took his
B.A. 8th July 1577; then went to London, and 26th April
1578 was admitted at Lincoln's Inn.   On 22nd July 1579
Gosson's *School of Abuse* was entered S. R., and on 7th Nov.
his *Ephemerides of Phialo;* on 29th Dec. 1579, for E.
White (not 1580, as Hazlitt has it), Lodge's *Epitaph on his*

mother (now lost). Soon after his mother's death Lodge " privily printed " *A Reply to Stephen Gosson's School of Abuse, in Defence of Poetry, Music, and Stage Plays.* On 23rd Oct. 1581, S. R., Barnaby Rich's *Simonides* was entered. This book had verses by Lodge, in which he speaks of his " long distress." In 1582, Mar. [April] 6, S. R., Gosson's *Plays confuted in* 5 *Actions* was entered, in which he attacks Lodge as " little better than a vagrant." Lodge complains of this in his *Alarum against Usurers*, S. R. 4th Nov. 1583, by T. Este for Sampson Clarke. In 1587 he got into debt with one Toppin, and then, as he says himself, being " first a student, and afterwards falling from books to arms," he " with Captain Clarke made a voyage to Terceras and the Canaries, where he wrote *Rosalynde ; Euphues' golden Legacy,* " found after his death in his cell at Silexedra, bequeathed to Philautus' sons, nursed up with their father in England. Fetcht from the Canaries by T. L., Gent." This was entered S. R. 6th Oct. 1590 for Nicholas Ling and John Busbie, and dedicated to Lord Hunsdon, with two of whose sons he had been contemporary at Oxford. This " Euphues," of course, means Lyly, and his " death in his cell " means his retirement in 1590. Compare Spenser, *Tears of the Muses,* 1590 :—

> " Our pleasant Willy, ah, is dead of late . . .
> Doth rather choose to sit in idle cell. . . ."

But this title may have been a second thought, and the story itself written before 1590. What, then, was the date of this voyage with Clarke ? In 1589, Sept. 22, S. R., Lodge was in England publishing *Scylla's Metamorphosis* (written while he was at Oxford ; see the opening lines), and promising a better poem (in his Dedication to R. Crane, &c.) by " next term." In 1587–8 he was, as we shall see, writing plays. Had Clarke's ship been one of Cavendish's squadron in his 1588 voyage (S. R. Nov. 3), I think Cavendish would have been mentioned. I rather think it must have been under Drake that Clarke sailed. Drake was at Cadiz 19th April 1587 (see S. R. 15th June 1587), and visited Terceras and the Canaries in this same year. This would agree with Lodge's having fallen from books to arms; and in *Wily Beguiled* Churms, who is, in my opinion, Lodge, has been at Cadiz. At the end of *Rosalynde* Lodge again mentions his promised poem (by name this time) as *The Sailor's Calendar*, intended, I suppose, to be a pendant to Spenser's *Shepherd's Calendar*. In the *Scylla* Glaucus binds Lodge by oath—

"To write no more of that whence shame doth grow,
  Or tie my pen to penny knaves' delight,
  But live with fame, and so for fame to write ;"

which certainly means to write poems instead of plays; but that this should have been taken as a binding promise, or anything more than a transient intention, is to me astonishing. Lodge was certainly in England 1st Feb. 1589, when he prefixed verses to Greene's *Spanish Masquerado*, and 1st Dec. 1589, S. R., when Peter Bale's *Writing Schoolmaster* was published with verses by him. On 2nd May 1591, S. R., *Robert 2 of Normandy*, "Robin the Devil," was published by N. Ling and J. Busbie, with a Dedication to Mr. Thomas Smith; but from 6th Aug. 1591 till 1593 Lodge was with Cavendish, and while in the Straits of Magellan wrote his *Margarite of America*. During his absence his *Catharos*, or *Diogenes in his Singularity*, "a Nettle for Nice Noses," was published (S. R. 17th Sept. 1591, "for H. Chettle") by J. Busbie; and so, S. R. 17th Feb. 1592, was *Euphues' Shadow*, "The Battle of the Senses," by J. Busbie. Greene supervised this latter book, and shortly after addressed Lodge in his *Groatsworth of Wit* as one that had "lastly writ with

him a comedy," viz., *The Looking-glass for London*, finished
by Greene after Lodge's departure. When he returned Greene
was dead. In 1593 *Phillis* and *Elstred*, dedicated to the
Countess of Shrewsbury, were published together by J.
Busbie, and *William Longbeard*, "with other histories," by
R. Yardley and P. Short, with a Dedication to Sir W. Webbe
(Lord Mayor in 1591). In 1594, June 7, S. R., *A Spider's
Web* (now lost, but extant 1725) was entered for N. Ling.
Hazlitt gives this date as July; wrongly. On 2nd April
1595 *A Fig for Momus* (Satires, Eclogues, and Epistles)
was entered S. R. for Clement Knight. About May 1595
Lodge was arrested at Topping's suit for his debt incurred
in 1587. This tailor's affair is so important in fixing dates
for Lodge's career that I must treat it in detail.

There are five documents extant :—

  i. Topping's [first] complaint to [Henry] L. Hunsdon,
     L. Chamberlain [c. June 1595].

  ii. Henslow's [second] answer to a further complaint
      of Topping's [to L. Cobham, c. Dec. 1596].

  iii. Topping's [third] complaint to [George] L. Huns-
       don [c. May 1597].

  iv. Henslow's [third] answer [c. June 1597].

  v. George L. Hunsdon's final order, 29th Jan.
     1598.

William Brooke, Lord Cobham, succeeded Henry Lord
Hunsdon as Chamberlain 22nd July 1596. George L.
Hunsdon succeeded him 17th April 1597.

It appears from i. that Lodge incurred a debt to R.
Topping, of the Strand, tailor, of £7 odd in 1587, "this
eight years due" that c. May ("half a year now past," ii.).
Topping arrested him to the Clink. Henslow, as his bail,
was bound for him for £12 odd (including expenses), but
refused either to pay or to disclose Lodge's whereabouts ; and

being "her Majesty's servant," and not subject to arrest,
he would keep Topping "from it this seven years." Topping
seeks leave to arrest Henslow. The matter was evidently
interrupted by Henry Hunsdon's death, and had to be
renewed by a second complaint to L. Cobham. This
Henslow answered in ii., that he had bailed Lodge from the
Clink, but that the action had been removed by *Habeas
Corpus* to the King's Bench, and new bail put in by Lodge,
but that Topping had persisted in proceeding in the Clink
by a *procedendo*. Brooke decided against Henslow, but
nothing was done by him; so after Brooke's death, c. May
1597, Topping made a third complaint to George L. Hunsdon. From this, iii., we find that the suit was begun in 1594,
"about 3 years past," when the debt had been "7 years for-
borne." The two previous complaints are mentioned *seriatim*,
and it is stated that Henslow's answer to the first complaint was a promise of payment. In iv. Henslow, who
in ii. had said that Topping "knoweth where Lodge is, and
how he may easily come by him," alleges that he himself
had tried to attach Lodge, but by no means could attain
to him, for that he is [note *is*, not *was*] passed beyond the
seas." In v. Hunsdon decides against Henslow.

The dates which I have put as c. May and c. June must
lie between 17th April and 22nd July; the year dates
are certain. This iv. document is the one into which
Mr. Collier foisted the words "as a player." Dr. Ingleby
proved this in 1868. Comment is not needful.

The Fig for Momus was "by T. L., of Lincoln's Inn;" but
Lodge never again claimed that designation. He was no doubt
expelled immediately after his arrest in 1595, say at Midsummer. In that work he addresses Drayton as "Golde:"
it was dedicated to the Earl of Derby. In 1596 Lodge

was "in hiding," and his publications [1] do not appear in S. R.; they are, however, dated. On 15th April *The Devil Conjured* (by Adam Islip for William Mats); dedicated to Sir John Fortescue. On 4th May *A Margarite of America* (for John Busbie); dedicated to Lady Russel; written while voyaging with Cavendish, 1591–2. On 5th Nov. *Wit's Misery and the World's Madness,* "discovering the Devils Incarnate of this age" (by A. Islip for Cuthbert Burby); dedicated to N., H., and J. Hare, and dated from Low Leyton; but before it was circulated Lodge was off to Avignon to get his degree as Doctor of Physic. He soon returned, and for his career for the next few years see below, under the University plays of *Wily Beguiled* and *The Return from Parnassus.*

In 1602 Lodge's translation of *Josephus* was dedicated to Lord Howard of Effingham, and in the same year (according to Hazlitt) *Paradoxes against common opinion* (for S. Waterson). On 25th Oct. he was incorporated at Oxford. In 1603 *A Treatise of the Plague,* by "Thomas Lodge, Doctor in Physic" (for E. White and N. L[ing]), was dedicated to the Lord Mayor. In 1614 his translation of *Seneca* was dedicated to T. Egerton, Baron Ellesmere. On 10th Jan. 1616 he, with one Henry Sewell, gent., obtained a pass "to travel into the Archduke's Country" to recover debts, and return within five months. In Mar. 1619 he was arrested by Alleyn (Collier, *Alleyn,* p. 47). In 1620 he dedicated an edition of his *Seneca* to the Earl of Suffolk, and in 1622 wrote an Address for the Countess of Lincoln's *Nursery.* In Sept. 1625 he died in the parish of St. Mary Magdalen, Old Fish Street. He had lived in Warwick Lane in 1602,

---

[1] As Dr. Ingleby rejects Lodge's authorship of *Prosopopeia, The Tears of Mary the Mother of God,* 1596 (for E. White; dedicated to the Countesses of Derby and Cumberland), I relegate it to this place. Not having seen the book, I am not in a position to oppose so great an authority.

and at Lambert Hill in 1609. His wife was Mrs. Joan or Jane Aldrid.

Mr. Collier is said to have had a medical MS. "corrected" by Lodge, and dedicated to Lady Arundel; but are the "corrections" genuine?

1. *The Wounds of Civil War.* "Lively set forth in the true tragedies of *Marius and Sylla.*" "Publicly played in London" by the Admiral's servants. "Written by Thomas Lodge, Gent. *O vita, misero longa, fœlici brevis.*" There is little doubt that this stage play, with its interminable list of characters, echo scene, French Pedro, &c., was produced in 1587. Lodge used the motto "*O vita, &c.,*" from 4th Nov. 1583 till 22nd Sept. 1589. The chariot drawn by four Moors in Sc. 3 is an evident copy from *Tamberlane.* Civil war was dreaded in England in 1587. I call attention to two phrases especially in this play, the prosaic medical "cooling card" in iv. 1, and the "rasors of Palermo" in v. 3, as characteristic of Lodge, who uses them not once or twice, like other men, but persistently in his works.

2. *Mucedorus,* "the King's son of Valentia," *and Amadine,* "the King's daughter of Arragon," with the merry conceits of Mouse. "Sundry times played in the honorable city of London." The earliest copy known dates 1598; but the date of first publication is unknown, as no entry in S. R. has yet been found. The date of first presentation is also unknown, but the older play on John (see further on) was played "in the honorable city of London" by the Queen's men. I do not know of plays of any other company played "in the *honorable* city of London." This points to c. 1588 as the date and the Queen's men as the company. A mask of shepherds presented by Lord Julio is referred to in i. 1, but this is *The Shepherds' Mask* of James

I.'s time, and the mention of it comes in the additions made in 1606 (though not so marked by the editors) when the play was revived by the King's men ; it had probably passed to Lord Strange's men along with many other plays in 1591–2, although it does not appear among their 1592 revivals. The original play was acted before Queen Elizabeth at Court; see the prayer at the end; and the arrangement for performance by eight players in the title also points to a very early date. As to authorship, the Induction is, I think, by the same hand as that to *The Warning for Fair Women ;* there are many coincidences in expression with *Marius and Sylla,* and the " cooling card " trade-mark is found in Sc. 17. No other author but Lodge is known in connexion with the 1587 Queen's men who could have written it; it is certainly not by Marlow, Peele, Green, or Dekker. That it was revived by the Chamberlain's men c. 1600 is likely. One of the "play scraps " in Marston's *What you will,* 1601, ii. i., is—

"Ha ! he mount chival on the wings of Fame ! "

where Halliwell prints " chirall." Compare—

" And raise his chival with a lasting fame " (Induction),

to which line Quadratus (Jonson) evidently refers. The Envy presentation of Jonson's *Poetaster* is adapted from this play.

In 1610 (and beyond doubt in the lost edition of 1606) *Mucedorus* was issued with new additions, as acted before the King at Whitehall on Shrove Sunday night by the King's servants usually, playing at the Globe. This title must belong to the 1606 edition, for there were no performances at Court at Shrovetide 1610 on account of the plague ; and this is further proved by the allusions to the *Eastward Ho* restraint in the added parts, " a trap for boys, not men " (Induction at the end of the play), and to " our unwilling error So late presented," in which a " raven with a needy beard," . . . " a lean and hungry meagre cannibal " had written a comedy with dark sentences and high abuse pleasing to factious brains ; Jonson's *Fox*, in which the King's miraculous healing powers by touch are perhaps ridiculed as Oglio del Scoto, and the ravens Corbaccio and Corvino are chief characters. Moreover, " usually at the Globe " implies a date before the taking over of the Black-friars by the King's men at Christmas 1609. From its shortness I conjecture that this play may have been one of the *Four plays in one* of 1605–6, with the *Yorkshire Tragedy*, *The Merry Devil of Edmonton*, and *Cloth Breeches.*

Lodge next appears as a coadjutor to Greene for the Queen's men, and this part of his career should be studied with Greene's, under whom I have noticed 3. 2 *Henry* 6 ; 4. *James* 4 ; 5. *George a Greene*, in all which Lodge, I think, had a hand.

6. The True Chronicle History of *King Leir and his three daughters*, " Goneril, Ragan, and Cordelia," was published 14th May 1594 ; it had been acted April 6–8 as an old play at the Rose by the Queen's and Sussex' men together. As it is the only play in Table C. p. 97 of my *History of the Stage* which does not occur in A and B, it may be fairly assigned to the Queen's men. The latter part, Sc. 11–30, is clearly by Lodge. " Cooling card " occurs in Sc. 11, " Razors of Palermo " (cf. *Marius and Sylla*) in Sc. 12, and there are coincidences of expression with his undoubted work too numerous to quote. The earlier part containing Skaliger is certainly by another hand, who in Sc. 7, 10 makes Leir dissyllabic, and in Sc. 1 writes Britanye (cf. Brittaine, Sc. 21, 24). I think this second hand was Marlow, or an imitator of him ; that he left this play

unfinished on leaving the Queen's men, and that Lodge finished it. Compare, for instance—

"She'll lay her husband's benefice on her back" (*Leir*, Sc. 6) ;
"She bears a duke's revenues on her back" (2 *Hen.* 6, i. 3, 83) ;
"He wears a lord's revenues on his back" (*Edw.* 2, i. 4, 406).

But the work is too poor for Marlow. I would suggest Kyd, his known imitator, and date his part 1588, Lodge's 1589.

This play was reprinted 1605 as "lately acted," doubtless in order that it might be taken for Shakespeare's *Leqr*. Note the "True Chronicle" in the title, which words also occur in *Cromwell* 1602, and the *Lear* Quarto 1608. In the 1594 S. R. entry of *Leir* we find "Most Famous" in place of "True."

7. *The Troublesome reign of John King of England*, " with the discovery of King Richard Cordelion's base son (vulgarly named the Bastard Fawconbridge). Also the Death of King John at Swinstead Abbey," was acted by the Queen's men "in the honorable City of London," soon after Marlow's *Tamberlane* (see Lines to the Gentlemen Readers), and therefore probably in 1588. See also the allusion to the threatened Armada at the end of the second part :—

"If England's peers and people join in one,
Nor Pope, nor France, nor Spain can do them wrong."

That the play is by several authors is clear from the varied spellings, Lewis and Lewes, the use of rhyme and prose, the quotations, and the allusions to Scripture. The surest guide in separating the authorship is the name Lewis. As I must consider both parts of the play in this matter, I now give the separate title of *The Second Part of the troublesome reiyn of King John*, " containing the death of Arthur Plantaginet, the landing of Lewes, and the poisoning of King John at

Swinstead Abbey." Part i. Sc. 1 (connected with ii. 8 by the use of the unusual expression " abbey lubbers ") and ii. 4–9 appear to be, in the main, by one hand, who writes (in the text) Lewes dissyllabic. This writer, I do not hesitate to confidently assert, is Lodge; the " cooling card " mark is in ii. 5 ; and the Scripture allusions, &c., are exactly like those in *The Looking-glass.* The " discovery of Cordelion's base son," i. 1, and the " landing of Lewes," ii. 4, 5, 7, 9, and the " poisoning of King John," ii. 6, 8, are included therein. But i. 2–9 (except a bit at the end of Sc. 9), 10–12, ii. 2, is by one who writes Lewis dissyllabic in the text. This is the main part of the play, and is, I think, by Peele. The remainder, i. 9 (bit at the end after the stage directions change from Lewis to Lewes), ii. 1, 3, are by a third hand, who writes Lewes, and pronounces it as a mono-syllable; he also writes Hughbert for Hubert. This in-cludes the " death of Arthur." I have little doubt that he is Greene, as Rosse and Percy, two of the unnecessary group of Lords who appear only in ii. 3, are also *Dram. Pers.* in *James* 4. This division of the play differs but slightly from that in my edition of it, made before I had succeeded in separating the authors of *Henry* 6. The " poisoning," how-ever, ii. 6, 8, may have been by Marlow ; but whoever wrote that I think wrote i. 1. These two plays were reprinted in 1611 as " by W. Sh.," and 1622, when Shakespeare was dead, as " by William Shakespeare," palpably with the deceitful intention of selling the play as his *King John,* which was most likely revived at both those dates, they being times when Spanish alliances were negotiating for a son of King James. The likeness of the title to *The trouble-some reign of Edward* 2, &c., seems to me to indicate Mar-low as the chief plotter.

9. *A Looking-glass for London and England* was published

as by T. Lodge and R. Greene, "*in Artibus Magister*," a style which Greene used from Sept. 1587 to Oct. 1590. The subject of this play is alluded to in Greene's *Mourning Garment*, S. R. 2 Nov. 1590, the first work in which he introduced "*utriusque Academiæ*" into his designation. The play probably dates just before this. It is certainly the one referred to in his *Groatsworth of Wit* as that which he had "lastly" written, and for the sharp lines in which he reproves Lodge [not Nash, as some would have it]. It was probably acted, like all Greene's plays, by the Queen's men. The part written by Greene is assuredly that of Rasni unrepentant, to which we must add Sc. 2, where the Clown (Adam) is called Smith, and the two scenes where Thrasybulus and Alcon are named Young Gentleman and Poor Man. This gives Greene Sc. 1–5, 6*b*, 12. Lodge wrote the rest, and left England in the next year, 1591. This play was revived by L. Strange's men at the Rose in Mar. 1592.

10. *A warning for Fair Women* (the murder of George Sanders in 1573) was acted by the Chamberlain's men "lately," before its publication 17th Nov. 1599. In the Prologue the theatre is called a "round" and a "fair circuit" —rather the Globe than the Curtain, one would think. The Induction should be compared with those to *Mucedorus* and *Two Tragedies in One*. For my reasons for assigning to Lodge a period of return to playmaking c. 1598–1601 see *The Return from Parnassus*. This play is a murder-play, like *Arden of Feversham* and *Page of Plymouth* and *Beech's Tragedy*. The other writers for the Chamberlain's men at this time were Shakespeare and Jonson. Objectors to my hypothesis of Lodge's authorship may adopt one of these, or (the usual resource) imagine some unknown playwright not elsewhere heard of. But I cannot state too emphatically that any attribution of this and the ensuing play to Lodge

is conjectural, and founded less on positive evidence than on the method of exhaustions.

11. *A Larum for London*, or *The Siege of Antwerp*, " with the venturous acts and valorous deeds of the Lame Soldier." This was acted by the Chamberlain's servants before the S. R. entry 29th May 1600 ; probably in 1599. Time is the Presenter. For the lame soldier compare *Liberality and Prodigality*, *The Shoemaker's Holiday*, &c. ; for the title the end of the *Looking-glass*, " The larum rings," &c. The date of the siege was 1576.

See also *Richard* 3, Anon., 242 ; *Selimus*, Anon., 240, Greene, 10.

LOWER, Sir WILLIAM. (Plays.)

   1. *The Phœnix in her Flames*, T., by Thomas Harper for Michael Young, 1639.

   Polyeuctes, or *The Martyr*, T., 1655. (Founded on P. Corneille, *Polieucte*, 1641.)

   Horatius, T., 1656. (Founded on P. Corneille, *Les Horaces*, 1641.)

   The Three Dorothies, or *Jodelet Box'd*, c. 1657. (Founded on P. Scarron, *Jodelet, duelliste, ou Les Trois Dorothées*, 1648.)

   Don Japhet of Armenia, C. In MS. (Founded on P. Scarron, *Don Japhet d'Armenie*, 1654.)

   The Enchanted Lovers, P. Hage, 1658 ; London, 1659.

   The Noble Ingratitude, P. T. C. Hage, 1659. (Founded on Quinault, *La généreuse Ingratitude*, 1657.)

   The Amorous Phantasm, T. C. Hage, 1660. (Founded on Quinault, *Le Fantome Amoureux*, 1657.)

Born at Tremare, Cornwall. Lived at the Hague from the time of the Civil War till his death in 1662.

   1. *The Phœnix in her Flames* is the only one of these plays that comes within my time limit. The others are

enumerated merely to show the use made of French plays
under the Commonwealth.

LOVELACE, RICHARD. (Plays.)

Son of Sir William Lovelace of Woolwich, Kent. Born
c. 1618. From Charter House School he went as gentleman commoner to Gloucester Hall, Oxford, 1634; was made
M.A. 1636, when the King came to Oxford; and afterwards
became a soldier under Lord Goring's patronage. His subsequent career till his death in 1658 does not concern us
here.

1. *The Scholar*[s], C., was acted at Gloucester Hall, Oxford (Query in 1636), and at Salisbury Court (Query by
the Queen's men). The Prologue and Epilogue are given
in *Lucasta*, 1649.

2. *The Soldier*, T. As the titles of these plays indicate,
considering Lovelace's own career, that this was the later
play of the two, it also was probably acted at Salisbury
Court by the Queen's men.

LUPTON, THOMAS. (Morality.)

1. 1577, Nov. 25, for Roger Ward. *All for money.*
" Plainly representing the manners of men and fashion of
the world nowadays," 1578. Query, is this *The Devil and
Dives?* See the list of characters in *Biog. Dram*. This
interlude is reprinted in *Literature of the* 16*th and* 17*th
Centuries illustrated*, 1851.

M., W. (Play.)

1. *The Lanching of the May*, or *The Seaman's honest
Wife*, written by W. M., Gent., in his return from East India,
A.D. 1632. Brit. Mus., Egerton MS., 1994. Licensed by
Herbert 1633, June 27. "All the Oaths in the Action to be
left out, as they are crost in the book, and all other Reforma-
tions strictly observed." A mere laudation of the East India
Company. An extract is given in Bullen's *Old Plays*, ii. 432.

MABBE, JAMES. (Translation.)

1. 1630, Feb. 27, for Ralph Mabbe. *The Spanish Bawd represented in Celestina*, or the tragic comedy of *Calisto and Melibœa*, 1631. Translated (apparently by a relation of the publisher) from the Spanish of Montalvan. In twenty-one acts. Its only importance for us is the connexion in subject with *The Beauty of Good Properties of Women* (*q.v.*).

MACHIN, LEWIS. See Markham, and Anon., 295*.

MANUCHE, COSMO. (Plays.)

An Italian; and a major in Charles I.'s army.

1. *The Just General*, T. C., 1650. Dedicated to the Earl of Northampton and his wife. Scene, Sicily.

2. *The Loyal Lovers*, T. C., 1652. Satire on the Committee-men.

These plays seem not to have been acted, and if they were they lie beyond my date limit; but I wish to include every play possibly lying within it.

MARKHAM, JERVIS or GERVASE. (Plays.)

1. 1608, Oct. 6, for John Bache. *The Dumb Knight*, C., 1608, 1633.

2. 1622, Feb. 22, for Matthew Rodes. *Herod and Antipater*, T., 1622.

Gervase, third son of Robert Markham of Cotham, Nottinghamshire, soldier and scholar. He fought in the Low Countries, and served under Essex in Ireland along with his brothers Francis and Godfrey; was a good classical scholar, and perfect master of French, Italian, and Spanish. For forty years at least, beginning in 1593, he poured forth a flood of books on various subjects, which lie beyond my scope—some thirty in number.

1. *The Dumb Knight* was acted by the children of His Majesty's Revels, probably in 1607. It was published with Markham's name as author on the title-page, and an Address

by Lewis Machin to the Understanding Reader, from which
it appears that "strange constructions" had been made of
this play; in modern language, it was regarded as a satirical
libel. As to Machin himself, he merely laughs at the
accusation. As to his "partner in the wrong," he is of
approved worth, and knows how to answer for himself. His
partner's answer was to withdraw his name from the book,
which may be taken as a tacit confession that he was the
author of the satirical part, viz., the underplot in i. 2,
ii. 1, iii. 2, 4; iv. 2, v. 2 (part), containing the story of
orator Prate, his wife Lollia, the bawd Collaquintida, his clerk
Precedent, his clients Velours and Drap, and the carpen-
ters Chip and Shavings. None of these characters appear
in the serious part of the play, which is founded on a novel
of Bandello's. Who is satirised as orator Prate I know not;
but the foul-mouthed clerk Precedent, who is coarser and
filthier in his talk than almost any character in our coarsest
plays, is in iii. 4 represented as a diligent reader of "*Maid's
Philosophy*, or *Venus and Adonis*," from which he quotes the
most luscious bits. The evident intention is to set down
Shakespeare as merely an immoral writer, just as people
used to treat Byron by quoting *Don Juan*.

2. For *Herod and Antipater*, "with the death of Fair
Mariam," see Sampson, W.

But Markham has a further, though indirect, connexion
with the drama through Shakespeare. On 23rd April 1593
his *Thyrsis and Daphne* (now lost, but evidently an amatory
poem like *Venus and Adonis*, *Hero and Leander*, *Procris and
Cephalus*, all written by 1593) was entered S. R. for Widow
Charlewood. He was one of the rivals of Shakespeare along
with Chute and Marlow, to say nothing of earlier poems,
such as Fraunce's *Phillis and Amintas*, 1591. In 1595,
Sept. 9., S. R., was entered *The most honorable tragedy of*

Sir Richard Grenvile, Knight, for J. Roberts. This book
had four Dedications—1. to L. Montjoy, 2. to the Earl of
Sussex, 4. to Sir E. Wingfield, and 3. to Henry Wriothesley,
Earl of Southampton. In Shakespeare's *Sonnets,* 78–86,
which were certainly addressed to Southampton, mention
is made of an "alien pen" (78), worthier (79) and better
(80) than Shakespeare's; as being learned (78) and well
refined (85), who lends Southampton virtue (79), whose
spirit is taught to write by spirits above a mortal pitch
(86). The phrase "both your poets" (83) implies that
these two, Shakespeare and the worthier pen, were the only
two poets who had since 1593, when Shakespeare first invoked Southampton's muse (78), dedicated works of any
pretension to him. Nor is any other such poet certainly
known, Nash's prose being out of the question, and Barnes'
Parthenophil (May 1593) too early. Moreover, Markham
addresses Southampton as "Lamp of Virtue," and he invokes
the spirit of Grenvile to

"Sit on my hand and teach me to indite;"

which the spirit evidently does, for at the end of the poem
it is Grenvile's style, not Markham's, that obtains immortal
verse; and surely a more "affable, familiar ghost" (86)
never guided a poet's pen. If Markham was not the "poet"
aimed at in the *Sonnets,* at any rate no other candidate for
that position yet proposed by others has nearly so good a
claim; if he was, the bitter allusion to *Venus and Adonis* in
The Dumb Knight is accounted for. And yet (see under
Marlow and Shakespeare) other, and, I think, still preferable, candidates will be found in G. Harvey and M. Drayton.

MARLOW, MARLEY, or MERLIN, CHRISTOPHER. (Plays.)

1, 2. 1590, Aug. 14, for Richard Jones. 1, 2 *Tam-*
berlane, The Scythian Shepherd, T., 1590, 1590–2,
1605–6.

9. 1593, July 6, for Richard Jones. *Edward 2*, H., 1594, 1598, 1604, 1612, 1622.

6. 1594, Mar. 12, for T. Myllington. 1 *York and Lancaster*, H., 1594, 1600, 1619.

4. 1594, May 17, for T. Myllington. *The rich Jew of Malta*, T., 1633.

8. 2 *York and Lancaster* (*Richard Duke of York*), H., 1595 (for T. Myllington), 1600, 1619.

10. *The Massacre of Paris*, T., n.d., for E. White [c. 1595].

7. 1595, Nov. 26, for Cuthbert Burbye. *Edward 3*, H., 1596–1599, 1609, 1617, 1625.

3. 1601, Jan. 7, for Thomas Bushell. *Doctor Faustus*, T., 1604, 1609, 1611, 1616, 1620, 1624, 1631, 1663.

Christopher Marlowe, son of John Marlowe, shoemaker (and clerk of St. Mary's?), was baptized at St. George the Martyr's, Canterbury, 26th February 1564. He was an exhibitioner at the King's School, Cambridge, and as such, from Easter to Christmas 1579, received three quarterly payments of £1 each. In 1581 "Marlin," on 17th Mar., matriculated at Benet College (now Corpus Christi). "Xrof Marlyn" took his B.A. degree in 1583. "Chr. Marley" was made M.A. in 1587, and translated *The Rape of Helen* from Coluthus (Coxeter's papers). He then came to London, and, after six years' play-writing, was killed by one Francis Archer in a tavern broil, and buried at St. Nicholas, Deptford. After his death his two sestiads of *Hero and Leander* were published in 1598 for E. Blunt (see Chapman).

1, 2. *Tamburlaine the Great*, "the Scythian Shepherd and the Scourge of God" (see editions for full title), in two discourses, was acted by the Admiral's men on stages in the City of London in 1587. "Atheist Tamburlan" is referred to in Greene's *Perimedes*, S. R. 29th March 1.588. The Prologue depreciates "rhyming mother wits."

3. *The Tragical History of Dr. Faustus* was acted by the Admiral's men in 1588. The ballad founded on it was entered S. R. 28th Feb. 1589, and *The Taming of a Shrew*, which contains a line imitated from it, was satirised in Greene's *Menaphon*, S. R. 23rd Aug. 1589. This play is by Marlow and Dekker. Marlow wrote Sc. 1, 3, 5 (except ll. 134–138, 141–148, 163–end); Sc. 6 (except ll. 4–10, 33–end; ll. 80, 83 are, however, Marlow's); Sc. 7 (altered); Sc. 11, ll. 1–9, 39–44; Sc. 13, ll. 18–end (except 36–39). I refer for a fuller discussion of this question to my Appendix A. in Ward's excellent edition. The variant version of the later editions was made up by S. Rowley and Bird 22nd Nov. 1602. The copyright was transferred to J. Wright, S. R. 13th Sept. 1610. The new title, *The Tragical History of the Life and Death of Dr. Faustus*, first appears in the 1616 edition.

4. *The Jew of Malta* was first performed after the death of the Guise 23rd Dec. 1588. "Now the Guise is dead," says Machiavel in the Prologue. This play was in 1593 acted by L. Strange's men at the Rose. It had, therefore, if we may judge by the history of the other plays acted then and there, been originally produced by the Queen's men. From L. Strange's it passed to Sussex' players, and from them to the Admiral's in 1594. Alleyn played the Jew's part. The extant version of 1633 was edited by T. Heywood after it had been played by Queen Henrietta's men at the Cockpit, and before the King and Queen at Whitehall, R. Perkins taking the part of Barabbas. In the scenes with Bellamira and Pilia Borza there is a good deal not by Marlow. This is not due to original collaboration, but to

alteration by Heywood c. 1632. Compare *The Captives* (the part with the friars).

5, 6. 1, 2 *Henry* 6 were probably produced in 1589 by the Queen's men. Marlow had a share in writing these plays, which I have discussed in my *Life of Shakespeare*, Section V., more fully than it would be justifiable to reproduce here.

1589, Aug. 23, Greene's *Menaphon* was entered S. R. Many allusions in Nash's Address prefixed thereto have been referred to Marlow, which really concern Kyd. It is a fashion to make Marlow responsible for everything where blank verse is mentioned or glanced at. I cannot find any direct allusion to Marlow in *Menaphon*, and I have no doubt that, had he still been writing for the Queen's men, he would have been mentioned as well as Peele. This silence is to me evidence that he had left the company, or was on the eve of leaving it. In Greene's *Never too late*, which dates before Nov. 1590, Tully (Greene) says to Roscius (Wilson), "If the Cobler have taught thee to say *Ave Cæsar*," which must, I think, refer to the next-mentioned play.

7. *Edward 3 and the Black Prince, their wars with King John of France.* This play, which passed to the Lord Chamberlain's men in 1594, no doubt with the other Pembroke's men plays, was, I feel sure, originally written by Marlow on the foundation of Holinshed's *Chronicle*. Shakespeare inserted in it, i. 2*b*–ii. 2, the story of the Countess taken from *The Palace of Pleasure*, just as he did the Talbot scenes in 1 *Henry* 6. In i. 1 "*Ave Cæsar*" occurs, a phrase which I cannot find elsewhere in any play that can be placed earlier than Greene's *Never too late*. On all these Marlow plays compare my *Life of Shakespeare*, Section V. It would be unfair to the purchasers of that work to repeat that Section here *in extenso*.

8. *The True Tragedy of Richard Duke of York and the death of good King Henry 6*, "with the whole Contention of the two Houses of Lancaster and York," was acted by the servants of the Earl of Pembroke, and must be referred to the date 1589–91. It was, in my opinion, an acting version abridged from 3 *Henry* 6, and beyond question by Marlow. See my *Life of Shakespeare, ut supra.*

9. *Edward* 2 (for the long full title of which see the editions, and note that these long titles are characteristic of Marlow throughout his career) was also acted by Pembroke's men 1590–1. This play they did not part with. It remained with them when they became successively Worcester's and Queen Anne's men, and in 1622 was issued as "acted by the late Queen's Majesty's servants at the Red Bull." They were at that time called The Company of the Revels. For a number of parallelisms between *Edward* 2 and *Henry* 6 see my edition of this play ; which, however, requires correction in many other matters, which, being stereotyped, it is not likely to obtain. The passages are too lengthy to quote here. Before September 1592 (probably at the opening of the Rose 19th Feb.) Marlow joined L. Strange's men, for whom Peele was also writing. Hence the Address to him, Peele, and Lodge in *Greene's Groatsworth of Wit*, which was intended to induce these men to leave that company. It did not produce that effect.

10. *The Massacre at Paris*, "with the Death of the Duke of Guise," was produced by Lord Strange's men 30th Jan. 1593 as a new play. It passed, like *Faustus*, to the Admiral's men, and was revived by them on 19th June 1594, in Nov. 1598 (*Diary*, pp. 110, 113), and again in Nov. 1601, p. 202, where "Webster" (a forgery, for the little tailor's name was Radford) is inserted by Collier. It was

published (probably in 1594) from an abridged acting copy as played by the Admiral's servants. A MS. of a portion of the omitted parts was in the possession of Mr. Collier, which, like the similar MS. of Greene's *Orlando*, no doubt properly belonged to the Alleyn papers at Dulwich College. This MS. contains a bit of the Guise's part as played by Alleyn in the original version for the L. Strange's company. These instances show how the plays were cut down for revivals, and strongly confirm my view of the nature of the early Quartos of 2, 3 *Henry* 6, with regard to which I may here note that Myllington never published any play unconnected with Marlow except *Henry* 5, and that was immediately transferred to T. Pavier.

11. *The tragedy of Dido, Queen of Carthage*, was published after Marlow's death. Written by Marlow and Nash. See Nash.

12. *Titus Andronicus*, a new play in 1594, may be Marlow's. See *Titus Andronicus*, Anon., 128.

13. *Richard* 3 was, in my opinion, based on a play by Marlow. See my *Life of Shakespeare*, Section V.

14. *The Maiden's Holiday*, C., was entered 8th April 1654 S. R. as by Marlow and Day. As the MS. was destroyed by Warburton's servant, we cannot ascertain the truth as to the authorship of this play.

15. *Lust's Dominion* was published 1657 as by Marlow. See Haughton; *Spanish Moor's Tragedy*.

16. *The true History of George Scanderbage* was played by the Earl of Oxford's servants, and entered S. R. 3rd July 1601, but is not known to be extant. In G. Harvey's *Sonnets*, at the end of his *New letter of notable contents*, after allusions to Charlemagne (? *The Distracted Emperor*), Guise (*The Massacre at Paris*), and *Tamberlane*, Harvey satirises Marlow for having made Paul's work of *Tamberlane*.

This publication of plays not performed at Court was as yet almost unprecedented.   He then goes on :—

> "is that Gargantua mind
> Conquered and left no Scanderbeg behind ?
> Vowed he not to Paul's a second bile ? "

This seems to indicate an affected surprise that Marlow had not published *Scanderbeg* as well as *Tamberlane,* and surely attributes its authorship to Marlow.   The dates would suit very well, for a play performed by the Earl of Oxford's men could not be later than 1588 ; and Harvey would be likely to know of such plays of Marlow's as were written at Cambridge and taken with him to London in 1587.   This may, then, have been a play performed, before any of Marlow's extant plays, in 1587 ; and Marlow may have "vowed a second bile" to Paul's by an intended publication of it.   The date of this effusion is Sept. 1593. But this *Sonnet* is far more interesting in another way, for the "Familiar Sprite" who buzzes Epitaphs into Harvey's head as he lies in bed before the dawn, and gives him the false news that Marlow died of the plague, is surely the "familiar ghost Who nightly gulls him with intelligence" of Shakespeare's *Sonnet* 86 ; and if so, this identifies Shakespeare's rival of *Sonnets* 78–86 with Gabriel Harvey. Shakespeare's known respect for Marlow's memory shows how he would resent such an attack on it as Harvey's.   See under Markham and Shakespeare for alternative hypotheses.

16. *The Troublesome Reign of King John, q.v.,* was in the end portion partly written by Marlow, in Dyce's opinion. See under *John* on this matter.   Malone attributed the whole play to him.   Mr. A. H. Bullen, whose edition of Marlow is mostly a *rifacciamento* of Dyce's, thus alludes to Dyce's view :—"Earless and unabashed must be the critic who would charge Marlow with any complicity in *The Trouble-*

some Reign of King John." I am proud that in this same book a slight magazine article of mine is described as a "titanic absurdity, gross as a mountain, open, palpable." Mr. Bullen has at one stroke placed on record his gratitude for the trouble I bestowed in correcting his inaccuracies and his superiority to Mrs. Malaprop in "derangement of epitaphs."

MARMION, SHACKERLEY. (Plays).

1. 1632, Jan. 26, for John Grove. *The Leaguer*, C., 1632, 1633. "The reformations to be strictly observed."
2. 1633, June 15, for Richard Meighen. *A Fine Companion*, C., 1638.
3. 1640, Mar. 11, for John Williams and Francis Egglestone. *The Antiquary*, C. 1641.

Born Jan. 1602 in the manor house of Aynho, Northamptonshire; educated under Richard Boucher at the free school, Thame, Oxfordshire; gentleman commoner of Wadham, Oxford, 1617; M.A. 1624. His father had dissipated the family property, and sold Aynho in 1618. He fought in the Low Countries; returned to England; wrote plays and the fine poem *Cupid and Psyche*, which was presented to the Prince Elector 1637; was admitted into Suckling's troop in the Scots expedition, but fell sick at York, returned to London, and died 1639.

1. *Holland's Leaguer* (or *The Leaguer*, S. R.), C., was acted by Prince Charles' servants at Salisbury Court; it had been "lately and often acted" between the 10th and 26th of Jan. 1632. The Prologue acknowledges the superiority of the King's men and the Queen's men, but implies the inferiority of the other companies, the Revels of the Fortune and the Outsiders of the Bull. The impostors Agurtes and Autolichus are J. Williams and T. Dixon. See ii. 3, where

the abortive project of these worthies in 1626 to build an amphitheatre in Lincoln's Inn Fields is plainly alluded to.

2. *A Fine Companion*, C., was also acted by the Prince's men at Salisbury Court, and before the King and Queen at Whitehall, before May 1633. The plays alluded to in the Prologue as contemned by the vulgar are—1. Jonson's *Magnetic Lady*, licensed 12th Oct. 1632 (but not published till 1641) for the King's men; 2. Shirley's *Ball*, licensed 18th Nov. 1632 (published 1638) for the Queen's men; 3. Ford's *Love's Sacrifice*, acted by the Queen's men, which was published 21st Jan. 1633, with an Epistle Commendatory by Shirley, who addresses Prynne in it as "voluminously ignorant." Compare the expressions in Marmion's Prologue—

> "And then ascribed it to their ignorance ;"

and—

> "With some
> Commendatory Epistles
> Fly to the press to vindicate your credit."

3. *The Antiquary*, C., was acted by the Queen's men at the Cockpit; therefore before 12th May 1636. But the play was revised before publication, the scene being changed from Venice to Pisa, and Bravo's character being altered in iii. 1 and v. 3. The King's occasional attendance (or is it the Queen's only ?) at the theatre is alluded to at the end of the play. For iv. 3 compare *Ram Alley*, *The Parson's Wedding*, and *Woman's a Riddle*.

4. *The Crafty Merchant*, or *The Soldiered Citizen*, C., is mentioned as Marmion's in Warburton's list; but see Bonen.

In Halliwell's *Dictionary*, copied, as usual, without verification from *Biog. Dram.*, which he exploited and then abused, *Holland's Leaguer* is said (as if it were a part of the title-page) to have been "performed at Court." This is probably a mistake arising from the title-page of *The Fine Companion*.

MARSTON, JOHN.   (Plays and Masks.)

   4. 1600, Sept. 8, for Felix Norton. *Jack Drum's entertainment*, C., 1601, 1616.

   5, 6. 1601, Oct. 24, for Matthew Lownes and Thomas Fisher.   1, 2 *Antonio and Mellida*, 1602.

   9. 1604, July 5, for William Aspley and Thomas Thorpe. *The Malcontent*, T. C., 1604.

   8. 1605, June 26, for John Hodgets. *The Dutch Courtesan*, C., 1605.

   13. 1605, Sept. 4, for William Aspley and Thomas Thorpe. *Eastward Ho*, C., 1605.

   11. 1606, Mar. 12, for William Cotton. *The Fawn*, 1606.

   10. 1606, Mar. 17, for Eleazar Edgar. *The Wonder of Women*, or *Sophonisba*, T., 1606.

   7. 1607, Aug. 6, for Thomas Thorpe. *What you will*, 1607.

   1. 1610, Oct. 31, for Thomas Thorpe. *Histriomastix*, 1610.

   12. *The Insatiate Countess*, T., by T. S. for Thomas Archer, 1613.

   16. *The Mountebanks*, Mask. MS.

   15. *Lord and Lady Huntingdon's Entertainment*. MS.
Collected *Plays*, 1633, for William Sheares.

John Marston of Coventry (doubtless the dramatist) was born c. 1576.   Commoner or fellow-commoner at Brazennose, Oxford, 1591; B.A. Feb. 1593; married Mary, daughter of William Wilkes, chaplain to James I. Died 25th June 1634, and was buried in the Temple Church near his father, who had been a counsellor in the Middle Temple.

Marston's earliest works were not dramatic.   On 1598, May 27, *The Metamorphosis of Pigmalion's Image and cer-*

tain Satires was entered S. R. for Edmond Mattes; on 1598, Sept. 8, *The Scourge of Villany,* "three books of Satires," for James Roberts; on 30th Mar. Hall's *Virgidemiarum* had been entered; and on 3rd May *Seven Satires applied to the Week,* by W. Rankins; so that Marston was the Third English Satirist; but as he seems to have been acknowledged as the Second, Rankins' book probably appeared after his. Marston's *Satires* are very important for Dramatic History. They were indirectly the origin of the three years' stage war between Jonson and Marston, Dekker, &c. There is no trustworthy modern edition of Marston to which I can refer the reader. In 1599 *The Scourge* was reprinted with the addition of "new satires." In the first book he had attacked Hall (Grillus) somewhat violently, and defended Markham, Southwell, Sackville, Daniel, Drayton, &c., against him. In *The Scourge* he again attacked Hall, Davis, Barnes, and, I think, Donne. In the second edition he inserted a new Satire (x.), in which he again attacks Hall on pretext of self-defence. But in all these Satires I find no one attacked but rival satirists, and no trace of enmity to Jonson or any playwright. Gifford, rash and inaccurate as usual, says that Marston in *The Scourge* ridiculed Jonson's words, "real, Delphic, intrinsicate," &c., "which are all to be found in his earliest comedies;" but when *The Scourge* was written not one of Jonson's extant comedies had been published, and scarcely one acted. More concerning these Satires will appear under the Dramatic Works, to which I now turn.

1. *Histriomastix,* or *The Player Whipt.* This play was produced before Jonson's *Every man out of his Humour,* 1599, in which it is satirised. In i. 1 Clove (who is not Marston, but a talker of "fustian" derived from his works), at the end of his principal fustian speech, quotes its title, " as

you may read in Plato's *Histriomastix*—you conceive me, Sir;" and the authorship is certain, for Clove not only uses fustian words, " Zodiac, Ecliptic, Tropic, Mathematical, i. 1 ; Paunch of Esquiline, iii. 4, which occur in *Histriomastix*, but also " synderesis " (*Scourge*, viii.), mincing capreal (*Scourge*, xi.), circumference (*Scourge*, x.), intellectual (*Scourge*, " To Detraction "), which I have not found in *Histriomastix*. This identifies the Plato who wrote *Histriomastix* with the Don Kynsader or Theriomastix, who wrote *The Scourge*. All the indications of date agree with this, and the year being thus settled, the fear of Spanish invasion, " The Spaniards are come," v. 4, would seem to fix the very month of production, for it was in August that this dread was excited. But this must not be pressed too far, for the play has a double ending, one for the public stage, in which Plenty, &c., resign their Sceptres to Peace in Dumb Show, and the other for a Court performance, in which Astræa personates the Queen herself in enthroned Majesty; and the extra-metrical words, " The Spaniards are come," seem to have been inserted for this performance when the fear had passed away. The only companies who performed at Court 1599–1600 were the Chamberlain's, the Admiral's, and Derby's. The plays by the Admiral's men were *Fortunatus* and *The Shoemaker's Holiday*. This one could not have been acted by the Chamberlain's men, as it is satirised by Jonson in a Chamberlain's play. It was, therefore, necessarily that acted by Derby's men, who at this time occupied the Curtain, from which another company had been ousted and driven to travel. The shareholders among these latter, there is little doubt, were Kempe, Beeston, Duke, and Pallant, who had just left the Chamberlain's men, and this company is, I think, satirised in *Histriomastix*. The poet who accompanies them is a " pageanter,"

iv. 3 ; has been a ballad-writer, v. 2, vi. 5 ; ought to be employed in matter of state, ii. 2 ; is great in plotting " new " plays that are old ones, ii. 2 ; and uses " no new luxury or blandishment, but plenty of Old England's mother words." He is certainly Antony Monday. Moreover, we have Jonson's direct assertion that his quarrel with Marston began thus, " that Marston represented him on the stage." There is no play of Marston's possibly anterior to *Every man out of his Humour* in which any personation of Jonson can be detected except the present, in which I have no doubt that Chrysoganus means Jonson. The " translating scholar " who can " write a stabbing Satire or an Epigram," ii. 1, and is refused by the strollers as their playwright in favour of Posthaste Monday, iii. 4, and whose speech on Envy, iv. 2, is so thoroughly Jonsonian in purport, can hardly be any one else. But Marston evidently meant to compliment Jonson, not to abuse him ; and the indirect compliment to the man who had been rejected by the strollers, and was now poet to the chief company in London, second only to Shakespeare, was as delicate as it was deserved. Nevertheless Jonson took offence ; he could not tolerate being made to talk fustian, and his scholarly service to all the sciences implied in i. 1 did not compensate for that. Hence his abuse of Marston ; but not as Carlo Buffone, The Grand Scourge or second Untruss of the Time (Hall being the first) ; for Carlo was Dekker : see under Jonson. The satire on Monday as Posthaste was also, I think, meant to be acceptable to Jonson, who had exhibited him as Antonio Balladino, the pageant poet, in *The Case is Altered*. Posthaste, like Monday, can sing extempore, ii. 4 ; but his principal business is to refashion other men's plays, such as *The Prodigal Son* (the play existing in the German version, published 1620, and probably taken abroad by Kempe's company in 1600) and *Troilus and Cressida* (from Dekker and Chettle's play of 1599). The allusion "when he shakes his furious Spear" in this latter, ii. 4, cannot, unfortunately, be fully explained, as the Dekker play is not extant; but it probably refers to something therein anent Shakespeare's drama on the subject in its earlier form. I do not suppose that the Post-haste company were actually impressed as soldiers; but it is just worth mention, as confirming the date assigned to this play, that such presses as that in vi. 5 began to be made in Jan. 1599. See *Stow*, p. 788. The alteration for the Court seems to have introduced a good deal of confusion between Fourcher and Voucher in iv. 1, vi. 3. Incle was also imperfectly expunged when Gulet and Clout were added; but there is no shadow of reason in supposing any dual authorship. *Histriomastix* is of little value as literature, but as a portion of Dramatic History it is invaluable, and, like Marston's other works, sadly requires editing by a competent hand.

2. 1599, Sept. 3, 15, 16, 27, *Robert 2, King of Scots.* Marston has been thought to be the "other gentleman" who wrote this play in conjunction with Chettle, Dekker, and Jonson. If so, *Histriomastix* must, I think, date in October 1599, which is unlikely.

3. 1599, Sept. 28, Henslow paid Mr. Maxton or Marston, the new poet, £2 in earnest of a "book." If this play were ever finished and acted, it was probably burned at the Fortune in 1624.

4. *Jack Drum's entertainment,* or *The comedy of Pasquil and Katherine,* was acted by the children of Paul's, then recently re-established, v. 1; in a Leap-year, or "women's year," i. 1, *i.e.,* in 1600, about May (compare i. 1, "'Tis Whitsuntide"); while Kemp's morris, Feb. 11–Mar. 11, was the nine

days' wonder of the time, i. 1. That the author was Marston there can be no doubt. As Mr. Simpson said, his vocabulary betrays him. As this is important, especially in confuting the identification of Jonson's Crispinus with Shakespeare published by Mr. Jacob Feis, and commended for its research by Dr. Karl Blind, I give here a list of the words vomited by Crispinus with references to such of them as I have noticed in Marston :—

barmy froth. *Scourge, In Lectores,* To Perusers, vi. *Drum.,* i. 1, v. 1.

chilblained. *Drum.,* ii. 1.

clumsy. *Drum.,* ii. 1. *2 Ant.,* Prol.

clutcht. *2 Ant.,* i. 1, v. 1.

conscious. *Scourge,* viii.

damp. *Scourge,* vii.

defunct.

fatuate.

furibund.

glibbery. *Drum.* i. 1. *1 Ant.,* i. 1, ii. 1, iv. 1.

incubus. *2 Ant.,* iv. 4.

inflate.

lubrical.

magnificate. *Scourge,* Proem. ii.

oblatrant.

obstupefact.

prorumped.

puffy. Sat. ii. *Scourge, In Lectores,* iv.

quaking custard. *Scourge,* ii.

reciprocal.

retrograde.

snarling gu[s]ts. *2 Ant.,* Prol.

snotteries. *Scourge,* ii.

spurious.

strenuous.   1 *Ant.*, Induction.   2 *Ant.*, v. 1.

turgidous.

ventosity.

In this play I have little doubt that young Brabant is, as Mr. Simpson conjectured, Marston; but that the elder Brabant can be meant for Jonson is, I think, disproved by Jonson himself, who says, in his *Conversations:* " He had many quarrels with Marston; . . . the beginning of them were that Marston represented him in [on] the stage in his youth given to venery; . . . a man made his own wife to court him, whom he enjoyed two years ere he knew of it, and one day finding them by chance, was passingly delighted with it." This astounding story is identical with that of Monsieur John fo de King in this play, and this French reprobate is, therefore, strange as it may seem, Jonson. The two brothers Brabant are the brother Satyrists, Hall and Marston. Sir Edward Fortune is surely Edward Alleyne, who was then building the Fortune Theatre; the agreement was made 8th Jan. 1600. Timothy Tweedle seems very like Antony Monday, and Christopher Flawn I take to be Christopher Beeston. John Ellis, with his similes, is a gross caricature of John Lyly. But I must not pursue this question of personal satire too far in a place where I have not space for full proof. I hope to complete a monograph on the subject. The identification of the " fustian " which Jonson had imputed to Marston with the " compliment " which Jonson introduced in his own plays, " compliment is as much as fustian," iii. 2, is not merely a good *quid pro quo*, but shows that this play is an answer to *Every man out of his humor.* Pasquil is perhaps Nicholas Breton. His Pasquil's *Madcap and his Message,* 20th Mar.; *Foolscap* (signed N. B.), 10th May; *Mistress, Pass and Passeth not,* 29th May; *Swollen Humors,* 22nd Aug.; all appeared in 1600.

5. *The History of Antonio and Mellida* (Part i.) was acted by the children of Paul's. Jonson early in 1600, in *Cynthia's Revels*, v. 2, "played the painter, and limmed to the life" Anaides, Hedon, and Amorphus. Now Anaides is acknowledged to be Marston. He also wrote the additional scene with the Painter in it in Kyd's *Spanish Tragedy*, which was perhaps acted by the Chapel children 1599–1600 (see Induction to *Cynthia's Revels*), wherein Jeronymo requires "a doleful cry" to be painted. Marston hits both these by introducing a painter who in 1599 had "limmed" one picture, and in 1600 had represented Marston at twenty-four years old in the other. Balurde requires him to paint "Uh!" (a belch), and a reeling song. There is no reference whatever to *Hamlet*, as some have supposed. Antony Scoloker seems to have been offended by this scene, for in his *Daiphantus*, 1604 (Address to the Reader), he says, "As for Momus, if the Noble Ass bray not, I am as good a knight-poet as *Ætatis suæ* [Marston], Master *An. Dom.'s* son-in-law." Cole and Norwood, who acted Andrugio and Lucio, iv. 1, are the only two actors of Paul's whose names have come under my notice.

6. *Antonio's Revenge* (Part ii.) was also acted by the Paul's boys in 1600. It is the last of Marston's plays in which the words satirised by Jonson in *The Poetaster* 1601 frequently occur. In 1601 Marston left the Paul's boys and wrote for the Chapel children. At the same time Jonson left the Chapel children, who were now in disgrace, and returned to the Admiral's men. The stage quarrel, as far as Jonson is concerned, between them here ended; but see further in the next play. This play is a "revenge for a father" play, like Shakespeare's *Hamlet*, 1601, and Chettle's *Hoffman*, 1601–2. Revenge-plays were very popular just then; cf. Chapman's *Revenge of Bussy;* also Kyd's *Jeronymo*

(revived 1599–1600), which, with his *Hamlet*, were the roots from which all these sprang. *Jeronymo*, like *Antonio*, *Hoffman*, and *Bussy*, was in two parts, the second part containing the Revenge; so, in my opinion, was Shakespeare's *Julius Cæsar* in its original shape. The continual allusions to "round" and "ring" in the Prologue show that the Paul's boys' building, *i.e.*, Whitefriars, was not a square room, but round, like the Globe. Andrugio's ghost appears v. 5, "between the music houses." This is one of many plays in which the revenge is brought about in a mask. Compare especially *The Revenger's Tragedy*. Chester's *Love's Martyr*, 1601, in which Marston, Chapman, Jonson, and Shakespeare appear as writers, marks the end of the war of the stages.

7. *What you will* has no company of actors named in the title; it was, I think, acted by the Chapel boys before the reconciliation with Jonson was complete. Its date is probably 1601, after Jonson's *Poetaster* (which does not quote ány "fustian" words from it), but before the final reconciliation between Jonson and Marston. In ii. 1 Lampatho is called Don Kynsader, which identifies him with Marston; and there can be little doubt that Quadratus is Jonson. His Papist belief is alluded to in iv. 1, "He and I are of two faiths." He writes Epithalamiums, like Horace in *Satiromastix*, ii. 1. He proposes to "present the end of Cato Utican," but is interrupted. Possibly this is the play of *Cæsar and Pompey*, afterwards finished by Chapman, but not acted. On 3rd Dec. 1597 Jonson obtained money on the plot of a play, and Chapman made two acts on this plot before 23rd Oct. 1598. If so (which I do not admit), the hypothesis that this play was *Mortimer* is wrong. The "moral play" of Dame Temperance is one of several allusions to Chapman's *May-day*. The Signor Snuff, Monsieur

Mew, and Cavaliero Blirt of the Induction, I think, mean
Armin, Jonson, and Middleton. Shakespeare's *Twelfth Night*,
or *What you will*, which introduces Malevole [Marston] as
Malvolio, and addresses him in an anagrammatic way as
M. O. A. I., *i.e.*, Jo. Ma. (John Marston), I take to be his
rejoinder to the two plays *What you will* and *The Malcontent*
in 1601–2. But Marston's play as we have it has evidently been much altered. Albano and Belezzo, Francisco
and Soranza, though often appearing in duplicate, are proved
by the metre to be really alternative names : and the pages'
names are a mass of confusion : Battus and Trip, Phylus and
Nous, Doit and Slip (Albano's page), Bydett and Nathaniel
(probably Field), seem to be identical. There is further
confusion between Lucea and Celia, Adrean and Andrea.
The alteration would seem to have been made for a Court
performance ; cf. iv. 1, where the Court play is said to be by
Lampatho : probably that of 21st Feb. 1601. Compare
for the time of year v. 1, " I may go starve till Midsummer
Quarter." The stage on which it was publicly acted was a
small one (see the Induction), not the " round " of Paul's.
Philomuse in the Induction is, I think, Daniel, whose Muso-
philus was written 1599. For

> "Ha ! He mount chival on the wings of Fame" (ii. 1),

see *Mucedorus*. The plot is founded on an Italian play : so
Mr. Daniel tells me.

8. *The Dutch Courtesan* was acted by the children of Her
Majesty's Revels, *i.e.*, Queen Anne's, c. 1604, but was produced originally by them, I think, when they were the
Chapel children of Queen Elizabeth. There are allusions to
a lottery in iii. 1, 4, which, I think, refer to the Lottery presented to the Queen by Sir J. D[avies] at York House in
the summer of 1601. Compare " July " in iii. 2. The

play is full of echoes from Shakespeare's *Henry* 5, *Merry Wives of Windsor*, &c.; but the latest I have traced is from *Hamlet*, "Wha, ha, ho! come, bird, come," i. 2. This also points to 1601 as the date. The title would seem, from passages in the Epilogue and iv. 1, iv. 4, v. 3, to have been originally *All's Well*. I think it was altered in consequence of the production of Shakespeare's *All's Well that ends Well* in 1601. The subject of the play is "the difference between the love of a courtesan and a wife." Compare Jonson, *Conversations*, xiii., "He thought the use of a maid nothing in comparison to the wantonness of a wife." In 1613, Dec. 12, the Lady Elizabeth's men revived this play at Court as *Cockledemoy* before Prince Charles. *Pasquil's Mistress*, or *The Worthy and Unworthy Woman*, had appeared in 1600.

9. *The Malcontent* was acted by the Blackfriars (Chapel) children in 1601. For proof of this see the Induction, whence we learn that the actors were in *decimo sexto*, and that they acted at Blackfriars. Cf. "Blackfriars (the playhouse) hath spoiled Blackfriars (the locality) for feathers;" and iii. 1, "the horn growing in the woman's forehead twelve years since," S. R. 15th Oct. 1588, which fixes the date as between Oct. 1600 and Oct. 1601. The reference to Don Diego in ii. 3 is to 1597; but the *Hamlet* bits, i. 2, iii. 2, necessitate our taking the latter part of the year 1601. It further appears from the Induction that in 1604 (no doubt on the reconstitution of the Blackfriars boys as the Queen's Revels children in January) they "lost" this play, which was appropriated by the King's men in retaliation for the boys' having stolen their *Jeronymo* and acted it c. 1600. Sly, Sinkler, Condell, Lowin, and Burbadge (Malevole) appear in this Induction, which was "written by Webster;" the "additions" by Marston seem, from

internal evidence, to be rather restorations of passages left out to lessen the number of actors when the boys performed, Passarello being omitted. The reference in the Epilogue to Jonson's forthcoming play is to *The Fox*, not to *Sejanus*, as Gifford supposed. Arrogant and inaccurate Gifford always was, but it is a surprise to find him taking Thalia to be the Tragic Muse. The Epilogue is Marston's for the 1604 revival.

10. *The wonder of Women*, or *The tragedy of Sophonisba*, was acted at the Blackfriars, probably by the Chapel children. Had it been by the Revels' boys, I think they would have been named. The date is 1602–3; it could not have been earlier than 1602, and the plague closed the theatres in June 1603. When published in 1606 Marston distinctly contrasted it with *Sejanus*: "To transcribe authors, quote authorities, and translate Latin prose Orations into English blank verse hath been the least aim of my studies." Hard this upon *Benjamini Jonsonio, poetœ elegantissimo, gravissimo, amico suo candido et cordato*, "to whom he had dedicated *The Malcontent* in 1604." But Jonson meanwhile had published *Sejanus*, and not dedicated it to Marston. The title is taken from an Admiral's play 15th Oct. 1595, *The Wonder of a Woman*. The plot is semi-historical. Marston writes, he says, as a poet.

11. *Parasitaster*, or *The Fawn*, was acted at Blackfriars by the children of Her Majesty's Revels, undoubtedly in 1604, when this company lost the Queen's Patronage in 1605. It was transferred [by Kirkham] to the Paul's boys ("and since at Paul's" 1606, second edition), and then probably the alteration of name (Frappatore to Baldonzozo) was made. The mask v. 1 is very like *Histriomastix*. The whole plot reminds us of *Measure for Measure*, which this play was meant to rival. The presence of

women at executions, iv. 1, does not refer to the 1606 executions, but to those of 1604, as I have repeatedly pointed out. The Frappatore story is taken from *The Scourge*, x., and undoubtedly refers to some personal scandal of the time. Hence the change of name in this character. In the Address to the Reader, 12th Mar. 1606, Marston brazens out his real difficulties arising from the 1605 imprisonment, and professes to be most "fortunate in these stage-pleasings;" but it is clear that it had led him into "detractions" and quarrels with Jonson and Chapman; and no play of his later than *Eastward Ho* exists, nor, in my judgment, ever existed. The tragedy promised in the Address is merely the *publication* of *Sophonisba*.

12. *The Insatiate Countess* was acted at Whitefriars, as we have it, 1610–1613; but it has manifestly been greatly and clumsily altered. The names, 1. Rogero; 2. Guido; 3. Mizaldus; 4. Thais; 5. Abigail, have been introduced (but only partially) in place of 1. Guido; 2. Mizaldus; 3. Rogero; 4. Abigail; 5. Thais; and the result is a confusion that would seem unsurpassable had not modern editors managed to make it worse. The play, which bears Barksted's name in some copies, seems to have been condensed by him from two others, one a Tragedy, the other a Comedy; and this curious union of two complete plays, one of each kind, in one, together with the "abuses" mutually bandied by the Jew and the Apothecary, induce me to identify it with *The Abuses*, *q.v.*, acted by the Paul's boys in 1606. We have seen that *What you Will* and *The Fawn* were altered in a similar way, though in a less degree, and we know that *The Fawn* passed to the Paul's boys. I think that all three plays did, and that Barksted, when he left the King's Revels' children, who succeeded Paul's, carried them with him to the Lady Elizabeth's, whereunder we

find mention of the present play as Baxter's or Barksted's Tragedy. The date of the original play or plays was, I think, 1604. *The Miseries of Enforced Marriage* seems to be glanced at in i. 1. The tragic plot is from an Italian play.

That the whole comic plot is personally satirical I am certain. Claridiana, the apothecary, compiles *The Snarl*, a book of Satires againt women, iii. 1. T. M. in 1599 published *Microcynicon, Six Snarling Satires*, one of which is especially against women. This T. M. was Thomas Moffat, an "apprentice in Physic," who had written *The Silkworms and their Flies*, 1599, and in 1604, Jan. 3, issued his *Father Hubbard's Tales*, or *The Ant and the Nightingale*, and in 1604, Mar. 22, *The Black Book*. Dyce, who assigns these to Middleton in a doubtful way, says that Nash being alive in the book published in March, and dead in that published in January, must have died in the interim: a singular piece of inference. Surely this is a lesson for critics. W. C. Hazlitt rightly assigns both these to Moffat. I wonder he did not see from internal evidence that *The Snarling Satires* were also his. I think that Marston took offence at one of the 1604 books, and then wrote his play. Another satirical book, which is said to be a reply to Rowland's, but also to attack Marston, "the Cynick Satyre," is *The Whipping of the Satyre*, 1601, by I. W. [Query John Weever. I have not seen this book]. I have not at present identified the Jew-Onocentaur. The end of the third plot (Lady Lentulus) has been omitted by the adapter.

13. *Eastward Ho* was acted by the Revels children in 1604–5. It was written by Marston, i. 1, 2; ii. 1; Chapman, ii. 2; iii. 1, 2, 3; iv. 1; and Jonson, iv. 2; v. 1, 2, 3, 4, after *Volpone*. The date of production lies between that of *Westward Ho*, 1st Nov. 1604, and of *Northward Ho*, early in 1605. See the Prologue and i. 1. The footman in iii. 2

was doubtless acted by Robert Hamten or Hamlet, which
gives Gertrude, who parodies Ophelia in this scene, oppor-
tunities for filthy puns. Potkin's "Hamlet, are you mad?"
fixes the allusions. For this play the authors were imprisoned; they had satirised the Scots. One passage in iii.
3 (Chapman) on the industrious Scots, who are friends to
England when they are out on't, still remains in a few
copies; but as the play was evidently reformed before
printing, and this passage was cancelled and reprinted,
many other allusions were no doubt repressed. Allusions
to Scotch dress still remain in i. 2 (Marston), and to Scotch
knights, ii. 1 (Marston), and to Scotch dialect, iii. i. (Chapman). This agrees with Jonson's account that Chapman
and Marston had written the offensive part among them.
See further on this matter under Jonson. For the identification of Quicksilver with Luke Hatton see *Athenæum*,
13th Oct. 1883.

14. Marston also wrote *The City Pageant*, " on the occasion of the visit paid by the King of Denmark to James I."
in 1606 (July 31), in very bad Latin verse.

15. *The Lord and Lady Huntingdon's Entertainment of
their Right Noble Mother, Alice Countess Dowager of Darby,
the first night of her honor's arrival at the House of Ashby*,
dates August 1607 (Nichols, ii. 145).

16. *The Mountebanks' Mask* has been attributed to
Marston by Collier on the ground that his name is written
on the MS. in pencil, &c. But this is merely a portion of
the *Gesta Graiorum*, 1617, and Marston belonged to the
Temple. The Shakespeare Second Folio forgeries were
made in pencil; probably by the same hand.

MASON, JOHN. (Play.)

1. 1609, Mar. 10, for John Busby, jun. *The Turk*,
"with the death of Borgias," T., 1610, 1632.

B.A. of Catherine Hall, Cambridge, 1606; M.A.

1. This "worthy tragedy," as the title calls it in 1610, or, as the 1632 edition has it, "An excellent tragedy of *Mule asses the Turk, and Borgias, Governor of Florence*, full of interchangeable variety beyond expectation," was acted by the children of His Majesty's Revels 1607–8.

MASSINGER, PHILIP. See FLETCHER, JOHN.

MAY, THOMAS. (Plays and Latin.)

    2. *The Heir*, C., 1622, 1633.

    3. *Antigone, the Theban Princess*, T., for B. Fisher, 1631.

1638, Oct. 26, for T. Walkley.
{
5. *Julia Agrippina, Empress of Rome*, T., 1639,
4. *Cleopatra, Queen of Egypt*, T., 1639,
} 1654.

    1. *The Old Couple*, C., 1658.

Son of Sir Thomas May of Mayfield, Sussex; born 1595; B.A. of Sidney, Sussex, Cambridge, 1612; admitted at Gray's Inn 6th Aug. 1615. He wrote many non-dramatic works between 1626 and his death on 13th Nov. 1650. His dramatic career does not appear to have extended far beyond the reign of James; his translation of Lucan's *Pharsalia* was entered S. R. as early as 1626, April 18, and his translation of Virgil's *Georgics* still earlier, in 1622.

1. *The Old Couple.* I place this comedy before *The Heir*, because there is in it a passage, ii. 3, which also occurs in a modified form in *The Heir*, iii. 2. *The Heir* version is diluted, and far less suited to the occasion than the other, which I take to be the original. The lines near the end which occur also at the close of Suckling's *Goblins* were certainly taken by him from May, and not conversely.

2. *The Heir* is definitively stated to have been acted by

the Revels Company in 1620. Probably *The Old Couple*
was also acted by them.

3. *Antigone* was dedicated to Endymion Porter.

4. *Cleopatra* was acted in 1626.

5. *Julia Agrippina* was acted in 1628.

6. *Julius Cæsar*, T., a Latin play. "The MS. is in the
possession of Mr. Stephen Jones" (*Biog. Dram.*, 1812).

7. The fact that *Nero*, T., 1624, was transferred along
with May's *Heir* and his *Lucan* translation, S. R. 1633,
Oct 24, by T. Jones to Matthews makes me suspect that it
also was by May. These two plays alone out of six mentioned in this entry had been originally licensed independently
of the Stationers by the Master of the Revels. A careful
examination of May's undoubted tragedies might clear up
this matter.

MAYNARD, Sir JOHN. (Masks.)

1. 1619, Jan. 6. A mask while Jonson was in Scotland
was performed. "Young Maynard" danced in it, and bore
the bell. He was probably also the author (Nichols, iii.
521).

2. 1623. Nov. 18. A mask given at York House by
the Duke of Buckingham on the Prince's return, which
offended the Spaniards (Nichols, iii. 941). See Jonson.

3. 1624, Aug. [1]. A mask at Burley on the Hill
(Buckingham's), "with a great approbation" (Nichols, iii.
985).

MAYNE, JASPER. (Plays.)

1. *The City Match*, C., Oxford, 1639. ⎫ Oxford, 1658,
2. *The Amorous War*, T. C., 1648. ⎭　　1659.

Born in 1604 at Hatherleigh, Devonshire; educated
at Westminster School; servitor at Christ Church, Oxford,
1623; student 1624; B.A., M.A.; took Holy Orders; D.D.
1646. Died 6th Dec. 1672.

1. *The City Match* was acted at Whitehall before the King and Queen by the King's command in 1639, and afterwards at Blackfriars by the King's men.

2. *The Amorous War*, being published in London, was probably also acted at Blackfriars.

MEAD, ROBERT. (University.)

1. *The Combat of Love and Friendship*, 1654.

Born in Fleet Street, London, 1616; educated at Westminster; student of Christ Church, Oxford, 1633–4; M.A.; afterwards a soldier. Died 12th Feb. 1652. The play was written when he was an undergraduate, c. 1636, and represented by the members of his own college.

MEASE, PETER. (Latin).

1. *Adrasta Parentans sive Vindicta*, Brit. Mus., MS. addit. 10,417. Dedicated to Launcelot Andrews, Bishop of Winchester. Plot from Herodotus. The date must be between 1618 and 1627.

MEWE, ———. (Latin).

Of Emanuel, Cambridge.

1. *Pseudomasia* T. C. MS. in Emanuel Library. Scene, Mantua.

MIDDLETON, THOMAS. (Plays, Masks, Pageants.)

ROWLEY, WILLIAM. (Actor and Playwright.)

2. 1602, June 7, for Edward Aldee. *Blurt M. Constable*, C., 1602, for H. Rockitt.

9. 1604, Nov. 9, for Thomas Man, jun. 1 *Honest Whore*. See Dekker.

19. 1607, June 29, for John Wright. *Three English Brothers*, H. See Wilkins.

11. 1607, May 9, for Arthur Johnson. *The Phœnix*, C., 1607, 1630.

10. 1607, May 15, for Arthur Johnson. *Michaelmas Term*, C., 1607, 1630.

14. 1607, Aug. 6, for George Elde. *The Puritan Widow*, C., 1607.

12. 1607, Oct. 7, for George Elde. *A trick to catch the old one*, C., 1608 (twice ; the second sold by H. Rockitt), 1616.

15. 1607, Oct. 12., for John Brown and John Helme. *The Family of Love*, C., 1608.

16. 1608, Mar. 22, for Richard Bonyon. *The five Witty Gallants*, C., n.d.

13. 1608, Oct. 4, for W. Burre and E. Edgar. *A mad World, my Masters*, C., 1608, 1640.

9. 1608, April 29, for T. Man, jun. *2 Converted Courtesan.* See Dekker.

18. *The Roaring Girl*, 1611. See Dekker.

28. *A Fair Quarrel*, C., 1617, for J. T[rundel] (twice ; the second with additions), 1622.

31. 1619, July 10, for John Brown. *The Temple Mask*, anno 1618, 1619.

33. 1620, July 4, for G. Purslowe and J. Trundle. *The World tost at Tennis*, Mask, 1620 (sold by E. Wright).

36. 1624, June 28, for John Wright, *The Spanish Gipsy*, C., 1653 ; for R. Marriot, 1661.

48. *A Game at Chess*, 1625 by Jan Massey, at Leyden (three editions), and a fourth [London].

21. 1630, April 8, for F. Constable. *A chaste Maid in Cheapside*, C., 1630.

38. 1631, Nov. 24, for F. Constable. *A new wonder, or a woman never vexed*, C., 1632.

37. 1632, Sept. 27, for Thomas Harper. *All's lost by lust*, T., 1633.

17. 1633, Jan. 15, for William Sheares. *A match at Midnight*, C., 1633.

20. 1637, Nov. 28, for John Okes. *A shoemaker is a*

gentleman, " with the life and death of the cripple that stole the weathercock at Paul's," 1638.

46. 1647, Feb. 14, for Humphrey Moseley. *The Maid of the Mill.* See Fletcher.

49. *The Widow,* 1652, for H. Moseley.

35. 1653, Sept. 9, for H. Moseley. 52. *The Fool without Book.* [Query *The Changeling,* 1653, for H. Moseley; 1668.]

51. 1653, Sept. 9, for H. Moseley. *The Knave in print,* or *One for another.*

55. 1653, Sept. 9, for H. Moseley. *The Puritan Maid, Modest Wife, and Wanton Widow.*

Fortune by Land and Sea, 1655, for Sweeting and Pollard. See Heywood.

1. *The Old Law,* or *A new way to please you,* 1656, for E. Archer.

22. *No Wit (Help) like a Woman's,* 1657, for H. Moseley. Two new plays, viz. :—

40. *More Dissemblers besides Women,* ⎫ 1657, for H.
23. *Women beware Women,* ⎭ Moseley.

39*. *The Witch of Edmonton,* 1658. See Ford.

1660, June 29, for H. Moseley, ⎰ 53. *The Nonesuch* [Query *The Woman never vexed*].
⎱ 54. *The four honored Loves.*

7. *The Mayor of Quinborough,* C., 1661, for H. Herringman.

29. *A Cure for a Cuckold,* C., 1662, for F. Kirkman.

The Thracian Wonder, 1662, for F. Kirkman. See Heywood.

5. *The Birth of Merlin,* T. C., 1662, for F. Kirkman and T. Marsh.

45. *Anything for a quiet life,* C., 1662, for F. Kirkman and T. Marsh.

41. *The Witch.* MS.

MIDDLETON'S PAGEANTS.

24. 1613, *The Triumphs of Truth.* Thomas Middleton's mayoralty.

27. 1616, *Civitatis Amor :* The City's Love. At Prince Charles' creation, 4th Nov.

30. 1617, *The Triumphs of Honor and Industry.* G. Bowles' mayoralty.

32. 1619, *The Triumphs of Love and Antiquity.* W. Cockayn's mayoralty.

39. 1621, *The Sun in Aries.* E. Barkham's mayoralty (Drapers).

43*. 1622, *The Triumphs of Honor and Virtue.* P. Proby's mayoralty.

47. 1623, *The Triumphs of Integrity.* M. Lumley's mayoralty.

50. 1626, *The Triumphs of Health and Prosperity.* C. Hackett's mayoralty.

Thomas, son of William Middleton and Anne daughter of William Snow, was one of two children (the other, Avicia, married, 1, John Empson; 2, Alan Waterer) born in London. William Middleton's arms were, " Argent on a Saltier engraved Sables, a Castle of the first; " his crest, assigned in 1568 by Sir Gilbert Dethick, Garter King-at-Arms, was, " On his Torce argent and sables an ape passant with a collar about his neck and chain gold mantled argent double gules." One Thomas Middleton was admitted at Gray's Inn in 1593; another in 1596. In 1597 V. Sims published *The Wisdom of Solomon paraphrased,* written by Thomas Middleton. Various other works, *Microcynicon, Six Snarling Satires,* 1599, by T. Creede for T. Bushel; *Father Hubbard's Tales,* or *The Ant and the Nightingale,* S. R. 1604, Jan. 3, by T. C[reede] for T. Bushel (but another edition, also in

1604, was printed by T. C[reede] for W. Cotton, much abridged, and usually regarded as the first edition); *The Black Book*, S. R. 1604, Mar. 22, by T. C[reede] for J. Charlton, have been assigned by Dyce, Collier, &c., to Middleton; they were all written by T. M[offat]; the authorship of *The Snarl*, *i.e.*, *Microcynicon*, is distinctly assigned to Claridiana, the apothecary, in *The Insatiate Countess*, iii. 3 : Moffat was " an apprentice in Physic " (see the title-page of his *Silkworm*): Middleton was an Inns of Court man, and he always put his name in full to all publications authorised by himself.   Dyce, taking the Piers Penniless in *The Black Book* to be Nash, places this tract after *The Ant and the Nightingale*, in which Nash is mentioned as dead, and argues that Nash must have died in 1604.   He died in 1601.   Piers Penniless is just as much Nash as Harold Skimpole is Charles Dickens, and the order of the S. R. entries entirely upsets Dyce's argument.   In or before 1603 Middleton married Maria, daughter of Edward Marbeck, one of the six clerks in Chancery.   His only son, Edward, was born in 1604.   In 1620 he was appointed chronologer to the City of London.   In 1627, July 4, he was buried at Newington Butts.   His second wife Magdalen was buried in the same place 1628, July 18.

William Rowley was born somewhere about 1585.   In 1607 he wrote for the Queen's men.   His *Search for Money* was entered S. R. 1609, May 10.   He acted with the Duke of York's company (afterwards Prince Charles') 1610–16. His name is second in the original patent, 1610, Mar. 30; first in the documents quoted in my *Stage History*, p. 265, which date 1616, Feb., Mar.   In the *Mausoleum*, 1613, there is a tribute by him to the memory of Prince Henry. In 1614 he wrote an epitaph on Thomas Greene (see *Greene's Tu Quoque*), and in 1621 an elegy on a fellow-actor who died 21st Sept. In that year he joined the Lady Elizabeth's men, and in 1623 removed to the King's. In 1625 his name occurs in the 27th Mar. list as a Prince's man at the King's funeral, but in the 25th June patent as a King's man, and so in the title-page to *The New Wonder*, S. R. 1631, Nov. 24, although not in the 1629 patent-list. He probably retired from the stage at Middleton's death, July 1627. They had been closely connected from 1613 onwards—so closely that to treat them separately would be the next worse thing to treating Beaumont apart from Fletcher. In 1637 Rowley married Isabel Tooley at Cripplegate, and, I think, died shortly after.

MIDDLETON, 1599–1612.

1, 34. *The Old Law.* Middleton's part dates late in 1599; probably acted by the Paul's boys 1600. See further on.

2. *Blurt Master Constable,* or *The Spaniard's Nightwalk,* C., was acted by the Paul's boys 1600-1. From "Garlic and the rest follow strongly!" iv. 3, I infer that Garlick, who afterwards made such stir as a player at the Fortune, was at this time a Paul's boy. There are many allusions to the titles of Admiral's men's plays; and a passage in the text, i. 1, is clearly paraphrased from *Romeo and Juliet,* i. 4. "The owl whose voice shrieks like the belman," iii. 1, is admitted even by Dyce to be probably a recollection of *Macbeth,* ii. 2, though this is entirely inconsistent with any hypothesis of the date of *Macbeth* except my own. The ridicule of the pronunciation *ch* for *s* in chitty, capachity, chick, &c., should be noticed, as showing the date of this affectation.

In 1602 Middleton wrote for the Admiral's men at the Fortune :—

3. May 22, *Cæsar's fall*, with ? Dekker, Drayton, Monday, Webster.

4. May 29, *The two harpes*, with Dekker, Drayton, Monday, Webster.

5. Oct. 21, *The Chester Tragedy ;* Nov. 9, *Randal Earl of Chester*, unquestionably the same play. Query Edol Earl of Chester, another name for a refashioning of the old play *Uter Pendragon*, afterwards remade into *The Birth of Merlin.* See further on.

6. Dec. 14, A Prologue and Epilogue for Greene's *Friar Bacon*, for the Court. He also received for Worcester's men at the Rose.

7. Oct. 3, "In earnest of a play called ———," 20s. Was this the altered *Hengist*, afterwards remade as *The Mayor of Quinborough ?* See further on.

8. In 1604 Middleton assisted Dekker (*q.v.*), then writing for the Prince's men, formerly the Admiral's, in *The Entertainment to King James.*

9. Mar. 15, 1 *The Honest Whore*. But by Dec. he had left the Prince's company and returned to the Paul's boys.

10. *Michaelmas Term.* Certainly written in 1604, the only available Leap-year, when "knaves wear smocks" (cf. ii. 1), and after 29th Nov., when Clarke was executed at Winchester. He and Watson were cut down and their bowels torn out while yet alive; "and Clarke, to whom more favour was intended, had the worse luck, for he both strove to help himself and spoke after he was cut down" (Sir Dudley Carleton). Cf. ii. 3, "help to rip up himself," and note the presence of ladies. The last scene is imitated from *Measure for Measure*, and the play, I think, contains personal satire.

11. *The Phœnix* was "presented before His Majesty." Founded on *The Force of Love*, a Spanish novel. The 1607

edition is from the Court copy (see the conclusion); the
1630 edition from an abridged stage copy. Proditor is, I
think, meant for Jonson; cf. v. 1, "the raven that was I,"
and compare *Mucedorus* and *Volpone*. The last scene is
travestied from *The Poetaster*, and the "oil of quiet" therein
from the Oglio del Scoto in *Volpone*.

12. *A trick to catch the old one* was also "presented before His Majesty on New Year's Night last;" not 1607, Jan.
1, as we should suppose from the S. R. entry, but 1606,
Jan. 1. The only entry for Paul's plays at Court, either in
the Privy Council Registers or the Office-books of the Treasurers of the Chamber, is (in the latter) for two plays paid
for 1606, Mar. 31, and no other Paul's plays but these two
of Middleton's are known to have been acted at Court at
this time. But the two plays in the Treasurers' entry were
presented before the Princes Henry and Charles, not the
King. It would seem, then, that economical James saved
a part of his expense, which was £10 a play for plays presented before him, £6. 13s. 4d. for those presented to the
Princes, and yet was present at the performance. This play
(and probably *The Phœnix*) was on the public stage in 1605,
for it is alluded to in *The Isle of Gulls* (*q.v.*).

13. *A Mad World, my Masters*, had "been lately in
action" in 1608; but as the Paul's boys were dissolved in
1607, it was probably produced in 1606, Mar., when Tuesday fell on the 11th, iv. 5. Acts ii. and iii. are separated
by a song and country-dance. A Succubus enters in iv. 1.
The Bold Beauchamps (see Heywood) is mentioned v. 2;
Smug on the white horse in *The Merry Devil of Edmonton*,
v. 2. Dumb Shows are spoken of as popular v. 2, and
there are allusions to *Venus and Adonis*, &c. The title is
from Breton's dialogue of the same name, 1603.

14. *The Puritan*, or *The Widow of Watling Street*, was

published as " Written by W. S.," *i.e.* (with an equivocation)
written concerning William Shakespeare. The date is fixed
as in 1606 by the falling of 15th July on a Tuesday, iii. 6.
The plot is concerned with the jests of George Pyeboard or
Peele, but the purport of the play is to travesty those of
Shakespeare. With "the first chapter of Charity," i. 4,
compare *Twelfth Night*, i. 5 ; Sir John "accosts" Mary, ii. 1,
cf. *Twelfth Night*, i. 3 ; "Shooters and archers are all one,
I hope," ii. 1, cf. *Love's Labour's Lost*, iv. 1 ; "For shame, put
up, put up," ii. 1, cf. 2 *Henry* 4, ii. 4 ; "Jacks o' the clock-
house," ii. 1, cf. *Richard* 3, iv. 2 ; "The fescue of the dial
is on the chriss-cross of noon," cf. *Romeo and Juliet*, ii. 4 ;
" Let me entreat the corpse to be set down ! Bearers, set
down the coffin ! " cf. *Richard* 3, i. 2. The recovery of Oath,
iv. 3, is modelled on that of Thaisa in *Pericles*, iii. 2 (which
must have closely followed Wilkins' original version ; see
his novel) ; and, finally, " Instead of a jester will have the
ghost in the white sheet sit at the upper end of the table."
Certainly the ghost here is Banquo's, alluded to as well
known, "*the* ghost," and the only one I know of that sat at
the upper end of the table. Some of these allusions are
very slight, and singly would not be worth notice, but their
cumulation is remarkable. As to the authorship of the play,
any one who has read Middleton will not hesitate for a
moment. The whole style, plot, and metre is his. The
play cannot possibly be attributed to Day, Webster, or Beaumont, the only other authors then writing for these boys.
Among minor indications of Middleton's manner, note " The
Bear at the Bridge-foot in Heaven," i. 4, and compare *No
Wit like a Woman's*, vi. 1, and the use of almanacs, iii. 6,
the method of which is so different from that of Jonson and
others. This is the last of the series of five Paul's plays by
Middleton.

15. *The Family of Love* was acted by the children of His Majesty's Revels, and therefore (as I learn from Mr. Greenstreet's recent discoveries) at Whitefriars. This must have been early in 1607, after Middleton left Paul's, and before he joined the Blackfriars' Revels Boys. The boy-players in i. 3 called "*the* youths" are, of course, the King's Revels boys. The Paul's boys had been suppressed, and the Queen's Revels boys disgraced, and these were *the* youthful company during 1607 and 1608. But it appears from the Address to the Reader that this play had been performed with success some time before (probably by the Paul's boys in 1604, when the Family of Love were such objects of public attention), and marks of alteration are manifest in the extant version. Shrimp has been substituted for Smelt, and, *Dram Pers.*, Poppin for Exigent, v. 3, but the old names here and there are left unaltered. Near the end are several allusions to *Club Law* (*q.v.*). No other play by Middleton was acted by this company.

16. *Your Five Gallants* (or *Five Witty Gallants*, S. R.) was acted c. Dec. 1607 by the Blackfriars' boys (called the children of the Chapel in the S. R. entry, but usually at this time the children of the Revels; they had lost the Queen's patronage and appellation in 1605). The date of the incidents in the play is Nov. 1607, but the arrangement is very muddled; iv. 1, 2 ought to be transferred so as to begin Act iii., which is not marked. The Mitre nights in the play are Fridays, Nov. 6, 13, 20, 27. A new moon happens on Thursday, 5th Nov., which fixes the year to 1607. The plague-returns in that year fell below forty on 26th Nov.; compare i. 1. St. George's Day (April 23), iii. 5, seems to have been put in for St. Andrew's (Nov. 30), to avoid offending the King. In iii. 4 note "*subaudi*," and in iv. 8 the Quixotic fighting with a windmill, as

showing that Cervantes' work was well known in England before it was translated. This play sadly wants competent editing. Dyce seems to have been careless, because disgusted with it.

17. *A Match at Midnight* was certainly acted at this time by the same boys. See further on.

18. Middleton now gave up writing for boys, and were it not for his Address to *The Roaring Girl* (for which see Dekker) we could not even conjecture what he was doing from 1608 to 1611, but that Address shows that he was connected with Prince Henry's men at the Fortune. The loss of his plays during this time is not surprising, for most of their stage copies were burned in the Fortune fire in 1621. Perhaps the play called *The Puritan Maid, Modest Wife, and Wanton Widow*, S. R. 1653, Sept. 9, the MS. of which was destroyed by Warburton's servant, was one of these. The title suggests a date near *The Puritan* and *The Match at Midnight*.

ROWLEY: 1607–9, QUEEN'S; 1610–12, DUKE OF YORK'S.

19. *The Travels of the three English Brothers;* with Day and Wilkins. Acted at the Curtain by Queen Anne's men. See Wilkins.

20. *A shoemaker's a gentleman* ("with the life and death of the cripple that stole the weathercock at Paul's," S. R.). Acted at the Bull, therefore by the same company, in 1609, when they went to the Bull, and before 1610, when Rowley joined the Duke of York's. The plot is founded on *Crispin and Crispianus,* or *The History of the Gentle Craft,* 1598.

20*. *Hymen's Holiday,* or *Cupid's Vagaries,* was acted at Court 1612, Feb. 24, by the Duke of York's players; and again 1633, Dec. 16, as an "old play of Rowley's." It has long been attributed to S. Rowley, but William, not Samuel,

Rowley belonged to the Duke of York's men in 1612. Samuel was then with Prince Henry's. This play must have been by William.

MIDDLETON, 1612–1616. a. PLAYS.

21. *A chaste Maid in Cheapside.* Acted by the Lady Elizabeth's company at the Swan, and therefore between 1611 Aug. and 1613 Mar. As Middleton was probably writing for Prince Henry's men till his death, 1612, Nov. 6, and the time of action in the play is Lent, I place the production of it c. 1612, Christmas. The "wholesome laws," ii. 1, are those of 1610. The *grammatica est ars* joke occurs in iv. 1. I think the Master of the Revels corrected this play before publication.

22. *No wit, no help, like a woman's.* Shirley revived this play at Dublin as *No wit to a Woman's.* It was then somewhat altered. In iii. 1 Weatherwise, speaking in "1638, when the Dominical letter is G," says he has "proceeded in five-and-twenty such books of astronomy" (almanacs). The play was, then, first acted in 1613 or 1614, according as we read in i. 1 the "eleventh" day of June (with the old copy), or the "tenth" (with Dyce). It appears afterwards in the play that the day mentioned was a Friday. I think the text is right, the company the Lady Elizabeth's, and the year 1613, just after the junction of this company with the Queen's Revels boys (say about July); see iv. 2, "You attendants upon Revels." In v. 1 we meet with "The Bear at the Bridge-foot in heaven;" cf. *The Puritan.* The transit of Venus in v. ii., "Venus being a spot in the Sun's garment," must be one of Shirley's additions. The first transit observed (by Horrocks) was in Dec. 1639, and, except one, not observed, in 1631, there had not been one for a century.

The Epilogue is also Shirley's.   His Prologue is printed in his Works.

23. *Women beware Women*, T.   Of very doubtful date; but I place it provisionally in 1613 on account of the devil with one eye and fireworks at his tail in "the last Triumph," v. 1, which seems to allude to Envy and the fireworks in Dekker's *London Triumphing*, the pageant of 1612.   The Ward has a part in the Mask, and plays Slander.   Dekker's *Triumph* has Calumny in it.   Langbaine, quoted by Dyce, assigns the foundation of this play to [Hart's] *Hyppolito and Isabella*, S. R. 1627, Nov. 9.   Middleton died in 1627 July, but no doubt the romance and the play had a common origin.

b. Shows.

24. 1613, Oct. 29.   *The Triumphs of Truth*, for Thomas Middleton's Mayoralty, was Middleton's first pageant. No doubt family influence had been at work.   The 1612 pageant was Dekker's; but Monday was the regular pageant-writer before (1605, 1611) and after (1614–1616). I guess that the new Mayor was the dramatist's godfather. Monday is distinctly alluded to as "the impudent common writer" wanting in knowledge, and "freezing Art sitting in darkness with the candle out and looking like the picture of Black Monday," and is further personated as Envy on a rhinoceros.   Zeal is Middleton.   Monday furnished "the apparel and porters," H. Nichols the firework, J. Grinkin the "body of the Triumph."

25. *The Entertainment at the opening of the New River*, at the cost of Hugh Middleton, 1613, Sept. 29, was added to the second issue of the foregoing.

26. Two Masks, one being a Mask of Cupids by Middleton, and a play were presented 1614, Jan. 4, at Merchant Tay-

lors' Hall, at the Earl of Somerset's marriage. The "other shows" mentioned in the payment order (Nichols, ii. 732) certainly are exclusive of the second Mask, inclusive of the dances, &c., and perhaps of the play.

27. *Civitatis Amor*, *The City's Love*, "an entertainment by water at Chelsea and Whitehall, Monday, 1616, Nov. 4, at the receiving of Prince Charles and his creation as Prince of Wales," was partly written by Middleton, who contrived the shows.

MIDDLETON (M.) AND ROWLEY (R.), 1616–1627.

The companies of Lady Elizabeth and Prince Charles joined in 1614. This brought Middleton and Rowley together ; but I find no evidence of their writing in collaboration till after the death of Henslow, 1616 Jan., the separation of the companies, and the establishment of the Prince of Wales' men at the Curtain and Lady Elizabeth's at the Cockpit, probably at the creation of 4th Nov. 1616.

28. *A Fair Quarrel*, by M. and R., was acted by Prince Charles' men, and was evidently one of their first plays at the Curtain, for it was published in 1617, as it had been acted "before the King," probably at Christmas 1616–17. For the plot compare *The Complaisant Companion*, p. 280 ; and, for the Physician and Jane, Cynthio Giraldi, *Dec. 4, Nov. 5*. Bretnor appears as the Almanac-maker in v. 1, replacing Pond of the earlier plays. A second edition in 1617 contained the "new additions of Mr. Chaugh's and Trimtram's Roaring and the Bawd's song," in which the word "bronstrops" occurs. Is not this the same play as *A Vow, and a good one*, acted at Court 1623, Jan. 6, by the Prince's men ? Middleton wrote i. 1 (part); ii. 1, 3,; iii. 2 ; iv. 2, 3 ; v. 1 (part); Rowley, i. 1 (part) ; ii. 2 ; iii. 2 ; iv. 1, 4 ; v. 1 (part).

29. *A cure for a Cuckold*, published 1661 as by Rowley

and Webster, is certainly written in great part by Rowley; but Act i. is by another hand. It contains two marks of date, one in iv. 1, "a tweak, or bronstrops; I learned that name in a play." This must have been after (and I think not long after) *A Fair Quarrel*, 1617. The other, iii. 1—

> "Although the tenure by which land was held
> In villenage be quite extinct in England,"

is still more decisive. The last claim under this tenure was made in the 15th of James I. 1617—18. See Stephen's *Blackstone*, i. 220, 1886 edition. I assign this play, therefore, to 1618, and therefore to the Prince's company. Had it been later, the name of the King's or Queen's company was not likely to be omitted on the title-page. Rowley's coadjutor was most likely Middleton, certainly not Webster (*q.v.*). They never worked together; and as for Kirkman's statement, see *The Thracian Wonder*. Of much greater value is his allegation in the Address to the Reader that only about 700 plays had then been printed.

30. *The Triumphs of Honor and Industry* (M.) was the Mayoralty pageant of G. Bowles, 1617 (Grocers' company). Rowland Bucket, chief master of the work, was aided by Jacob Wilde and Henry Challoner.

31. *The Inner Temple Mask*, or *Mask of Heroes* (M.), presented (as an Entertainment for many worthy ladies) by Gentlemen of the same ancient and noble House, ("an. 1618," S. R.). This 1618 means 1618—19. Internal evidence shows that it was presented after Twelfth Night and before Candlemas in 1619. The past Christmas was on a Friday, *i.e.*, in 1618. The "ruin" of the Cockpit in 1617 is mentioned. Rowley, "the fat fool," acted Plum Porridge in it. Jonson's mask of *Christmas*, 1616, should be compared.

32. *The Triumphs of Love and Antiquity* (M.), was the

pageant for W. Cockayne's Mayoralty, 1619, Skinner's company. Garret Crismas and Robert Norman did the " workmanship."

33. A Courtly Mask: The Device called *The World tost at Tennis* (M. R.), acted divers times by the Prince's servants, and dedicated to Charles, L. Howard, of Effingham, and Mary, Lady Effingham, daughter of Sir W. Cockayne, Lord Mayor, must date in his Mayoralty, *i.e.*, between 1619, Oct. 29, and 1620, July 4, when it was entered S. R. It was performed before the King at Denmark (Somerset) House with a special Induction, when the Prince was practising "in armour" and troops were preparing for "most glorious wars" of the Palatinate expedition. There is small doubt that this was the "play" presented at Denmark House to the peers 1619, Mar. 4, when the Prince was practising at the ring against the King's Day (Mar. 25); Sir. H. Vere left for the Palatinate with his troops July 22. The "royal'st guest" in the Induction is James; the "owner," Charles: Dyce quite mistakes the whole matter. Rowley's share is the first part of the mask, Middleton's the last. Dyce, unfortunately, has altered the Rowleyan metre.

34. *The Old Law*, or *A new way to please you*, C., was published 1656 as by Massinger, Middleton, and Rowley. "Acted before the King and Queen at Salisbury House and several other places." A catalogue of plays is appended. The original play was certainly written by Middleton in 1599, late in the year, and it was probably acted by the Paul's boys early in 1600. It would from them naturally pass on to Prince Charles' men, and was possibly altered for them by Massinger c. 1615. I cannot recognise his hand in any considerable passage. The likeness to parts of *The Queen of Corinth* is unmistakable; but these do not occur in Massinger's part of that play, and I rather attribute them

to reminiscences by Field, who was, I think, part author in that one and actor in both plays. But whether Massinger had a hand in *The Old Law* or no, Rowley certainly had; the Creon and Antigone part, i. 1, ii. 1, v. 1, was inserted by him, and the date of his revival must have, I think, been before (not long before) the death of Dr. Butler in 1618. See ii. 1, end. When the play was acted at Salisbury House (the Earl of Dorset's) I have failed to ascertain. Was it at Prince Charles' christening, 1630?

Middleton makes no further appearance among Prince Charles' plays; but Rowley does in *The Witch of Edmonton*, 1621 April, for which see Ford. Later in 1621 they were both with the Lady Elizabeth's; Middleton had been appointed in 1620 Chronologer to the City.

35. *The Changeling* was acted at the Cockpit by the L. Elizabeth's players, and at Salisbury Court [by Queen Henrietta's after 1637]. Founded on *God's Revenge against Murder*, i. 4, which was entered S. R. 1621, June 7. The public production was certainly in 1621, before Middleton wrote for the King's men. A Court performance before Prince Charles at Whitehall 1624, Jan. 4, is noted by Herbert. Middleton's part is ii. 1, 2; iii. 1, 2, 4; iv. 1, 2; v. 1, 2; Rowley's i. 1, 2; iii. 3; iv. 3; v. 3.

36. *The Spanish Gipsy* was acted at the Cockpit by the L. Elizabeth's players, at Whitehall before Prince Charles 1623, Nov. 5, and at Salisbury Court after 1637 by Queen Henrietta's men. Founded on *The Force of Blood*, by Cervantes. The date of writing is certainly soon after that of *The Changeling*: "None but myself shall play the changeling," ii. 1. "The rarest wildgoose chase," i. 5, alludes to Fletcher's play, 1621. Jonson's *Gipsies metamorphosed* was presented in 1621 Aug. The whole play is, I think, Middleton's. There are two difficulties. First, the

play was certainly acted after the revival of *The Coxcomb* with Massinger's alterations: *Ped.* "Wilt thou ever play the Coxcomb?" *San.* "If no other parts be given me, what would you have me to do?" Compare iv. 2. *The Coxcomb* had been almost forgotten (see the Prologue to it), and could not before its revival have been thus alluded to. But Massinger was writing for the King's men till 1622, Oct. 24; and if Middleton wrote for the L. Elizabeth's after this, how could his *More Dissemblers besides women* have been licensed by Buck for the King's before May 1622? Secondly, Rowley's name appears as coadjutor on the title-page. My conjectural explanation is that Middleton left writing for the Cockpit 1621–2, and that Rowley afterwards touched up this play, which was not publicly acted till 1622 c. Christmas. Shortly after, in 1623, he rejoined Middleton at the King's. Being an actor, he held the same position as regards Middleton that Field did to Beaumont and Fletcher, and often introduced changes with a view to stage effect. I cannot explain the allusions to "elephants and camels" in ii. 2, iv. 1, but they do not refer to contemporary pageants, as Dyce supposes. Roderigo in iii. 1, who has just written "too sad a tragedy" (*The Changeling*), is for the nonce Middleton.

37. *All's lost by Lust*, T., by Rowley, was acted at the Cockpit c. 1622. Founded on *The Unfortunate Lovers*, Nov. 3. It, with *The Changeling*, *The Fair Quarrel*, *The Spanish Gypsy*, and *The World* [*tost at Tennis*, which was produced by the Prince's men] belonged to Queen Henrietta's players in 1639.

38. *A new Wonder*, or *A Woman never vexed*, C., was published as by "William Rowley, one of His Majesty's servants," in 1632, by Constable, who issued only L. Elizabeth plays (with one exception, *The Fatal Dowry*, a King's

play). It is clearly altered from an old rhyming play, the part from iii. 2 onward being slightly changed. The insertion in v. 1, "Good husband. Gentle brother. Dear uncle," and a passage in iv. 1 which originally stood thus—

> "But for his father, hang him !
> Brew.   Fie [fie] fie.
> Steph. By heaven !
> Brew.   Come, come, live in more charity !
>   He is your brother : if that name offend[s]
>   I'll sing that tune no more. Jane, bid your friends
>   Welcome.
> Jane.   They must be, sir, that come with you," &c.,

evidently prove a revision. Comparison with the modern copies will give a fair idea of the way in which this play has been edited. I think the original author was Heywood, whose *Fortune by Land and Sea* may also have been put on the stage, but certainly in no part written, by Rowley.

39. *The Sun in Aries* was Middleton's pageant for E. Barkham's Mayoralty, 1621 (Drapers' company). Garret Chrismas did the workmanship.

39*. *The Witch of Edmonton*, by Dekker, Ford, and Rowley. See Ford.

KING'S MEN'S PLAYS, 1622–1625.

40. *More Dissemblers besides Women*, C., was entered by Herbert 1623, Oct. 17, for the King's company as "an old play, allowed by Sir G. Buck," and therefore before Ashley succeeded him, 1622, May 22, but not, as Dyce says, "a considerable time" before. On the contrary, the play had probably not been yet acted; had it been, there would have been no need to refer it to Herbert at all. I cannot date it earlier than Christmas 1621, nor later than May 1622. "I had rather meet a witch far north,"

i. 2, looks as if Middleton were busy in his alteration of *Macbeth*.

41. *The Witch*, from a MS., with dedication by Middleton to T. Holmes and therefore not later than 1627, (probably prepared for publication, but interrupted by his death), is said to have been "long since" acted at Blackfriars; therefore in the early days of his connexion with the King's men, c. 1621–2. There are six witches in this play and six in *Macbeth* as altered by Middleton. Edward Fairfax in 1621 was prosecuting six witches. I do not think this coincidence is accidental. The plot is from Machiavel's *Florentine History*, and Middleton has drawn largely on R. Scot's *Discovery of Witchcraft*. The names of the imps, Titty, Tiffin, Suckin, Pigeon, Lyard, and Robin, are from *The Witches of St. Osees*, 1582. Dyce has pointed out six important coincidences with *Macbeth*.

42. *Macbeth* was altered by Middleton shortly after *The Witch* was acted. Two songs in the latter are referred to as if well known. See my *Life of Shakespeare*.

43. *The Mayor of Quinborough*, C., was also called *Hengist, King of Kent*, as appears from a MS. quoted by Halliwell, *Marriage of Wit and Wisdom*, p. 85. It seems to be an alteration of *Hengist*, an Admiral's play of 1597, June 22, which, not being marked as a new play, I take to be the same as the *Vortiger* of 1596, Dec. 4. Query, was this old play by Middleton? The chorus in *The Mayor of Q.* is imitated from *Pericles*. The King's men probably obtained the old play after the Fortune was burned, 1621 Dec. Note the Dumb Shows and compare the part with the players with *Sir T. More*. The date of the revival must be subsequent to Fletcher's *Wildgoose Chase*, 1621, which is mentioned among the "new names of late," v. 1. I should guess c. 1622.

43. *The Triumphs of Honor and Virtue*, Middleton's pageant for P. Proby's Mayoralty, is not extant.

44. *The Birth of Merlin*, or *The Child has lost a Father*, T. C. ("hath found his Father," Lownes), was published as by Shakespeare and Rowley 1662. It is clearly a refashioning by Rowley of an old play. The ascription to Shakespeare justifies my assigning it to the King's company. The "Joan Goto't" part is clearly Rowley's. The original may have been *Uter Pendragon*, an Admiral's play of 1597, April 29, obtained by the King's men along with the preceding. The present title is Rowley's. Who was the original author I cannot even guess. Mr. Daniel suggests Middleton, and adds compare *The Mayor of Quinborough*.

45. *Anything for a quiet life*, C., by Middleton. I date this 1623, before May 10, when Ashley's entries begin. Had it been later it would have appeared there, and it must have been before 1624, Sept. 3, when Heywood's *Captives* was licensed, as that play, iii. 3, alludes to its title. In ii. 1 is a clear allusion to *A cure for a Cuckold*.

46. *The Maid of the Mill*, by Rowley and Fletcher (*q.v.*), was licensed 1623, Aug. 29.

47. *The Triumphs of Integrity* was Middleton's pageant for M. Lumley's Mayoralty, 1623 (Draper's Company). The works by Garret Chrismas.

48. *A Game at Chess*, by Middleton, was acted 1624, Aug. 3. For its suppression, &c., see my *History of the Stage*, p. 266. I think the W. Q. Pawn may be Katherine, daughter of the Earl of Rutland, who was converted before her marriage to the Marquis Buckingham, 1620 May. It may be worth while to give a complete list of the characters, as Dyce has failed to identify so many :—

W. King. James I.	B. King. Philip IV. of Spain.
W. Knight. P. Charles.	B. Knight. Gondomar.
W. Duke. Buckingham.	B. Duke.
W. Bishop. Archbishop Williams.	B. Bishop. Father-General of the
W. King's Pawn.	Jesuits.
W. Bishop's Pawn. Carandeleto's	B. King's Pawn.
mistress.	B. Bishop's Pawn.
W. Pawn.	B. Jesting Pawn and another.
W. Queen. English Church.	B. Queen. Church of Rome.
W. Queen's Pawn.	B. Queen's Pawn. ? Mrs. Ward
	the Jesuitess.

Fat Bishop. Spalato and his pawn.

N. Butter is alluded to i. 1. From *The Staple of News*, iii. 1, it appears that the player of Spalato was dead in 1625.

49. *The Widow*, published as by Jonson, Fletcher, and Middleton in 1652, is evidently written by Middleton alone; but if, as I think, he ceased to write for the stage in consequence of the trouble about *The Game at Chess*, it is quite possible that Jonson revised his MS. for the King's men c. Christmas 1625. Dyce's argument for an earlier date, from the mention of yellow bands, is altogether wrong; and as to the imitation of a line by S. S. in *The Honest Lawyer*, how did Dyce know which was the imitator? A song in *More Dissemblers besides Women* (acted Oct. 1623), " come, my dainty doxies," is referred to in iii. 1, and I have no doubt that the " busy Coxcomb this fifteen year," ii. 2, refers to the original production of *The Coxcomb* in 1610. The Prologue mentions the production of *The Widow* as a Christmas sport. Fletcher died 1625 Aug.; he may have left the revision unfinished and Jonson have completed it. The play is not mentioned in Herbert's entries for 1624. For the marriage of Martha compare Jonson's *New Inn*.

50. *The Triumphs of Health and Prosperity* was Middleton's last pageant for the Mayoralty of C. Hacket, Draper's company. Garret Chrismas did the works, as usual.

51. *The Knave in print.* 52. *The Fool without book.* 53. *The Nonesuch.* 54. *The four honored loves* are known only from Moseley's S. R. entries, already given. He ascribed them to Rowley. In *The Thracian Wonder* and *Fortune by Land and Sea* I believe that Rowley had no share. See Heywood.

55. *The Puritan Maid, Modest Wife, and Wanton Widow* was entered by Moseley as Middleton's. The MS. was destroyed by Warburton's servant.

MILTON, JOHN. (Masks.)

   1. *Comus*, M., 1637, 1645.

   2. *Arcades*, 1645 (in his Works).

Born at Milton, Oxfordshire, 9th Dec. 1608; educated at Paul's, London; entered at Christ College, Cambridge, Feb. 1625; B.A. 1628; M.A. 1632; left Cambridge to live with his parents at Horton, Buckinghamshire, and remained there till early in 1638. This is the only part of his career that concerns us. He died in 1674.

1. *Comus* was presented 29th Sept. 1634 at Ludlow Castle before John Egerton, Earl of Bridgewater. Viscount Brackley, the landlord of Milton's father, the Lord Egerton, Mr. Thomas Egerton, and Lady Alice Egerton acted in it.

2. *The Arcades* was part of an entertainment presented to Alice Spencer, Countess Dowager of Derby, at Harefield. This lady was mother-in-law to the Earl of Bridgewater, and the mask was acted not long after *Comus* by some noble persons of her family.

MONDAY, ANTONY. (Plays and Pageants.)

   1. 1584, Nov. 12, for Thomas Hackett. *Fidele and Fortuna*, C. [1584].

   3. 1595, Dec., MS. *John a Kent* and *John a Cumber.*

10. 1600, Aug. 11, for Thomas Pavier. 1 *Sir John Oldcastle*, H., 1600.

2. 1600, Oct. 7, for Richard Olyffe. *The Weakest goeth to the Wall*, 1600, 1608.

5. 1 *Robin Hood*, 1601. ⎱ Licensed 28th Mar. 1598
6. 2 *Robin Hood*, 1601. ⎰ (*Diary*).

19. *Reunited Britannia*, pageant, 1605.

20. *Chrysothriambos*, pageant, 1611.

21. *Old Drapery*, pageant, 1614.

22. *Metropolis Coronata*, pageant, 1615.

23. *Chrysanaleia*, pageant, 1616.

Antony, son of Christópher Monday, Draper, London, was born 1553–4, according to the copy of his epitaph in Stow's *London*. He was a stage-player before 1576. In that year (his father being dead, and he of some twenty-two or twenty-three years old), on 1st Oct., he was apprenticed to John Allde, Stationer, for eight years, as from 24th Aug. In the next year, 1577, he made his first appearance as an author. According to *The true Report of the Death and Martyrdom of M. Campion*, 1581, this time " he well served with deceiving of his master." At any rate he did not serve two years, for in 1578 he, " wandering towards Italy by his own report, became a cosener in his journey." On this journey he was robbed between Boulogne and Abbeville, visited Paris, Venice, Padua, Naples, and Rome, where he met Stukeley (who was killed 4th Aug. 1578), and was " the Pope's scholar at the Seminary at Rome." But he did not deceive his master, for Allde gave him a certificate in 1582 that while he was his servant he did his duty in all respects. Moreover, they had relations in publishing matters after Monday's return in 1578–9. He then became a player again, played extempory, and was hissed off. Then he wrote a ballad against plays (1580, Nov. 10), then again took to acting. The company for which he played was the Earl of Oxford's, c. 1579–1584. He was messenger of Her Majesty's chamber c. 1584–1592. We shall find him writing for the Admiral's men 1594–1603. He was chief City pageant-writer 1605–1616, and probably much earlier, c. 1592, for in 1618 he had been twenty-six years "in the City's service." He had been while a playwright at enmity with Jonson, who was offended at Meres' mention of him in 1598 as our best plotter. Under *Histriomastix* I state my reasons for believing that from Aug. 1598 to Oct. 1599, when he was away from Henslow's theatre, he was travelling with Pembroke's company. He was buried 10th Aug. 1633 in St. Stephen's Church, Coleman Street. The subjoined list of his non-dramatic works (the full titles, &c., of which it would be useless to repeat here—they will be found in Hazlitt's *Handbook* or the Shak. Soc. edition of *John a Kent*) will aid the reader in co-ordinating the events of a career which, of little import in itself, is very important in connexion with greater dramatic poets, especially Jonson.

MONDAY'S NON-DRAMATIC WORKS.

S. R., 1577, Nov. 18, for J. Charlewood. *The Defence of Poverty*, &c., not extant.

Verses to *The Gorgeous Gallery of Gallant Inventions*, edited by Thomas Proctor, 1578.

Verses to *News from the North*, by F. Thynne, 1579 (printed by Allde).

Galien of France [1579], dedicated to the Earl of Oxford. Not extant.

1579, Oct. 10, for R. Ballard. *The Mirror of Mutability*, &c., printed by Allde; dedicated to the Earl of

Oxford, with verses by Thomas Proctor, William Hall "his kinsman," &c.

1580, Mar. 8, for J. Charlewood. A ballad of *The Encouragement of an English Soldier to his mates.*

1580, April 27, for W. Wright. *A view of (sundry) Examples,* "meet to be perused by all faithful Christians." This contains an account of the murder on which *A Warning for fair Women* is founded, and of the Earthquake of 6th April, *Honor alit artes.* Reprinted by Shak. Soc. In the body of the work Monday is repeatedly called Servant to the Earl of Oxford.

Zelauto, the Fountain of Fame, &c., "an Entertainment to Euphues at his late arrival into England" (and therefore after the spring of 1580, when Lyly's second part of Euphues was published), was dedicated to the Earl of Oxford (before 10th Nov., when the ballad against players appeared, I suppose), by A. M., his servant, *Honos alit Artes,* 1580, for J. Charlewood.

1580, Oct. 17. Dedication and Address to *The Pain of Pleasure. Honos alit artes.* Dedicated to Lady Douglas Sheffield. But the book was compiled by N. Britten, S. R. 1578, Sept. 9.

1580, Nov. 10, for E. White (no doubt Monday's ballad against plays)—

"A ringing retreat, courageously sounded,
Wherein plays and players are fitly confounded."

This was the first *Blast of Retreat.*

1581, Feb. 13, for J. Charlewood. *Palmerin of England* (translation). *Patere aut abstine,* 1596.

Love and Learning was dedicated to Mr. George Gifford and his lady; 1581, by J. Charlewood for Henry Carre.

1581, July 4, for W. Wright. *A brief discourse of the*

taking of Edmund Campion, &c. An answer to this was published soon after as *A very true report of the apprehension and taking of the Arch Papist Edm. Campion,* &c., by George Ellyot, " a controlment of a most untrue former book by one A. M., alias Antony Monday."

1582, Mar. 12, for E. White (but dated in the book 29th Jan.). *The Discovery of Edmund Campion,* &c., by A. M., " some time the Pope's Scholar, allowed in the Seminary at Rome amongst them."

1582, Mar. 12, for E. White (by J. Charlewood). *A Brief Answer to two seditious pamphlets,* " the one printed in French, the other in English, containing a defence of Edm. Campion, &c. *Honos alit artes.* Dated 22nd Mar. 1582, from the Barbican. This was answered by *A true Report of the Death and Martyrdom of M. Campion,* &c., Douay, 1582, by a Catholic Priest which was present thereat (Query Parsons). This answer contained the personal attack on Monday already noticed. The priest calls him a " boy; " he was twenty-eight. This is noticeable as showing that Greene's use of the term to Lodge was quite in conformity with the custom of the time.

1582, May 31, for W. Wright. *A brief and true report of the execution of certain Traitours at Tyburn,* 28th, 30th May 1582. Gathered by A. M., who was there present (compare the " Death and Martyrdom " title). *Honos alit artes.*

1582, June 21, by J. Charlewood for N. Ling. *The English Roman Life,* by A. M., some time the Pope's Scholar, &c. *Honos alit artes.*

1583, Aug. 9, for J. Charlewood. *The Sweet Sobs and Amorous Complaints,* &c.; not extant. See W. Webbe's *Discourse of English Poetry.*

A Watchword to England, &c., for T. Hacket, 1584. Dedicated to the Queen.

1584, July 6, for T. Hacket. *A Banquet of Dainty Conceits*, 1588, by A. M., servant to the Queen.

The godly exercise of Christian families, 1586; not extant. But compare S. R. 1584, Dec. 7, *The daily exercise of a Christian.*

The ballad of *Untruss.*

1587, Nov. 20, for E. Allde. *Histoire Palladienne*, by Claude Collet, to be translated. *Palladine of England. Patere aut abstine.* By A. M., Messenger of the Queen's Chamber. *Palmerin d'Oliva*, Part i., 1588. *Patere aut abstine.* By A. M., Queen's Messenger.

1509, Jan. 9, for J. Charlewood. *Palmendos and Primaleon. Patere aut abstine.* By A. M., still Queen's Messenger.

1589, Jan. 15, for E. Allde. *Amadis de Gaule*, Book i. Verses to Hakluyt's *Voyages*, 1589.

1592, Feb. 28, for J. Charlewood. *The Mask of the League and the Spaniard discovered. Patere aut abstine.* From the French, 1592; called in 1605 *Falsehood in Friendship*, &c.

1592, April 10, for J. Wolfe. *Amadis de Gaule.* Book ii. (iii., iv., v. to be done), by L[azarus] P[iot], *i.e.*, Monday. *The Defense of Contraries, Paradoxes*, &c., 1593, by R. Wendet for S. Waterson; from the French [of Sylven or Van den Bush], by A. M., Messenger of Her Majesty's Chamber. *Patere aut abstine.* The motto and the signature assure me that this was not the first imprint. In 1590, Aug. 25, S. R., fifty-five of Sylven's *Tragical Cases* had been licensed to E. Aggas and J. Wolf, as translated by E. A. This book contains the Declamation of the Jew who would have his pound of flesh.

1595, Mar. 10., for W. Leake. *Palmerin of England*, Book iii. Only in part by Monday. The 1602 edition has verses by Dekker, Webster, &c.

1596, July 15, for A. Islip. *Silvain's Orator* (*Cent Histoires Tragiques*), by L[azarus] P[iot]; an enlarged edition of the *Paradoxes*.

Translation of *The Book of Physic*, by O. Gabelhoner, 1599 (Dort). Surely he must have been at Dort when this book was printed.

Verses to Bodenham's *Belvidere*, 1600.

1601, Mar. 30, for Francis Hanson. *Don Sebastian of Portugal*. Dated 6th Jan. in the book.

1603, Oct. 29, for J. Roberts. *The* (*fasting*) *Maiden of Confolens*. Poictiers. Translation; with verses by Dekker.

Assinati's *Dumb Divine Speaker*. 1605; translation.

A brief Chronicle, &c., 1611, for W. Jaggard; a chronological Handbook.

An Epitaph on Sir J. Pemberton, 1613.

Additions to Stow's *Survey of London*, 1618. Compiled by order of the Corporation given to him in 1606. Stow's edition dates 1603. Monday, Dyson, and others made further additions up to 1633; but Monday died before the 1633 edition passed the press.

I now turn to Monday's dramatic career.

1. *Fidele and Fortunio* (or *The Two Italian Gentlemen*): "The Deceit in Love discoursed in a Comedy of Two Italian Gentlemen." Translated into English. Dedicated to John Heardson, Esq., by A. M. Title-page not extant. In rhyme. Captain Crackstone, one of the characters, is alluded to in Nash's *Have with you to Saffron Walden*, 1596, along with Basilisco (from *Soliman and Perseda*). Probably not acted. A song from it printed by Collier (*Annals*) is said by Hazlitt to be a "Prologue spoken before the Queen"! Date 1584.

2. *The Weakest goeth to the Wall* was acted by the Earl of Oxford's servants. As this company is only heard of in

London from 1584 to 1587, and Monday is the only playwright known in connexion with the company (except the Earl of Oxford himself, who may have written *George Scanderbag* and *Agamemnon and Ulysses*), I have little doubt that Monday was the author. The internal evidence of style, &c., is quite consonant with this supposition. The play has been most foolishly attributed to Webster. The date is probably c. 1584.

3. *John a Kent and John a Cumber.* The extant transcript is dated 1595 December, but this need not be the date of production, although it is the date of transcription. John of Kent Church or Kent Chester is the "wise man" of the play (iv. 1), and the scene is placed at West Chester. I have no doubt that it is the same as *The Wiseman of West Chester* produced by the Admiral's men at the Rose 2nd Dec. 1594. The ballad of *British Sidanen*, on which it was founded, is of much earlier date. See S. R. 13th Aug. 1579. Raynulf, or Randolph, or Randal, Earl of Chester, is a character in this and other plays.

4. 1597, Dec. 22, 28; 1598, Jan. 3. *Mother Redcap* (with Drayton).

5. 1598, Feb. 15. *The Downfall of Robert Earl of Huntingdon*: afterward called *Robin Hood of Merry Sherwood*, "with his love to Chaste Matilda, the Lord Fitzwater's daughter, afterwards his Fair Maid Marian." Altered (for Court performance) by Chettle 18th Nov., then called 1 *Robin Hood*. The part added by Chettle for the Court palpably includes the Induction, in which the play is turned into a Court performance, ostensibly presented by Sir T. Mantle to Henry VIII., but really to Elizabeth. The Skelton rhymes are Chettle's; so are the scenes where Matilda is called Marian before she assumes that name, and those where "the Friar" of Monday takes the name Tuck. But in all this (i., ii.,

iii. 3, 4) Chettle only altered Monday, while the Induction and the Skelton bits scattered through the play are purely his own. I think the play was founded on *The Pastoral Comedy of Robin Hood and Little John*, S. R. 1594, May 14, and that the allusion, iv. 2, to the "merry jests" of a previous play refers to this "pleasant comedy." The reference to the forthcoming Second Part, and to Cordelion's funeral at the end, could only have been spoken at the Rose before June 1598, and would have been absurd at Court at Christmas. The copy printed from is probably that used for correction, and not the prompter's copy, but a mixed version. It was licensed (with the Second Part) Mar. 28 (*Diary*), but the publication was probably stayed on account of its being selected for Court performance.

6. 1598, Feb. 20, 25, 28; Mar. 8. *The Death of Robert Earl of Huntingdon*, otherwise called *Robin Hood of Merry Sherwood*, "with the lamentable tragedy of chaste Matilda, his fair Maid Marian, poisoned at Dunmowe by King John." This play (2 *Robin Hood* of Henslow) consists of two plays in one. The second (the Matilda part) is clearly by Chettle, but has been altered by Monday (clumsily), probably being the comedy revised by him for the Court on 9th Aug. He has in many places introduced Salisbury for Oxford, while leaving Aubrey de Vere in the text, in order to assimilate this character to the Salisbury of Part i. In like manner he has confused Hugh Burght and Hubert, Chester and Winchester, Young Bruce and Young Fitzwater (who really does not appear at all), the Nun and the Abbess, &c; but I cannot, not having the original Quarto by me, disentangle all these discrepancies, owing to the shamefully inaccurate editing of Collier and his followers. The first "short play," the death of Robin Hood, is (except the bit of Induction at the beginning) plainly from the same hand as the *Downfall*,

Salisbury and Oxford were no doubt played by one actor in the same dress; hence the desire to assimilate the characters.

7. 1598, June 13, 14, 15, 17, 21, 23, 24, 26. *Richard Cœur de Lion's Funeral* (with Chettle, Drayton, Wilson). This play, with the two preceding, formed a Trilogy.

8. 1598, July 19. *Valentine and Orson* (with Hathway). Probably founded on the Queen's men's play, S. R. 1595, May 23.

9. 1598, Aug. 19, 24. *Chance Medley* (with Chettle (or perhaps Dekker), Drayton, Wilson).

For more than a year Monday is away: probably with Pembroke's men and in the Low Countries.

10, 11. 1599, Oct. 16, Dec. 19. 1, 2 *The true and honorable history of the life of Sir John Oldcastle, the good Lord Cobham* (with Drayton, Hathway, Wilson). The first part (which only is extant) was published as by William Shakespeare, but this was afterwards withdrawn. It was, as is evident from the Prologue, written against Shakespeare's *Henry* 4, in which Sir John Oldcastle was the original name of Falstaff, and, in my belief, a caricature of Brook, Lord Cobham. But it was not written till Shakespeare had been compelled to change the name, which he did early in 1598, and so in iii. 5 we find Falstaff, Poins, and Peto mentioned *nominatim.* The authorship is very hard to distinguish, but I think that i. 2; ii. 3; iii. 4; iv. 2, 3, 4, which comprise events which happened in 1413, but are scattered through the play without regard to chronology, must be by one hand, probably Wilson; the 1415 events of iii. 1, v. 1 by another, probably Hathway: i. 1 and v. 2—end, I have no hesitation in assigning to Monday; while the bulk of the play, comprising the 1414 events of ii. 2, iii. 2, iv. 1, as well as the series i. 3; ii. 1; iii. 3, 4, 5; iv. 2, 3, 4, are almost certainly by the author of *The Merry Devil of Edmonton ; i.e.*, Drayton. The proof of the title to the crown in iii. 1 should be compared with the corresponding passages in Shakespeare. Drayton wrote three-quarters of the Second Part.

12. 1600, Jan, 10. *Owen Tudor* (with Drayton, Hathway, Wilson).

13. 1600, June 3, 14. 1 *Fair Constance of Rome* (with Dekker, Drayton, Hathway).

14. 1601, Oct. 10; Nov. 6, 9, 12. *The Rising of Cardinal Wolsey* (with Chettle, Drayton, Smith).

14*. 1602, May 5. *Jephtha* (with Dekker).

15. 1602, May 22. *Cæsar's Fall* (with [Dekker], Drayton, Middleton, Webster).

16. 1602, May 29. *"The two harpes"* (with Dekker, Drayton, Middleton, Webster).

17. 1602. July 9; Aug. 26; Sept. 2, 11. *The Widow's Charm*, by "Antony the poet," which means, I think, poet to the City Corporation, for whom Monday wrote nearly all the pageants from this time to 1616.

18. 1602, Dec. 2. *The Set at Tennis.*

Monday now left writing plays for the Admiral's men, by whom all the above, from 1594, were produced. Of his pageants the following are known:—

19. 1605. *The Triumphs of reunited Britannia.* Leonard Holliday, Merchant Taylor, was the Mayor. Monday now signs "Citizen and Draper;" but I do not know when he acquired the freedom of this Company.

20. 1611. *Chrysothriambos, the Triumphs of Gold.* James Pemberton, Goldsmith, was the Mayor.

21. 1614. *The Triumphs of old Drapery*, or *The rich Clothing of England.* Thomas Hayes, Draper, was the Mayor.

22. 1615. *Metropolis Coronata, The Triumphs of ancient*

Drapery, or *Rich Clothing in England,* "in a second year's performance." John Jolles, Draper, "the first [Society] that received such dignity in this City," was the Mayor. Jason and Robin Hood are introduced in this show.

23. 1616. *Chrysanaleia,* or *The Golden Fishing,* or *The Honour of Fishmongers.* John Leman, Fishmonger, was the Mayor.

MONTAGUE, WALTER. (Pastoral.)

 1. *The Shepherd's Paradise,* P. C., 1659 (1629 in a few copies; a misprint).

Second son of Henry Earl of Manchester; born at St. Botolph without Aldersgate; member of Sidney College, Cambridge. After writing this pastoral comedy he travelled in France, became a Roman Catholic, then a Benedictine monk. He was busy in political matters later on, and died 1669.

1. *The Shepherd's Paradise* was acted at Court 8th Jan. 1633 by the Queen and her Ladies before Charles I. at Denmark House. The *Dram. Pers.* in MS. Sloane 3649 gives their names, but I have not seen this MS. It was for abusing the women's acting of this play in his *Histriomastix* that Prynne was so severely punished. Suckling ridiculed it as unintelligible in his *Session of the Poets.*

MORREL, ——. (Latin.)

 1. *Hispanus,* C., acted at Cambridge 1596. MS. Douce 234, in the Bodleian.

NABBES, THOMAS. (Plays.)

1636, Aug. 6, for Thomas Greene.

 3. A Moral Mask [*Microcosmus*], 1637.
 4. *Annibal and Scipio,* T., 1637.

 2. 1637, April 5, for Thomas Greene. *Tottenham Court,* C., 1638, 1639.

1. 1637, May 28, for Thomas Greene. *Covent Garden*, C., 1638, 1639.

5. 1637, June 23, for Thomas Greene. *The Spring's Glory*, &c., 1638.

7. 1639, July 8, for Laurence Blaiclock. *The Bride*, C., 1640.

8. 1639, Nov. 4, for Daniel Frere. *The Unfortunate Mother*, T., 1640.

1. *Covent Garden* was acted by the Queen's men "1632" [at the Cockpit]. It appears from the Prologue, which defends the author from stealing the play's name, that it was written after Brome's *Covent Garden weeded*, and also that "Lent is at hand," i. 4. The date of performance is therefore c. Jan. 1633. From i. 1 it seems that *Guy of Warwick* was still acted in the country. The "draining Marsh land with a windmill" is alluded to i. 4. "Her features transcend Mopsa's in the Arcadia," i. 6, shows the actor who personated Susan had played Mopsa in Shirley's *Arcadia* at the Cockpit in 1632. Wither's *Abuses Stript and Whipt* is alluded to in ii. 3, where also we meet with "Secretary Susan," in allusion to Jonson's Secretary Prue in his *New Inn* of 1631. The "reputed wit," Littleword, whose whole part consists in the *little word* "No" in iv. 6, is an evident exaggeration of Day's Signor No in *The Spanish Soldier*. In these allusions, which help us in stage history, the whole value of this otherwise worthless play consists; yet none of these are noticed in its recent reprint (it would be a misnomer to call such hurried work editing) by Mr. A. H. Bullen. As it is unlikely that this thing will ever see the light in a more perfect shape, I note here a few of the most flagrant blunders in this modern reissue. Vol. i., p. 23, "eares" is printed "cares;" p. 37, there should be a full stop after "welcome," and the

semicolon after " hope " and the ridiculous " [now] " should be
deleted; p. 101, for " but " read " let; " p. 102, for " Ay we "
read " Ay me; " p. 170, *dele.* the note on " best hand," which
is exactly equivalent to " first hand " (*i.e.*, without middle-
man) of our present time; p. 217, *dele.* another absurd note
and restore the old reading. As for such misprints as
p. 208, counfailours; p. 243, feemed; p. 208, polcy; p.
231, bewitch (for bewitcht), there are too many to be here
noticed. This play was dedicated to Suckling.

2. *Tottenham Court* was acted at Salisbury Court " in
1633," or rather early in 1634. *The Lancashire Witches*
(who were tried Feb. 1633–4) are alluded to i. 2. " There
was a Tub at Tottenham: you know the success of it "
refers to Jonson's *Tale of a Tub*, licensed 7th May 1633,
but performed at Court 14th Jan. 1634, and " not liked."
It is this performance that Nabbes means. Booker's Almanacs are also mentioned i. 6, and Swetnam the woman-hater
ii. 2. The company who acted this play must (from the
date) have been the King's Revels, not the Prince's men.

3. *Microcosmus.* This moral mask was also acted at
Salisbury Court, no doubt by the same company. There
is nothing remarkable in this tedious production, unless it
be the persistent misprinting, pp. 165–200, of Bellamina
for Bellanima: only to be paralleled by the editors of Lovelace, who, in like manner, persist in giving Aramantha for
Amarantha. Complimentary Verses by Brome are prefixed.
Date 1634–5.

4. *Hannibal and Scipio* was acted 1635 by the Queen's
men at the Cockpit. Founded, no doubt, on the old
Fortune play of the same name by Rankine and Hathway,
Jan. 1601. For the subject compare also Marston's
Sophonisba.

5. *The Spring's Glory* I think more likely to have been

written, and if so, privately acted, during the closure of the theatres, 1636–7, than at any other time. It vindicates Love by Temperance against the tenet *Sine Cerere* &c. Nabbes seems to have utilised this long vacation of the stage, 12th May 1636–17th Aug. 1637, in printing all that he had yet written; but this fourth volume was interrupted by the reopening after the subsidence of the plague, and was not issued till after 29th May 1638.

6. *The Presentation on the Prince's Birthday* was included (with date as above) with *Spring's Glory*, which proves the preceding statement; but this presentation was "intended" only, and apparently never made. The only noticeable allusion in it is that to *Chronomastix*.

7. *The Bride* was acted by the King's and Queen's men at the Cockpit 1638. It contains allusions to Tottenham Court, ii. 4; Martin Parker's *Ballads*, ii. 4; Coryat, v. 7; and has a bit of personal allusion taken from Brome's *Asparagus Garden*, 1635, ii. 1. There are bad mistakes in the text as reprinted p. 11, "wore" for "worse;" "expection" for "expectation;" p. 17, "propethick" for "prophetick;" p. 25, "dumbs" for "dumps;" p. 50, "almode" for "*la mode;*" p. 76, "for" for "sor" (sword).

8. *The Unfortunate Mother* was not acted, being refused by the actors [Beeston's boys]. It was written in rivalry to Shirley's *Politician*, which was acted by the Queen's men at Salisbury Court 1638–9. See the Proem and v. 1. Its date is therefore 1639, about autumn.

All that I need say of Nabbes' minor poems is that they show him to have been a friend of Marmion, R. Chamberlain, Tatham, and Jordan, and probably a denizen of Worcestershire.

Having pointed out a few of Mr. Bullen's inaccuracies, I am bound to confess my own. In my *History of the*

Stage, p. 321, will be found "Hamilcar" for "Himilco," "Gorgon" for "Gisgon," and "Hatfield" for "Stutfield" (so in p. 372). These were printed from an indistinctly written copy taken for me from *Hannibal and Scipio* by some friend in 1875, when I lived in Yorkshire, and could not get to the British Museum. I ought to have verified when I had the opportunity; but my erroneous reading had so long remained unnoticed, although it was published in 1881, that I trusted to its accuracy.

NASH, THOMAS. (Plays).

1. *Dido, Queen of Carthage,* 1594, by Widow Orwin for Thomas Woodcock.
2. 1600, Oct. 28, for C. Burby and W. Burre. *Summer's last Will and Testament,* 1600 (by Simon Stafford for W. Burre).

PROSE WORKS.

1588, Sept. 19, for T. Hackett. *The anatomy of absurdities,* 1589. Not published till after 23rd Aug. 1589. Dedicated to Sir Christopher Blunt.

1589, Aug. 23. The Address to the Gentlemen Students of both Universities prefixed to Greene's *Menaphon.* 1589.

Pasquil of England: "a countercuff for Martin Junior:" privately printed Aug.–Sept. 1589; "within a mile of an oak," *i.e.,* by N. Okes. 1589.

Pasquil of England: his return and meeting with Marforius: privately printed Oct. 1589, "by Pepper Alley." 1589.

1589, Dec. 22, for John Wolf. *A Mirror for Martinists.* "Nash, it is said."

Pasquil's Apology, c. July 1590, privately printed.

An Astrological Prognostication for 1591, by Thomas Scarlet. 1590–1.

The Address before Sidney's *Astrophel and Stella* (first and surreptitious edition), for T. Newman. 1591.

1592, Aug. 8, for Richard Jones. *Pierce Penniless, his Supplication to the Devil.* 1592 *bis*, 1593, 1594.

1593, Jan. 12, for John Danter. *The Apology of Pierce Penniless,* or *Strange news of the intercepting certain letters,* &c. 1592, 1593.

1593, June 30, for John Danter. *The Terror of the Night,* or *A discourse of Apparitions,* by J. Danter for W. Jones. 1594.

1593, Sept. 8, for Alice Charlewood. *Christ's Tears over Jerusalem,* 1593, by J. Roberts for A. Wise. 1594 (with the new Epistle), 1613. Dedicated to Elizabeth, daughter of Sir George Carey (Daniel's Delia).

1593, Sept. 17, for John Wolf. *The Unfortunate Traveller,* or *The life of Jack Wilton,* 1594, by T. Scarlet for C. Burby. Dedicated to L. Southampton.

1594, Oct. 25, for John Danter. *The Terror of the Night* (second entry ; by mistake, I suppose, for *Have with you to Saffron Walden,* or *Gabriel Harvey's Hunts-up,* &c. The Motto, " instead of *Omne tulit punctum, Pacis Fiducia nunquam.*" 1596).

1599, Jan. 11, for C. Burby. *The Praise of the Red Herring* (Nash's *Lenten Stuff*), 1599, for N. L[ing] and C. B[urby].

Thomas, son of William Nash, minister, and Margaret, his wife, was baptized at Lowestoft, Suffolk, Nov. 1567 (Sh. Soc. *Papers,* iii. 178). He was descended from the Nashes of Herefordshire. As he resided at St. John's " seven years together, lacking a quarter" (*Lenten Stuff*), and was in London before Sept. 1588, he must have gone to Cambridge a year before his matriculation, and resided while preparing for it, just as Lyly did. Ignorance of this custom has mis-

led all his biographers into errors of date for his whole
career. In Oct. 1582 he matriculated " as a sizar of St.
John's," was elected Lady Margaret's scholar in 1584, and
took his B.A. early in 1586. He " forsook Cambridge,
being Bachelor of the third year," c. July 1588 (not 1587
or 1589, as usually stated), having " had a hand in a show
called *Terminus et non Terminus*, for which his partner in it
was expelled the College. . . . He played in it the Varlet
of Clubs." This was probably the play of *The Cards* mentioned by Harrington in his *Apology of Poetry*, 1591. He
then came to London, and for Greene wrote his *Menaphon*
Address, S. R. 1589, Aug. 23. The direct praise of Greene
and Peele in this, combined with that of Lyly in Upchear's
subsequent verses, sufficiently indicates the one faction in
this quarrel; while the satire of Marlow and Kyd points
out the other. That of Marlow is universally recognised;
but as there are still some eccentric persons who think
Shakespeare is alluded to as the author of the early *Hamlet*,
I here gather up what is implied of him. He had no learning; was "nourisht in a servingman's idleness;" was an
" ironical censurer;" wrote " *Got*-hamist barbarism;" was no
Sabæan to refresh himself with the scent of " *Goats*' beards
burnt;" had left "the trade of *Noverint*," whereto he was
born; used "English Seneca," and was like the "Kid
in Æsop."

The Anatomy of Absurdity was published shortly after,
but entered as early as 1588, Sept. 19, with dedication to
Sir C. Blunt. It was, p. 8, "begun in my infancy," *i.e.*, in
1588, in a love disappointment "two summers since."
Nash's infancy ended 1588, Nov. 17. In p. 13, "let
them," the authors of eloquence who euphuise in the Honor
of Women, "alter their posies of profit with intermingled
pleasure," must, I think, allude to Greene's motto, "*qui*

miscuit utile dulci;" but this pamphlet cannot be one of "the paper bucklers" out of which it was beaten, for *Perimedes*, in which Greene's statement occurs, was entered 1588, Mar. 29. In p. 22, again, "with Greene colors seek to garnish such Gorgon-like shapes" is certainly aimed at Greene. Nash and he must have quarrelled since the publication of *Menaphon.* In p. 27 Stubbs' *Anatomy of Abuses,* 1583, is ridiculed; "pretend to anatomise abuses and Stubb up Sin by the roots." This pamphlet was published c. Sept. 1589, and a copy with 1589 on the title is extant in the Bodleian.

Next followed Nash's four anti-Martinist pamphlets.

A Countercuff given to Martin Junior by Cavaliero Pasquil of England was probably printed by N. Okes for R. Field; "within a mile of an Oak and not many Fields off, &c." The running title is *Pasquil of England to Martin Junior;* date 1589, Aug.–Sept.

The Return of Cavaliero Pasquil, or *Pasquil's Return to England,* dates 1589, Oct. 20, p. 136. The well-known passage of Martin and Divinity on the Stage occurs p. 123, and the "sly practice used in restraining of *Vetus Comedia,*" p. 135.

The first part of Pasquil's apology was entered 1589, Dec. 22. In p. 216 *Plain Percival* is mentioned. This is the first allusion to any of R. Harvey's works.

[*Martin's Month's Mind* has been printed as Nash's in the Huth Library, but without shadow of reason assigned or existing. It is written in a style so unlike Nash's that no one who has once read it could ever take it for his, and is written by Marphoreus to Pasquin, *i.e.,* Nash, who, however, always writes "Pasquil."]

A Mirror for Martinists, published by T. T., which was entered for J. Wolf S. R. 1509, Dec. 22, with marginal

comment, "Nash, it is said," being the only tract of this
nature with direct external evidence of Nash's authorship,
is not included in the Huth Edition.   I have not had opportunity to see this pamphlet; but Arber, in his *Sketch of
Martin Marprelate*, pp. 140, 200, suppresses the reference
to Nash, and gives it as written by T. T.; but was not this
T. T[horpe] the publisher, although his name does not occur
in S. R. till 1594?

An Almond for a Parrot, or *Cuthbert's Curryknave's alms*
[1590], has also been attributed to Nash by Mr. J. Petheram.
It appears to me to be by the same author as *Martin's Month's
Mind*, not by Nash nor by Lyly.   Some stage allusions in
it may, however, be noticed here.   In p. 3 (Petheram's reprint) it is dedicated to " Cavalier Monsieur du Kempe,
Jestmonger and Vicegerent-General to the Ghost of Dick
Tarleton," the " curtain " of whose countenance is mentioned.
This, I now think, indicates that Kempe, and therefore L.
Strange's men, were in 1590 acting at the Curtain, not at
the Crosskeys, as I guessed in my *History of the Stage*, p.
86.   "A man cannot write *Midas habet aures asininas* in
great Roman letters but he shall be in danger of a further
displeasure," p. 4, alludes to the offence given by Lyly in
his *Midas* (*q.v.*).   In p. 5 the author was in Venice last
summer, and took Bergamo in his way homewards.   In p.
17 the preacher in Ipswich who had been a player, and
will now " brandish a text against bishops," may be Stephen
Gosson, but he was parson at Great Wigborow, Essex.   Will
Tong, p. 22, had acted Martin, " attired like an ape on the
stage."   The Cambridge M.A., p. 28, who challenged the
degrees he never took for making *clari* a passive at Wolf's
printing-house, is, of course, Gabriel Harvey.   In p. 50 we
find " Wily-guilies," and p. 52 that Martin had called
Antony Monday Judas, and that Martin must beware of

Monday's laying open his "false carding to the stage of all men's scorn." Was Monday Marphoreus, the author of these two tracts? He was certainly involved in this controversy, and as Queen's Messenger in 1589 may have been in Italy.

Before noticing Nash's next work I must digress to give a short view of Gabriel Harvey's position at this time.

Gabriel Harvey was born c. 1545 at Saffron Walden, Essex, one of six children of a ropemaker, the others being Richard, John, Mercy, and two with whom we have no concern here. He was a "cousin" of Sir T. Smith of Audley End, Essex. Before 1565 he entered at Christ's, Cambridge; 1570, Nov. 3, he was made tutor at Pembroke; and 1575 Jan. 1, Fellow, iii. 93 (Grosart's edition, to which all references in this article are made). Before 1576 he was Lecturer on Rhetoric. In 1577, Oct. 3, S. R., he published his *Rhetor*, 1577, for H. Binneman; then his *Ciceronianus*, 1577, for H. Binneman; in 1578, Jan. 16, S. R., for H. Binneman, his *Smithus*, or *Musarum Lacrimæ*; 1578 Sept. his *Gratulationum Valdinensium Libri* iv. He was elected Fellow of Trinity Hall 1578, Dec. 13. He wrote Almanacs, "much in esteem." In 1579 he was refused his grace for his M.A. by Dr. Young of Pembroke, but ultimately obtained it. He failed in his candidature for the Public Oratorship. Spenser's letter to him, 1579, Oct. 5, from Leicester House contains mention of "my *Slumber*," i. 8; of Sidney, Dyer, Spenser, Drant, and Harvey as hexametrists, and of Spenser's poetical names *Benevolo* and *Immerito*. He calls Harvey "*multis jamdiu nominibus clarissimum*," p. 12; alludes to his going to Italy next week, pp. 12, 16; and applies to him "*Omne tulit punctum, qui miscuit utile dulci*" in his Latin verses. He had the "*dulce*," not the "*utile*;" Harvey had both, p. 15. Another letter from Harvey to Spenser

dates 1579, Oct. 23. These were published 1580, after June
19. On 4 Nones April 1580, Spenser, in a letter to Harvey, mentions his *Epithalamion Thamesis*, p. 37; his *Dream*
(finished, with its glossary); his *Pelican* (finished), p. 38;
his *Fairy Queen* (beginning), p. 38, cf. p. 94; his *Calendar*,
and his *Stemmata Dudleiana*, " not to be lightly published."
On April 7 Harvey writes to Spenser on the Earthquake,
mentions the great rain of Michaelmas 1579, p. 43, and his
nine English Comedies, pp. 67, 95. On 9 Kal. May 1580,
Harvey writes to Spenser on Hexameters. These three
letters were entered S. R. June 3, and published with Harvey's address, dated June 19, before the two letters mentioned above, which came late to the printer's hands. From
Harvey's Letter-Book it appears that in 1580, Aug. 1,
Spenser had published, with Dedication to Edward Dyer,
Harvey's " *Verlayes*," and other poetical *devises* (p. 111), at
which Harvey pretends to be annoyed, and writes to him
thereon 1579, [Aug.] 10 (*sic.*, p. 120). The J. W., p. 112
(" whoever he was," says Dr. Grosart), is, of course, J. Wolf,
the printer. In this letter I note that Harvey began the
childish game of replacing G. H., Gabriel Harvey, by G. H.,
Grandis Hostis, of which more hereafter. In p. 121 he mentions Wilson and Tarleton as extemporal players; in p. 125
Leicester's, Warwick's, L. Rich's, and Vaux's as the four
theatrical companies in London (but Vaux's men do not appear elsewhere, and Rich's were of earlier date); and "the
Theater or other painted stage" as their play-places. In
another letter, " before Pentecost approaching," p. 129, he
speaks of " my familiar," the fere of that " which attended
on M. Phaer in Kilgarran forest when he translated Virgil's
Æneidos" (the " affable familiar sprite" of Shakespeare's
Sonnets, I think); but Harvey adds, " by his familiar he
[Phaer] meaneth most likely his paper book "). In 1582

Harvey was appointed Junior Proctor, and in 1585 LL.D. of Oxford, and Advocate of the Prerogative Court at Canterbury.

Many points here noted may seem trivial, but they all have a bearing on the history of the Drama.

As to Richard Harvey, his *Discourse on the conjunction of Saturn and Jupiter*, 1583, April 28, "with the effect of the late eclipse of the sun," 1582, was entered S. R. 1583, Jan. 22, for. H. Bynneman; and an addition to it 1583, April 12, for R. Watkins; *A prognostical judgment* on the same by R. Tanner, and an anonymous *Judgment of the Star* [? by Elderton; cf. *infra*], having meanwhile been entered Mar. 11. The prophecies of these astrologers would seem to have been unsuccessful, for in 1583, May 3, S. R., a ballad appeared:—

"Trust not the conjunctions or the judgments of men,
  When all that is made shall be unmade again;"

and June 13, *A Defensitive against the poison of supposed prophecies*. In 1583 he also published his *Ephemeron, or Pæan to the Earl of Essex*, and in 1584 his *Leap Year*, "a compendious prognostication for 1584." But note that 1584, April 7, S. R., was entered for R. Watkins (R. Harvey's then publisher) *An almanac and prognostication* "for 1585, first from the Leap-year, which is from the creation of the world 5547; Gabriel Frene authore." Is this the same book? If not, who is Gabriel Frene? See *infra*, p. 142.

Of Mercy Harvey, "the milkmaid," I need only note that she had a love affair with Phil[ip], my Lord A. S. [Query Assistant Secretary], a young married nobleman, in 1574, Nov. 29–1575, Jan, 1; Gabriel's *ex parte* and evidently false account of which, with irreconcilable dates (whatever Dr. Grosart may allege to the contrary) will be found in

Harvey's *Works* (Grosart), iii. 73, &c. The " urring tauye " which " the Editor can't elucidate," p. 202, by the bye, is the familiar " orange tawny." I may now proceed with the Nash *v.* Harvey controversy.

On 1588, Feb. 27, S. R., for R. Watkins, was entered *A discoursive problem concerning Prophecies*, by John Harvey, diametrically opposed to the pretensions of R. Harvey's *Astrological predictions* of 1583. In 1589 R. Harvey published his *Plain Percival* anonymously, c. Sept. On 1589, Oct. 23, S. R., for W. Ponsonby, *The Lamb of God and his enemies*, by R. H[arvey]. In 1589 c. Aug. Lyly had issued his *Paphatchet*, and Nash his *Pasquil of England*. On 1589, Nov. 5, G. Harvey wrote *An advertisement for Paphatchet and Martin Marprelate* (published as part of *Piers' Supererogation*, 1593, Sept., iii. 124–221). Soon after this MS. got abroad, Peele, Nash's friend, represented Harvey as Huanabango in *The Old Wife's Tale*, and Nash issued his *Astrological Prognostication* for 1591, in ridicule of R. Harvey's 1583 tracts; but this was only in retaliation for *The Lamb of God*, 1589, and not the beginning of the quarrel: R. Harvey, not Nash, was the aggressor. Also in 1591 Nash wrote his Address for the surreptitious issue of Sidney's *Astrophel and Stella*. On 1592, July 21, S. R., Greene's *Quip for an upstart courtier* was entered, in which he alluded to the Harveys as the sons of a ropemaker at Saffron Walden. On 1592, Aug. 8, S. R., for R. Jones, *Piers Penniless, his supplication to the Devil*, was entered The allusions in this book require detailed notice. Harvey, in his *Advertisement for Paphatchet*, 1589, Nov. 5, had disclosed Lyly's authorship of that work. In it he calls Lyly Paphatchet, p. 124; I'll, I'll, I'll, pp. 128, 219; V. V., p. 129; a playmonger, the fool of Oxford, the stale of London, p. 132; Cock a lilly, or The white son of the black art, pp. 210, 217; Vice-

master of Paul's [school], fool master of the Theater, p.
212; [1] Dia-Pap, Dia-Fig, Dia-Nut, p. 216. It appears
from p. 131 that Harvey had been thought to be Martin;
from p. 211 that Lyly had called Harvey " No-body " (cf.
the play of *Nobody and Somebody*), and made him "a cart of
Croydon" (a collier's cart). In p. 217 Harvey refers to
Huff, Ruff, and Snuff (see Preston's *Cambyses*) as "the
three tame ruffians of the church." Nash, in his *Supplication*, does not reply to Harvey at once, but attacks Monday.
His ballad of *Untruss* is first mentioned p. 12, the authorship of which is determined by a letter of Nash's published
in Collier's *Stage Annals*, i. 305, first edition. In p. 26 he
describes him as the greasy son of a clothier, an *Inamorato
Poeta*, *Italianato* in his talk, a traveller, with a sharp spade-
peak. In p. 29 he attacks a prodigal young Master, a waste-
good at the Inns of Court, who will to the Sea. This appears to be directed against Lodge. In p. 34 the Cobbler's
Crow, who cries but *Ave Cæsar*, alludes, I think, to Marlow's
Edward 3 (*q.v.*). In p. 37 he that grows to a mountain in
a moment by carrying tales or playing the doughty pander
is, I, fear, W. Shakespeare. In p. 44 Polyhistor Rimerus,
who wrote a ballad of blue starch and poking-sticks, S. R.
1590, July 4, has not been identified; he may be Monday
or Elderton. In p. 45 the yeomen of the vinegar-bottle
suggest a very different interpretation to the entrance of
Nash with a vinegar-bottle in *The Return from Parnassus*
from that usually assigned. In p. 60 Daniel's *Rosamond*,
S. R. 1592, Feb. 4, is praised. In p. 61 Henry Smith's
poems are praised, and his death, causing the " general tears
of the Muses," mentioned. See Fuller's *Church History*, ix.
142. Entries of his *Sermons* occur S. R. 1591, July 19,
26, Aug. 18, Oct. 4; 1592, April 10, May 19; 1593,

---

[1] "Dia" is a medical prefix; cf. dia-margaritam, dia-ambre, i. 267.

Mar. 18. At last, p. 65 *seq.*, R. Harvey is assailed. This ropemaker's son, when B.A., had his hood turned over his ears for painting Aristotle on the school gates with asses' ears; this jade of the Press had published his *Pœan* anonymously; this student in Almanacs had written a book set forth in his brother's name [What book is this? Is it John Harvey's *Discoursive Problem?*]; this prognosticator's prophecies had been hissed in the University, jested at by Tarlton at the Theater, bear-baited in Elderton's ballads; had written *The Lamb of God,* and attacked Lyly in it as Paphatchet. He had need to follow his father's occupation and "make a rope" to hang himself; cf. Polly-make-a-rope-lass-it-does in Peele's *Old Wife's Tale.* The "new laureate," p. 70, is unknown to me. In p. 88 *seq.* Nash defends historical plays, mentions the Talbot scenes in 1 *Henry* 6, acted 1592, Mar. 3, and Henry 5 leading the French King prisoner, and the Dolphin swearing fealty in the old *Victories of Henry* 5, acted by the Queen's men; also the merriment of *The Usurer* (Dives) *and the Devil.* He says our plays show "the ill success of treason [*Jack Straw*], the fall of hasty climbers [*Edward* 2], the wretched end of usurpers [*Richard* 3], the misery of civil dissension [*Marius and Sylla*], and how just God is evermore in punishing of Murder [*Arden of Feversham*]. He reproves the plays beyond sea in which common courtesans play women's parts, and extols Tarlton, Allen, Knell, and Bently. In p. 132 he glorifies Amintas, omitted in the Sonnet-list of *The Fairy Queen.* This cannot mean the dead Walsingham, Watson's Amintas, and I think Collier is right in suggesting the Earl of Southampton: to no other nobleman fulfilling the required conditions did Nash afterwards dedicate any of his works. Note that the lending of periwigs to bald pates, p. 133, applies to plagiarists, not to actors, and disproves

Simpson's interpretation of the passage in the Address prefixed to *Menaphon*.

1592, Dec. 4, S. R., for J. Wolf. *Four letters and certain Sonnets touching R. Greene*, &c., were published by G. Harvey; but the Address to the Reader is dated Sept. 16. Letter 1, from C. Bird to E. Demetrius, Aug. 29, is on Greene's *Quip*, Greene being as yet alive. He calls Greene Robin Goodfellow and Greensleeves, p. 161. Letter 2, from G. Harvey to C. Bird, Sept. 5, after Greene's death, gives the well-known description of the decease of "Mrs. Isham's Nightingale," and the pickle-herring banquet that caused it. In Letter 3, To the Reader, Sept. 8, 9, p. 182, Harvey denies having been in the Fleet, but admits that Sir James Croft had been incensed with him till pacified by Secretary Wilson and Sir Walter Mildmay; he also denies having attacked the Earl of Oxford as the Mirror of Tuscanism. In p. 188 we learn that John Harvey, deceased, was M.D. Cantab.; and p. 189 Harvey calls Greene the second Toy of London (the first Toy being, not the actor in *Summer's last Will*, as Grosart says, but Tarlton, who wrote the *Toy*), the stale of Paul's (the press, not the theatre), the ape of Euphues (Lyly), the Vice (or Iniquity) of the Stage (*i.e.*, in the old Moralities), &c. He accuses him of atheism p. 190, and parallels him with Babington p. 193; mentions the playing of Tarleton's *Seven Deadly Sins* at Oxford (Query in 1585) p. 199; says that Nash had cried a mercy of Churchyard in print p. 199; and mentions Dr. Caius p. 215. In Letter 4, Sept. 11, 12, he calls Greene and Nash Grasshopper and Cricket, p. 222 (cf. *Merry Wives of Windsor*, v. 5, *The Maid's Metamorphosis*, and *Wily Beguiled*), and uses the phrase "old lad of the castle," p. 225, for a stage fool (cf. ii. 44 and 1 *Henry* 4, i. 2).

On 1592, Dec. 8, Chettle published *Kindhart's Dream;*

and on 1593, Jan. 12, S. R., for J. Danter, Nash answered Harvey in *Strange News of the intercepting certain letters and a convoy of Verses as they were going privily to victual the Low Countries*, 1592. This was entered as *The Apology of Piers P.*, or *Strange News*, &c., and was printed in one issue (in my opinion the first, not the second, as Hazlitt says) with that title. See *infra*. It has an Epistle to M. Apislapis [Bee-stone] and an Address to The Gentlemen Readers. In p. 177 Harvey is called Doddipol and fellow-coach-horse with Shakerley for the Queen's fool-taker. In p. 179 John Davies' *Soul* (S. R. 1599, April 14) is alluded to; this poem must have circulated in MS.; Davies had published his *Sir Martin Marpeople* 1590, Oct. 20, S. R. In p. 185 Nash says he was attacked by R. Harvey "about two years since" [it was really more than three years] because in his alphabet of idiots he had overskipt the H's; in p. 186 he uses the term "paper buckler" for a pamphlet, which shows how wrongly Simpson interpreted this word in Greene's *Perimedes*. In p. 190 he attacks Gabriel's phrases "entelechy" and "addulce" as hermaphrodite. In p. 193 he mentions Piers' father [Lyly] as Dame Lawson's poet, who wrote of her in *An Almond for Parrot;* and bids Gabriel *respice funem* [not *finem*, as Grosart gives it], "look back to his father's house." Compare *Errors*, iv. 4, 46, "the prophecy like the parrot, beware the rope's end," absurdly obelised in the *Globe Shakespeare*. In p. 194 he says that he had never derogated from Dr. Harvey, *i.e.*, Gabriel, till now, and thought him of another family; and p. 196 that Richard, in Jack of both sides Percival, had snarled at Paphatchet [Lyly], Pasquil [Nash], &c.; and then again had gleeked at them and Greene as make-plays and make-bates in his *Lamb of God*, which had been preached by him without book three years before he put it in print [1587]. Then

Greene, being chief agent for the company [the Queen's men], for he writ more than four other [Kyd, Peele, Marlow, Lodge], canvassed the three brothers in seven or eight lines in his *Cloth Breeches and Velvet Breeches*, and him Gabriel had attacked when dead :—

"So Hares may pull dead lions by the beards.

Memorandum,—I borrowed this sentence out of a play " [*The Spanish Tragedy*]. In p. 199 he gives a list of books quoted by Gabriel. In p. 202 we find that John Harvey, who died at Lynn in July last, and whom Greene, not knowing him dead, had attacked July 21, was the "almanac-maker," not Gabriel; in the same page the play on "smiter" and "scymiter," the original of many such in Jonson, &c., makes its first appearance. In p. 207 he refuses to allow that Gabriel is a D.D. when he had not "done his acts." [What would Nash have said of the literary swarm of Doctors 300 years later?] In p. 210 he calls Elderton the father of Stubbs, Deloney, and Armin, and says that he wrote the "judgment" of Earthquakes against Gabriel in 1580. [I find no such "judgment" in S. R. 1580. Can this be the "*Judgment of the Star*" of 1583, Mar. 11?] In p. 211 Hoddy Doddy (Dr. Doddipol again) is going to set forth his "Paraphrase upon Paris Garden, wherein he will so tamper with the interpreter of the Puppets." In p. 232 Coppinger and Arthington (the false prophets) are mentioned. In pp. 233, 235 G. H. is said to have been in Newgate and the Fleet. In p. 240 Dr. Butler (M.D.) is mentioned, and the statement that little Paphatchet (Lyly) had incenst the Earl of Oxford against G. H. is evaded. In 243 Nash disclaims being Greene's companion for more than a carouse or two. In p. 244 he says that Harvey's *Musarum Lacrymæ* was flouted in Winkfield's *Pedantius* (*q.v.*) at Trinity College.

In p. 252 he says the old quarrel with Churchyard shall
not be renewed; he loves him unfeignedly and admires his
Shore's Wife [originally published in *The Mirror for Magistrates*, but entered as enlarged S. R. 1593, June 16]. In
p. 255 the charges against R. H. are repeated. In p. 263 a
list of the inkhornisms of G. H. is given; and John Tell-
truth's Chronicle (Stow's) is quoted against R. H. In p.
283 Nash first knew Greene about town (in 1589), but has
been two years together and not seen him (*i.e.*, c. 1590
July to 1592 July). Note that "*cat* in the pan" is printed
"eat" in Grosart's most inaccurate text, and "the cat" in
his Index. *Ex uno disce omnia.*

Shortly after this book (Jan. 12) and before Mar. 25 (for
the second issue of *Piers Penniless* is dated 1592) Jones had
transferred to Jeffes the copyright of *P. P's Supplication*,
and Nash wrote a letter to the new publisher before he
reissued it:—"Had you not been so forward in the republish-
ing of it you should have had certain epistles . . . to
insert; . . . and lastly to the ghost of Robert Greene, telling
him what a coil there is with pamphleting on him after
his death." This must have meant Harvey's *Four letters*
(Dec. 4), Chettle's *Kindhart's Dream* (Dec. 8), and Nash's
Strange News (Jan. 12); Nash would not have written to
Greene's ghost until he had a share in the "coil" himself.
He bids Jeffes cut off the long-tailed title of Jones' edition
(which he accordingly did), and denies that he is writing a
second part; some "obscure imitators" are doing that. Nash
promises, if he has leisure, to write The Return of the Knight
of the Post from Hell with the Devil's answer to the· Supplication; but he never did; it was done in 1606 by a
"near companion" of his. There is no trace in S. R. of
any second part of *P. P.*, but I think there can be little
doubt that the announcement of one was the reason of

Nash's omitting "The Apology of Piers P." from the title of
the second issue of *Strange News*. He further denies that
he had anything to do with *Greene's Groatsworth of Wit*, and
says that he is still "the plague's prisoner in the country,"
where he had been with my lord [Query Archbishop Whitgift at Croydon] since 1592 July. The plague lasted (with
a short relaxation in Jan.) till 1593 Dec.

Pierce's Supererogation, or *A new praise of the old ass*,
"a preparative to certain larger discourses entitled Nash's
S. Fame," by G. Harvey, was published by J. Wolf 1593,
with dedication to Barnaby Barnes, John Thorius, Antony
Chute, &c., and is dated July 16. Barnes' letter, p. 19, is
dated June; it contains a Sonnet by [Dr. Raphael] Thorius.
Other Sonnets are affixed, one on Nash by Parthenophil
(Chute, according to Wolf, p. 25), and one on Harvey by
Parthenope (Fregevil Gautius, author of *Palma Christiana*,
1593, and translator of *The Spanish Counsellor*, p. 14).

With the same title (*Piers' Supererogation*, &c.) a much
larger work appeared soon after. I think that this was
originally called Nash's S. Fame, "already finished," p. 25,
but that the title was altered to give the reader the impression that a still larger tractate was "presently to be
published," p. 25. This book was written by April 27,
p. 331, but not printed till July. The name Doddipol,
which seems to have specially offended Harvey, is referred
to pp. 63, 90. The "familiar spirit" of *Piers' Supererogation*, as Harvey "newly christened" *The Strange News*, is
mentioned p. 84; the title of a later work of Nash's is
taken from "his Lenten stuff, like the old pickle-herring,"
p. 115. The Advertisement for Paphatchet, pp. 124–221,
of 1589, Nov. 5, thrust into the midst of this pamphlet as
makeweight, has been already noticed. In p. 222 we find
the often-quoted "Nash the ape of Greene, Greene the ape

of Euphues, Euphues the ape of Envy." A passage in p.
227 probably gave Lodge the title of his *Spider's Web*,
1594, June 7. In p. 240 Nash is called Tom [not Jack]
Drum. Grosart in iii. 138 has muddled this Tom Drum
with Marston's "famous" play, of which he does not even
know the title. In p. 242 G. H. puns on the "boys," the
Chapel children, for whom Nash was now writing "by her
favor who hath made him a Sultan Tom-um-*boi*-us, and
another, Al-*man*-us Hercules, the great captain of the *boys*,"
but "only in her Bello Eu-*boi*-ico or main battle of scolds."
It seems from p. 282 that Gabriel had not given up his
astrology; he claims to have been a true prophet in his
"prognostication" of the last year, *i.e.,* 1592. In S. R. I
find entered for J. Wolf, Harvey's publisher, April 3, *A
prophecy for* 8 *years yet to come,* and April 8, *Gargantua, his
prophecy.* Nash calls him Gargantua, and I think this was
Harvey's prognostication. In p. 290 there is a list of poets
commended by Harvey, among them Monday and Daniel.
In p. 297 the Fox (one of his chief enemies, p. 23) is identified with Dr. Perne, who died 1586, April 26; the other
enemy, "the ass," is Nash. Harvey revels in his wretched
pun on a Nash and an Ass, *sh* being pronounced as *s* at that
time, as I have abundantly proved, although Mr. A. J.
Ellis held a contrary opinion. In p. 322, &c., the praises
of Mary Countess of Pembroke are rung once more: see i.
267; ii. 100, 266. Harvey expected her to write against
Nash, but she was better advised. In p. 325 Tarlton's
Toy ["the first Toy of London," I suppose] is mentioned.

Christ's Tears over Jerusalem, "with a comparative admoni-
tion to London," was entered S. R. for Alice Charlwood, but
was printed by J. Roberts for A. Wise. In the Epistle to
the Reader Nash asks G. H. for "reconciliation and pardon;"
he had "rashly assailed" his fame, though after provocation;

acknowledges his scholarship, courtesy, and judgment; "only with his mild gentle moderation hereunto he hath won me." Dedicated to Elizabeth, wife of Sir. G. Carey.

The Terrors of the Night, "a discourse of apparitions," by Nash, S. R. 1593, June 30, for J. Danter, was dedicated to Elizabeth, wife of Sir G. Carey (Delia; see Daniel). "Tarlton's *Toy*" is mentioned p. 216.

The Unfortunate Traveller, or *The Life of Jack Wilton,* S. R. for J. Wolfe 1593, Sept. 17, was printed by T. Scarlet for C. Burby. Note how often Nash's works are entered for one publisher and issued by another. Dedicated to Lord Southampton. "I knew two or three good wenches" of the name of Mercy alludes to Mercy Harvey, p. 19. The orator of Wittenberg, who addresses the Duke of Saxony in a speech stolen out of Tully, and ends his sentences with *esse posse videatur,* is surely a caricature of Harvey, p. 67. Acolastus, the prodigal child, p. 71, is Fulton's play, which was translated into English 1540. "Chastity's first martyr, Lucretia," p. 80, may refer to Shakespeare's poem in MS., but it was not entered till 1594, June 7. "Which music, the philosophers say, in the true heaven, by reason of the grossness of our senses, we are not capable of," p. 120, was probably the origin of *The Merchant of Venice,* v. 1, 62–4.

A new letter of notable contents, "with a strange sonnet entitled Gorgon or the Wonderful Year," by G. Harvey, was entered for J. Wolf 1593, Oct. 1, but dated Sept. 16, and therefore written before *Jack Wilton* was published. In p. 259 he refers to the publication of Barnes' *Parthenophil,* S. R. May 10; Chute's *Shore's Wife,* June 16; *The Articles of Accord,* Aug. 18; and *The Remonstrance to the Duke of Maine,* Sept. 4: all sent to him by Wolf the publisher. In pp. 270 *seq.* he abuses Nash more scurrilously than

ever, rejects his proffered peace, and declares war to the
death.   For the concluding sonnets see under Marlow and
my *Life of Shakespeare*.

Early in 1594 Nash reissued his *Christ's Tears* with a
new Address.   Nash withdraws his apology to Harvey,
and intimates that it had been obtained from him by ad-
vances for reconciliation and professions of regret privately
made by G. H.

On 1594, Oct. 25, *The Terrors of the Night* is again entered
S. R. for J. Danter, the most unlikely man to pay a fee
twice over.   I believe that the title is a mistake for the
next book published in 1596, which had then been two years
in preparation.   Perhaps the title had not been fixed in
1594, and it was desirable to secure an entry of some kind.
The second title in this entry, " an apparition of dreams," is
inaccurate, and looks as if dictated from memory.

Have with you to Saffron Walden, or *Gabriel Harvey's Hunt
is up,* " containing a full answer to the eldest son of the
Haltermaker, or Nash his confutation of the Sinful Doctor,
The Mot or Posie, instead of *Omne tulit punctum* [Greene's
motto ; cf. Harvey's poem, i. 15, and Greene's *Perimedes*],
Pacis fiducia nunquam.   As much as to say as I said I
would speak with him," was printed by J. Danter 1596.
This is the cardinal work in this controversy.   It is dedicated to Richard Lichfield, the Trinity barber.   In p. 9
Nash attributes to Richard Harvey *A defence of Short Hair
against Synesius and Pierius* (S. R. 1593, Feb. 4, for J.
Wolf).   In p. 14 " being not only but also two brothers "
ridicules Harvey's continual use of " not only, but also ; " cf.
p. 73, and *Locrine.*   In p. 17 *Richard* 3 (*q.v.*), and the actor
who cried *Ad urbs* is mentioned ; in p. 18 Doctor Doddipol
again ; in p. 19 " Old Tooley " and his pronunciation.   Is this
Nich. Tooley, the actor ?   In p. 20 *seq.* Harvey's words

connive wink), cosmologised and smirked (recreated), omnisufficiency, enthusiastical (rich), entelechy (capacity), are jeered at.[1] In the Address to the Readers, pp. 25, 27, he has been "two or three years" at this book, ever since the hanging of Lopus (condemned 29th Feb. 1594). Tocrub, p. 29, is, of course, Dr. Burcot. In the body of the work, p. 36, we learn that Nash had been writing "toys" for private gentlemen during this time; from p. 39 that he dated the Creation 4000 B.C., not 3960, as Dekker did. In p. 44 it appears that Nash's "toys" were love-ditties for amorous new-fangles written in poverty; from p. 47 that Dick Lichfield had turned *Piers Penniless* in Macaronic verse, and that it had been maimedly translated into French. In p. 50 Simpson's interpretation of "periwig" is again disproved, and in p. 51 *Piers. P.* had passed six editions (four only of which are now extant). In p. 52 *Ha' y' any work for Cooper?* 1589, is alluded to. In p. 55 the picture of Gabriel as he is ready to let fly upon A-jax is given. Harington's *Metamorphosis of Ajax* was entered 1596, Oct. 30, and I think Nash's book must date c. Nov. In p. 59 Dick Harvey's word tropological in *The Lamb of God* is ridiculed; in p. 67 the suppression of the Paul's boys is mentioned; in p. 80 G. H. is "of the age of 48 or upwards;" in p. 93 he wrote verses on the Months, "extant in Primers and Almanacs," and was a sizar at Christ's; in p. 96 he ends every sentence with *esse posse videatur :* this identifies him with the Wittenberg orator already mentioned in *Jack Wilton,* and proves that Nash, after his proffered reconciliation in *Christ's Tears,* still continued to attack Harvey in ambuscade. *Jack Wilton* was entered a fortnight before Harvey's *New letter.* This shows that Harvey's refusal to

---

[1] In p. 23, instead of "sit on his skirts," Grosart prints "fit on his skirts," as if Nash were a man-milliner.

accept Nash's articles of peace was justifiable, and that all the biographers have totally misunderstood the merits of the case. In p. 97 Nash says Harvey was nicknamed Gabriel *Ergo* at Cambridge; in p. 98 that he writ verses in all forms, from gloves to pothooks; in p. 101 that he hexametrised the Earl of Oxford, and then wrote almanacs under the name of Gabriel Frend; in p. 107 his hobby-horse revelling when the Queen was at Audley End, 1578, is mentioned; the Queen said he looked something like an Italian, and ever since he is an insulting Monarch above Monarcho the Italian, who wore crowns on his shoes. See the commentators on *Love's Labor's Lost*, iv. 1. In p. 115 the charge of Harvey's having been in the Fleet is renewed; in p. 117 he is said to have been ridiculed as a schoolmaster in Wingfield's *Pedantius* at Trinity (1590), the three brothers at Clare Hall in *Tarrarantantara, turba tumultuosa Trigonum, Tri-Harveyorum Tri-Harmonia*, and Dick H. at Peterhouse in *Duns Furens* (Dick Harvey in a frenzy), whereupon Dick broke the College windows, and was set in the stocks. Gabriel's first hexameters were through his love to Kate Cotton and the wife of Widdows, the St. John's butler. John Harvey, p. 119, was a wencher, a tutor in fustian, at Meade's house; stole his daughter; to pacify him dedicated to him an almanac. With her G. H. quarrelled after John's death. In p. 123 note the dearth (1596), and Deloney's authorship of *John for the King*. Dick H., p. 124, wrote *The miracle of the burning of Brustem and his wench* for Bynneman, which afterwards proved to be an ordinary murder, by the murderer's own confession. The Aristotle story is again mentioned. Dick was pastor of Chiselhurst, but lost his benefice and his wench both at once. Kit Marlow called him an ass. He wrote (as above) against baldness: this may throw some light on the Jon-

son speech in Dekker's *Satiromastix*. G. H., while shut
up at Wolf's in the plague of 1593 (p. 127), got him to
publish *Parthenophil*, S. R. May 10; by Barnes; *Shore's
wife*, June 16, by Chute (an attorney's clerk and captain's
boy, p. 157); and Chute's *Procris and Cephalus*, Oct. 22.
In p. 135 "remuneration of gratuities" is ridiculed as a Har-
veyan phrase; "remuneration" is Armado's phrase in *Love's
Labor's Lost*, iii. 1, v. 1 (nine times repeated); and "gratillity"
is the clown's word in *Twelfth Night*, ii. 3. In p. 196 Nash
"half a year since," *i.e.*, c. April 1596, had not been in
Cambridge "in six years before," *i.e.*, since 1590; but he
left Cambridge 1588. He probably visited it afterwards,
or this part of his book may have been written in 1594.
He began to write it then, but delayed publishing till he could
get "more intelligence of his (G. H.'s) life and conversation,"
pp. 25, 41. Nash had been staying in Lincolnshire in 1595.
In 1592 he was at Christmas in the Isle of Wight [at Sir
George Carey's]. At that time, p. 141, Harvey incensed
the Lord Mayor against him, and incited a preacher at Paul's
Cross to denounce woe on him and Lyly. In p. 151 Nash
says Chute wrote a comedy on the transformation of the
King of Trinidado's two daughters, Madam Panachæa and
the Nymph Tobacco. In p. 159 Nash confesses his obligations to Sir Roger Williams for a year and a half before his
death. Note the phrase *summ' tot'* in p. 160. Campion
wrote an *Epigram* on Barnes, p. 162. In p. 163 "Is he
like a Tinker that never travels without his wench and his
dog?" Compare Jonson's Puntarvolo. In p. 169 a list of
titles of plays to be written against G. H. is given; "more
than half of one of these I have done already" [of course
The Isle of Dogs], to be acted in Candlemas Term [Feb.
1597]. The ballad of *The Devil of Dowgate*, p. 179, was
entered S. R. 1596, Aug. 5. Note the derivation of Pander

from Pandora. In p. 189, "It is well known I might have been Fellow of St. John's." "See him and see him not I will," p. 191, is probably the origin of the wrongful assignment to Nash of the authorship of *Hans Beerpot*. In p. 194, "I never abused Greene, Marlow, Chettle, in my life," and he prints Chettle's letter giving Harvey the lie on this point. In p. 196 one Valentine Bird writ against Greene, imitated Nash, and stole "six lines at a clap" from *Piers Penniless*. I do not recognise this tract. In p. 202 the great dearth of 1596 is mentioned; and in p. 204 Lyly in the time he spends in one week in taking tobacco will compile what will make Gabriel repent all his life. Before leaving this series of references to matters (all of which will be found to concern our history, and will be alluded to in some part of my book) I will note a few of the Tucca-like appellations of G. H., coined in imitation of his *Grandis Hostis*, noticed above: Gorboduc Huddle-duddle, p. 32; Gobin-a-grace ap Hannakin, p. 45; Gregory Huldrick, p. 45; Gurmo Hidruntum, p. 95; Graphiel Hagiel, p. 158; Gnimelf Hengist, p. 193.

The Trimming of Thomas Nash by Don Ricardo de Medico Campo (Leech-field) was published by Philip Scarlet, but entered S. R. 1597, Oct. 11, for C. Burby. It accuses Nash of suffering from a shameful disease, p. 9, and of having been imprisoned with one Lusher; contains a string of Epigrams like those of Horace in *Satiromastix*, p. 36; acknowledges that G. H. had attacked Harington as Ajax, and in retaliation for his portrait in *Have with you*, gives one of Nash in fetters with no beard, long hair, and a love-lock by his ear: he also calls him "deformed," pp. 37, 40, 53. All this identifies Nash with Deformed in *Much Ado about Nothing*, iii. 3. Nash had written his *Isle of Dogs* in the Dog-days of 1597, and warrants were out for his apprehension, pp. 50–54. "Nine or ten years since," *i.e.*, 1588 c. April, he being a bachelor of the third year, forsook Cambridge for London ; but had previously acted as the Knave of Clubs [Query in 1587] in *Terminus et non*. His partner in that play [Query Marlow] was expelled, p. 67. There are contradictions in this tract about Nash's imprisonment, but these disappear if the part "Here let" p. 50—"cut" p. 64 be supposed to have been an insertion of Sept., the rest of the pamphlet being a little earlier, say in Aug.

In 1598, May 8, Harvey at Walden wrote to Cecil asking that the election to the Mastership of Trinity Hall might be stayed ; the then Master was dangerously sick.

Nash's Lenten Stuff, &c., was entered S. R. 1599, Jan. 11, for C. Burby, as *The praise of the Red Herring*, and published for N. L[ing] and C. B[urby]. From p. 192 it appears that Nash was in Ireland serving in the war ; from p. 193 that the gallants of the Court often had two plays in one night ; from p. 195 that Humfrey King's *Hermit's Tale*, or *Robin the Devil*, was expected. The earliest known edition is for N. Ling, 1607 ; the third edition, by T. Thorp, assigned from E. Blount, dates 1613. Nash's dedication is to this Humphrey King, tobacconist. From p. 199 that Nash wrote only the Induction and Act i. of *The Isle of Dogs*, the players [What players ? The entry in Henslow's *Diary* is a forgery] having added Acts ii.–v. ; he threatens an answer to *The Trimming*, to be called the " Barber's Warming-Pan;" says that he was at Yarmouth six weeks in the autumn [1597, when the arrest was out against him] as a *mendicus* [printed *medicus* in the Latinless modern reprint] ; in p. 235 there is a list of recent waste poems worth further investigation ; in p. 245 Domingo Rufus and Sacrapant [redfaced] Herring are made synonymous : Domingo or Domine Mingo is therefore a herring [cf. *Summer's Last Will*,

Monsieur Mingo, and 2 *Henry 4*, v. 3, 79, "Sa[n] Mingo. Is't not so ?"], the great provocative to drink; in p. 252 "the 600 witches executed in Scotland Bartelmew tide was twelve month," 1597, Aug. 27, are not otherwhere known to me; in p. 288 "he that proclaims himself Elias" and Don Sebastian "raised from the dead" are mentioned; in p. 299 plays *The Case is altered* [by Jonson], and Philip's *Venus, the white tragedy*, or *the green Knight;* the former right merry, the latter absurd.

1599, June 1. Orders were given by J. Whitgift, Cantuar, and R. Bancroft, London, S. R., iii. 677, that the following books should be burned, that no unallowed plays should be printed, and that all Nash's and Harvey's books be taken wheresoever found, and none of them printed hereafter. [*Christ's Tears* was, however, reprinted in 1613.] No Satires or Epigrams to be printed hereafter :—

> Hall's *Virgidemiarum*, 1598, Mar. 30.
> Marston's *Pygmalion*, &c., 1598, May 27.
> Marston's *Scourge of Villany*, 1598, Sept. 8.
> *Shadow of Truth*, 1598, Sept. 15.
> [Moffat's] *Microcynicon*, 1599.
> Cutwode's *Caltha Poetarum*, 1599, April 17.
> {Davies' *Epigrams*.
> {Marlow's *Elegies*.

> R. T.[ofte]'s *Of marriage and wiving* (against women),
>   1599, Mar. 6.
> *The xv joys of marriage*, 1599, Feb. 5
>   (S. R., ii. 829).

On June 4 the asterised books were burned in the Stationers' Hall. *Virgidemiarum* and *Caltha Poetarum* were "stayed," and so was Willobye's *Avisa* of 1594, Sept. 3 [but it was transferred 1611, Sept. 11]. *Summer's Last Will* was published (by Nash himself, I think) 1600, Oct. 28;

it has no note of Nash's death. He was dead when Fitz-
geffrey's *Affaniæ* was printed at Oxford 1601, and when
The Return from Parnassus (*q.v.*) was acted. G. Harvey
died 1630, Feb. 7, and was buried at Walden Feb. 11. I
have only to add that the letter from Nash to Sir R. Cotton, Collier's *Annals*, i. 302, edition 1831, is undoubtedly
genuine, and must have been written shortly before 30th
Oct. 1596, when Harington's *Ajax* was entered. See my
History of the Stage, p. 157. Dr. Grosart unfairly brands
it as "suspect," because Collier published it; Collier's
publications were not all forgeries.

1. *Dido, Queen of Carthage*, T., written by Marlow and
Nash, was acted by the children of the Chapel, perhaps at
Croydon, in 1591, and published in 1594, no doubt in consequence of Marlow's death in 1593. It is usually supposed
to have been finished by Nash, having been left incomplete by
Marlow; but it seems to me to have been made in collaboration with him, and to have been an early work written at
Cambridge before either author left the University, possibly
founded on the Latin *Dido* by Halliwell 1564, in rivalry
to the Oxford Latin play by Gager 1583. Marlow in his
later career did not from 1590 onwards work with a coadjutor, nor can I trace him in connexion with Nash in London;
but the coincidence of dates makes it likely that he was the
second author of *Terminus et non*, T., who was expelled
from Cambridge in 1587. A list of actors (characters) is
printed in the title, a mark of early work. Marlow spells
Cloanthus, iii. 1, iv. 3, v. 1; Nash Cloanthes, v. 2 and title:
iv. 4 is certainly by Marlow. I conjecturally assign the
authorship thus—Marlow, i. 1*a*; ii. 1, 2; iii. 3; iv. 3–4;
v. 1, 2: Nash, i. 1*b* (which should be marked as a new
scene); iii. 1, 2, 4; iv. 1, 2, 5. Woodcock published no
other plays. Whether this play was the same as the *Dido*

and Æneas acted by the Admiral's men in 1598 Jan. is very doubtful.

2. *Summer's last Will and Testament*, C., was acted by the Chapel children at Croydon 1592 Aug., before "my Lord," p. 17, &c. (probably Archbishop Whitgift), and the Queen. The place is undisputed, being repeatedly alluded to in the play; but the date, rightly assigned by Collier, has been disputed on the most frivolous grounds by Dr. A. Grosart and Dr. B. Nicholson. I owe an apology to Mr. P. A. Daniel for associating his name with this absurd hypothesis in my *History of the Stage*, p. 78; he informs me that he did not "aid Dr. Grosart," as I stated, and is in no way responsible for anything connected with this date. Nevertheless, Dr. Grosart did avail himself of Mr. Daniel's reputation, and did in his edition introduce his name as assisting his assistant, Dr. Nicholson, which I ought to have carefully distinguished from assisting Dr. Grosart himself. I have the greatest respect for Mr. Daniel's work, and wish we had more of it disconnected from the very inferior names in conjunction with which his so often appears; and I do not at all object to the omission of my own name (as in the notorious case of *Lingua*): rather than have it placed by the side of certain others, I wish the present N.S.S. practice of omitting it altogether and leaving the reader to infer that they, the N.S.S., have done work really done by me, to continue in the future as it has done for fourteen years. The plague of 1592, the holding the term at Hertford (p. 90 Hazlitt's *Dodsley*), the Queen's progress to Oxford, pp. 22, 89, and, above all, the low state of the Thames caused by the drought, p. 37, are conclusive as to the date. Ned, Dick Huntley, Harry Baker, p. 17, Robert Toy, pp. 16, 59, are mentioned as performers. The acting of the children in 1591 is alluded to p. 17; the

satirical plays of the common stage p. 18. The Falanta burden satirised by Harvey in 1593 Sept. occurs p. 24. In the same page note Nash's phrase, *Summ' tot'*, for this is the true reading; cf. *supra.* From p. 30 it appears that the Queen's men were still acting at the Theater; "Go to a Theater and hear a Queen's Vice." In p. 34 *The Prodigal Child* (*Acolastus*) is mentioned as if still on the stage; in p. 39 the "hieroglyphical" Euphuists are satirised; in p. 47 comes the first hint of the future *Isle of Dogs*; and in p. 73 the periwig for baldness alludes not so much to Abraham Fleming's translation of *Synesius* 1579 as to Richard Harvey's *Defence of short hair against Synesius,* on which see *Have with you to Saffron Walden,* pp. 7, 9. See also *The Return from Parnassus.*

3. *The Isle of Dogs,* and 4. *Terminus et non Terminus,* have already been noticed sufficiently.

NEALE, THOMAS. (University.)

1. 1637, Sept. 16. *The Ward,* T. C. A dated MS. in the Bodleian Library, MS. Rawl. Poet. 79.

NEVILE, ROBERT. (Play.)

Fellow of King's, Cambridge.

1. *The Poor Scholar,* C., 1622, 1662.

This play has Commendatory Verses.

NICCOLS, RICHARD. (Play.)

Born in London 1584; student at Magdalen, Oxford, 1602; B.A. 1606. Wrote *Poems* and other works 1603–1610.

1. *The Twins,* T., was acted at Court 1612–13, and perhaps earlier, 31st Dec. 1611. It was entered S. R. 15th Feb. 1612. See RIDER.

NORTON, THOMAS. (Play.)

Lived at Sharpenhoe, Bedfordshire. A Calvinist barrister; Counsel to the Stationers' Company.

1. *Ferrex and Porrex* (Gorboduc).   See SACKVILLE.

PARSONS, PHILIP.   (Latin.)

1. *Atalanta*, C.   Brit. Mus., MS. Harl. 6924.   Dedicated to Laud, president of St. John's, Cambridge.   Scene, Arcadia.

PEAPS, WILLIAM.   (Pastoral.)

1. *Love in its Extasy*, or *The Large Prerogative*, P., 1649. Written while a student at Eton, but not acted and unprinted for many years.   Scene, Lilybæus.

PEELE, GEORGE.   (Actor, Playwright, Pageant-writer.)

1. *The Arraignment of Paris*, P., 1584, by Henry Marsh.

2. *Pageant*, for W. Dixie, 1585, by Edward Allde.

11*. *Polyhymnia*, triumph at tilt, &c., 1590, by R. Jones.

16. *Descensus Astrææ*, pageant, for W. Webbe; 1591, for W. Wright.

3. 1591, July 26, for Richard Jones.   *The Hunting of Cupid*, P., "by G. Peele."

14. 1593, Oct. 8, for Abel Jeffes.   *Edward* 1, H., 1593 (by A. Jeffes and J. Danter; sold by W. Barley), 1599.

4. 1593, Oct. 23, for John Danter.   *Jack Straw*, H., 1593 (by J. Danter; sold by W. Barley), 1604.

6. 1594, May 14, for Edward White (A. Islip's name being crossed out).   *David and Bethsabe*, T., "by George Peele," 1599 (by Adam Islip).

8. *Alcazar*, T., 1594, by Edward Allde for Richard Bankworth.

11. 1595, April 16, for Ralph Hancock.   *An Old Wife's Tale*, "by G. P.," 1596 (by J. Danter; sold by R. Hancock and J. Hardie).

12. 1600, Oct. 7, for Richard Oliffe.   *Doctor Doddipoll*, C., 1600.

17. 1606, Nov. 12, for Clement Knight. *Wily Beguiled*, C., 1606, 1623, 1635, 1638.

13. *Alphonsus of Germany*, T., 1654 (for H. Moseley).

See also *Locrine*, Anon., 257 ; *The troublesome reign of John*, Lodge, 7, 8 ; and *Richard* 3, Anon., 242.

George Peele, gentleman, probably a Devonian, was born c. 1558. He was a member of Broadgates Hall (Pembroke College) c. 1572 ; student of Christ Church " 1573 or thereabouts " (Wood) ; B.A. 12th June 1577 ; determined in Lent ; M.A. 6th July 1579. He then went to London. In 1582 Lines by him were prefixed to Watson's *Hecatompathia* in flowing blank verse, a matter in which he certainly anticipated Marlow. On 29th Mar. 1583 he was summoned to Oxford to make a deposition in the University Court, from which it appears that he was then twenty-five years old, had been in London about two years, and at Oxford for nine years previously. In June 1583 he was still at Oxford assisting Dr. Gager in presenting Latin plays for the entertainment of Albertus Alasco, Polish Prince Palatine, at Christ Church. See *Rivales* and *Dido*. Peele then returned to London and pursued his playwriting. On 18th April 1589, S. R., was entered *A Farewell: to Sir J. Norris and Sir F. Drake*, by George Peele, M.A., Oxon. ; printed by J. C[harlewood] for W. Wright ; to which *The Tale of Troy* (probably written at Oxford when he was helping in preparing *Dido*) was appended. He calls it "an old poem of mine own." The fact that Gager wrote the lines to him by which alone his translation of Euripides' *Iphigenia* (at Tauri or Aulis ?) is known would seem to fix the date of this lost work also in 1583. In the year 1589, Aug. 1, S. R., there is another entry, this time for R. Jones, of an *Eclogue gratulatory to Robert Earl of Essex, his welcome into England from Portugal.* The inter-

locutors are Piers (Peele) and Palinode (the Palin of
Spenser's *Shepherd's Calendar*, *i.e.*, the Roman Catholic,
Francis Constable). Malone and others have quite wrongly
identified Palinode with Peele. On 26th June 1593 (S. R.,
by Widow Charlewood for J. Busbie) he dedicated *The
Honor of the Garter* to the Earl of Northumberland. This
poem contains a passage addressed to the Earl of Southampton, which should be studied in connexion with Shakespeare's
Sonnets. Also, in 1593, *The Praise of Chastity*, by Peele,
appeared in *The Phœnix' Nest. Anglorum Feriæ, England's
Holidays*, dedicated to Katherine Countess of Huntingdon,
has been printed from MS. It celebrates the 17th Nov.
1595, and may have been the ballad on *The Running at
Tilt* entered S. R. 18th Nov.; compare the two following
entries. On 17th Jan. 1596 he sent his *Tale of Troy* to
Lord Burghley " by his eldest daughter, Necessity's servant,"
when in sickness and poverty. In Meres' *Palladis Tamia*
(S. R. 7th Sept. 1598) he is said to have died of the pox.

1. *The Arraignment of Paris*, Peele's " first increase," as
Nash called it in 1589, was presented to the Queen by
the Chapel children, and therefore before 1582. The only
vacant place for it in the payment-list is that of 5th Feb.
1581. Colin and Hobbinol in it are, of course, Spenser
and Harvey. Thestylis is Spenser's Rosalynde (Rosa
Dinley); Diggon, I think, Churchyard; Paris and Œnone,
Leicester and Lady Sheffield; Helen being the Countess of
Essex. The ease of the blank verse at this early date is
especially noticeable.

2. *The Device of the Pageant for Woolston Dixie*, Mayor,
29th Oct. 1585, marks Peele's first appearance as Pageant
poet. Children and a Moor on a luzern appear in it.

3. *The Hunting of Cupid* is only known by a few frag-
ments printed in Dyce's edition.

4. *The life and death of Jack Straw, a notable Rebel,* &c., was written in 1587. In 1586 there had been an insurrection of apprentices. In 1587 there was great distress, and money and ships were raised by Elizabeth in London. That the play does allude to contemporary events is clear to me, especially in Sc. 2, where "this last benevolence of the King" is mentioned. The Armada is not noticed. The S. R. entry is next to that of *Edward* 1; one of the printers and the publisher were the same for both plays. This points to Peele as at least part-author, and I think the internal evidence of style confirms this. Peele's sign-manual, "sandy plain," is found near the end; and as Oxford scholars, who should know something of logic, have sneered at my use of this phrase in detecting Peele's work on the ground that any author might call a plain sandy, I may here say, once for all, that my point is that Peele, whether in or out of place, persists in calling plains sandy, which is a very different matter.

5. *The Turkish Mahomet and Hiren the Fair Greek,* the "famous play" mentioned in the *Jests* of Peele, is not extant. It is supposed to be ridiculed in 2 *Henry* 4, ii. 3, "Have we not Hiren here?" and to be the *Mahomet* of Henslow's *Diary,* 1594 Feb.–1595 Feb., which was then an old play.

6. *The love of King David and Fair Bethsabe,* "with the tragedy of Absalom," may fairly be dated c. 1588. The situations in the play are strikingly suggestive of Elizabeth and Leicester as David and Bathsheba, Uriah as Leicester's first wife, and Absalom as Mary Queen of Scots. The disguise of political allusions by a change of sex was not unknown to the early stage; witness Lyly's plays and the representation of Elizabeth as Richard II. This was an Admiral's men's play revived in Oct. 1602, when we find

Ḥenslow making an entry for "pulleys and workmanship for to hang Absalom, 14d."

7. *The device of the Pageant for Martin Colthorpe, Mayor*, was entered S. R. for R. Jones 29th Oct. 1588, "George Peele the author." Mr. Carew Hazlitt, *quoting* this entry, fabricates three other publishers' names, and attributes it "to Peele on conjecture." This is really too bad.

8. 1588–9, *The battle of Alcazar*, "fought in Barbary between Sebastian King of Portugal and Abdelmelec King of Morocco, with the death of Captain Stukeley," was acted by the Admiral's servants after the Armada, iii. 1, and before *The Farewell*, 18th April 1589, in which there is a singular enumeration of Admiral's plays then on the stage :—

> "Bid *Mahomet's pow* and mighty *Tamberlane*,
> 　King *Charlemain*, *Tom Stukeley*, and the rest,
> 　Adieu."

Mahomet's pow is the "ould Mahomet's head" in Greene's *Alphonsus of Arragon ; Tamberlane* is Marlow's play ; *Charlemain* is, I think, "The distracted Emperor ; " and *Tom Stukeley, The Battle of Alcazar.* "Feed and be fat, my fair Callipolis," 2 *Henry* 4, ii. 4, which refers to a line in ii. 3, would not, I think, have been written by Shakespeare had Peele then been recently deceased. For further ridicule of this play see Jonson's *Poetaster*. "Sandy plains" occurs in v., near the end. There are Dumb Shows and a Presenter in *Alcazar*, which is a "*Vindicta*" or Revenge play.

9, 10. 1, 2 *Henry* 6. For Peele's share in these Queen's men's plays see my *Life of Shakespeare*, Section V. Peele left the Admiral's men and joined the Queen's c. 1589.

11. *The Old Wife's Tale* was acted by the Queen's men. The date is clearly c. 1590. On 5th Nov. 1589 G. Harvey had attacked Lyly, Peele s friend. This attack (fortunately

it is dated) was circulated in MS. prior to its publication in 1593. In this play Huanebango (a name travestied from Huon o' Bordeaux) is palpably Harvey. In Sc. 8 he speaks in hexameters—nay, in Harvey's own hexameters ; and names for the stock of Huanebango are adapted from Plautus, Polymachæroplacidus (from *Pseudolus*), Pyrgopolinices (from *Miles Gloriosus*), in shapes which inevitably suggest English puns indicating Harvey's ropemaking extraction, Polly-make-a-rope-lass, and Perg-up-a-line-o. Three lines near the end are from Greene's *Orlando*. The name Sacrapant is from the same plays. Erastus is from Kyd's *Soliman and Perseda*. The play is evidently full of personal allusions, which time only can elucidate.

For *The Troublesome reign of John King of England* see Lodge, 7, 8.

11*. *Polyhymnia*, the Triumph at Tilt, 1590, Nov. 17, with Sir Henry Lea's resignation of honor at Tilt to Her Majesty, received by the Earl of Cumberland.

12. *The Wisdom of Doctor Doddipoll* was published in 1600, as acted by the children of Paul's. It is clearly an older play. It is not written by Marston or Middleton, who at that time were the writers for these boys, and is probably one of " the musty fopperies of antiquity " alluded to in Marston's *Pasquil and Katherine*, v. 1, as revived by them in 1600. It was most likely one of their old plays produced originally c. 1590. One song in it, " What is Love ? " i. 1, is by Peele, being taken from his *Hunting of Cupid*, and I see no reason for depriving him of the rest of the play. The Enchanter is very like the one in *The Old Wife's Tale ;* the metre is that of *David and Bethsabe ;* the publisher is the same as for *The Maid's Metamorphosis*. The plot is taken from Lucian's *Zenothemis and Menecrates*. The Doctor is, I think, a caricature of Dr. John Harvey, Gabriel's

brother.   Other plays seem to have been produced later on
the same story.   *The Painter*, or *The Wandering Lovers*,
S. R. 9th Sept. 1653, entered as Massinger's, seems more
likely to have been *The Dutch Painter*, or *The French Branke*
[Query Brinch or pledge-drink ; cf. ii. 1], which was licensed
10th June 1623 for the Prince's men, than *The Wandering
Lovers* (or *Lovers' Progress*), licensed for the King's men 6th
Dec. 1623.   The 1653 entries are frequently wrong as to
authorship; and for the wandering cf. iii. 1, "I will restless
wander," &c.

13. *Alphonsus, Emperor of Germany.*   The external evidence is certainly in favour of Peele's authorship of this
play.   It was published as Chapman's in 1654 by Moseley,
who attributed authorship in a most reckless way.   See my
Life of Shakespeare, pp. 358–360.   On the other hand,
Wood and Winstanley, "misled by former catalogues," says
Biog. Dram., attribute it to Peele.   Surely the former catalogues are a better authority than Moseley.   The play is
palpably an old one, dating c. 1590.   It was revived 5th
May 1636 at Blackfriars " for the Queen and the Prince
Elector."   Chapman died in 1634, and therefore had nothing
to do with the revival.   This is a revenge-play, and would
seem to be the " *Richard Conqueror* " alluded to in *The Taming of the Shrew*, Ind., which has given the commentators
so much trouble; cf. v. 1, " If we be conquerors or con-
quered."   As it was in 1636 a King's men's play (chosen
for performance before the Prince Elector on account of the
Teutonic part in it), it probably was originally produced by
the Lord Strange's men for presentation before some ambassador from Deutschland.   I do not find any evidence in
the foreign tongue introduced that the author must have
visited the Continent.   I have not found any allusion to
Richard, Emperor of Germany, in old plays, except in

Peele's *Edward* 1, Sc. 1, "Your brave uncle, Almain's Emperor."

14. *The famous chronicle of King Edward* 1, *sirnamed Edward Longshanks,* "with his return from the Holy Land. Also the life of Llewellyn, rebel in Wales. Lastly, the sinking of Queen Elinor, who sunk at Charing Cross, and rose again at Pottershithe, now named Queenhith," was also, I think, acted by Lord Strange's players. In Sc. 4—

> "*King of Scots.*   Shine with thy golden head,
>   *Shake* [thou] thy *spear* in honor of *his name,*
>   Under whose royalty thou wear'st the same,"

surely implies that the part of Edward was acted by Shakespeare : "his name" is very forced on any other interpretation : Edward's name was not Shakespeare, and without an allusion to this name we should expect "in honour of the King," or something equivalent thereto. Shakespeare, we know, on the authority of John·Davies, did act "kingly parts." Several lines in this play are taken from *Polyhymnia,* 17th Nov. 1590, which fixes the date approximately as 1590—1.

15. Speeches by Peele were recited to the Queen, when she visited Burghley, at Theobald's, 10th May 1591. As L. Strange's men were at this time the Court actors *par excellence,* it is not likely that the request to furnish these should have been made to any other company.

16. *Descensus Astrœœ, the device for the pageant for W. Web's Mayoralty,* 29th Oct. 1591, was by G. Peele, M.A.

Greene's Address in his *Groatsworth of Wit,* 1592, appears to me to imply that Peele and Marlow were then connected with L. Strange's men ; but I cannot trace him in connexion with them after their reconstitution as the Chamberlain's company in 1594. There are some indications of his having then gone to the Admiral's. On 14th Aug. 1594 his *Mahomet* was revived by them. On 29th Aug. 1595 they produced *Longshank*, a new play, but surely a reformed version of his *Edward* 1 ; and on 11th Dec. 1596, 16*. *Captain Stukely* (part of which is evidently by Peele), for which see under Dekker.

I see no possibility of attributing to him *Clyomon and Clamydes*. As for the inscription on the title in an old handwriting, it is sufficient to remark that its discovery was made in the time of Collier and his compeers.

16*. For *Stukeley* see Dekker, 40.

17. *Wily Beguiled*. "A pleasant comedy. The chief actors be these : A poor Scholar, a rich Fool, and a Knave at a Shift." No company or theatre mentioned. Possibly a University play. I give my account of it (corrected of many gross misprints) from *Shakespeariana* for Mar. 1885. I do not find Knight the publisher in connexion with any other play :—

Wily Beguiled has all the air of a play written for a London audience, and adapted for a University performance. Compare, for instance, the allusion to " Momus' mates " in the Prologue with the Induction to *The Return from Parnassus*. That this play of *Wily Beguiled* is a personal satire I tried to show in 1876, and still maintain my theory as to the identity of the chief personages.

That Churms, for instance, who has (i. 1) been "at Cambridge, a scholar; at Calais, a soldier; and now in the country, a lawyer, and the next degree shall be a coney catcher," is Lodge there can be small doubt. Lodge wrote the greater part of *The Looking-glass for London*, alluded to in the Prologue, in which the " calf-skin jests " imitated in this play are introduced. He also, in my opinion, in conjunction with Greene, wrote *The Pinner of Wakefield*, from which Churm's name, *Wily*, has been taken; and see Sc. 8, where George sits despairing and Jenkin comes in and says he is a juggler. This is the origin of the Prologue to *Wily Beguiled*. All through the play the character of Churms should be compared with Philomusus, in *The Return from Parnassus*.

But since that essay of mine was published I have found more definite evidence as to the authorship of this play. In the Prologue a juggler enters and offers to "show tricks." Now, in the second scene of Dekker's *Satiromastix*, Captain Tucca says to Horace, *i.e.*, Jonson, "I'll teach thee . . . to tell gentlemen I am a juggler, and can show tricks." I have searched in vain for any passage either in Jonson's works or any play in which he could possibly have had a hand corresponding to this description except this Prologue, which must therefore, I think, be assigned to Jonson, the author of the play itself being the "humorous George" of the Prologue, *i.e.*, George Peele, as Dyce suggested, not Chapman, as I formerly thought when I accepted the hypothesis of Mr. Daniel of a later date for the play. But the humorous George of the Prologue, "as melancholy as a myrtle tree," is the Sophos of "melancholy dumps" in the play—in other words, the author of the play himself, George Peele; and his friend Fortunatus, who has come back from the wars, is evidently Jonson. Robin Goodfellow, Churm's friend, is Drayton, the author of *The Merry Devil* and *Nymphidia*. He was often satirised under that name. Peter Plodall, Lelia's third suitor, I cannot as yet identify, but there are characters in other plays with whom he is identical. That the original date of this play is 1596–7 I have no doubt. It contains passages distinctly parodying *Romeo and Juliet* (c. 1595–6, but still on the stage in 1598), and *The Merchant of Venice*, 1596–7, but no allusion to any later play of Shakespeare.

As to Will Cricket, the "fool," whose dancing is so highly commended, he is, as I conjectured in 1876, undoubtedly William Kempe, but the date now assigned to the play affords additional evidence of the truth of this conjecture, for in Nov. 1597 Kempe, who was (together with Burbadge and Shakespeare) at the head of the Chamberlain's players, was acting at the Curtain. I agree with Mr. Halliwell that this interpretation must be given to the "Curtain plaudites" assigned to *Romeo and Juliet* in Marston's 1598 *Satires*. But I now think him entirely wrong in supposing that in 1596 that company acted at that playhouse. The lease of the theatre granted to J. Burbadge in 1576 expired in April 1597, and Giles Allen refused to renew it according to covenant. The Burbadges, however, retained possession till Dec. 1598, when they removed the timber, &c., of the theatre to build the Globe. That the companies with which the Burbadges were connected acted at the Theater which was James Burbadge's property may be looked on as certain; no doubt the Queen's company acted there from 1583 to 1591, and the Chamberlain's from 1594 to 1597, but we find no notice of any plays performed at the Theater after July 1597, and a positive statement that it was "deserted" and empty in 1598. (See Halliwell's *Illustrations*.) Some time in the latter part, then, of 1597 the Chamberlain's men left the Theater and went to the Curtain. But in Oct. of that year Pembroke's men joined the Admiral's at the Rose, and as they were the only then existing company who could have occupied a public theatre (excepting the Chamberlain's and the Admiral's, who were otherwise located), and as the Curtain was the only theatre they could have occupied, there is no doubt that they had used that house from 1594 to 1597. In the play before us Cricket complains that old Plodall (the landlord of his house, Giles Allen) has given him notice to quit, and says, "If you discharge me, I'll discharge my pestilence at you, for to let my house before my lease be out is cutthroatery, and to scrape for more rent is poll-denery." Surely this alludes to the refusal of Giles Allen to continue the letting of the Theater to Kemp and his company according to the covenants of the original lease.

It may be worth noting that the plot of this play is identical with the Anne Page story of the *Merry Wives of Windsor*, where Dr. Caius is the counterpart of Churms, Fenton of Sophos, and Slender of Plodall. I do not intend here to follow out these identities, but I may point out that the name Cricket is the same as that of the fairy of that appellation in Shakespeare's play, and that it seems not unlikely that that part was acted by Kempe.

There is in Sc. 13 a passage which, if my interpretation be right, throws great light on several obscure points in the Shakespearian drama: "As long as Hunks with the great head has been about to show his little wit in the second part of his paltry poetry." Hunks was a Paris Garden bear, and here may mean a writer of Paris Garden plays. There is no play known in dramatic annals of which the second part was unissued in 1597 except Dekker's *Fortunatus*, of which the first part was acted as an old play in Feb. 1596, but the complete play was not performed till Nov. 1599. The first part cannot date later than 1593, and probably, as the theatres were shut in that year, not later than 1592. Had it been produced in the interim, it would be found in Henslow's *Diary* under its proper date. This would imply that Dekker was a much earlier writer than has been supposed, but it is still more likely that Daniel's *Civil Wars* is intended. Books i.–iv. appeared in 1595, Book v. in 1599. That Gripe represents Henslow in this play, and that all its details are satiric, I doubt not; but further investigation into these details must be left for the present.

PERCY, WILLIAM. (Plays.)

The dramas of this sonnetteer, Barnes' friend, are preserved in MS. in the Duke of Devonshire's library.

1. 1602, *The Aphrodisial,* or *Sea Feast.*

2. 1601, *Arabia Sitiens,* or *A dream of a Dry Year,* T. C.

3. 1601, *The Cuckqueans and the Cuckolds Errants,* or *The Bearing Down the Inn,* C. Printed by the Roxburgh Club.

4. 1602, *A Country Tragedy in Vacuniam,* or *Cupid's Sacrifice,* T.

5. 1601, *The Fairy Pastoral,* or *Forest of Elves,* P. Edited by Haslewood, 1824.

6. c. 1601–2, *Necromantes,* or *The Two Supposed Heads:* a comical invention, acted by the children of Paul's.

PESTELL, THOMAS. (Latin.)

Vicar of Packington, Leicestershire.

1. *Versipellis,* C., MS.; acted at ? Cambridge. A list of the performers is given in *Biog. Dram.*

PETT.

1. *Strange news out of Poland.* See HAUGHTON.

PHILIP.

1. *Venus, the white tragedy,* or *The Green Knight,* is mentioned in Nash's *Lenten Stuff,* 1599 (*q.v.*).

PICKERING, JOHN. (Play.)

1. *Orestes,* H., 1567.

See my *History of the Stage,* p. 61.

PORTER, HENRY. (Plays.)

3. *The 2 Angry Women of Abingdon,* for Joseph Hunt and William Ferbrand, 1599.

1596, Dec. 16, p. 77. Dd. unto Mr. Porter £5.

1597 (not 1598), Mar., p. 77.   Lent unto Mr. Porter £4.

1597, Aug. 23, p. 98.   This entry about Nash's *Isle of Dogs* is a forgery.

1. 1598, May 30.   *Love Prevented.*

June 26.   Becomes security for Chettle *re* 2 *Black Batman.*

2. Aug. 18.   *Hot Anger Soon Cold* (with Chettle and Jonson).

3. Dec. 22.   2 *Two Angry Women of Abingdon.*

4. 1599, Feb. 28.   *Two Merry Women of Abingdon.* He promised Henslow that he should have all his books, whether written by him alone or with others.

5. Mar. 4.   *The Spencers* (with Chettle).

April 7, p. 147.   Borrows 20s.

April 11, p. 94.   Borrows 2s. 6d.

April 16, p. 261.   He took an *assumpsit* of Henslow, for 12d. then given him, to forfeit £10 if he did not pay on the 17th the 25s. he then owed.   The 12d. is crossed out p. 94.   He therefore paid up.

May 5.   Borrows 2s. 6d.

May 15.   Borrows 2s. 6d.

May 26.   Owes 10s., and we hear no more of him; but he is mentioned in Meres' *Palladis Tamia*, 1598.

3. *The Pleasant History of the two angry women of Abington,* "with the humorous mirth of Dick Coombes and Nicholas Proverbs, two serving-men," was published twice in 1599, the second time for Ferbránd alone; but not entered in S. R.   I believe it to have been the same play as *Love Prevented:* compare the speech about the "crossing of true love" in the last scene.   As it was lately acted by the Admiral's men, it must be in the *Diary* somewhere.   See also my *History of the Stage,* p. 107.   In the Prologue Porter alludes to his needy circumstances.   This play was

the First Part; the Second Part does appear in the *Diary*.

PRESTON, THOMAS. (Play.)

 1. 1569–70, for John Allde. *Cambyses.*

M.A.; Fellow of King's, Cambridge; D.C.L.; Master of Trinity Hall.

 1. *Cambyses.* See my *History of the Stage*, p. 64.

PUTTENHAM, GEORGE. (Plays.)

In his *Art of English Poesy* (S. R. 1588, Nov. 9, for Thomas Orwyn) he mentions the following plays as his own :—

 1. *Lusty London*, interlude; quoted pp. 183, 208 (Arber's edition).

 2. *The Wooer*, interlude; quoted pp. 212, 233.

 3. *Gynæcocratia*, C.; described p. 146.

QUARLES, FRANCIS. (Private play.)

 1. *The Virgin Widow*, C., 1649, 1656.

Born 1592 at Stewards, near Romford, Essex; son of James Quarles. At Peterhouse, Cambridge; migrated to Christ Church; member of Lincoln's Inn; Cupbearer to the Queen of Bohemia; Chronologer to the City of London; Secretary (in Ireland) to Archbishop Usher; returned with him to England 1641. Died in London 8th Sept. 1644.

 1. *The Virgin Widow*, a sort of interlude, was privately acted by young gentlemen at Chelsea.

RANDOLPH, THOMAS. (Plays : University and London.)

1630, Mar. 26, for John Mariott. $\begin{cases} 1.\ \textit{Aristippus,} \\ 2.\ \textit{The Pedlar.} \end{cases}$

 1, 2. 1630, April 8, for Robert Allot. *The Conceited Pedlar*, "by R. Davenport," 1630 (with *Aristippus*).

 3. *The Jealous Lovers*, C., Cambridge, 1632, 1634.

5. *The Muses' Looking-glass.*
4. *Amyntas,* P.
} Oxford, 1638, 1640, 1643, 1652 (with poems).

7. 1638, Mar. 30, for Harper and Slater. *Cornelianum Dolium,* L. C., 1638.

Works, 1664, 1668.

Thomas, son of William Randolph of Hammes, Sussex, steward to Edward Lord Zouch, was born at the house of his grandfather, Thomas Smith, at Newnham-cum-Badley, Northampton; baptized 15th June 1605; King's scholar at Westminster; matriculated as pensioner at Trinity, Cambridge, 8th July 1624; B.A. Jan. 1628; minor-fellow 22nd Sept. 1629; major-fellow and M.A. 23rd Mar. 1632; *ad eundem,* Oxford, 1632. On 15th June 1629 he wrote his poem on *Six maids bathing* at Cambridge. Up to that date his residence was probably uninterrupted; but from Nov. 1629 to Nov. 1630 there was a plague at Cambridge, and the scholars were dispersed. This interval he probably spent in London, where he arranged for his first publication. On 26th Feb. 1630 he prefixed verses to Shirley's *Faithful* or *Grateful Servant,* both of which titles he recognises, advising him to aim at the laureateship; but this was granted to Jonson 26th Mar. On 1st May he wrote Latin and English quatrains *on the birth of Prince Charles;* but he probably became acquainted with Jonson, and was adopted as one of his "sons" before returning to Cambridge in the winter, for in 1631 he answered his *Ode* concerning *The New Inn.* In 1632 he wrote his verses *on the fall of the Mitre Tavern* at Cambridge, in which he mentions the fire at London Bridge which happened 13th Feb. (Maitland); also his *Oratio Prevaricatoria.* After the King's visit to Cambridge in March Randolph came to London, and "tended the flock of Coridon." About the end of 1633 he left London, and after after some stay at his father's at Little Houghton he went to William Stafford's of Blatherwick, where he died, and was buried 17th Mar. 1635. He had the smallpox some years before, and had lost one finger in a fray. Many of these details are trifles; but in this instance it is only by trifles that we can trace the poet's dramatic career. The "poems" of 1648 were given to the press by his brother Robert.

1. *Aristippus,* or *The Jovial Philosopher,* a private show, was presented at Cambridge, where "shows had long been forbidden by authority for their abuses." It was entered by Mariott, but published by Allot. Medico de Campo is, of course, Leech-field or Lichfield: an allusion missed by Mr. Halliwell in his enumeration. On the other hand, he invents "a ridicule of the Prologue of [*sic*] Shakespeare's *Troilus and Cressida.*" This is pure delusion.

2. *The Conceited Pedlar* was another Cambridge show, entered S. R. with *Aristippus* for Mariott, and again as "by R. Davenport," by Allot, who published the two together.

3. *The Jealous Lovers* was presented by the Trinity students to the King and Queen in March 1632 (Fuller).

4. *Amyntas,* or *The impossible Dowry,* was acted before the King and Queen at Whitehall, and also in public, for the Prologue and Epilogue were evidently not meant for a Court audience.

5. *The Muses' Looking-glass* was originally acted (Query at Court) as *The Entertainment.* Editors say the scene is laid "in the Blackfriars playhouse," but the play itself says only "the playhouse:" and I believe Salisbury Court is the one meant; for, although this recently erected theatre is distinctly alluded to in i. 1, "they build . . . more shops of

Satan;" and again, "playhouses increase, . . . one begets another," it is the only one omitted in the "zealous prayers" just after. The mistake probably arose from Bird and Flowerdew dwelling "by Blackfriars College." Moreover, in the Eclogue to Jonson (Tityrus) Damon (Randolph) tells him that he left Cambridge to keep the flock of Corydon :—

> "A flock it was that would not keep together,
> A flock that had no fleece when it came hither ;
> Nor would it learn to listen to my lays,
> For 'twas a flock made up of several strays."

This would apply to Prince Charles' men at Salisbury Court, 1632 Jan.–1633 May, but not to any other company of the time. I interpret the passage as meaning that Corydon was the director of the theatre, and Randolph manager under him. Randolph's London career exactly coincides as to dates with the Prince's men's occupation of this playhouse; and of the date of the present play there can be no doubt, for the device of draining the Fens by Dutch Windmills (see Nabbes) in 1632 is alluded to as contemporary, and in iii. 2 Inigo Jones is ridiculed as Chaunus, evidently after Jonson's quarrel with him in 1631. The allusion to Jonson's mask as being named *Fortunate Isles* from Jones, the Fortunate carpenter, is so plain that I wonder the editor could miss it. There are many other allusions of interest, but not of dramatic matters.

6. *Plutophthalmia Plutogamia*, C., entitled *Hey for Honesty, Down with Knavery*, may have been founded on a translation of the *Plutus* of Aristophanes by Tho. Randolph, but in its present state is certainly more like the work of an imitator. Hardly a page is free from allusions of later date than Randolph's death, and I believe that F. J., who "augmented and published" it, wrote it altogether, using Randolph's name to cover his attack on the

Roundheads It has no publisher's name to it, being surreptitiously printed, and Robert Randolph shows no knowledge of it. It is an interesting play, but outside my date limit.

7. *Cornelianum Dolium*, C., "auctore T. R." in title, and " by T. R." in the S. R. entry, has been attributed to Braithwaite by Mr. Crossley. I, as always, prefer to adhere to the external evidence. Braithwaite was certainly not " *ingeniosissimo hujus ævi Heliconio.*" It is, however, quite possible that the play was altered after Randolph's death.

RANKINS, WILLIAM. (Plays.)

This author in 1587 published *A Mirror of Monsters*, "wherein is plainly described the manifold Vices and spotted enormities that are caused by the infectious sight of Plays, with the description of the subtle sleights of Satan making them his instruments."

1588, *The English ape, the Italian imitation, the footsteps of France.*

1598, *Seven satires applied to the Week*, &c.

But immediately after he sells to Henslow for the Admiral's men at the Rose :—

1. 1598, Oct. 3, *Mulmutius Dunwallow* for £3 ; an old play therefore, and not necessarily of his own writing; but in 1601 he certainly did help in writing plays, viz., 2. *Hannibal and Scipio;* 3. *Scogan and Skelton;* 4. *The Conquest of Spain.* For these see HATHWAY.

RAWLINS, THOMAS. (Play.)

1. 1639, Nov. 20, for Daniel Frere. *The Rebellion,* 1640, 1654.

Rawlins was engraver at the Mint, and wrote other plays after the Restoration. Died 1670 (?).

1. *The Rebellion* was acted nine days together by His Majesty's company of the Revels. In v. 2, "An' we do

not act with any players in the Globe of the world, let us be baited like a Bull for a company of strutting coxcombs," seems to imply that the play was acted at the Bull : probably the remains of the Revels men, after the best of them had been chosen to strengthen the Queen's men at Salisbury Court in 1637, still retained the name, and took this the only theatre open to them. There is no absolute evidence of date, however, in the play. The phrase, "Kings and Queens," v. 3, is oddly used, and, I think, must allude to the name of Beeston's young company. One Golding, actor "of the beggars' theatre," is also mentioned v. 2. The Commendatory Verses are by Richards, Davenport, Chamberlain, J. Gough, Tatham, C. G. (unquestionably Christopher Goad, not Charles Gerbier), and five others.

RICHARDS, NATHANIEL. (Play.)

    1. 1639, Oct. 3, for Daniel Frere. *Messalina, the Roman Empress,* 1640.

LL.B. of Caius College, Cambridge, 1634.

1. *Messalina* was acted by His Majesty's company of the Revels. This play has a list of the actors. Among these are William Cartwright, senior, who had acted at the Fortune, and Christopher Goad, who had, up to 1636, acted with the Queen's men. I infer that this play must date after the plague of 1637, instead of just before it, as I once conjectured. It has introductory verses by Jordan (who acted in it), John Robinson (who also acted in it), T. Rawlins, R. Davenport, and two others. Frere published this play, Rawlins' *Rebellion,* and Nabbes' *Unfortunate Mother* (not acted) all in this year. The inference is that the King's Revels company dissolved at Michaelmas 1639.

Richards published *Sacred and Satirical Poems* in 1630, 1641.

RICHARDS, THOMAS. (Play.)

   1. *Misogonus*, 1560, for which see my *History of the Stage*, p. 58, has been (I think wrongly) assigned to him.

RICKETS, J. (Latin.)

Byrsa Basilica sive Regale Excambicum, C., *in honorem Thomæ Greshami, militis*, 1570. Bodleian, MS. Tanner, 207.

RIDER, WILLIAM, M.A. (Play.)

   1. *The Twins*, T. C., 1655.

This was acted at Salisbury Court, which was built in 1629. Nevertheless, I suspect that it was only a revival of Niccols' play (*q.v.*). The authority of title-pages after 1650 is next to *nil*.

RIGHTWISE, JOHN. See HALLIWELL, EDWARD.

RIVERS, Mr. A Jesuit.

The authorship of Shirley's *Traitor* was in 1692 shamelessly claimed for this man. Halliwell, of course, accepts the honour for the Jesuit, which Dyce, with unnecessary elaboration, vindicated for Shirley in his edition of that author.

ROBINSON, ———. See CHETTLE, *Femelanco*.

ROLLINSON, ———. (Latin.)

   1. *Silvanus*, C., acted at Cambridge 1596. MS. Douce, 234, Bodleian.

ROWLEY, SAMUEL. (Actor; Plays.)

   4. 1605, Feb 12, for Nathaniel Butter. *Henry 8 (When you see me you know me)*, H. "If he get good allowance before he begin to print it." 1605, 1613, 1622, 1632.

S. Rowley belonged to the Admiral's company at the Rose 8th–13th March 1599, Henslow's *Diary*, p. 120; and on Nov. 16 he, with Charles Massey, engaged to play solely with that company until Shrovetide 1601, *Diary*, p. 260.

1. 1601, Dec. 20–24. He, with Bourne, was paid £6 for *Judas*.

2. 1602, Sept. 27. He was paid £7 for *Joshua*.

3. 1602, Nov. 22. He, with Bourne, received £4 for additions to Marlow's *Faustus*; these are the new parts of the 1616 edition.

4. *When you see me you know me*, or *The Famous Chronicle History of Henry* 8, "with the birth and virtuous life of Edward Prince of Wales," was acted by the high and mighty [Henry] Prince of Wales his servants, and written for them after the close of Henslow's *Diary*, May 1603, before the S. R. entry Feb. 1605.

5. 1612, Feb. 24, Shrove Monday, *Hymen's Holiday*. See ROWLEY, WILLIAM, 20*.

6. 1623, July 27. Herbert licensed a tragedy of *Richard* 3, or *The English Profit*, "with the Reformation [alteration] written by Samuel Rowley," for the Palsgrave's men [at the Fortune]. Whether Rowley wrote the reformations or only the whole play does not appear. This may have been only an alteration of Jonson's *Richard Crookback* of 1602.

7. 1623, Oct. 29. Another license of Herbert's. For the Palsgrave players [at the Fortune]. A new Comedy called *Hard Shift for Husbands*, or *Bilbo's the Best Blade*.

8. 1624, April 6. Another license. A new Comedy called *A Match or no Match*. The large gap in Rowley's career, from 1602 to 1624, was no doubt filled by writing plays, which were destroyed when the Fortune was burned in 1621. His name never occurs in connexion with a second company, for the Admiral's, Prince Henry's, and

the Palsgrave's are merely successive names for one company only.

9. For *The Noble Spanish Soldier* see Dekker.

ROWLEY, WILLIAM. See MIDDLETON, T.

RUGGLE, GEORGE. (Latin.)

  3. 1615, April 18, for Walter Burre. *Ignoramus*,
   L.C., 1630, 1659.

George Ruggle, eighth child and fifth (youngest) son of Thomas Ruggle of Lavenham, Suffolk, was baptized 13th Nov. 1575 ; educated at the free school there ; pensioner of St. John's, Cambridge, 20th June 1589 ; scholar of Trinity 11th May 1593 ; B.A. ; M.A. in 1597 ; took Holy Orders ; Fellow of Clare Hall 1598 ; taxer in the University 1604 ; *ad eundem* M.A. of Oxford Aug. 1605, at the King's visit ; in 1611 the Cambridge town Mayor and the University Vice-Chancellor contested the right of precedence. The Privy Council in 1612 decided in favour of the Vice-Chancellor. Brakyn, Recorder of Cambridge, was active in this matter, and was ridiculed there-for in *Ignoramus* 1614. Ruggle's will was proved 3rd Nov. 1622 ; executed 6th Sept. 1621. He had resigned his Fellowship in 1620.

  1. *Club Law,* ridiculing the townsmen, was acted at Clare Hall 1598. " A merry but abusive comedy," Fuller. Dr. Farmer had the MS.

  2. *Re Vera*, or *Verily*, was written against the Puritans.

  3. *Ignoramus* was acted before James I. 8th Mar., and again 13th May 1615. David Drummond, the King's second fool, was the hobby-horse in the Prologue : Brakyn, the Recorder, was the prototype of Ignoramus. The plot (not the characterisation) was taken from the *Trappolaria* of Giambatista Porta, 1596. It took five hours to act.

RUTTER, JOSEPH.

    1. 1635, Jan. 19, for John Benson. *The Shepherd's
Holiday*, P.T.C., 1635.

    1638, Jan. 29, for Thomas Walkley.

        2. *The Cid* (Part 1), T., 1637, 1650.

        3. *The Cid* (Part 2), T., 1640.

Tutor to the son of the Earl of Dorset, and at some time
lived with Sir Kenelm Digby.

    1. *The Shepherd's Holiday* was acted before their Majesties
at Whitehall by the Queen's men; also in public [at the
Cockpit]. It was published as by J. R. Kirkman interprets
this as Joseph Rutter (*Biog. Dram.*). But is there J. R. on
the title-page? Hazlitt does not give it. The Commendatory Verses are by Jonson, who calls the author "his
dear son" and this his first play, and by May. An *elegy on
Lady Venetia Digby* (who had a son by Dorset) is published
with it. Is she the Stella and he the Mirtillus of v. 1?
There are certainly personal adventures alluded to in the
play. See the Prologue and Epilogue. Lady V. Digby
died in 1633.

    2. *The Cid*, Part 1, was translated from Corneille by
Rutter at Dorset's command, who showed it to the King,
who ordered the translation of 3. Part 2, which was made
accordingly.

    S., J. (Play.)

    1. *Andromana*, or *The Merchant's Wife*. The Scene,
Iberia. 1660, for John Bellinger, "by J. S.," not James
Shirley. Founded on Sidney's *Arcadia*, the Plangus story.
Compare *Cupid's Revenge*. Written after the publication of
The Sophy, 1642. See iii. 5. Not acted.

    S., S. (Play.)

    1. 1615, Aug. 14, for R. Redmere (but assigned to R.
Woodriffe on the same day). *The Honest Lawyer*, C.,

1616. Acted by the Queen's Majesty's servants. Scene, Bedford.

S., W. (Play.)

1. The famous history of *Petronius Maximus*, "with the tragical death of Ætius, the Roman General, and the misdeeds of Valentinian, the Western Emperor, now attempted in blank verse by W. S., 1619," by W. Brent for N. Butter. See Constable's *Edinburgh Magazine*, 1821 July, Vol. 88.

S., W. See under DRAYTON and SHAKESPEARE.

SACKVILLE, THOMAS. (Play.)

1. 1565, for William Griffith. *Gorboduc*, 1565, 1569, 1571, 1590.

Born 1536; son of Richard Sackville, Esq., of Buckhurst, Withiam, Sussex; removed from Hart Hall, Oxford, to Cambridge; M.A.; student of the Inner Temple. His subsequent illustrious career as Lord Buckhurst and Earl of Dorset is beyond our scope. Died 19th April 1608.

1. *Ferrex and Porrex* (as it is called in the only genuine impression printed by John Daye, 1570) was acted 18th Jan. 1562 by the gentlemen of the Inner Temple before the Queen. In the spurious editions, 1565, 1590, Acts. i.–iii. are said to have been written by T. Norton, but this is very doubtful. Compare my *History of the Stage*, p. 59. This is the earliest English Tragedy; it has Dumb Shows, &c., and is built on classic lines.

SADLER, J. (University Mask.)

1. *Masquerade du Ciel*, M., 1640. "Presented to the great Queen of the little world: a Celestial Map of the heavenly bodies through the years 1639, 1640," by J. S., of Emmanuel College, Cambridge. Archbishop Sancroft gave the name of the writer in full.

SALTERNE, GEORGE, of Bristol. (Latin.)

1. *Tomumbeius sive Sultanii in Ægypto imperii evasio*,
T. Bodleian, MS. Rawl., Poet, 75.

SAMPSON, WILLIAM. (Plays.)

1. 1622, Feb. 22, for Matthew Rhodes. *Herod and Antipater*, T., 1622.

3. *The Vow Breaker*, T., for J[ohn] N[orton], 1636.

A retainer of Sir Henry Willoughby, Richley, Derbyshire. He published other works.

1. *Herod and Antipater;* with the death of Fair Mariam, by Gervase Markham and William Sampson, was acted at the Red Bull [by the Revels company].

2. *The Widow's Prize*, C., by Sampson, was licensed by Herbert (according to Halliwell, *Dictionary ;* but I cannot find the entry in S. R., Malone, or Chalmers): "For the Prince's company a new play called *The Widow's Prize*, which containing much abusive matter, was allowed of me on condition that my reformations were observed." Halliwell's date is 25th Jan. 1625. If this means, as it usually does in his book, 1625-6, there was no Prince's company at that time; if it mean 1624-5, where did he get it from? The play, however, was entered S. R. 9th Sept. 1653, and the MS. was destroyed by Warburton's servant.

3. *The Vow Breaker*, or *The Fair Maid of Clifton in Nottinghamshire*, T., was divers times acted by several companies with great applause.

SAVILE, JOHN, published an account of King James' Entertainment at Theobald's 1603-4, which is reprinted in Nichols, and, having no right to a place in this book, is only mentioned to prevent mistakes, Halliwell having given it a position in his Dictionary of *Plays*.

SHANK, JOHN. (Actor and Jig-writer.)

This actor was a member of Prince Henry's company c.

1610; then of the Palsgrave's; one of the King's men in 1619, with whom he remained till his death. He was buried 27th Jan. 1636 in St. Giles', Cripplegate, where he had lived throughout his career. The earliest known mention of him in that register occurs at the date 1610, Dec. 31, Buried a son of John Shanckes, player. He acted in *The Prophetess* 1622; Sir Roger in *The Scornful Lady* c. 1625, when the King's men had it; Hilario in *The Picture* 1629; a servant in *The Wildgoose Chase* 1632. For his share in the 1635 lawsuit see my *History of the Stage*, p. 324. Collier, after Malone, *Variorum*, iii. 221, says that Shank's *Ordinary*, "written by Shank himself," was licensed by Herbert for the King's company 16th Mar. 1623–4. The fee was £1. See further in my *History of the Stage*, p. 375.

SHAKESPEARE, WILLIAM. (Actor and Playwright.)

Born 1564. Theatrical career 1587–1610. Died 1616.

It would be useless to repeat here *in petto* that to which I have devoted a volume of this series. Nevertheless, a list of the plays must be given. To avoid repetition, I give it in the shape of a copy of the title-pages of the earliest editions, and in the chronological order which seems best for continuous study.

PLAYS probably acted by L. STRANGE'S MEN, 1589–1591, in which SHAKESPEARE was most likely a coadjutor, but which have not reached us in their original shape.

1. c. 1589–90, *Love's Labour's Lost.* See below, 1597.

2. c. 1590, *Love's Labour's Won.* See below, *Much Ado about Nothing.*

3. c. 1590, *Errors.* See below, 1594.

4. c. 1591, *Romeo and Juliet.* See below, 1596.

5. c. 1591, *Two Gentlemen of Verona.* See below, 1595.

PLAY in which SHAKESPEARE was a coadjutor, acted at the ROSE by L. STRANGE'S MEN, 1592.

6. 1592, Mar. 3. The first part of *Henry 6*, the new additions of the Talbot scenes being very probably Shakespeare's.

PLAYS in which SHAKESPEARE was probably a coadjutor, acted perhaps by Lord STRANGE'S MEN at NEWINGTON BUTTS, 1592, Autumn.

7. c. 1592, *All's Well that ends Well*. See below, 1601.

8. c. 1592. *Troylus and Cressida*. See below, 1601.

PLAYS in which SHAKESPEARE was probably a coadjutor, acted by L. STRANGE'S MEN at the ROSE, 1593 Jan.–May.

9. 1593, Jan. 5. *The Jealous Comedy*. See below, *The Merry Wives of Windsor*.

10. c. 1593, *Twelfth Night*. See below, 1602.

Thus far, on grounds more or less conjectural, we have rather a possible hypothesis than a statement of ascertained facts. But one thing is certain, every play as yet mentioned was revised from an earlier version by Shakespeare at a subsequent date.

PLAYS by MARLOW, with additions by SHAKESPEARE, acted by the CHAMBERLAIN'S MEN at the CROSS KEYS, &c., 1594 April, May, July, Sept.

11. c. 1594, *The Reign of King Edward 3*, "as it hath been sundry times played about the City of London." London. Printed for Cuthbert Burby, 1596 (S. R. 1595, Dec. 1). Another edition (with considerable variations), 1599, by Simon Stafford for Cuthbert Burby. Shakespeare's part is the Countess of Salisbury's story. The alterations in the

second edition should be carefully compared with those in
Richard 3.

12. c. 1594, *The tragedy of King Richard* 3, "containing his treacherous plots against his brother Clarence, the
pitiful murder of his innocent nephews, his tyrannical
usurpation; with the whole course of his detested life and
most deserved death. As it hath been lately acted by the
Right Honorable the Lord Chamberlain, his servants." At
London. Printed by Valentine Sims for Andrew Wise, 1597
(S. R. 1597, Oct. 20). This title is unlike that to any undoubted play by Shakespeare, nor was any play by him
alone published as "*lately* acted." His name, however, appeared as author in the 1598 edition. The title in the
Folio is *The Tragedy of Richard* 3, "with the landing of
Earl Richmond and the battle at Bosworth Field." No other
history in the Folio is entitled a tragedy. These minutiæ
are significant.

PLAYS probably acted by the CHAMBERLAIN'S MEN at the THEATER,
1594 Oct.–1597 July.

3. 1594, Dec. 28. *The Comedy of Errors.* Folio 1623.
Altered from an earlier version. Acted as the play of
Errors 1604, Dec. 28.

12*. 1595 (? Jan. 26). *A Midsummer night's dream,* as
it hath been sundry times publicly acted by the Right
Honorable the Lord Chamberlain, his servants. Written
by William Shakespeare (S. R. 1600, Oct. 8, for Thomas
Fisher). 1600, two editions: one "by James Roberts,"
the other "for Thomas Fisher." Fisher's has the best readings, but Roberts' is more correctly printed, and was the
copy used for the Folio reprint. The concensus of critical
opinion is that Roberts pirated his copy from the earlier
Fisher edition; but it would be a unique phenomenon had

this been allowed to pass without inhibition or, at least, protest. All the evidence lies the other way. Better readings are usually found in later editions, whenever these are produced in the lifetime of the author. Printer's errors are far more likely to have been introduced than corrected in a second edition; while the fact that "the *Exits* are more frequently marked" in the Roberts edition, *i.e.*, in ii., i. 244, and iii. 2, 101, of which the Cambridge editors make special notice, is too trifling to weigh for a moment. In both instances the *Exit* is sufficiently indicated in the text. It seems to me far more likely that Roberts printed the play for Fisher, who did not, for some reason unknown to us, care to put his name on the first issue; but finding the edition quickly exhausted, and the play popular, he then appended his name as publisher. The only other instance in which I have found Fisher's name on a play title-page is Marston's *Antonio and Mellida*, 1602. Compare carefully the very similar instance of *The Merchant of Venice*, below.

13. c. 1595. *The Tragedy of King Richard 2*, "as it hath been publicly acted by the right Honorable the Lord Chamberlain, his Servants." London. Printed by Valentine Simmes for Andrew Wise, 1597. In 1598 "By William Shakespeare" appeared on the title-page; in 1608 (but only in part of the edition) "With new additions of the Parliament Scene and the deposing of King Richard;" but these additions were only restorations of a scene disallowed under Elizabeth. They are given most correctly in the 1623 Folio, wherein the play is entitled *The life and death of King Richard 2*.

5. c. 1595. *The Two Gentlemen of Verona.* 1623 Folio. Altered from an earlier version.

6. c. 1596. *The Life and death of King John.* 1623 Folio. Somewhat compressed for representation.

7. c. 1596. *The [most] excellent History of the Merchant of Venice.* " With the extreme cruelty of Shylock the Jew towards the said Merchant in cutting a just pound of his flesh : and the obtaining of Portia by the choice of three chests [as it hath been divers times acted by the Lord Chamberlain, his servants]." Written by W[illiam] Shakespeare, 1600. This edition was printed by J[ames] R[oberts] for Thomas Heyes. Another edition, also dated 1600, omits the words in brackets, and was " printed by J. Roberts," who had entered the play S. R. 1598, July 22, as " *The Merchant of Venice,* otherwise called *The Jew of Venice ;* " but it is added, " Provided it be not printed without license first had from the Lord Chamberlain." In the S. R. entry of " Haies' " edition, 1600, Oct. 28, the words " by consent of Mr. Roberts " occur. I have no doubt that the license was obtained from the Lord Chamberlain in 1600, and that on the exhaustion of the " Roberts " edition the copyright was sold by him to Heyes on condition that Roberts should have the printing of the play. L. Heyes had the copyright in 1637. T. Heyes appears nowhere else as a play publisher. The Folio was printed from the Roberts Quarto.

4. 1596, July 22–1597, April 17. " An excellent conceited Tragedy of *Romeo and Juliet,* as it hath been often (with great applause) played publicly by the right Honourable the L. of Hunsdon, his Servants." Printed by John Danter, 1597. This is the version of the play as acted up to 1596–7, and, in my opinion, thrown aside when the ultimate version, in which Shakespeare replaced by his own lines his original 1591 coadjutor's work, was fashioned. Danter had up to this time been a frequent publisher of plays, but never afterwards. This is his only play publication not entered in S. R. I infer that this play had been

surreptitiously obtained, and that the players declined any
further dealings with him. "The most excellent and lamentable tragedy of *Romeo and Juliet*. Newly corrected, augmented, and amended as it hath been sundry times publicly
acted by the right Honorable the Lord Chamberlain, his
Servants." Printed by Thomas Creede for Cuthbert Burby,
1599. This was the final version as acted at the Curtain from
1597 Oct. onwards. Note the insertion of "most" in the
second edition title, and compare the instance of *The Merchant
of Venice*. This play, like *Love's Labour's Lost*, also published
by Burby, does not appear as originally licensed in S. R.; but
they must have been authorised (probably by the Master of
the Revels), because in 1607, Jan. 22, they were, with *The
Taming of a Shrew*, duly entered as transferred to N. Ling.
Shakespeare's name never appears as author of this play or
of *Henry* 5 in any edition anterior to the Folio, in which it
is called *The Tragedy of Romeo and Juliet*.

14. c. 1597. *The History of Henry 4*, "with the battle
at Shrewsbury between the King and Lord Henry Percy, surnamed Henry Hotspur of the North. With the humorous
conceits of Sir John Falstaffe." Printed by P[eter] S[hort]
for Andrew Wise, 1598. Entered S. R. 1598, Feb. 25, for
A. Wise. This play was published sooner after representation than usual, to show that Oldcastle had been replaced by
Falstaff. It was acted before King James, 1612–13, as *Hotspur*. Shakespeare's name as author first appeared in the
1599 edition. The Folio title is *The First Part of Henry
4*, "with the life and death of Henry, surnamed *Hotspur*."

PLAYS acted by the CHAMBERLAIN'S MEN at the CURTAIN,
1597–1599.

11. 1597–8, Christmas. "A pleasant conceited Comedy
called *Love's Labour's Lost*, as it was presented before her

Highness this last Christmas. Newly corrected and augmented by W. Shakespeare." Imprinted by W[illiam]
W[aterson] for Cuthbert Burby, 1598. Not in S. R. (see
Romeo and Juliet). This is the first appearance of Shakepeare's name on a play title-page. Until a Court version of
a play of his was issued he kept his anonymity. In this
case there can be no dispute that an earlier version existed ;
but that "newly corrected," &c., implies an earlier edition
I deny. Compare, for instance, the title-page of *Locrine*,
which was certainly a first edition. This play was published immediately after the Court performance, as usual
in such cases.

15. c. 1598, before July. *Much Ado about Nothing.* "As it
hath been sundry times publicly acted by the right honorable
the Lord Chamberlain, his servants. Written by William
Shakepeare." Printed by V[alentine] S[ims] for Andrew
Wise and William Aspley, 1600. S. R. 1600, Aug. 23.
Probably a rewritten version of *Love's Labour's Won.* Called
Benedict and Bettris when acted before King James 1612–13,
although presented to Prince Charles, the Palatine, and Lady
Elizabeth that same Christmas under its proper name. It
may be noted that the eleven plays last noticed, together
with *Titus Andronicus* (which see), make up the twelve in
Meres' 1598 list, which clearly includes all plays reputed
to be Shakespeare's acted by the Chamberlain's men up to
that date.

16. c. 1598, July. *The Second Part of Henry* 4, " continuing to his death and coronation of Henry 5. With the
humours of Sir John Falstaffe and swaggering Pistol. As
it hath been sundry times publicly acted by the right
honorable the Lord Chamberlain, his servants. Written by
William Shakespeare." Printed by V[alentine] S[ims] for
Andrew Wise and William Aspley, 1600. S. R. (with *Much*

Ado about Nothing) 1600, Aug. 23. This was a much less popular play than the first part. The Folio title is *The Second Part of Henry* 4, "Containing his Death and the Coronation of King Henry 5." The Quarto, with its first Epilogue (down to "pray for the Queen"), is evidently a version abridged for Court performance. This Epilogue, "of mine own making," must have been spoken by Shakespeare himself [in the character of Prince John ?]; the second Epilogue (for public performance) is spoken by a dancer, and refers to "our author." The Folio, which has been expurgated of many oaths, &c. (probably by the Master of the Revels), is the received stage copy of James' time. The 1623 editor, not seeing that there were two Epilogues in the prompter's copy, has mixed them by transferring the "pray for the Queen" to the end of the second one.

PLAYS acted at the GLOBE by the CHAMBERLAIN'S MEN, 1599–1603.

17. 1599. *The Chronicle History of Henry* 5, "with his battle fought at Agin Court [*sic*] in France. Together with Antient Pistol. As it hath been sundry times played by the Right honorable the Lord Chamberlain, his Servants." Printed by Thomas Creede for Tho. Millington and John Busby 1600. But it was not entered for them in S. R. On 14th Aug. 1600 (previously to which the first edition must have been printed) the copyright was transferred to T. Pavier, who published the 1602 edition. The publication is proved by this transfer to have been an authorised one, although it had been "stayed" on 4th Aug., along with those of *As you like it, Every Man in His Humour,* and *Much Ado about Nothing. As you like it* was not published; the others were, on 14th Aug., with due authority; but

every play by a different publisher. It seems clear that the delay, of which so many hypothetical interpretations have been offered, was simply to enable Millington and Busby, who probably had the copyrights of all four plays, to complete their sales thereof to the other publishers. The Folio title is simply *The life of Henry* 5. The Quarto appears to me to be merely an abridged version, probably made for acting in the country, or possibly a first sketch; but there are differences in historic statement, which make the first view more likely. As Shakespeare's name appears in none of the Quartos, he personally had probably nothing to do with the publication.

18. 1599. *As you like it.* Stayed, S. R. 1600, Aug. 4. First printed in 1623 Folio.

19. 1600. "A most pleasant and excellent conceited comedy of *Sir John Falstaffe and the Merry Wives of Windsor.* Intermixed with sundry variable and pleasing humors of Sir Hugh, the Welsh Knight, Justice Shallow, and his wise Cousin M. Slender. With the swaggering vein of Ancient Pistoll and Corporal Nym. By William Shakespeare. As it hath been divers times Acted by the right Honorable ·my Lord Chamberlain's servants, both before her Majesty and elsewhere." Printed by T[homas] C[reede] for Arthur Johnson, 1602. S. R. 1602, Jan. 18, for John Busby: with an assignment to Johnson. Comparing Busby's assignment of *Henry* 5 to Pavier in Aug. 1600, I incline to the opinion that this was one of the batch of plays then held by him and Millington, and that it had been performed at Court c. Shrovetide 1600; if not, it must have been at Christmas 1600–1, for there were no Court performances 1601–2. Probably, the copy being so crude, he could not meet with a purchaser immediately. The text is just what we might expect in an alteration of the old "*Gelyous Comedy,*" hurriedly

made by command; and I do not think (although it was no
doubt much improved for public representation in the interval) that the play received the author's final touches till
its Court performance before King James, 26th Dec. 1604.
In its final state it appeared in the 1623 Folio as *The Merry
Wives of Windsor;* but when acted before Prince Charles,
the Palatine, and the Lady Elizabeth, 1612–13, it retained
the other part of its original title, *Sir John Falstaffe.*

20. 1600, *The tragedy of Julius Cæsar.* First printed in
the 1623 Folio; but it contains Cæsar's "Revenge," as well as
his "Tragedy," and seems to me to be a condensation of two
plays into one, made after Shakespeare's retirement. *Cæsar's
Tragedy* was played at Court 1612–13, before Prince Charles,
the Palatine, and Lady Elizabeth. I think *The Tempest* and
Julius Cæsar both assumed their final shape at this time.

21. 1601, *The Tragical History of Hamlet, Prince of Denmark.* "By William Shakespeare. As it hath been divers
times acted by his Highness' servants in the City of London:
as also in the two Universities of Cambridge and Oxford,
and elsewhere." At London; printed for N[icholas] L[ing]
and John Trundel, 1603. The S. R. entry is for James
Roberts, 22nd July 1602. Roberts probably sold his right
to Ling and Trundell, and printed this edition for them.
This differs much from *The Tragical History of Hamlet,
Prince of Denmark.* "By William Shakespeare. Newly
imprinted and enlarged to almost as much again as it was,
according to the true and perfect copy." Printed by J[ames]
R[oberts] for N[icholas] L[ing], 1604. A third form of
the play is in the 1623 Folio, where the title is *The Tragedy
of Hamlet, Prince of Denmark.*

The facts that N. L. published both these Quartos, and
that no fresh entry was required in S. R. for the second one,
show that the 1602 entry refers to the 1603 edition, and

not, as usually taken for granted, to that of 1604 only. The reference to the acting at Cambridge, Oxford, and elsewhere indicates that the copy was a version used when the company were travelling; and the text, ii. 2, 343, &c., shows that this travelling was an exceptional thing with this company. It must, therefore, be referred to the only known instance between 1594 and 1602 of such absence from London, viz., that in 1601, when we know that they went even as far as Scotland. The "humour of children," Q. 1, in the "private" theatres could hardly be termed a "novelty" at a later date. It began to be fashionable in 1600, when the Paul's boys' performances were revived, and Evans (in September) got his lease of Blackfriars for the Chapel children. The playing "in the City of London," not at the Globe, which was not in the City, has not received the notice it deserves. The forty performances of *Richard 2* in 1601, for which the Chamberlain's men got into trouble at Essex' trial, were "in open streets and houses" in the City, and I have little doubt that *Hamlet* was performed in the same way during the same time. These players were evidently thought to be acting in the interest of Essex and James, who "for some time after his accession considered Essex as a martyr to his title to the English crown" (*Criminal Trials*, L. E. K., i. 394). Roberts got his entry licensed, but Ling did not find it expedient to issue the play till after James' accession. The title was, in fact, not printed till the players had obtained their patent as "his Highness' servants," 17th May 1603. The copy used was apparently a MS. of the old play by Kyd, as hurriedly altered by Shakespeare for the occasion, but with the omission of many speeches which, being written on separate papers, had passed into the hands of the several actors, their defect being made up as best might be. In the meanwhile Shakespeare had completed his version of the play, and the company, not liking an issue so imperfect to be their first appearance in print in the new King's reign, supplied a "true and perfect copy" to the publisher.   Noticeable is it that they did not do this for *The Merry Wives of Windsor* (nor, indeed, for *Henry* 5), and that, excepting that one play and *Hamlet*, no play by Shakespeare was published between 1600 Oct. and 1607 Nov.   The 1604 and 1623 editions are both abridged from Shakespeare's full MS.; the Folio considerably so (some 200 lines), evidently for stage pur poses; the 1604 Quarto only here and there.   Two Quarto omissions are important : one, ii. 2, 244–266, in which Denmark is called a prison, and one of the worst, which would have displeased Queen Anne; the other, ii. 2, 351– 379, about the boy-players, omitted in 1604, when the Queen had taken them under her special protection, but probably restored c. 1613, when boy companies ceased to perform, and the very boys here alluded to had "grown to common players," and been (in 1610) adopted into the King's company.   The necessity of adopting the date 1601 for the "travelling" in this passage, and the inseparable connexion of the "inhibition" with the travelling, compels me to withdraw the explanation of "the late innovation" advanced in my *Life of Shakespeare*, p. 227, and to adopt the view that the recent setting up of children's companies is referred to on the surface, but with an under-reference to Essex' insurrection, the real cause of their absence from London.   This requires that they should have been actually inhibited from performing there, which I doubt not was the case.   Note the unique allusion, l. 342, to "the tragedians of *the City*."   They had not, till this Essex affair, performed in the City since 1594.   Of course, this alteration of view implies a date for the perfect play of 1602, although metrical tests require this play to come after *The taming of the Shrew* ; but date of production on the stage is not necessarily quite identical with that of writing.

7. 1601, before going to Scotland. *All's Well that ends Well*. Folio 1623. A recast of an earlier play.

22. 1601, c. Oct., in Scotland. *The Tragedy of Macbeth*. This is the date, in my opinion, of this play in its first form; but it was certainly revised by Shakespeare c. 1606, on the public stage 1610, and reduced to the form in which it appears in the 1623 Folio by Middleton c. 1622.

8. 1601, c. Nov. *The History of Troylus and Cressida*. "As it was acted by the King's Majesty's servants at the Globe. Written by William Shakespeare." Imprinted for G. Eld for R. Bonian and H. Walley, 1609. Q. 1.

The Famous History of Troylus and Cresseid. "Excellently expressing the beginning of their loves, with the conceited wooing of Pandarus, Prince of Licia. Written," &c. [as above], 1609. Q. 2.

The Tragedy of Troylus and Cressida. Folio 1623.

When I wrote my *Life of Shakespeare* I omitted to refer, as I should have done, to the Cambridge edition, and accepted Halliwell's later statement, taken from Collier, that Q. 2 was the first edition; but Clarke and Wright have shown conclusively that the leaf with the Preface, with its new signature, was not cancelled in Q. 1, but inserted in Q. 2. This fact modifies largely the view set forth in my previous work. In S. R. 1603, Feb. 7, the play was entered for James Roberts as to be printed "when he hath gotten sufficient authority for it," and "as it is acted by my Lord Chamberlain's men." Roberts did not get sufficient authority, and the play was not then printed, as is shown by its having to be re-entered 1609, Jan. 28, for Bonion and

Whalley; but the copy used by them was probably purchased from Roberts in the same way as in the previous
instances: cf. *The Merchant of Venice, Midsummer Night's
Dream,* and *Hamlet.* They accordingly repeated the statement that the Chamberlain's men (now the King's) had
acted it, which there is no reason for doubting, but added
"at the Globe." This was evidently denied by the company, and they had to cancel the title and insert a Preface
that it was "never staled with the stage, never clapper-
clawed with the palms of the vulgar," but was (to the
reader) "a new play." At the same time they intimate
that "the grand possessors," *i.e.,* the King's company, had
been opposed to its publication. But if not publicly acted,
where was it presented? There is no indication of a Court
performance; nor is it suited for a private marriage or the
like. My hypothesis is that the "physic" given to "the
great Myrmidon," i. 3, 378; iii. 3, 34, is identical with the
"purge" administered by Shakespeare to Jonson in *The
Return from Parnassus,* iv. 3, and that the setting up of
Ajax as a rival to Achilles shadows forth the putting forward Dekker by the King's men to write against Jonson
his *Satiromastix.* The subsequent defection of Thersites
from Ajax to Achilles would then agree with the reconciliation of Marston and Jonson in 1601, when they wrote
together in *Rosalind's Complaint.* See further under these
authors' names, and compare in this play i. 3, 140–196;
ii. 1; ii. 3, 85; iii. 3, 241–end. In ii. 3, 23, "Devil Envy,
say Amen!" refers to the end of *Mucedorus,* but not necessarily to the later version. Envy must have said Amen in
the earlier one, see the last lines, which show that this was
acted at Court before Elizabeth. This Envy Induction in
Mucedorus was imitated in Jonson's *Poetaster,* and the armed
Prologue in the *Poetaster* by Shakespeare (?) in the present

play (see the reference in l. 23 to the "well-erected confidence" of Jonson's Prologue) ; so that these three plays
are connected, and should be studied together. But the
authorship of the *Troylus* Prologue is very doubtful. Passing from this conjectural matter, I think that, in any case, this
play was acted at Cambridge, as we know that *Julius Cæsar*
and *Hamlet* were ; and if so, it was almost certainly in 1601,
·n the return from Scotland c. November, before *The Return
from Parnassus.* If it be objected that I assign too many
plays to this year, I would answer that they were all plays
refashioned from older versions, and that four such revivals
involve less expense of energy than two entirely new plays.
That the present play was altered from an older one on the
loves of Troylus and Cresseid I have shown in my previous
works ; and the altered title of Q. 2 proves that the King's
men (and that here means Shakespeare himself) were
anxious to emphasise this as the main subject of the
play, and to divert attention from the satirical underplot.
The play is not called a Tragedy till the 1623 Folio,
and this title is only applicable to the alternative ending
after v. 3.

10. 1602, Feb. 2. *Twelfth Night,* or *What you Will.*
Folio 1623 ; a recast of an earlier play.

PLAYS acted by the KING'S MEN at the GLOBE,
1603–1609.

23. 1603, after March. *The Taming of the Shrew.*
Folio 1623. Only the Petruchio and Katherine scenes
by Shakespeare.

24. 1604. *Measure for Measure.* Folio 1623. Acted
before King James 26th Dec. 1604.

25. 1604. *The Tragedy of Othello, the Moor of Venice.*

Folio 1623. Acted before King James 1st Nov. 1604. S. R. for Thomas Walkley 6th Oct. 1621. The title of the 1622 edition is *The tragedy of Othello, the Moor of Venice,* "as it hath been diverse times acted at the Globe and at the Black-Friars by his Majesty's Servants. Written by William Shakespeare." Printed by N[icholas] O[kes] for Thomas Walkley, 1622.

26. c. 1605. "Mr. William Shak-speare, HIS True Chronicle History of the life and death of *King Lear* and his three Daughters. With the unfortunate life of Edgar, son and heir to the Earl of Gloster, and his sullen and assumed humor of Tom of Bedlam: as it was played before the King's Majesty at Whitehall upon St. Stephen's night in Christmas Holidays. By his Majesty's servants, playing usually at the Globe, on the Bankside." Printed for Nathaniel Butter, 1608. S. R. for N. Butter and Jo. Busby 26th Nov. 1607; therefore performed at Court 26th Dec. 1606. Clearly from a copy altered for this Court performance, and, as usual with these altered copies, none too legible. The stage version is that of the Folio 1623. The title with "HIS" in capitals and the author's name conspicuous at the top was meant to distinguish it from the older *Leir,* reprinted 1605 as "The True Chronicle History of *King Leir and his three Daughters,* &c.," but entered S. R. 1594 as "The most Famous Chronicle History of *Leir, King of England.*" The 1605 title had evidently been accommodated to that of Shakespeare's play for manifest reasons; and, doubtless, partly to vindicate their own play as a new one, partly to advertise a play that had pleased the King, this issue was allowed by the company.

27. c. 1606. *The life of Tymon of Athens.* Folio 1623. Only partly written by Shakespeare.

28. 1607. *The Tragedy of Anthonie and Cleopatra.*

Folio 1623. S. R. 1608, May 20, with *Pericles*, but not then printed.

    29. 1608. *The tragedy of Coriolanus.* Folio 1623.

    30. 1608, c. May. "The late / and much-admired Play / Called / *Pericles, Prince* / *of Tyre.* / With the true relation of the whole History, / adventures, and fortunes of the said Prince. /

As also /

The no less strange and worthy accidents / in the Birth and Life of his Daughter /

MARIANA.

As it hath been divers and sundry times acted by / his Majesty's Servants at the Globe, on / the Bankside. / By William * * Shakespeare. /" Imprinted for Henry Gosson, / 1609.

    Entered S. R. 1608, May 20, for Edward Blount. As no new entry was required before publication by Gosson, this was probably an entry for the copy as published. *The true history of the play of Pericles,* "as it was lately presented by the worthy and ancient Poet, John Gower," was published 1608 by Nat. Butter as *The Painful Adventures of Pericles, Prince of Tyre,* written by George Wilkins, who undoubtedly wrote the first two acts of the play; but this book does not appear in S. R. I feel certain that its appearance was the cause of the company consenting to the publication of the play itself, the title of which is so arranged as to throw into unusually prominent relief the name of Shakespeare and the distinct separation of his part of the play, viz., the Marina story. This disappears in the 1664 Folio, where the words "As . . . Bankside" are omitted. The 1623 Folio does not contain the play, Pavier, who then held the copyright, having probably refused his assent. "The Painful Adventures" in Wilkins' title is taken from Twine's

Apollonius [1576], but the play professes to be founded on Gower's *Prince of Tyre*, printed 1483.

31. c. 1609. *The tragedy of Cymbeline.* Folio 1623. But the historical part dates earlier, probably c. 1606. As we have it, the play has been touched up by a second hand. Perhaps it was not acted in 1609, that being a plague-year, and was not finished for the stage till after Shakespeare's retirement.

PLAYS acted at the GLOBE or BLACKFRIARS, 1610–11.

32. 1610. *The Winter's Tale.* Folio 1623. Acted before King James 5th Nov. 1611, 7th April 1618; and before Prince Charles, the Palatine, and Lady Elizabeth 1612–13.

33. 1610. *The Tempest.* Folio 1623. Acted before King James 31st Oct. 1611; and before Prince Charles, the Palatine, and Lady Elizabeth 1612–13, when it was probably abridged by Beaumont to its present state and the Mask inserted.

34. c. 1611. *The Famous History of the Life of King Henry* 8. Folio 1623. Probably completed by Fletcher, and produced as a new play 1613 at the Globe. Massinger had also a hand in this; but was the remaining part by Shakespeare or Beaumont?

These notes are avowedly supplementary, and should be read with what I have previously published in my *Life and Work of Shakespeare;* they are inserted here only to complete the chronicle of the Drama, which would not allow of their omission. The consideration of the title-pages of the Quartos is new matter. I could not enter on it until after the publication of my *History of the Stage,* because no sufficient collection had been elsewhere made of the details of connexion between publishers and dramatic publications.

On the Prologues, Epilogues, &c., in Shakespeare.

1. *Midsummer Night's Dream.* This play has certainly alternative endings: one a song by Oberon for a marriage, and then *Exeunt*, with no mark of Puck's remaining on the stage; the other an Epilogue by Puck, apparently for the Court (cf. "gentles" in l. 436). It might seem, as the Epilogue is placed last, that the marriage version was the earlier, and so I took it to be when I wrote my *Life of Shakespeare;* but the compliment to Elizabeth, ii. 1. 148–168, was certainly written for the Court; and this passage is essential to the original conduct of the play, which may have been printed from a marriage-version copy, with additions from the Court copy. This would require a date for the marriage subsequent to the Court performance. One version must date 1596, for the weather description, ii. 1, 88–118, which can be omitted without in any way affecting the progress of the play, requires that date. I believe this passage was inserted for the Court performance in 1596, that on the public stage having taken place in 1595; but that the marriage presentation, being subsequent to this, was most likely at the union of Southampton and Elizabeth Vernon in 1598–9. In any case, this was Shakespeare's first Epilogue now extant.

2. *Romeo and Juliet* has a Sonnet Prologue (mutilated in Q. 1): this must date c. 1596–7. See my *Life of Shakespeare*.

3. *2 Henry 4* has an Induction Prologue, presented by Chorus, in blank verse, and an Epilogue in prose, by a Dancer, with alternative endings. The position of the stage version thereof in Q. 1, after the Court ending, with its "pray for the Queen," shows that here, as in the case of *Midsummer Night's Dream*, that Quarto was probably printed

(with additions) from the Court performance MS. Date, 1598.

4. *Henry* 5 has a Chorus presentation to each act, with the Epilogue in Sonnet form. Date, 1599. This is the last Sonnet and the last Chorus.

5. *As you like it*, 1599 (or 1600), has an Epilogue, spoken by Rosalind, in prose.

6. *All's well that ends well*, 1601, has an Epilogue in couplets, spoken by the King.

7. *Troylus and Cressida*, 1601, has a Prologue "armed" with special references to Jonson, and an Epilogue spoken by Pandarus. Shakespeare after this introduced neither Prologue nor Chorus. The Induction in *The Taming of the Shrew* was adapted from the old play. The Gower Chorus in *Pericles* was originally devised by Wilkins; the Prologue and Epilogue in *Henry* 8 are not by him; they are usually attributed to Fletcher, but in my opinion were by Jonson. The rhymes "see, storey" and "in, women" are not in accordance with Fletcher's system; Jonson continually uses them; *e.g.*, "he, body" in *Hymenæi*. Yet Mr. Addington Symonds rejects one of his most characteristic poems expressly on account of such rhymes.

8. *The Tempest*, 1610. This final play of Shakespeare's fitly closes with an Epilogue by Prospero, the only one after the 1601 *Richard* 2 trouble; for I cannot attach any import to the Fool's jig-song at the end of *Twelfth Night*, which is of most uncertain authorship. Of course, I do not "assume" (as Elze maliciously accuses me of doing in such cases) that we have all the evidence before us; but from what we have, it seems that Shakespeare gave up writing Epilogues as a habit in 1601.

On the Division of Shakespeare's Plays into Acts and Scenes.

There are no divisions in any of the Quartos 1597–1619; but one play, *Othello*, S. R. 1621, Oct. 6, has a division into acts only. In the 1623 Folio there is great variation. The numbers prefixed to the plays in the following list refer to the order in which they were therein printed :—

i. *Plays without Division.*

a. Comedies. None.

b. Histories. 7. *2 Henry 6*; 8. *3 Henry 6*. Imperfect versions of both these were in 1622 in the possession of T. Pavier.

c. Tragedies. 3. *Romeo and Juliet*, printed from the 1609 Qto.

4. *Troylus and Cressida*, printed from the 1609 Qto.

5. *Timon of Athens.*

11. *Anthony and Cleopatra*, perhaps printed from the copy prepared for press 1608, May 20, but not published.

It is clear that up to 1609 Shakespeare introduced no division into Acts or Scenes, and I think we are justified in concluding that all such divisions were made after his retirement in 1610. The printing of 4, 5 requires special notice. As the Folio was issued the signatures and pagination are irregular. The back-leaves of pp. 73, 75, sig. gg, gg2, of *Romeo and Juliet* have been cut off; then follow pp. 79 (*Romeo*), 81 (*Timon*), 81, sig. Gg, gg2, gg3, where the pages 79, 81 (the first 81) are evident misprints for 77, 79 : after this all goes on regularly to the end of *Timon*, where, in *Julius Cæsar*, a new signature, kk, and pagination, 109 (missing 101–8), suddenly begins. This would correspond with sig. gg, p. 73, as the sheets have

two insets. The *Dram. Pers.* of *Timon* are unpaged, manifestly to cloak the deficiency in pagination; and the verso
is a blank page. Turning to *Troylus*, which is thrust in
between the Histories and Tragedies, and not included in
the Catalogue of Contents, we find, first, 4 pp. with no signature (back-leaves that have been cut off), the second of
which is paged 79; then a new set of signatures of odd
sorts, ¶, &c., but no pagination. Along with the new signatures comes a change of running title, "The tragedy of"
being omitted. It is quite clear that *Troylus* (which fills
29 pp.) was at first intended to fill up (with a page of
Dram. Pers., perhaps) the 31 pp. between *Romeo* and
Cæsar; that after the sheets gg gg2 had been set, and
perhaps printed off, the editors discovered that *Troylus*
was not a tragedy. They then utilised the printed copies,
if any, by cutting off the back-leaves; and, if not, rearranged
the *pages* of set type, and then made up as well as they
could with *The life of Tymon of Athens*, which is scarcely
more a tragedy than *Troylus.* This minute examination
confirms entirely what I advanced in 1874. In 1884
Mr. G. Gould, a practical printer I believe, advocated (I
have no doubt quite independently) a similar explanation; but he was quite wrong in supposing a cancel of
36 pp. The following comparison will make the whole
thing clear to the reader's eye:—

ROMEO AND TIMON.		TROYLUS.	
Page.	Signature.	Page.	Signature.
first leaves { 73	gg	...	...
75	gg2	...	...
{ [77]. 79	Gg	n. p.	n. s. } back-leaves
new sig. { [79]. 81	gg2 [Gg2]	79	n. s. }
81	gg3 [Gg3]	n. p.	¶ new sig.

Note that the Prologue to *Troylus* was an after-insertion to replace, p. [*77*], *Romeo*, which would otherwise have been blank, and may probably not, at first, have been meant for publication. Other Prologues may, in like manner, have been omitted.

ii. *Plays divided into Acts only.*

a. Comedies. 5. *Errors.*

6. *Much Ado about Nothing*, printed from the 1600 Qto.

7. *Love's Labor's Lost*, printed from the 1598 Qto.

8. *A Midsummer Night's Dream*, printed from the 1600 Qto.

9. *The Merchant of Venice*, printed from the 1600 Qto.

11. *The Taming of the Shrew.*

12. *All's well that ends well.*

b. Histories.

5. *Henry 5.* In this instance, and this only, the Folio division is quite wrong. Having missed Act ii., the editor divided iv. into two acts, making iv. 1–6 the first of them. The Chorus-presenter clearly marks the true divisions.

c. Tragedies. 1. *Coriolanus.*

2. *Titus Andronicus*, printed from the 1600 Qto., with addition of iii. 2.

3. *Julius Cæsar.*

This ii. group, so far as the printing from Quartos is concerned, is taken from those of 1598–1600; the previous i. group from those of 1607–9.

The only play requiring special notice is *The Taming of the Shrew.* Act ii. is not marked: Act iii. includes iii. 1–iv. 2 of the modern editors; Act iv., iv. 3–v. 1. The extremely short fifth act was in all probability made up in the original by a concluding Induction Scene, with the replacing of Sly on the heath, and his awaking. It is much to be regretted that editors should take liberties with the old copies merely to accommodate the plays to the modern stage. Much valuable evidence is suppressed by such procedure.

iii. *Plays divided into Acts and Scenes.*

a. Comedies. 1. *The Tempest*, with *Dram. Pers.* Not inserted, like the *Dram. Pers.* in *Timon* and *2 Henry 4*, merely to fill up, but added, as in all other instances, by some careful reviser.

2. *The Two Gentlemen of Verona*, with *Dram. Pers.*

3. *The Merry Wives of Windsor.*

4. *Measure for Measure*, with *Dram. Pers.* Scenes i. 2, 3 are made one scene by modern editors because the place of action is the same in both. In the old time scenes were divided, not by changes of decoration, but by *Exeunt omnes*, and rightly so. On the other hand, iii. 2 is not marked as a new scene; the Duke did not leave the stage. iii. 1 was acted as in the prison; the traverse was then drawn, and the Duke was supposed to be in the street outside.

10. *As You like it.*

13. *Twelfth Night:* p. 276 at the end is blank. Query, has an Epilogue been cancelled?

14. *The Winter's Tale*, with *Dram. Pers.*

b. Histories. 1. *John.* The modern editor has here been at work with a vengeance. He has turned i. 2 into ii.; ii. into iii., i. 1—74. It is evident that, either from some accident to the MS., some mishap in printing, or some correction by the Master of the Revels, a considerable part of Act ii. has been lost. There is no *Exeunt* at the end of it; and in iii. 1, where we have "Enter . . . Constance" in the Folio, Salisbury and Arthur are not on the stage, as the modern editors, with one exception, have them. I am the exception, and deserve praise for my courage, or blame for my rashness, in adhering to the version of Shakespeare's fellows. iii. 3 is not marked in the Folio, but is by modern editors, in direct opposition to their practice in *Measure for Measure*, i. 2, 3. The omission in the Folio arose from the common mistake of printing *Exit* for *Exeunt* at the end of iii. 2. The MS. had probably *Ex.* The new scene is proved by "Enter John, Arthur, Hubert" in iii. 3. It should be edited as iii. 2*b*, to preserve the old notation through the act. "*Actus Quartus*" for "*Quintus*" is merely a misprint.

2. *Richard* 2, printed from the 1615 Qto. v. 4 [v. 3*b*] is not marked—an accidental omission of the editor.

3. 1 *Henry* 4, printed from the 1615 Qto. v. 3 is not marked in the Folio; nor is it needed.

4. 2 *Henry* 4, with *Dram. Pers.* and Epilogue, to make up 2 pp. and hide the blundering printers' errors in miscalculating their matter, inserting a supernumerary sheet, sig. gg., with three insets, and starting *Henry* 5, sig. h, with page 69 instead of 85. Of course, the printing of *Henry* 5 was begun before that of 2 *Henry* 4 was finished. The Induction is counted as i. 1. This should be retained. iv. 2 is not marked; nor should it be: Mowbray, &c., do not leave the stage, but walk about it to indicate their passage to "just distance 'tween our armies." iv. 3 [iv. 1*b*] should have been marked, but is of slight consequence. The change of chamber iv. 2, 132 (*i.e.*, iv. 5 of modern editors) was indicated by the traverse being drawn and the King being disclosed on a bed behind. The actors did not leave the stage, and no new scene should be marked.

6. 1 *Henry* 6. A very remarkable instance. No scenes marked in i., ii.; scenes rightly marked in iii.; the six Tal-

bot scenes [by Shakespeare] inserted without mark between
iv. 1 and iv. 2 ; scenes after iv. 3 not marked. The insertion of the Talbot scenes, and the consequent omission of
matter (in Act v. ?) to make room for them, produce an extremely short fifth act. Hence modern editors alter the
arrangement, beginning Act v. at iv. 2, and thus conceal
the evidence, which I regard as of considerable importance,
that even before the Talbot scenes were introduced this play
must have been divided into acts and scenes. The bearing
of such facts on the determination of doubtful authorship
will not be fully appreciated till modern editors learn to
follow Dyce's example in his editions of Marlow, &c., and
refrain from inserting falsifications of the old copies in their
stage directions and scene divisions. These should be
marked, but all variations from the originals should be
between crotchets.

9. *Richard* 3. iii. 5, 6, 7 ; v. 3, 4, 5, not marked, as
they should have been : iv. 3 not marked, *Exit* for *Exeunt*
immediately preceding. Compare *John*, iii. 2. I believe
that the copy for this play was an imperfect MS., and that
iii. 5–7 and v. 3–5 were printed from a Quarto.

10. *Henry* 8. v. 3 of the modern editors is wrongly
inserted. The actors do not leave the stage. The King is
on the upper stage, Cranmer behind the traverse below,
which represents the door of the council-room. " Draw the
curtain close " is a stage direction to hide Cranmer, not the
King, while the table, &c., are brought in. Line 34 should
run—

> " Let 'em alone ; we shall hear more anon."

" *Exeunt* " is an unwarrantable insertion of modern editors.

c. Tragedies. 7. *Macbeth*. v. 8 is unnecessarily inserted
in modern editions.

8. *Hamlet*. Only i. 1, 2, 3 ; ii. 1, 2, are marked.

9. *Lear.*   ii. 3, 4 are not marked, evidently from care-
lessness.   iv. 3 of the modern editions does not appear in
the Folio, but its place is left for it, for *Scena Septima*
succeeds *Scena Quinta.*   It was *Scena Sexta* evidently, and
when in the play probably closed the fourth act, iv. 7
being then v. 1.   Its true position is fixed by the words
"Lear's i' th' town, and by no means will yield to see his
daughter," l. 40, which must be after the attendants have
taken him in, Sc. 5 (Sc. 6 in the modern editions), and
before Sc. 7, when he does see her.   The authority of the
Folio, the regular stage copy, is far above that of the Court
Quarto copy, and the omission of the scene was probably
accidental.   The hypotheses of Eccles and Daniel that the
position of Sc. 5 [Sc. 4 Folio] should be changed are without support in the old versions, and seem to be founded on
study of the play as arranged by the modern editors.

10. *Othello.*   Printed from a stage copy, with *Dram.
Pers.*: ii. 3 is accidentally omitted in the marking: another
instance of the editor having marked his scenes by preceding
"Exeunts."   In this instance the preceding "Exit" is that
of the Herald; not a misprint, as in the other cases.   In the
Quarto of 1621, Oct. 6, the acts are marked, not the
scenes.   Act. iii. is accidentally omitted.   This shows, I
think, that act divisions in all the plays were introduced in
the stage copies at some time after Shakespeare's retiring in
1610, but before 1621; while the scenes were not divided
till the Folio was prepared in 1622.   I venture to guess
that Fletcher marked the act divisions, but that Jonson
added the scene divisions for Group iii., which would agree
with the usual practice of both these men in their own plays;
and we know that Jonson had a hand in editing the Folio.

12. *Cymbeline.*   i. 1, 2 are made one scene by modern
editors, exactly as in *Measure for Measure*, i. 2, 3.   The old

arrangement should not be interfered with. ii. 5 is not marked, nor (although it may seem preferable) need it be so necessarily. iii. 6, 7 are rolled into one by the modern editors, but the stage is clear at l. 27. The case is parallel to that of i. 1, 2.

Pericles. Mr. Daniel has pointed out that the Gower Choruses must mark new acts, but I cannot agree with him (until he proves it by other instances) that a play with seven acts was ever represented on the English stage in Shakespeare's time. The Quarto has no divisions, and the Folio of 1664, which has acts but no scenes, is post-Restoration and of no authority. The following table will show the problem to be solved :—

Gower Entries.	Folio Acts.	Modern Editors.	Fleay Divisions.
i.	i.	Gower	i.
		i. 1–4	
ii.	ii.	Gower	ii.
		ii. 1–5	
iii.		Gower	iii.
		iii. 1–2	i.*b.*
	iii.	iii. 3–4	
iv.		Gower	iv., ii.*b.*
		iv. 1	
		[iv. 2]	
		iv. 3	
v.	iv.	[iv. 4 (Gower)	iii.*b.*
		iv. 5–6	
vi.		Gower]	iv.*b.*
		v. 1, 1–240	
	v.	v. 1, 240–256	
vii.		v. 2 (Gower)	v., v.*b.*
		v. 3	
viii.		Gower epilogue	

It is clear that the Folio acts are wrong, not coinciding with Gower entrances, and may be discarded at once. The play as it stands would require seven acts, as Mr. Daniel pointed out. I cannot believe that such a unique arrangement was adopted, and propose the following hypothesis:—

When the play was altered by Shakespeare, by his insertion of his Marina story in place of Wilkins' version, the brothel part did not exist; soon after, iv. 2, 4, 5, 6 were inserted as an alternative arrangement in place of Acts i. ii., so that Wilkins' part of the play would entirely disappear. When the play was published, 1609, these arrangements were patched together, so that the reader would be in possession of both versions. The brothel insertions I have enclosed in crotchets in the table; they are not alluded to in any other part of the play, not even in the recapitulatory Epilogue, and I cannot believe that, with such a representation of Lysimachus as that contained in them, Shakespeare would have married him to Marina. I have in the last column given the acts as I suppose them arranged for each method of presentation. These alternative versions are not uncommon. See, for instance, that in *Troylus and Cressida*. But, passing from this relatively unimportant matter to the more interesting question, Why was not *Pericles* printed in the 1623 Folio, since it is undoubtedly in great part written by Shakespeare? I will firstly note the S. R. entries. The Quartos "entered to other men" were manifestly placed at the disposal of the 1623 editors (for a consideration, of course) for their Folio, although the other men retained their right to issue subsequent Quartos, as they did in many instances. But to this rule there is one exception, that of Thomas Pavier. He allowed (perhaps could not prevent) their printing perfect copies of 2, 3 *Henry* 6 and *Henry* 5, of which he had issued most insufficient versions; but of other plays he deliberately retained an obstinate grasp. *The Contention of York and Lancaster* was " set over " to him, 1602, April 19, by T. Millington, " *salvo jure cujuscunque*," which may have reserved the right of the " grand possessor " to print a more perfect version; and *Henry* 5 on 1600, Aug. 14, by the same T. Millington and T. Busbie, no doubt with the same reservation. But in the 1602 entry another play, *Titus and Andronicus*, is mentioned; and on 4th Aug. 1626 his widow assigned to Brewster and Bird the " play " of *Henry* 5, " Master Pavier's right to Shakespeare's plays, or any of them, and *Titus and Andronicus*." What the " Shakespeare's plays " here mentioned were appear from Bird's assignment to Cotes, 1630, Nov. 8, of *Henry* 5, *Titus and Andronicus, Pericles,* and *The Yorkshire Tragedy*. Now, this *Titus and Andronicus* could not have been the play that has come down to us, for Quartos of that had been issued in 1600 and 1611. It does not appear at first sight that it ever was printed, and yet surely it must have been; it would be strange indeed for an unprinted MS. to be entered in S. R., and to have been assigned three times over. The persistent use of " and " in the title would point to an identification of this play with the original form of *Titus and Vespasian,* acted by L. Strange's men in 1592, from which the German extant version of *Titus and Vespasian* (on the Andronicus story) was derived. My own belief is that Pavier would not come to terms with Hemings and Condell for the printing of either *Pericles, Titus and Andronicus,* or *The Yorkshire Tragedy,* and that, not being able to get at the true Simon Pure, they arranged with White or his assigns to print the extant version instead. We know that they did not print *Pericles,* which had, as F. 3 says, been "published in Shakespeare's lifetime;" and surely they would have if they could. I have little doubt that Pavier's

version was Shakespeare's play as acted when he was with
Strange's men in 1592. The extant play was acted *for the
first time* in 1594 by a rival company (Sussex'), and was no
doubt bought up by Derby's, afterwards the Chamberlain's,
men, to prevent its clashing with their own. If Marlow
wrote it, Shakespeare would certainly have been unwilling
to appear in such direct rivalry with the "dead shepherd."
As to *The Yorkshire Tragedy*, the external evidence for its
being by Shakespeare is very strong. It was entered for
Pavier S. R. 1608, May 2, as "written by William Shakespeare;" published 1608 as "by W. Shakespeare," while
Shakespeare was still a prominent dramatist and sharer at
the Globe: reissued 1619 as by "W. Shakespeare." Two
other plays not in the Folio were, it is true, published as by
Shakespeare, but neither *Sir John Oldcastle* nor *The London
Prodigal* were entered S. R. with the author's name, which
was withdrawn by a cancel from the *Oldcastle* title-page;
and the publication of the second part thereof (though duly
entered) seems to have been prevented; while the *Prodigal*
was surreptitiously printed without any entry at all, and as it
was not reprinted, may, for all we know, have been called in.
I have repeatedly, even in this volume, expressed my intense
difficulty to admit that Shakespeare wrote this little play
about the same time as *Lear*, in the zenith of his power, and
have tried hypothesis on hypothesis to find another author
for it; but the external evidence is too strong. *The Yorkshire Tragedy* and the lost *Titus and Andronicus* must, like
Pericles, be included among the plays of Shakespeare in
which Pavier had an interest.

It is very difficult to form any hypothesis which will
explain this *Yorkshire Tragedy* difficulty. The second title,
All's one, certainly looks as if it were connected in subject
with the other three plays which made up *The Four plays*

in one, of which it formed a part; and the first scene, which
has nothing to do with Calverly's wife, but refers to the
lady with whom he broke off his engagement, must (one
would think) have been part of the first of these three
plays. Nothing extant in dramatic form refers to this
Calverly story except Wilkins' *Miseries of enforced Marriage ;*
and it is certainly singular that this play should contain
three distinct motifs, viz., 1. the tragedy of Clare Harcop,
i. 1—ii. 4; 2. the prodigality of Scarborow, iii. 1, 2, 4;
3. the comedy of the marriage of Scarborow's sister, iii. 3,
iv. 1—v. 1. The ending, v. 2, is certainly not consistent
with the title of "Miseries," and looks like an alteration.
This is confirmed by the unusual words on the title, "as it
is *now* acted ; " not "lately acted," which is the customary
form. Moreover, the S. R. entry, 1607, July 31, expressly
says "a tragedy ; " and a tragedy it surely was when performed in 1605 (it could not be earlier, for it contains an
allusion to fighting with a windmill, iii. 4, and *Don Quixote*
was published in that year); but as "now acted " in 1607
it has become a comedy. This suggests the inference that
the original tragic ending was *The Yorkshire Tragedy*, and
that the representation of this domestic crime had been
inhibited, as too closely reproducing such recent facts,
through the influence of the Brook family. The "now
acted " of 1607 ; the disguise of the names in Wilkins'
play ; the separate publication of one only of *The Four
plays in one* with no character-names at all; the meaning
of the first scene of *The Yorkshire Tragedy*, which would
come between ii. 1 and ii. 2 of the *Miseries,* would all be
accounted for on this hypothesis. It must not be forgotten
that immediately after this Shakespeare altered Wilkins'
play of *Pericles* (possibly in retaliation for his altering this
Shakespeare part of the Yorkshire play); that no one has

succeeded in tracing any author but Shakespeare who could have written this little tragedy in connexion with the King's men at this date; and that Wilkins, by issuing the *Miseries* after he had left the King's men, began the series of publications, certainly not of a friendly nature, traced under *Pericles* in my *Life of Shakespeare.*

Nevertheless, although I give way before this external evidence, and reluctantly admit Shakespeare's authorship of this *Yorkshire* play, I have not cancelled my previous efforts to find another author. There may be some possibility that such author may be found, though I do not dare to hope for it. The external evidence of authorship is exactly the same for *The Yorkshire Tragedy* as for *Pericles*, and both are connected with the play-writing of G. Wilkins.

Excursus on Shakespeare's Sonnets.

No impartial reader can doubt that these *Sonnets* consist of two series, distinct in the persons addressed, yet connected in subject-matter. These series are separated by the *Envoy*, wrongly numbered as Sonnet 126, which consists of twelve heroic lines. The former series, 1–125, is addressed to a youth; the latter, 127–154, to a woman. The connexion lies in the woman-allusions in 40–42. That the youth was Lord Southampton is beyond doubt. The "Lord of my love" (26), to whom Shakespeare sends his "written embassage" as a vassal "to witness duty," whom (78) he has invoked as a Muse, and under whom others have, like Shakespeare, dispersed their poetry in "dedicated words" (82), the only "one" (76, 105) to whom his songs have been addressed, is out of all question the Lord to whom "love without end" was dedicated with *The Rape of Lucreece.* Every sentiment and almost every word in that dedication is repeated in Sonnets 26, 84, 108, 75, 117, 16, &c. Only dilettanti or faddists of a clique can resist the clear and conclusive arguments of Drake on this point, or suppose that Queen Elizabeth, the Earl of Pembroke, Anne Hathaway, William himself, William Hart, or William Hughes is the object of the poem. I shall not here gibbet the names of the authors of those wild guesses, which are mostly founded on the dedication in 1609 of the Sonnets to "Mr. W. H." This Dedication was written by Thomas Thorpe the publisher, not by Shakespeare, and as the only hypothesis worth controverting turns on the identification of W. H. and William Herbert, Earl of Pembroke, it is worth while to dispose of this point before proceeding further. It has been noticed by others that a translation of S. Augustine's *City of God* was in 1610 dedicated " To the Honorablest patron of Muses and good minds, Lord William, Earl of Pembroke," &c.; but it has not, to my knowledge, been observed that the reference in this Dedication, by " your late imaginary but now actual traveller, then to most conceited *Viraginia*, now to almost concealed *Virginia*, then a light but not lewd, now a sage and allowed translator. . . . He that against detraction beyond expectation then found your sweet patronage," &c., is to *The Discovery of a New World, or A Description of South Indies hitherto unknown, by an English Mercury.* This book, entered S. R. 1609, Jan. 18, is a translation of Joseph Hall's *Mundus alter et idem sive Terra Australis antehac semper incognita. Authore Mercurio Britannico.* This translation was issued as printed by E. Blount, but the S. R. entry is for T. Thorpe. Both translations, *The City of God* and *The New World,* were made by John Healey, and their Dedications, to the Earl of Pembroke with all his titles displayed, were both signed T. Thorpe. As *The New World* preceded, and *The City of God* followed, the publication of

Shakespeare's *Sonnets*, I presume that the question as to "Mr. W. H." being possibly intended for Lord William Herbert, Earl of Pembroke, Knight of the honorable order, &c., is finally disposed of. I may add that for other publications by T. Thorpe we have to go back to Chapman's *Byron*, 1608, or forward to *Histriomastix*, 1611.

But here I am met by the fact that the "Mr. W. H." to whom the *Sonnets* are dedicated is said to be their "only begetter." If begetter mean direct cause as addressee, the Dedication would require this begetter to be Southampton, which is absurd. If begetter mean obtainer for the press, it must be shown that "begetter" can mean "getter." It is said that Minshew shows this; but although he says that *get* can be used for *beget*, he nowhere asserts the converse; and his statement that *woorthbringen* in Low Dutch may mean *to beget* does not imply that *bring forth* is admissible for *beget* in English. It is true that Dr. Karl Elze says "that *to beget* can be used in this sense admits of no doubt;" but, like most of his statements (when not stolen from other men), no proof is attached to this one: nor has an instance of such use ever been given of later date than Robert of Gloucester. But that a dedicatee might be termed a begetter, as being the cause of publication or production to the outer world, is, I think, evident from W. Rowley's Dedication of *The Fair Quarrel:* "This child of the Muses is yours; whoever begat it, 'tis laid to your charge: and for aught I know, you must father and keep it too." I do not think the poet is here meant by "whoever begat it," but rather the suggester of the plot, the patron who commanded the play to be written. Compare also Chapman, *Chabot*, v. 2, "The corruption of a captain may beget a gentleman-usher, and a gentleman-usher may beget a lord, whose wit may beget a poet, and a poet may get a thousand pound a year," where *beget* means simply *produce* (cf. just before "a tumult may beget a captain"); but when the meaning *obtain* is wanted, *get* is the word used. I infer from these passages, and from the general use of the word *begetter*, that it means here not the obtainer for the press, but the dedicatee at whose expense they were produced to the public, and possibly the original suggester of their being written.

Before drawing any inference as to the personality of Mr. W. H., the date at which the *Sonnets* were written must be considered. They were certainly written after 1594, May 9, the date of publication of the *Lucreece* Dedication, which is so often paralleled in them. But the earliest internal reference of definite date is in 14, where the conjunction "of plagues, of dearths, of season's quality," seems to point to the plagues of 1592 and 1593, succeeded by the dearths of 1594, 1595, 1596, and the irregularity of the seasons in 1595, 1596, alluded to more fully in *A Midsummer Night's Dream*, ii., i. 87 *seq.* Possibly this Sonnet may date 1595, but 1596 seems more likely. In 21 Spenser's *Amoretti*, S. R. 1594, Nov. 19, are certainly intended (compare especially *Amoretti*, 9, 15, 84): this would imply also a date of 1595 at the earliest. The latest definite internal date is in 107, in which the moon's eclipse (the fears for the Spanish invasion and the safety of the Queen and her kingdom) has passed over, "and peace proclaims olives of endless age." This can hardly be made to fit with any date but that of the peace of Vervins, 1598 April. Any such reference to Cynthia-Elizabeth could not have been written during the reign of her successor. Most of the Sonnets were then written (unless we adopt the unnecessary hypothesis that we may change their order as we please) before the notice of them in Meres' *Palladis Tamia*, S. R. 1598, Sept. 7, as "sugared sonnets among his private friends."

To me, then, it seems that " Mr. W. H." must be sought
for; not among Shakespeare's relations, for he had certainly
nothing to do with the publication—he would not have
left the Dedication to the bookseller, nor allowed such a
conceited "forewords" as Thorpe's: nor among Thorpe's
literary connexions, for he seems to have none but Chapman and Healey about this time: but among Southampton's
friends.   We must seek for one likely to get at the MS.; to
publish it, of course with Southampton's consent; to accept
the Dedication; and yet to demand that his incognito should
be preserved.   Such a person was Mr. William Hervey, afterwards created an Irish baronet, 1619, May 31, but in 1609
the widower of Southampton's mother.   Surely there is
nothing extravagant in supposing that Southampton, unwilling that these, the finest of all the English Sonnets
written in connective series, should be lost to posterity,
equally unwilling to publish them himself on account of the
black lady episode, should have induced his stepfather to
issue them without mention of Southampton's name, whence,
I think, came the insertion of the word "only" in "the
only begetter."   Southampton had really inspired them, but
W. H. had to father them.   W. H., so long a riddle to us,
was in all appearance equally so to his contemporaries, and
assuredly to the publisher.   Were it otherwise, allusions to
him would have been discovered.   In fact, G. Withers'
Dedication to [1] *Abuses stript and whipt*, 1613, Jan. 16, " To
himself G. Wither wisheth all happiness," which certainly
parodies the Sonnet Dedication, looks as if he understood
W. H. to be William Himself, or a misprint for W. S.   If
so, he anticipated the great Teutonic discovery of Barnstorff

[1] Elze makes the interval from 1609 May 20 to 1613 Jan. 16 "two
years." This deficiency of elementary arithmetical knowledge explains his
aversion to "metrical tests." He was always amusing to look at when
scanning and counting on his fingers.

and Karpf. But was this interpretation mischievously inspired by W. Hervey? *Abuses stript* was printed by G.
Eld for F. Burton, and so was Southwell's *Fourfold Medita-
tion*, 1606, May 21, which was procured for publication by
" W. H." See *Athenæum*, 1873, ii. 528, 661. Marston's
Scourge of Villany was also dedicated to " his most esteemed
and best-beloved self," but this was in 1598, and can have
no reference to the 1609 publication of the *Sonnets*.

It will be evident by this time that I believe the Sonnets
1–125 to have been written in one series, addressed to
Southampton c. 1595–8, and dedicated to Mr. William
Hervey in 1609. It remains to test this hypothesis by an
examination of the allusions in the *Sonnets* themselves. I
give a preliminary list of known dates, to which I shall be
able to refer in confirmation of my explanation of them:—

1563. Drayton born. *Ætatis* 31 in 1594.

1564, April c. 23. Shakespeare born. *Ætatis* 32 in 1596.

1573, Oct. 6. Southampton born. *Ætatis* 22 in 1595.

1592, Feb. 4. Daniel's *Delia* published.

1592, Aug. 8. Nash's *Piers Penniless' Supplication*
published with Sonnet to Amyntas.

1592, Sept. 22. Constable's *Diana* published.

1593. Lodge's *Phillis* with the Elstred Sonnets published.

1593, April 18. *Venus and Adonis* published.

1593, April 23. Markham's *Thyrsis and Daphne* published.

1593, May. 10. Barnes' *Parthenophil* published with
verses to Southampton, but dedicated to W. Percy.

1593, Sept. 17. Nash's *Jack Wilton* published with
prose dedication to Southampton.

1593, Oct. 1. G. Harvey's *Letter* published with
Sonnet to Southampton.

c. 1594, June. After the *Lucreece* Dedication Shakespeare becomes personally acquainted with Southampton.

1594, May 9. *Lucreece* published with Dedication to Southampton.

1594, May 30. Drayton's *Idea* Sonnets published.

1592 June–Dec., 1593 Feb.–1594 Oct. Shakespeare's company without settled theatre: "travelling;" in 1592–3 on account of the great plague.

c. 1594. *Edward* 3 revived with Shakespeare's addition of the Countess of Salisbury's story before the *Heroical Epistles.*

1594, Sept. 3. *Willobie his Avisa* published.

1594, Nov. 19. Spenser's *Amoretti* published.

1595, Sept. 20. Markham's *Sir R. Grenville* published with Sonnet Dedication to Southampton.

1595, Sept. 23. Southampton in love with E. Vernon.

1595, Nov. 17. Peele's *Anglorum Feriæ* contain blank verse lines on Southampton.

1595, Dec. 1. *Edward* 1 published.

1596, Feb. 13. Peter Colse's *Penelope's Complaint* published just before the second edition of *Avisa.*

1596, Mar. 2. Florio's *Dictionary* published with prose Dedication to Southampton.

1596, July 22. Henry Lord Hunsdon died.

1596, Aug. 11. Hamnet Shakespeare buried. Shakespeare probably at Stratford.

1597, Easter. New place purchased. Shakespeare at Stratford.

1597, Mar. 5. G. Carey, Chamberlain. 1 *Henry* 4 produced soon after, and Shakespeare's company "travel" in June. They were at Bristol and Dover in September: probably in trouble for the Oldcastle-Falstaff affair.

1597, July–Oct. Southampton away with Essex.

1597 Oct.–1598, Feb. 8. Southampton in Parliament: in Nov. his blow to Willoughby was given.

1597, Dec. 19. Rudolph Graphium's *Prognostication* published.

1598, April The Peace of Vervins.

1598, Feb. 10–Nov. Southampton abroad: soon after his return he married E. Vernon.

1598, Sept. 7. Meres' *Palladis Tamia* published.

1599. *The Passionate Pilgrim* published, containing Sonnets 138, 144.

1599, June 4. *Avisa* called in.

c. 1600. *The Fair Maid of the Exchange* [? by Markham] acted.

1607, Nov. Southampton's mother died.

1608, Oct. 6. *The Dumb Knight*, by Markham and Machin, published.

1609, Jan. 18. J. Healey's translation of Hall's *Mundus alter et idem* published.

1609, May 20. The *Sonnets*, with *A Lover's Complaint*, published.

1610. J. Healey's translation of S. Augustine's *City of God* published.

1619, May 31. Mr. W. Hervey created an Irish baron.

In this list all dates are exact except the few to which " c." is prefixed.

Now returning to the *Sonnets*: in 14 there is the reference to " plagues, dearths, and season's quality," which I have already fixed as written in 1595–6 at the earliest; in 21 the palpable allusions to Spenser's *Amoretti*, which cannot have been written till after 1594 Nov.; in 23 the " books " mentioned must be *Venus and Adonis* and *Lucreece*, and therefore this Sonnet must be later than 1594 May. Their " eloquence and dumb presagers " of " silent love " is a pal-

pable hit at the "silent rhetoric" and "dumb eloquence"
of Daniel's *Rosamond*, S. R. 1593, Feb. 4. The last line
of the Sonnet—

> "To hear with eyes belongs to love's fine wit,"

is to my mind not serious, but a very delicate thrust at
Daniel's lines, often, but more roughly, burlesqued by subsequent writers, Jonson among them. The repeated references to the *Lucreece* Dedication do not help us as to date
further than to show that 18, 26, 34, 81, 108, &c., were
written after 1594 May. In 27, 48, 50 the "travel" is
doubtless that of the company when strolling in the pro-
vinces, and must refer to that of 1593 or 1597. As that
of 1593 would be anterior to the *Lucreece* Dedication, and
preceding Sonnets require a later date, I would refer this to
1597, when Shakespeare was "in disgrace with Fortune
and men's eyes" for the Oldcastle plays. The Sonnet was
certainly contemporaneous with the "travel," as is clearly
shown by the use of the present tense. I date it c. June,
after the production of 1 *Henry* 4 c. April, and before
Southampton's leaving in July. The "precious friends"
deceased in 30 certainly include Marlow, who died 1593,
and possibly his son Hamnet, who died 1596 Aug.

The batch 33–42 appear to me to absolutely necessitate
the assumption of the theory that Southampton is addressed,
he who "was but one hour mine," 33; who "made me
travel forth without my cloak" (appear publicly as an
author), 34, can be only Southampton, to whom the poems
were dedicated; while

> "I may not evermore acknowledge thee
> Lest my bewailed guilt should do the shame,
> Nor thou with *public* kindness honor me" (36),

as clearly indicates a refusal to accept any further dedication by him from Shakespeare; they are henceforth to be "twain." Nevertheless these Sonnets were to be published, even without a Dedication; for how could "my slight Muse please these curious days" if unpublished? and to "thy praise" too? 38. How else could they promise "eternity" to the youth addressed? The eclipses (35) of the moon (Cynthia–Elizabeth) and the sun (Southampton; cf. 33, last line, and 34) are, I think, conclusive of a date when Shakespeare was temporarily out of favour with both Court and Patron, and no such date can I find but 1597, c. June. I will treat of 40–42 along with the second series, 126–154. In "when thou art gone," 44, there is again a clearly definite date, if my general view of the *Sonnets* be a true one. This one must have just preceded Southampton's leaving England in July 1597. In 47, 50 we find the "travel" [of 1597, I suppose] still continuing; in 53 a distinct intimation that Adonis in *Venus and Adonis* was in 1593 intended for a portrait of Southampton, then disinclined to love: the early Sonnets, 1–17, being, in my judgment, written after he had met Elizabeth Vernon in 1595. I think it more likely that the poet should encourage his known passion by urging marriage on him than that he should venture to initiate such a subject before his own inclination had been disclosed.

Shakespeare's "age" and wrinkled brow, 13, have been adduced as proofs of a late date for the poem; but whoever has traced the continual allusions to his predecessors' Sonnets will, I think, see nothing more in this than an allusion to Drayton's *Idea*, 44, "Age rules my lines with wrinkles in my face." Shakespeare in 1597 was *ætatis* 33; Drayton in 1594 was 31: this is a similar reference to the Daniel allusion in 23. The "shame" in 72, like the "motley" in 110 and the "brand" in 111, cannot, I think,

mean, as they are usually interpreted, simply the quality of
acting which Shakespeare professed; he was never ashamed
of that: rather they indicate some particular occasion of
his having, as an actor, ("motley,") and playwright ("that
which I bring forth," 72, cannot mean acting merely), got
into disgrace for his "public manners," 111, as a satirist.
All this agrees with the 1597 date and the Falstaff-Oldcastle trouble. Again, in 76 Shakespeare defends himself
for writing in the "noted weed" of Sonneting, and not
"glancing aside with the time to new-found methods."
Sonnets were popular till 1595. Spenser's *Amoretti* were
the last important series published before their revival by
Drummond in 1616. Thus again we are driven to a
date not long after 1595.

I now reach the decisive crux of all Sonnet theories, the
"alien pen" of 87. Who was he? He was some one who
had "dedicated" some poem to Southampton, and the Dedication was in verse, 79. He had praised his "virtue" and
"beauty," 79; had a "proud sail," 80; was "taught by
spirits," by an "affable familiar ghost," 86; and there is a
strong presumption that the Dedication was in Sonnet form:
it must have been after Shakespeare's *Venus and Adonis*,
1593 April, and probably after *Lucreece*, 1594 May.

Nash's lines to Amyntas in 1592 (suggested by Collier,
and adopted by me in an ill-advised attempt to "arch-
angelise" Shakespeare, as others had attempted for Shelley)
are too early; his Dedication of *Jack Wilton* is in prose:
G. Harvey's Sonnet, 1593 Oct., for which I have said all I
could pp. 65, 128, &c., is possibly meant. Peele's *Anglorum
Feriæ* lines are not a Dedication, nor are those of Barnes;
and Florio's Dedication of his *Dictionary* is a prose one. I do
not think any of these are "*the* worthier pen," 79, though
some may be included under "every alien pen," 78: the

" better spirit " is much more likely to be Gervase Markham. His *Thyrsis and Daphne*, published five days after *Venus and Adonis*, and unfortunately not extant, was no doubt written in rivalry thereof. His *Sir R. Grenville*, 1595 Sept. (just the date required), contains explanations of most of the allusions to Southampton's " eyes, virtue," &c.; and though his beauty is not mentioned, that may have been descanted upon in the lost *Thyrsis*: he was " learned," had " proud sail " with a vengeance, and his poem was dictated by the " spirit " of Grenville. All this I have pointed out under Markham; but I did not then know that *The Fair Maid of the Exchange*, c. 1600, was probably written by him. In this play and in *The Dumb Knight* Markham ridicules *Venus and Adonis* in almost identical words in a way unparalleled in any other author, and this persistent satire against Shakespeare's poems, I think, distinctly indicates that Markham was, if not the second poet, at any rate one of the alien pens alluded to.

One more name in this very difficult question requires notice. Drayton in his *Matilda*, 1594, had inserted a complimentary allusion to Shakespeare's *Lucreece*, " lately revived to live another age." This allusion was retained in 1596, but omitted in all subsequent editions. By 13th Mar. 1598 he had left Shakespeare's company, for whom he had written *The Merry Devil*, and joined the Admiral's men. He was mixed up in the Falstaff-Oldcastle affair. He would suit the description of " a better pen," &c., better than Markham or Harvey. The only missing link (a most important one) is the absence of any dedicatory Sonnet to Lord Southampton. I cannot get access to the early editions of his works (as my health does not allow me to work at the British Museum), but it seems possible that his suppressed Sonnet to L. S. may have been addressed to L[ord] S[outhampton]. If so,

Olcon, whom I have identified conjecturally with Sir John Davies, would more probably be Shakespeare, whose influence at Court was undoubtedly considerable at the time of James' accession.   Were this one link discovered I should undoubtedly pronounce in favour of Drayton as *the* other poet. The reason for Shakespeare's taking his Sonnets as a model would be apparent at once.

In 83, 117 the reason for Southampton's refusal to accept a Dedication from Shakespeare (cf. 36, 38) slips out. He had been "silent," had written no poem for three years, and his lordship, now accustomed to frequent Dedications from others, thought himself neglected.   I suspect that Shakespeare had offered him the Dedication of a *play*.   The first authorised publication of a play by him was that of *Richard* 2, entered 1597, Aug. 29, and the offer would be made just before that date.   Southampton, who had (whatever we may think as to the truth of the story that he gave him £1000) most certainly befriended Shakespeare, may well have been glad to accept Dedications of poems, yet reject those of plays by the common players, as Sir T. Walsingham did in the parallel instance of Chapman's *All Fools*.   This would account for all the complaints of his "quality" as an actor in 111, and playwright, 72, &c.   Shakespeare wisely abstained from seeking another patron for his published plays, and after three years ceased to publish them at all. No publication after 1600 Oct. was authorised by him.

In 94 occurs the well-known line, "Lilies that fester smell far worse than weeds," taken from *Edward* 3 (S. R. 1595, Dec. 1), of which more hereafter.   In 97, 98 the absence of Southampton in the "summer" and early autumn exactly agrees with the date of his being away with Essex, 1597 July–Oct., and in 104 the three years "since first I saw you" must reckon from 1594 to 1597.   I think that Shakespeare's *personal* acquaintance with Southampton began with his waiting on him with a presentation copy of *Lucrcece* in May 1594, and that the exact date of Sonnet 104 is 1597 Oct., when Southampton returned. The careful avoidance of the change of *Summer* to Autumn in the Sonnet induces me to think this: there had been four such since 1594 May, when Southampton must have known Shakespeare personally (which he certainly did not in 1593; compare the tone of the Dedications of *Venus and Adonis* and *Lucreece*); but only three changes from *Spring* to Autumn, for Spring was reckoned to begin in March. In 107 comes what I take to be the allusion to the Vervins peace of 1598 April, and the mention of the mistaken "sad augurs." who had prophesied disasters to Elizabeth from an eclipse[1] of the moon, probably in Graphium's *Prognostication*, 1597, Dec. 19, which unfortunately is, I believe, not extant. I would date the final presentation of Sonnets to Southampton in 1598 Nov., on his return from abroad, and before his marriage. The *Envoy*, 126, marks their conclusion, and I cannot find any indication, however remote, of a later date, nor anything that indicates a want of chronological order in this series. Their not being arranged in order of subject rather confirms than disproves a chronological sequence. They all seem to have been written between 1595 and 1598.

I must now turn to the second series, 127–154, and those in the first series, 40–42, &c., connected with them in subject but not necessarily in date. I have in my *Life of Shakespeare* already treated of *Willobie his Avisa*, but can now give some further particulars. It was published 1594,

---

[1] For the "eclipse" compare Greene's *Menaphon*, Lyly's *Endymion*, but above all *Anthony and Cleopatra*, iii. 13, 154, "Our terrene moon Is now eclipsed, and it portends the fall of Anthony."

Sept. 3, and contains the story of one Avice, a young inn-keeper's daughter of the George in the Evesham vale: twenty years of age; married; tempted by a Frenchman, an Anglo-German, an "old player, W. S., who not long before had tried the courtesy of the like passion," and was in 1594 newly recovered; but she resisted all these. Then at first sight of her H. W. Italo Hispalensis was infected with a fantastical fit, and consulted W. S., who persuaded him it was a matter easy to be compassed; but the obtaining his purpose seemed impossible till Time and Necessity, if not healed, yet in part eased his malady. W. S. is univer-sally admitted to be the "old player," William Shakespeare; and until some other H. W. than Henry Wriothesley is found among his connexions at this date, I shall have no doubt that this Avisa story is the same as that of the black woman to whom this second series of Sonnets is addressed. She in like manner to Avisa has thrown over Shakespeare, who has courted her, in favour of H. W. All modern editors and critics (except Dr. Ingleby) appear to have believed that Henry Willobie was a genuine name; and even in 1595 W. Clarke in his *Polymanteia* mentions Willobie with Britton and Percy as then sweet singers at Oxford; but in 1596, Feb. 14, Peter Colse published his *Penelope's Complaint*, in which he says *Avisa* was by an "unknown author," and that she, the meanest of matrons, is "seeking by slander of her superiors to eternise her folly." (See Bridges' *Restituta*, iii. 532. I have not access to Colse's book, and cannot find a copy in the British Museum.) All this is in accordance with my interpretation. On 30th June 1596 the equally fictitious editor, Hadrian Dorrell, re-published *Avisa*, with a statement that Henry Willoby was dead, but had left a poem on Susanna; but his brother, Thomas Willoby, still alive, whose poem, *The Victory of*

English Chastity, is inserted after the "apology shewing the true meaning of" *Avisa*. As this Henry Willoughby is described in the 1594 edition as then a young man in Her Majesty's service and a scholar of good hope, but in 1596 is said to have written *Avisa* thirty-five years since, and again in the author's conclusion is said to "have not any further essayed: and whether he be alive or dead I know not," there can be no doubt whatever of his fictitious character. The 1596 edition of *Avisa* was called in, (S. R. 1599, June 4,) with Cutwode's *Caltha Poetarum* and Hall's *Satires*, all libellous productions: but that the copies were not destroyed, but reissued in 1605 with merely a new title-page will be evident on comparison of the parallel case of Hall's book, which was republished in 1602 with a new title-page for Books i.–iii., but the old 1599 title-page unaltered for Books iv.–vi. The strangest thing in connexion with this matter is Brydges' acceptance of Dorrell's equivocations on P. Colse as "pertinent remarks."

I take this second series of Sonnets 127–154 to have been written about 1595, contemporaneously with 40–42. They are all addressed to the lady, with whom, according to them, the "new actor" had been more successful than the "old player." The only one that can be interpreted into more than an eventless attack on Shakespeare's part is 152 ; and I cannot admit the punctuation of the modern editors. I would rather punctuate consistently with the old edition:—

> "But thou art twice forsworn to me (love) swearing ;
> In act—thy bedvow broke and new faith torn ;
> In vowing—new hate after new love bearing."

I take the "bedvow broke" to mean, not her unfaithfulness to her husband, but her refusal to fulfil a promised assignation with Shakespeare. So in 142 I would point—

"those lips of thine,
That have profaned their scarlet ornaments
And sealed false bonds of love, as oft as mine
Robbed others' beds' revenues of their rents."

"Their scarlet ornaments" occurs also in *Edward* 3, ii. 1 ; and as the line,

"Lilies that fester smell far worse than weeds" (94, cf. 69),

is taken from the same scene, the natural inference is that the second series is also later than the play: that 94 is later than the play is clear, for it cannot date, if the series is continuous, earlier than 1597, and the play was published 1595, Dec. 1.

I now pass to another and larger topic : Shakespeare's views as to Sonnet writing generally.

In *Love's Labour's Lost* he not only introduces two Sonnets proper which were published separately in *The Passionate Pilgrim* as poems by him, but uses the Sonnet form in the dialogue in several instances : I do not know where to find a parallel to this. At this time he was evidently smitten with this form of composition. The compilation of Sonnets in this play (iv. 3, 14, 134, 158) is spoken of as a serious means of gaining the favour of a mistress. In *All's Well that Ends Well* Helen's letter (part, no, doubt, of the older form of the play) is serious and in the Sonnet form (iii. 4). Yet even at this time he was struck with the absurdity of long series of Sonnets such as Sidney's *Astrophel and Stella*, Drayton's *Idea*, Daniel's *Delia*, &c., for he makes Armado say (*Love's Labour's Lost*, i. 1, 190)—

"Assist me, some *extemporal* god of rhyme, for I am sure I shall turn *sonnet*. Devise wit : write pen : for I am for *whole volumes in folio.*"

In the *Two Gentlemen of Verona* (iii. 2, 68, 92) the Sonnet is seriously recommended to Thurio by Proteus :—

"You must lay lime to tangle her desires
By wailful sonnets, whose composèd rhymes
Should be full-fraught with serviceable vows.
Say that upon the altar of her beauty
You sacrifice your tears, your sighs, your heart.

.   .   .   .   .

This, or else nothing, will inherit her."

Thurio approves of this, and says he "has a sonnet that will serve the turn;" and the Duke says that Proteus must have been in love to give such advice, and mentions the "force of heaven-bred poesy." Again, in 1598, c. Spring, he put two of the Choruses in his revision of *Romeo and Juliet* (Q. 2) in Sonnet shape; but after this we find no favourable allusion to Sonnets in any way. Passing over the mention of the *Book of Songs and Sonnets* in the *Merry Wives of Windsor*, we find a distinct sneer at Sonnet-writing in *Much Ado about Nothing* (1598, after Sept.), where Benedick promises Margaret "a sonnet in praise of her beauty in so high a style that no man living shall come over it" (v. 2); and Claudio produces one (v. 4) really written by Benedick, which he calls

"A halting sonnet of his own pure brain.

So in *Henry* 5 (iii. 7) we find the Dauphin quoting the Sonnet he had made in praise of his horse which began "Wonder of nature." The date of this play is also certainly 1599. Finally, in *Twelfth Night* (iii. 4) Malvolio mentions "the very true sonnet, *Please one and please all.*" The date of this play is also certain, namely, 1602. It is proven, then, that Shakespeare, who in his early plays was an admirer of the Sonnet, never uses this form of verse in dialogue after 1598, nor even mentions it with approbation. If he speak of it at all, it is rather disparagingly than otherwise, and after 1602 never even alludes to it in his plays in any way. It seems clear that at first he was fond of it;

then he ceased to care for it; lastly he despised it: all which is consistent with the date 1598 Nov. which I assign for his own latest productions of this kind.

I will now try to show that the *Sonnets* have a direct reference to Drayton's *Idea's Mirror*.

Sonnet 144 runs thus:—

> "Two loves I have of comfort and despair
>   Which like two spirits do suggest me still:
> The better angel is a man right fair,
>   The worser spirit a woman colour'd ill.
> To win me soon to hell my female evil
>   Tempteth my better angel from my side
> And would corrupt my saint to be a devil,
>   Wooing his purity with her foul pride.
> And whether that my angel be turn'd fiend
>   Suspect I may, yet not directly tell,
> But being both from me, both to each friend,
>   I guess one angel in another's hell.
> Yet this shall I ne'er know, but live in doubt
> Till my bad angel fire my good one out."

Drayton's 20th Sonnet is this:—

> "An evil spirit your beauty haunts me still;
>   Wherewith alas I have been long possest;
> Which ceaseth not to tempt me to each ill,
>   Nor gives me once but one poor minute's rest.
> In me it speaks, whether I sleep or wake,
>   And when by means to drive it out I try,
> With greater torments then it me doth take
>   And tortures me in most extremity;
> Before my face it lays down my despairs
>   And hastes me on unto a sudden death,
> Now tempting me to drown myself in tears,
>   And then in sighing to give up my breath.
> Thus am I still provokt to every evil
> By this good-wicked spirit, sweet Angel-Devil."

The possession of the dark woman by the angel-man exactly corresponds to that of Drayton by his angel-woman.

Compare next Drayton's 44th Sonnet with those in which
Shakespeare speaks of his old age :—

> "Whilst thus my pen strives to eternize thee,
>   *Age rules my lines with wrinkles in my face,*
>   Where in the *map* of all my misery
>   Is model'd out the world of my disgrace ;
>   Whilst in despite of tyrannizing rhymes
>   Medea-like I make thee young again,
>   Proudly thou scorn'st my world-out-wearing rhymes
>   And murther'st virtue with thy coy disdain :.
>   And, though in youth my youth untimely perish
>   To keep thee from oblivion and the grave,
>   Ensuing ages yet my rhymes shall cherish
>   Where I entomb'd my better part shall save ;
>   And, though this earthly body fade and die,
>   My name shall mount upon eternity."

When Drayton wrote this he was just of the same age
(thirty-one) as Shakespeare was in 1595. What becomes
of the argument that Shakespeare must have been old when
he wrote—

> "But when my glass shows me myself indeed
>   Beated and chopt with tanned antiquity,"
>
> *Sonnet 62,*

and similar passages ?

Compare also with line 3—

> "Thus is his cheek the *map* of days outworn,"
>
> *Sonnet 68,*

with lines 5, 6—

> "Against my love shall be as I am now
>   With Time's injurious hand crusht and o'erworn ;
>   When hours have drain'd his blood and fill'd his brow
>   *With lines and wrinkles :*
>   His beauty shall in these black lines be seen,
>   And they shall live and he in them be green,"
>
> *Sonnet 63,*

with line 8—

> "Love is my sin and thy dear virtue hate,"
>
> *Sonnet 142,*

with the latter lines—

> "The earth can yield me but a common grave
> When you entombed in men's eyes shall lie.
> Your monument shall be my gentle verse," &c.,
>
> *Sonnet* 81.

There are many other similar passages, *e.g.*, Sonnet 107.
Again, compare—

> "I myself am mortgaged to thy will .
> The statute of thy beauty thou wilt take
> Thou usurer that put'st forth all to use," &c.,
>
> *Sonnet* 134,

with Drayton's 3rd Sonnet—

> "My heart hath paid such grievous usury
> That all their wealth lies in thy beauty's looks ;
> And all is thine which hath been due by me,
> And I a bankrupt quite undone by thee."

Or Sonnet 133—

> "I being pent in thee
> Perforce am thine and all that is in me,"

with Drayton's 11th—

> "Since you one were, I never since was one,
> Since you in me, myself since out of me,
> Transported from myself into your being."

Or Sonnet 17—

> "If I could write the beauty of your eyes
> And in fresh numbers number all your graces,
> The age to come would say this poet lies,
> Such heavenly touches ne'er toucht earthly faces,"

with Drayton's 17th—

> "Pass on and to posterity tell this,
> Yet see thou tell but truly what hath been ;
> Say to our nephews that thou once hast seen
> In perfect human shape all heavenly bliss,
> And bid them mourn, nay more despair, with thee ;
> That she is gone, her like again to see."

Or Sonnet 141—

> " In faith I do not love thee with mine eyes . . .
>   Nor are mine ears with thy tongue's tune delighted,
> Nor tender feeling to base touches prone,
>   Nor taste nor smell," &c.,

with Drayton's 29th—

> " But he with beauty first corrupted sight,
>   My hearing bribed by her tongue's harmony,
> My taste by her sweet lips drawn with delight,
>   My smelling won with her breath's spicery,
> But when my touching came to play his part," &c.

Or Sonnet 142—

> " Be it lawful I love thee as thou lov'st those
>   Whom thine eyes woo as mine importune thee,"

with Drayton's 43rd—

> " Why should your fair eyes with such sovereign grace
>   Disperse their rays on every vulgar spirit,
> Whilst I in darkness in the self-same place
>   Get not one glance to recompense my merit."

Or Sonnet 112—

> " You are my all the world, and I must strive
>   To know my shames and praises from your tongue ;
> None else to me, nor I to none alive,
>   That my steel'd sense or changes right or wrong ;
> In so profound abysm I throw all care
>   Of other's voices, that my adder's sense
> To critic and to flatterer stopped are.
>   Mark how with my neglect I do dispense :
> You are so strongly in my purpose bred
>   That all the world beside methinks are dead,"

with Drayton's 47th—

> " In pride of wit, when high desire of fame
>   Gave life and courage to my laboring pen,
> And first the sound and virtue of my name
>   Won grace and credit in the eyes of men,

> With those the throngèd theatres that press
>   I in the circuit for the laurel strove,
> Where the full praise I freely must confess
>   In heat of blood a modest mind might move
> With shouts and claps at every little pause.
>   When the proud round on every side hath rung
> Sadly I sit unmoved with the applause,
>   As though to me it nothing did belong.
> No public glory vainly I pursue.
> All that I seek is to eternize you ; "

or, finally (for these comparisons might be extended to almost
every Sonnet in Drayton's sixty-three), compare Sonnets
87, 89—

> " Farewell ! thou art too dear for my possessing . . .
>   I will acquaintance strangle and look strange ;
>   Be absent from thy walks, and in my tongue
>   Thy sweet beloved name no more shall dwell,"

with Drayton's 61st—

> [1] " Shake hands, for ever cancel all our vows,
>   And when we meet at any time again
>   Be it not seen in either of our brows
>   That we one jot of former love retain."

There are similarities between Daniel's Sonnets and Shakespeare's : also between Spenser's and Shakespeare's ; but
Drayton's are evidently those he had specially in view. He
has at least three corresponding passages with him for one
with any other writer; and the likeness is much closer, especially in those parts of Drayton which are most removed from
commonplace. It is impossible here to give full evidence ;
but any one who will saturate himself with Shakespeare's
Sonnets, and then read Drayton's, will find, as I have done,
that hardly a stanza of Drayton has been left unused by
Shakespeare ; and as we cannot, from the manifest allusions
in the Sonnets of the latter, date them earlier than the

---

[1] This passage is conclusive as to the meaning of *Macbeth*, i. 2 :—
    " Ne'er shook hands nor bade farewell to him."

Dedication to *Lucreece* (1594), which was printed in the same year as *Idea's Mirrour*, we are necessitated to reject the alternative hypothesis that Drayton may have copied Shakespeare.

Summing up our evidence, then, we are certain of these points :—

That the publishing of series of Love-Sonnets culminated in 1594–5.

That of the series published that which has the greatest resemblance to Shakespeare's is Drayton's *Idea's Mirrour* (1594).

That Drayton was Shakespeare's *friend*—one of his Mermaid companions.

That after 1596 the writing of Love-Sonnets in a series, so as to form a continuous poem, was abandoned, after having been in continual favour for fifteen years at least ; the fashion having been followed by such men as Sidney, Watson, Spenser, Drayton, and Daniel.

Coupling with these data the utter failure of all attempts to explain the *whole* of these poems on any supposition of their being fragmentary compositions (although some of them may easily be accounted for on such a hypothesis) ; the singular intermingling of trivial matters with serious ; their *studied* obscurity ; and the fact that Shakespeare made no attempt to publish them ; I venture to conclude :

That both series were specially aimed at Drayton's *Idea's Mirrour*, but that in them, studiedly obscure as they are, there are enshrined some of the most delicately carved images, some of the most exquisitely designed ornaments, some of the most perfectly ethereal imaginations, that the hand of our greatest sculptural poet ever produced. They have, I believe, been a puzzle to posterity, because they were meant to be a puzzle to his contemporaries ; they have been overrated by some, who saw depth in those parts of them that were meant to be obscure; they have been underrated by more, who saw only their difficulty and could not appreciate their beauty; they have been abused by most, who could see their facts but not their metaphor, their biography but not their poetry.

I repeat, in conclusion, that if the slightest external evidence were forthcoming of any connexion between Drayton and Southampton, so that we might identify Drayton with the second poet of Sonnet 83, not a difficulty in the interpretation of the whole series would remain unsolved.

SHARPE, LEWIS. (Play.)

1. *The Noble Stranger*, C., 1640.

Acted at Salisbury Court.

SHARPHAM, EDWARD. (Plays.)

1. 1606, May 6, for John Trundle and John Busbye. *The Fleire*, 1607, 1610, 1615, 1621; but better authority and license was required, so on 21st Nov. Trundle's share was transferred to A. Johnson and Buck's license was obtained.

2. 1607, June 29, for John Trundle and Arthur Johnson. *Cupid's Whirligig*, C., 1607, 1611, 1616, 1630.

Sharpham was a member of the Middle Temple.

1. *The Fleire* was acted at the Blackfriars by the children of the Revels after they lost their right to the name of Queen's Revels: therefore in 1605–6.

2. *Cupid's Whirligig*, by E. S., was acted by the children of His Majesty's Revels in 1606 or 1607; most likely 1607. Founded on Boccaccio's *Decameron*, vii. 6. It contains an allusion to *The Valiant Welshman*.

SHIRLEY, JAMES.   (Plays and Masks.)

3. *The Wedding*, C., 1629, for J. Grove (cf. S. R. 1638, April 28), 1633, 1660.

6. 1630, Feb. 26. for J. Grove.   *The Grateful Servant*, C., 1630, 1637, n.d.

1. 1631, Feb. 25, for F. Constable.   *The School of Compliment*, C., 1631, 1637, 1667 (*Love Tricks*).

10. 1632, Feb. 9, for W. Cooke.   *The Changes*, C., 1632.

12. 1632, Nov. 9, for W. Cooke.   *Honor and Riches*, 1633, 1659 (*Honoria and Mammon*).

5. 1633, Jan. 15, for W. Cooke.   *The Witty Fair One*, C., 1633.

15. 1633, Mar. 19, for W. Cooke.   *The Bird in the Cage*, C., 1633.

19. 1634, Jan. 24, for W. Cooke.   *The Triumph of Peace*, mask, 1633 (three editions).

7. 1634, Nov. 3, for W. Cooke.   *The Traitor*, T., 1635, 1638.

11. 1637, April 13, for W. Cooke and A. Crooke.   *Hyde Park*, C., 1637.

24. 1637, April 13, for W. Cooke and A. Crooke.   *The Lady of Pleasure*, C., 1637.

17. 1637, April 13, for W. Cooke and A. Crooke.   *The Young Admiral*, T. C., 1637.

20. 1637, Oct. 18, for W. Cooke and A. Crooke.   *The Example*, C., 1637.

18. 1637, Oct. 18, for W. Cooke and A. Crooke.   *The Gamester*, C., 1637.

25. 1638, Mar. 13, for W. Cooke and A. Crooke.   *The Duke's Mistress*, T., 1638.

28. 1638, Mar. 13, for W. Cooke and A. Crooke.   *The Royal Master*, T., 1638.

23. 1638, Oct. 24, for W. Cooke and A. Crooke. *Chabot*, T., 1639.

13. 1638, Oct. 24, for W. Cooke and A. Crooke. *The Ball*, C., 1639.

2. 1639, April 12, for W. Cooke. *The Maid's Revenge*, T., 1639.

16. 1639, April 25, for W. Cooke and A. Crooke. *The Nightwalker*, C., 1640, 1661.

21. 1639, April 25, for W. Cooke and A. Crooke. *The Opportunity*, C., 1640.

9. 1639, April 25, for W. Cooke and A. Crooke. *Love's Cruelty*, T., 1640.

22. 1639, April 25, for W. Cooke and A. Crooke. *The Coronation*, C., 1640.

8. 1639, July 20, for W. Cooke. *The Humorous Courtier*, 1640.

14. 1639, Nov. 29, for J. Williams and F. Egglestone. *Arcadia*, P., 1640.

9. 1639, Nov. 29, for J. Williams and F. Egglestone. *Love's Cruelty.* (See *supra*.)

26. 1640, April 28, for R. Whitaker. *St. Patrick for Ireland*, 1640.

27. 1640, April 28, for R. Whitaker. *The Constant Maid*, C., 1640, 1661 (*Love will find out the Way*, 1667).

Six new plays. 37. *The Brothers*, C. 39. *The Sisters*, C. 35. *The Doubtful Heir*, T. C. 36. *The Imposture*, T. C. 38. *The Cardinal*, T. 40. *The Court Secret*, T. C., 1652. 41. *Cupid and Death*, mask, 1653, 1659.

30. *The Gentleman of Venice*, T. C., 1655.

29. *The Politician*, T., 1655.

42. *Ajax and Ulysses*, n.d. [1659 with *Honoria and Mammon*].

33. *The General.* MS.

4. *The Brothers* (*Dick of Devonshire*), T. C.   MS.

James Shirley, descended from the Shirleys of Sussex or
Warwickshire, was born near or in the parish of St. Mary
Woolchurch, London, 13th or 18th Sept. 1596.   On 4th
Oct. 1608 he was admitted into Merchant Taylor's School,
where he was, 11th Mar. 1612 eighth boy or last monitor :
c. 11th June 1612 he entered at St. John's, Oxford.   Dr.
W. Laud, then head of that house, objected to his taking
orders on account of a mole on his left cheek ; he therefore
migrated to Catherine Hall, Cambridge, where he took his
B.A. before 4th Jan. 1618, when his *Eccho*, or *Unfortunate
Lovers* (called in the 1646 poems *Narcissus*, or *The Self-
lover*) was entered S. R.   He was still B.A. when he wrote his
verses on Queen Anne's death, Mar. 1619.   He took his M.A.
and Holy Orders ; held a living in or near St. Albans, Hert-
fordshire ; became a Roman Catholic ; resigned his living ;
and in 1623 was master of St. Albans Grammar School.
In 1624 he removed to London and lived in Gray's Inn,
and took to playmaking.   In 1625, soon after 27th Mar.,
he wrote his *lines on the death of King James ;* in 1628
his *epitaph on the Duke of Buckingham ;* in 1630 his verses
for Massinger's *Renegado,* and *lines on the birth of Prince
Charles ;* in 1633 verses for Ford's *Love's Sacrifice ;* in 1634
lines to the Painter preparing to draw Mrs. Mary Hammond ;
in 1635 *An Elegy on Thomas Viscount Savage ;* in 1636,
c. May, his *lines to the Sisters, Lady B[ishop] and Dia[na]
Curs[on]* (daughters of Nicholas Tufton, Earl of Thanet), on
his departure for Ireland.   In April 1637 he was again in
England, but in October back to Ireland.   He returned
permanently to England between Feb. and 1st June 1640.
When the stage was interdicted in 1642 Shirley retired to
London, where T. Stanley "exhibited" to him.   In 1646
he published his *Poems,* and wrote verses for John Hall's

Horæ Vacivæ and Francis Hawkins' *Youth's Behaviour*; in 1647 verses on and address to the reader in the first Folio of Fletcher's plays. In 1649 he published *The way made plain to the Latin Tongue;* in 1650 wrote verses for Major Wright's *Loving Enemy;* in 1651 for T. Stanley's *Poems,* E. Prestwich's *poem,* and John Ogilby's *Fables of Æsop;* and in 1652 for Brome's *Jovial Crew.* In 1655 *Phyllis of Scyros* was translated by J. S. (not Shirley, I think). After the theatres were closed he had returned to his old trade of teaching, mostly in Whitefriars, and in 1656 he published his *Rudiments of Grammar.* He also assisted Ogilby in his various translations. On 29th October 1666 he and Frances, his second wife, were buried in St.-Giles-in-the-Fields. They died in one day, through " disconsolation at being driven into the fields from their house near Fleet Street by the great fire." Was his first wife the Odelia of his poems ?

1. 1625, Feb. 10. *Love Tricks with Compliments* was licensed for the Cockpit company, then occupied by the Lady Elizabeth's men. It was printed as *The school of Compliment.*

2. 1626, Feb. 9. *The Maid's Revenge* was licensed for the same company, now called the Queen's. The plot is from Reynolds' *God's Revenge against Murder,* ii. 7.

3. 1626, May 31. *The Wedding* must date between 1626, Feb. 9, when Shirley's " second birth " was licensed, and 1629, when it was printed. Cf. iii. 2, " In witness whereof I have hereunto put my hand and seal . . . the last day of the first merry month, and in the second year of the reign of King—Cupid." Verses Commendatory by May, Ford, Habington, &c.

4. 1626, Nov. 4. *The Brothers* was licensed. A play called *Dick of Devonshire* was printed from Eg. MS., 1994, by Mr. A. H. Bullen, and strangely assigned to Heywood,

to whose style it has not the slightest resemblance. This
play is expressly called (near the end) "the story of Two
Brothers : " it is certainly Shirley's, and the date shows
that it is the play now in question. For it is founded on
the adventures of one Richard Pike, the prose account of
whose exploits was published S. R. 18th July 1626. For
the play called *The Brothers* in 1652 (Shirley having determined not to publish this one) see under 1641.

5. 1628, Oct. 3. *The Witty Fair One* was licensed.

6. 1629, Nov. 3. *The Faithful Servant* was licensed.
It was published as *The Grateful Servant*, with verses by
Habington, Massinger, Randolph, &c. Randolph calls it
Servum Fidelem, which proves its identity with the licensed
play.

1631, May 4. *The Traitor* was licensed. It was in
1635 dedicated to the Duke of Newcastle, for whose connexion with Shirley in play-writing see CAVENDISH.

8. 1631, May 7. *The Duke* was licensed. The hero
of *The Humorous Courtier* (which does not appear on the
license-list, and which was not published under Shirley's
superintendence) is the disguised Duke of Parma. I have
no doubt this is the same play, for the license-list seems to
be quite complete. I may note here that every play published
under Shirley's inspection has a Dedication. This play has
not. It was doubtles *The Conceited Duke* of Beeston's 1639
list, absurdly identified by Halliwell, &c., with *The Noble
Gentleman*, a King's men's play.

9. 1631, Nov. 14. *Love's Cruelty* was licensed. It
was published 1640, with a Dedication (not Shirley's) signed
W. A. Can this mean W. Cooke and A. Crooke ? Jonson's
1630 masks are referred to in ii. 2.

All Shirley's plays up to this date were acted by the
Queen's men at the Phœnix.

10. 1632, Jan. 10. *The Changes*, or *Love in a Maze*, was licensed. It was acted by the Revels company at Salisbury Court, and published immediately. These men were evidently proud to get the great Queen's company playwright to write for them. Compare the Prologue and Epilogue, from which it appears that they were not successful at this playhouse. The Epilogue was printed with *Thierry and Theodoret* in 1649, and being accepted by Dyce as rightly there placed, has caused much trouble to critics to explain allusions which have no concern with that play. It appears from iv. 2 that "jigs" were still in fashion; and in i. 2,

"Has he any Fancies in him—can he ravish the ladies?"

surely alludes to Ford's *Francies Chaste and Noble*, then probably on the stage at the Phœnix.

11. 1632, April 20. *Hyde Park* was licensed for the Queen's men. The King's Revels had failed at Salisbury Court and removed to the Fortune. Shirley did not write for public theatres, and returned to his old " private house in Drury Lane," the Cockpit.

12. 1632, Nov. 9. *A Contention for Honor and Riches* was entered S. R. This moral was not acted nor meant to be. *Ubi quid datur oti illudo chartis* is its motto. Ingenuity seems to be Shirley himself. It was probably written during the plague, c. June 1631. It was greatly enlarged and republished in 1659 as *Honoria and Mammon*. Founded on *Decameron* v. 8.

13. 1632, Nov. 18. *The Ball* was licensed. Written by Shirley, says Herbert. Divers lords, &c., were personated so naturally that the license was given on condition of many things being left out. These were accordingly replaced by passages of Chapman's writing, and are easily traceable in

iv. 3 and v. 1, where Lionel, Stephen, and Loveall replace
Travers, Lamount, and Rainbow. In the Chapman part a
comedy called *Bartheme* (read *Bartleme*) is mentioned as
acted at the Bear Garden. Of course this is *Bartholomew
Fair*, acted at the Hope, the rebuilt Paris Garden, in 1614.
This might seem to fix the date of these substituted passages,
but the immediately subsequent allusion to the women actors
of 1629 shows that they were written in 1632. "This is a
Tale of a Tub," iii. 4, indicates that Jonson's play was already
looked for, though not licensed till May 1633. The draining of the fens and the iron-mills are mentioned ii. 2.

14. *The Arcadia*, a Pastoral, was acted by the Queen's
servants at Drury Lane, but was evidently originally presented at Court on a King's Birthday, 19th Nov.; cf. iii. 2,
"to celebrate your majestical birthday." It was not in
1633, for then *The Young Admiral* was presented. It
was before Nabbe's *Covent Garden*, 1632, for that contains
an allusion to the actor who personated Mopsa. Heywood's
Love's Mistress, the scene of which is also in Arcadia, which
was the King's day play of 19th Nov. 1634, is filled with
allusions to it. The most likely date is, therefore, 19th Nov.
1632. This play, being a Court play, does not appear in
Herbert's license-list. I suspect it was written by "command." It was, I think, the play for which Carew wrote
songs and choruses when presented at an entertainment
given by my Lord Chamberlain to their Majesties, for in
it there was "a lover in the disguise of an Amazon" and
"a lady rescued from death by a knight." For the subject
(Sidney's *Arcadia*) compare Day's *Isle of Gulls;* and see
further under Heywood's *Love's Mistress*.

15. 1633, Jan 21. *The Beauties* was licensed. Beyond
doubt the same as *The Bird in a Cage*. The date proves
this; for no other available title exists in the license-list

for this play to be identified with, and it must have been licensed. Compare also i. 1, "What Mantuan *Beauties* thou canst best Delight in, they shall serve thee." The title was changed to make it refer to Prynne, then in prison, to whom Shirley ironically dedicated the play : in which, in direct allusion to the cause of Prynne's imprisonment, he has introduced the Beauties of the Court as acting a play, iii. 3. *The Ring* (*Two Merry Milkmaids*) and *The Invisible Knight* (Query *Hans Beerpot*) are mentioned ii. 1.

16. 1633, May 11. *The Nightwalker*, a play of Fletcher's, was licensed as remodelled by Shirley. See FLETCHER.

17. 1633, July 3. *The Young Admiral* was licensed, with praise from Herbert for its freedom from oaths and obsceneness. It was acted at Court at St. James' 19th Nov., the King's day.

18. 1633, Nov. 11. *The Gamester* was licensed. Acted at Court 16th Feb. 1634. The King made the plot from Malespini's *Ducento Novelle*, Part ii. Nov. 96, or Queen Margaret's *Novels*, i. 8. "The King said it was the best play he had seen for seven years."

19. 1634, Feb. 3. *The Triumph of Peace* was performed at Whitehall by the Four Inns of Court. It was printed beforehand and passed three editions. Inigo Jones made the scenes and ornaments. The performance was repeated at Merchant Taylors' Hall by the King's command Tuesday, Feb. 11. The show through the streets was glorious.

20. 1634, June 24. *The Example* was licensed. The Prologue is interesting ; with allusions to smoking-seats on the stage and the attempt of C. Burbadge to monopolise the Drama by right of inheritance from his father.

21. 1634, Nov. 29. *The Opportunity* was licensed. The Dedication shows that this play (S. R. 1639 April, but not published till 1640, *i.e.*, after 25th Mar.) was emergent

from the press at Shirley's final return from Ireland, and thus refutes Dyce and Gifford, who place this return in 1638.

22. 1635, Feb. 6. *The Coronation* was licensed. It was published as Fletcher's 1640; claimed by Shirley 1652; retained in the 1679 Fletcher Folio. In iv. 3 there is a mask with Cupid in it: "This little gentleman Has troubled every Mask at Court this seven year;" especially in *Love's Triumph*, 1630; *Chloridia*, 1630; *Love's Welcome*, 1633; *Love's Welcome*, 1634, all by Jonson: *Love's Mistress*, 1634, by Heywood: *The Temple of Love*, 1635. by Davenant. From the Prologue it would seem the title had been altered. Cf. "tis become the title."

23. 1635, April 29. *Chabot the Admiral of France* was licensed. Written by Chapman and Shirley. Chapman wrote i., ii., and the prose speeches in iii. 1, v. 2, of the Proctor and Advocate. I think the play was an old one of Chapman's alluded to in *Northward Ho* and written c. 1604, and that Shirley altered and rewrote the latter part, iii., iv., v. The omission of proper names for the characters looks as if there were an under application intended. Could Chapman have written it concerning the Earl of Essex, and Shirley have twisted it to point at Francis Bacon?

24. 1635, Oct. 15. *The Lady of Pleasure* was licensed. In i. 1 there is an unmistakable claim to *The Ball* as a play of his making, for he promises a second part of it. The booths and bagpipes on Banstead downs are also noticed.

25. 1636, Jan. 18. *The Duke's Mistress* was licensed.

Thus far all Shirley's plays except *The Changes* were performed by the Queen's men at the Cockpit.

In 1635 a theatre was opened at Dublin. In May 1636 the theatres in London were closed on account of the plague. Shirley then went to Dublin.

26. c. 1636–7. *Saint Patrick for Ireland* was acted at Dublin. A second part was announced in the Prologue, but probably never written. The magic bracelet of iii. 1 is called in iv. 1 " a pretty toy." This may have been an allusion to the play called *The Toy*, for which Shirley there wrote a Prologue.

27. c. 1637–8. *The Constant Maid* was also probably acted in Ireland, as it was published with *Saint Patrick.* Neither of these plays appear to have been reproduced in England. In 1667 a second title, *Love will find out the way*, was added.

28. 1637. *The Royal Master* was acted in Dublin. The Dedication was written in Ireland before the restraint on the English theatres was removed, *i.e.*, certainly before 2nd Oct., and probably about Mar. 1637, " when the English stage shall be recovered from her long silence." The play had not at the time of writing this been " personated," but it was presented at Dublin Castle before Strafford, and still earlier at the Dublin theatre. Shirley also states that he is about to leave for England. He probably did so, but finding the plague still hot and the theatres still shut, returned to Ireland before Oct. 1637, leaving the dedicated copy of this play to be published in England. It was there issued 13th Mar. 1638, and licensed for performance 23rd April [at Salisbury Court, by the Queen's men, I suppose]. Shirley was not in England 13th Mar., for *The Duke's Mistress*, entered with this play, has no Dedication.

29. *The Politician* was acted at Salisbury Court by Queen Henrietta's men. As it was published with *The Gentleman of Venice*, which had been acted in Ireland, I think that this play was also there acted. It was not the same as *The Politic Father*, as Dyce is convinced it was, for that play was licensed in 1641 for the King's men. Dyce is unusually

careless and self-discrepant all through this Dublin campaign
of Shirley's. Neither was it published with *The Changes*, as
Gifford says. The plot is from the Countess of Montgomery's
Urania, Book i.

30. 1639, Oct. 30. *The Gentleman of Venice* was licensed
for the Queen's men at Salisbury Court. It appears from
the Dedication, 1655, that the MS. had been lost, and was
recovered with difficulty.

While Shirley was in Ireland the following eleven plays
were published without Dedications:—*The Example*, *The
Gamester*, *The Duke's Mistress*, *Chabot*, *The Ball*, *The Nightwalker*, *Love's Cruelty*, *The Coronation*, *Arcadia*, *St. Patrick*,
The Constant Maid. These plays were consequently not
corrected by him for the press, and in many of them the
text is very corrupt. On his final return to England [in
May 1640] he found *The Opportunity*, the publication of
which had been delayed for a year, "emergent from the
press," and hastened to prefix to it a Dedication. Only one
other play (except *The Royal Master*, already noticed), viz.,
The Maid's Revenge, is dedicated by him between Oct. 1637
and April 1640, and this exception, being entered for W.
Cooke only, had probably been in the publisher's hands since
1634, before A. Crooke joined him in these publications.
The Queen's men in the plague trouble had evidently been
selling Shirley's plays without his knowledge or consent;
and, worse still, they had sold *Love's Cruelty* twice over, and
The Coronation as a play of Fletcher's; and 31. *Look to the
Lady*, of which there is no other trace, was either not a play
of Shirley's or one of the extant ones under another name.
Williams and Egglestone, who entered this, had already been
victimised in the case of *Love's Cruelty*. Of 32. *The Tragedy
of St. Albans*, entered by W. Cook, and therefore probably
an early play, I am far less confident: I think it was

"stayed" by Shirley on his return. If it had anything to do with Bacon's career, or with the death of Clanrickard (1635), Earl of St. Albans, it may have been suppressed by authority. No wonder that Shirley left writing for a company that had treated his works in this way during his absence. The Dedications to the plays entered 13th April 1637 show that Shirley was about that time in England, and almost fix the date of his flying visit.

At Dublin, from Shirley's Prologues and Epilogues, we learn that *The Alchemist, The Toy*, 33. *The General*, and two plays of Fletcher's were acted under his management, as well as Middleton's *No Wit, No Help like a Woman's.* The date of revival of this last play (which see) is, fortunately, known to be 1638, and as Shirley says in his Prologue he had been two years in Dublin, the date of his leaving England is fixed to 1636. "The address to the Irish Gent[ry]" was no doubt a Prologue for *The Royal Master*, although Dyce makes The Irish Gent the name of a play. Compare the Epilogue to *The Doubtful Heir*, "You of the gentry."

34. 1640, c. May. *The Triumph of Beauty* (published with the poems 1646) was personated by some young gentlemen at a private recreation. From 1631 to 1639 Heywood had written the Mayors' pageants, except Taylor's show in 1634. Gerald Christmas had made for him the paper and wicker monsters that illustrated his speeches, and at Gerald's death his place was taken by his two sons. In his *Honor and Riches*, 1632, Shirley had satirised these shows. In 1634 Heywood retaliated by making his *Queen's Mask*, in which Shirley is Corydon the clown. Heywood then left the Queen's men and joined the King's company, with whom he remained till the 1636 plague. When Shirley returned from Ireland in 1640 Heywood had given up playwriting, and Shirley was about to succeed him as playwright

for the King's men. At this juncture he wrote the present mask, the date of which is proved by its allusions to Heywood's pageants up to 1639. Some of these I will mention. The whale, owls, ship, fiery dragons, Jason, Hercules, and the choice of Paris all occur in Heywood's pageants: note especially the shepherd with his scrip and bottle in the 1638 pageant, whence the names Scrip and Bottle (who is Heywood) in this *Triumph;* also what Bottle says, "You all know Paris the Prince of Troy,". and Crab's reply, "We know him now, but it was a mystery for many years;" and compare the burlesque account of the rape of Helen in *Love's Mistress,* ii. 3. The Jason story occurs in Heywood's 1639 pageant, the literary value of which may be estimated from one sample distich—

> "The Fleece of Aries trumpets to eternity
> The Drapers' hour due to that Fraternity."

Poor Heywood was old and worn at this time. This Jason story is especially ridiculed. Bottle is the Fleece, Crab Jason, Clout the Ship, Toadstool Medea, Shrub Hercules, Scrip the Dragon, and Hobbinol Absyrtus in the anti-mask. The whole of this is a weak echo of *Midsummer Night's Dream.*

35. 1640, June 1. *Rosania* was licensed for the King's men at the Globe. It had been previously performed in Dublin with the additional title of *Love's Victory;* and as it was not like the rest of the Dublin plays sent over to be acted by the Queen's men, I conclude that it was the last play there acted, and brought over by Shirley himself, who, on finding what the Queen's men had been doing in publishing his other plays, offered this one to the King's players. The Dublin Prologue mentions *Aglaura* and *Claricilla.* The Globe Prologue describes the difference between that stage

and the Blackfriars, where Shirley says this play " should have been presented." The Epilogue contains an allusion to Stephen Hamerton, the King's actor (on which Gifford is more absurd than usual). The ultimate name of the play was *The Doubtful Heir* in 1552.

36. 1640, Nov. 10. *The Imposture* was licensed. Acted by the King's men. The Prologue mentions Shirley's late return from Ireland : " He has been stranger long to the English Scene." Yet Dyce and Gifford will have it that he had been back in England two years and produced several plays.

37. 1641, May 26. *The Politic Father* was licensed for the King's men. This has been mistaken for *The Politician*, which belongs to the Queen's men ; but it is certainly the play published as *The Brothers*. " You show a provident father," says Francisco to Don Carlos in i. 1, and there is an allusion to the King's " Spanish plot " of 1641 in the Prologue.

38. 1641, Nov. 25. *The Cardinal* was licensed for the King's men. " A tragedy, the first that ever he composed for us," says Master Pollard in the Epilogue, which excludes *The Politician* from the King's plays and proves that *The Politic Father* was a comedy.

39. 1642, April 26. *The Sisters* was licensed for the King's men.

40. 1642, c. Sept. *The Court Secret* was written, but not acted. "The stage was interdicted," says Shirley in the Dedication. After this Shirley accompanied the Duke of Newcastle, whom he had assisted in his plays, which ought to be printed with Shirley's. One of them, *Captain Underwit*, was issued by Mr. A. H. Bullen as Shirley's. See CAVENDISH.

41. 1653, Mar. 26. *Cupid and Death* was presented before the Ambassador of Portugal.

42. *The Contention of Ajax and Ulysses for the Armour of Achilles* (published 1659 with *Honoria and Mammon*) was represented by young gentlemen of quality at a private Entertainment. The date is unknown, but the similarity of the personators to those of *The Triumph of Beauty* would suggest c. 1640.

SHIRLEY, HENRY. (Plays.)

1. 1638, Feb. 15, for John Okes. *The Martyred Soldier*, "with the life and death of Purser [and] Clinton," 1638.

The following plays were entered 1653, Sept. 9, S. R. :—

2. *The Spanish Duke of Lerma.*
3. *The Duke of Guise.*
4. *The Dumb Bawd.*
5. *Giraldo, the Constant Lover.*

1. *The Martyred Soldier* was a posthumous publication. It had been acted at the Cockpit [by the Queen's men] and other public theatres. The Address at the end was stolen from Heywood's *Royal King and Loyal Subject*, which had been printed by Okes and published in 1637 for James Beckett; but we are justified in concluding that this play to which it was affixed was an old one. It may have been originally acted at the Swan or the Hope by the Lady Elizabeth's men; but it is more likely to have been a Queen Anne's play, and so have reached Queen Henrietta's men through the Revels company, in which case the "other public theatres" would be the Bull and the Curtain. The likeness in subject to *The Virgin Martyr*, also acted by the Revels company, confirms me in this opinion. J. Okes published plays from 1637 to 1640, viz., W. Rowley's *Shoemaker is a Gentleman*, "with the life and death of the cripple that stole the Weathercock of Paul's." This had

been acted at the Red Bull [by Queen Anne's men] and
other theatres. *The Seven Champions of Christendom*, " with
the Life and Death of Jack Straw and Wat Tyler." This
had been acted at the Cockpit by Queen Henrietta's men,
and at the Bull, but not, like the other plays, by Queen
Anne's men; rather in 1637 by Prince Charles': and this
allows of the supposition that all these three plays had been
sold, when the Queen's men left the Cockpit, to the Prince's
men, who acted then at the Bull. But, as regards Shirley's
play, this would still leave the plural " other public theatres "
unaccounted for. Note that in these entries Okes seems to
have smuggled in some prose pamphlet without paying an
additional fee, as if it were part of the play. For instance,
Purser or Watton and Clinton, executed 1586 (cf. S. R.
Aug. 15), have nothing to do with this play. For further
details bearing on the preceding matters see HEYWOOD,
Fortune by Land and Sea and *Love's Mistress*. I think
Henry (considering dates) may have been James Shirley's
father; but certainly not his brother, as Wood imagines.
This play is dedicated to Sir Kenelm Digby by John Kirke,
who evidently procured this and other plays for Okes from
the players.

SIDNEY, Sir PHILIP. (Mask.)

Born 1554, Nov. 29; died 1586, Oct. 7. This is not the
place to describe the career of this illustrious gentleman,
with whom we are only concerned as the author of his first
work, viz. :—

1. *The Lady of the May:* presented to Queen Elizabeth
at Wanstead, Essex, the seat of Sidney's uncle, the Earl of
Leicester, in May 1578; printed with the *Arcadia* in the
3rd edition 1598, and reprinted in Nichols' *Eliz.*, ii. 94.
It is called a mask, but it is merely an entertainment, with
half-a-dozen characters and a little music.

SIMON, ——. (Latin.)

1. *Zeno.* Acted at Cambridge 1630–1.

SINGER, JOHN. (Actor and Jigmaker.)

One of the original company of Queen Elizabeth in 1583; with the Admiral's men 1594–1602. As to his authorship of *Quips upon Questions* see ARMIN.

1. 1603, Jan. 13. Henslow paid him £5 for his play called *Singer's Voluntary.* This must have been more than a mere jig; but from Day's *Humour out of breath,* iv. 3, I find that a "voluntary" means a song to music.

SMITH, WENTWORTH. (Plays.)

Nothing is known of this author outside of Henslow's *Diary.* He wrote for the Admiral's men at the Rose.

1. 1601, April 4, 11; May 2, 4; Aug. 5, 11, 26; Sept. 1. *The Conquest of the West Indies* (with Day and Haughton.)

2. 1601, Oct. 10; Nov. 6, 9, 12. *The Rising of Cardinal Wolsey* (with Chettle, Drayton, Monday).

3. 1601, Oct. 12, 22. 1 *Six Clothiers* (with Hathway, Haughton).

4. 1601, Nov. [3]. 2 *Six Clothiers* (with Hathway, Haughton).

5. 1601, Nov. 14; 1602, Jan. 6, 7. *Too good to be true,* or *The Northern Man* (with Chettle, Hathway).

6. 1602, May 4. *Love parts Friendship* (with Chettle).

7. 1602, Nov. 8, 17. *As merry as may be.* "For the Court" (with Day, Hathway), and for Worcester's men at the Rose.

8. 1602, Sept. 4. *Albert Galles* (with Heywood, *q.v.*).

9. 1602, Sept. 20. *Marshal Osric* (completed Sept. 30 by Heywood, *q.v.*).

10. 1602, Oct. 1, 11, 15. *The ii. (iii.) brothers* (in which it appears from the property entries there were a witch, devil, and spirits).

11, 12. 1602, Oct. 15, 21.　1, 2 *Lady Jane* (with Chettle, Dekker, Heywood, Webster).　See DEKKER and WEBSTER, *Sir Thomas Wyatt.*

13. 1602, Nov. 24, 26; Dec. 20.　1 *The Black Dog of Newgate* (with Day, Hathway, and " the other poet : " probably Haughton ; less likely Chettle or Webster).

14. 1603, Jan. 7, 10, 16, 19.　*The Unfortunate General,* " a French History " (with Day, Hathway, and the other poet).

15. 1603, Jan. 29, Feb. 3.　2 *The Black Dog of Newgate* (with Day, Hathway, and the other poet).

16. 1603, Mar. 7, 12.　*An Italian Tragedy.*　See *Orphans' Tragedy.*

This Smith is continually confused with William Smith by Halliwell, Collier, Hazlitt, and others ; he has also been conjectured to be the author of the plays by W. S. (*q.v.*). This supposition is baseless ; they were meant to be taken for Shakespeare's : they are :—

　Locrine (*q.v.*), probably belonging to the Chamberlain's men.

　Cromwell (*q.v.*), acted by the King's men.

　The Puritan (*q.v.*), acted by the Paul's boys.

The only play in which any of this Smith's writing has possibly come down to us is Heywood's *Royal King and Loyal Subject* (*q.v.*).

SMITH, WILLIAM.　(Plays.)

2. 1615, April 24, for Josias Harrison.　*The Hector of Germany,* or *The Palsgrave,* " is a harmless thing."　The words in quotation marks are not part of the title, but the Revels Master's verdict mistakenly copied as such and afterwards scored out.

1. 1614, Jan 4.　*The Freeman's Honour* was " acted by the Servants of the King's Majesty to dignify the worthy

company of Merchant Taylors." So we are told in the
Dedication of *The Hector of Germany.* This must, I think,
have been the play performed 4th Jan. 1614 at Merchant
Taylors' Hall at the marriage of the Earl of Somerset,
Nichols, *James*, ii. 732. It must have been very short, as
two masks for which (but not for the play : Nichols is wrong
in that) Middleton was paid on Jan. 18.

2. *The Hector of Germany*, or *The Palsgrave Prince
Elector :* " a new play, an Honorable History, as it hath
been publicly acted at the Red Bull and at the Curtain "
[not by Queen Anne's men, but] " by a Company of Young
Men of the City. Made by W. Smith. With new additions."
The date must be c. 1613, when the Palsgrave married the
Lady Elizabeth. The interesting point is not the play
itself, but the letting out the Queen's men's theatres to a
Citizen company. Halliwell adopts the absurd statement of
Biog. Dram. that this was the last play that we hear of as
acted at the Curtain. The play is dedicated to Sir John
Swinnerton, who was Lord Mayor in 1612–13, probably as
produced during his Mayoralty.

3. 1623, Nov. 28. Herbert licensed for a strange
Company at the Red Bull *The Fair Foul One*, or *The Bait-
ing of the Jealous Knight*, written by Smith.

4. *Saint George for England*, by William Smith, was one
of the MSS. destroyed by Warburton's servant.

I yet have a doubt as to these two Smiths. William
Smith could hardly be the William Smith who published
Chloris and other Poems 1596–1600, and the evidence
for any playwright existing except Wentworth Smith is very
slight, merely the " William " in Warburton's list : he is
only called W. Smith elsewhere.

SPEED, JOHN. (University.)

Son of John Speed the chronologer. Born in London

1595; educated at Merchant Taylors' School; scholar of St. John's, Oxford, 1612; Fellow, B.A., M.B., M.D. Died May 1640.

1. *Stonehenge*, P. Acted 1636 before Dr. R. Baylie, President, and the St. John's Fellows in their refectory.

SPENSE, ———. (Latin.)

Bellum Grammaticale sive Nominum Verborumque Discordia Civilis, C., 1635. Mentioned by Sir John Harington 1591. Performed before Queen Elizabeth 24th Sept. 1592 at Christ Church, Oxford; "meanly performed," Nichols, iii. 155. Entered S. R. 17th April 1634 for John Spenser as "by Master Spense."

SQUIRE, JOHN. (Pageant.)

1. *Tês Irênês Trophœa, The Triumphs of Peace*, for Nicholas Okes, 1620.

This was the pageant for the Mayoralty of Francis Jones of the Haberdashers' Company, 30th Oct. 1620. Reprinted in Nichols, iii. 619. Far more rich than former shows, all the metal adornments being of gold or silver.

STANLEY, WILLIAM, EARL OF DERBY. (Plays.)

In 1599 the Earl of Derby "was busy in penning comedies for the common players," *State Papers*.

STAPYLTON, Sir ROBERT. (Plays.)

1. 1653, Nov. 29, for R. Marriot. *The Royal Choice*.

Stapylton's other plays are post-Restoration, and his well-known career does not concern us in this book.

STEPHENS, JOHN. (Play.)

1. *Cynthia's Revenge*, or *Mœnander's Extasy*, T., for Roger Barnes, 1613.

This play (not entered in S. R., though a transfer of copyright 1635, July 4, is duly recorded) was [surreptitiously] published as by John Stephens, with Commendatory Verses by Jonson, &c. In one of these, by F. C., are the lines—

"One swallow makes no summer, most men say :
But who disproves that proverb made this play."

As " by John Stephens" was " removed" from the title-
page of most of the impression, Halliwell inferred that the
author's real name was John Swallow. The Dedication is
signed J. S. Founded on Lucan's *Pharsalia* and Ovid's
Metamorphoses. Very long and very tedious. Jonson
distinctly states that the publication was anonymous : —

"Who bluntly doth but look upon the same
Would ask what author doth conceal his name."

The name was no doubt inserted in the title-page after
this. "John Stephens, Esq., of Lincoln's Inn," author of
Essays in 1615, cannot be an assumed name. W. C.
Hazlitt and F. Cunningham have, of course, followed Halliwell's absurd conjecture. Compare Davies' "swallow"
allusion under DRAYTON.

STILL, JOHN. (Play.)

1. 1652–3, for Thomas Colwell. *Dyceon of Bedlam*,
C., 1575, 1661.

Son of William Still, Grantham, Lincolnshire. Born
1543 ; student of Christ's College, Cambridge ; M.A. ; Lady
Margaret's Professor 1570 ; held livings in Suffolk and
Yorkshire ; Master of St. John's 1574, then of Trinity
1577 ; prolucutor of the Convocation 1588 ; Bishop of
Bath and Wells 1592. Died 1607.

1. *Gammer Gurton's Needle* (which must be the same
play as *Dyceon of Bedlam*, for the 1575 edition was printed
for Thomas Colwell, and there is no other entry S. R. which
can apply to it) was acted [at Court 1562–3 by Leicester's
men], and at Cambridge 1566, according to *Biog. Dram.*
See my *History of the Stage*, p. 58. As it was printed as

"played not long ago in Christ's College in Cambridge, made by Mr. S., Mr. of Art," and no other Christ College M.A. whose name begins with S. has been discovered of the date required, the authorship has been all but unanimously ascribed to Still. But has not the search been made for too late a date, and was Still M.A. as early as 1562, when he was only nineteen? In the table p. 33 of my *History of the Stage* there is a bad misprint on this matter. See *Errata*. Hazlitt adds to his notice, "Written in 1551," I suppose through some confusion with *Ralph Royster Doyster*. Possibly the "Mr. of Art" may have been an addition in the title first made in the 1575 edition.

STRODE, WILLIAM. (University.)

1. *The Floating Island*, T. C., for H. Twiford, 1655.

Son of Philip Strode, who lived near Plympton, Devonshire. Born 1599; educated at Westminster School; admitted at Christ Church, Oxford, 1618; took Holy Orders; public reader 1629; admitted to read the sentences 1631; Canon of Christ Church and D.D.1638. Died 10th Mar.1644.

1. *The Floating Island* (which Wood calls *Passions Calmed*, or *The Settling of the Floating Island*) was acted by the Christ Church students before Charles I. at Oxford 29th Aug. 1636. The songs were set by Henry Lawes.

STUBBE, ———. (Latin.)

1. 1631, Sept. 28, for Richard Thrall. *Fraus Honesta*, C., 1632.

Stubbe was a Fellow of Trinity, Cambridge.

1. *Fraus Honesta* was acted at Trinity. A list of the actors is given in the MS. in Emanuel Library. Scene at Florence, 10th Feb. 1616.

SUCKLING, Sir JOHN. (Plays.)

1. 1638, April 18, for Thomas Walkley. *Aglaura*, T. or C., 1638.

3. *The Discontented Colonel* (*Brennoralt*, 1646), T., n.d. [1642].

2. *The Goblins*, C., 1646.

4. *The Sad One* (unfinished), T., 1646, 1659.

Son of Sir John Suckling, Comptroller of the Household to James I. Born at Whitton, Middlesex; christened at Twickenham 10th February 1609; matriculated at Trinity, Cambridge, 1623; travelled in 1628, and fought under Gustavus Adolphus 1631; returned to England c. 1632; published his *Session of the Poets* 1637, then wrote plays.; M.P. for Bramber 1640; joined in a plot to rescue Strafford 1641; was thereon accused of trying to bring over the French; fled to France, and there died before 1643.

1. *Aglaura* was acted at Blackfriars by the King's men, probably in 1637, after the reopening of the theatres in August. By altering the last act it can be performed either as T. C. or T. Brome wrote verses on it. From a letter 7th Feb. 1637–8 we learn that this play cost £300 or £400 setting out: "8 or 10 suits of new clothes he gave the players: an unheard-of prodigality."

2. *The Goblins* was also acted at Blackfriars by the King's men c. 1638.

3. *Brennoralt*, or *The Discontented Colonel*, was also acted at Blackfriars by the King's men: written after the breaking out of the Scotch rebellion (the Lithuanian rebels of the play) in 1639.

4. *The Sad One* was left unfinished c. 1640.

SWINHOE, GILBERT. (Play.)

1. *The Unhappy fair Irene*, T., 1658. Founded on Painter's *Palace of Pleasure*, Nov. 40. Painter took the story from Bandello, and he perhaps from Turkish history.

T., T. (Play.)

1. *The life of Mother Shipton*, C., n.d. Acted nineteen

days together with great applause; but see *Addenda*, THOMPSON. See Hazlitt's *Handbook*.

TAILOR, ROBERT. (Play.)

1. 1614, May 23, for Richard Redmer. *The Hog hath lost his Pearl*, C., 1614.

This play was "divers times publicly acted by certain London Prentices," according to a letter of Sir Henry Wotton's (*Rel. Wot.*, 1645, p. 402, 4th edition), at Whitefriars, the audience being chiefly rather the sixteen prentices' mistresses than their masters, who were admitted by ticket. The performance was unlicensed. The Sheriffs heard of it by chance, and took six or seven to perform the last act in Bridewell. The City thought the Hog meant Swinerton the Mayor, and the Pearl the late Lord Treasurer, William Cecil, Earl of Salisbury.

This play is a valuable storehouse of dramatic allusions. It appears from the Prologue that after its first performance at Whitefriars (which, being on a Sunday, and "Shrove Tuesday being at hand," i. 1, was probably on 14th Feb. 1613) it was "tossed from one house to another," until it had "a knight's license," and might range at pleasure, probably at the Bull and Curtain, which accounts for the "divers times acted" of the title-page. Compare Will. Smith's *Hector of Germany*. The "grunting at State affairs," and "invecting at city vices," *i.e.*, at Cecil and Swinnerton, is expressly disclaimed, yet I cannot help thinking that Haddit is a portrait. He has lost £800 a year by gambling, Fortune has "made a tennis-ball of him," and he is reduced to living at the house of Atlas, a porter, and writing jigs for the theatre. He has "some acquaintance with bricklayers and plasterers;" the actor who bargains with him "has acted king's parts any time these ten years," and does not understand Latin. All this reminds one of Dekker, who wrote

Forteion Tenes (*Fortune's Tennis*) for the Fortune Theatre, who had some acquaintance (in fact, more than he wanted) with Jonson, bricklayer and plasterer; and who in 1612 complained how Fortune, in her blind pride, had set her foot on his last play, *If this be not good, the Devil's in't,* which had therefore been transferred to the Red Bull. It appears that Dekker and R. Tailor were acquainted with Taylor the Water poet at this time, as appears from the complimentary verses by Dekker to *The Sculler* 1612, and of R. Tailor to *The Nipping or Snipping of Abuses* 1613, Dec. 7. But not to dwell on conjecture and come to certainty. The allusions in i. 1 fix the date of the revival of *Long Meg of Westminster,* and the personation of Garlic on the Fortune stage by an actor of that name points to the year 1612. Compare Dekker, *If it be not good,* &c., and Field, *Amends for Ladies;* also *The World's Folly,* by. J. H., S. R. 1615, May 10, quoted fully in *Dodsley* in the reprint of the present play. Another important allusion is that to W. Rowley's play, " as the learned Histriographer writes, *Hymen's Holiday* or nuptial ceremonious rites," ii. 1, which shows that *Hymen's Holiday* was written for a marriage, probably that of the Earl of Dunbar's daughter with Lord Waldon, interrupted by the Earl's death 29th Jan. 1612. It was acted at Court 24th Feb. Again, in iii. 3, " And you also; I could speak it in Latin, but the phrase is common," alludes to *Greene's Tu quoque,* then on the stage at the Bull. The lottery for the benefit of the Virginian Colonies, drawn 29th July 1612, in which Thomas Sharpliffe, a tailor, gained the £1000 prize (*Stow,* p. 1002), is mentioned, iii. 3, v. 1 ; and Wither's *Abuses Stript and Whipt* (S. R. 1613, Jan. 16) is alluded to in the Prologue ; and, finally, the success of *Pericles* on the stage is thus denoted in the Prologue :—

"We'll say 'tis fortunate, like *Pericles*."

TARLTON, RICHARD.   (Actor and Playwright.)
1. (Plot extant.)   2 *Seven Deadly Sins.*
2. 1594, May 14, for Thomas Creede.   *The Famous Victories of Henry* 5, " containing the Honorable Battle of Agincourt," H., 1598, 1617.

Tarlton was born at Condover, Shropshire (Fuller); was an apprentice and water-bearer in London (*Three Lords and three Ladies of London*).   According to *Tarlton's Jests*, he, with his wife Kate, kept a tavern in Gracechurch Street, and an ordinary in Paternoster Row.   His wife was of light reputation.   In 1570 he wrote *A ballad on the floods* in Bedfordshire, Lincolnshire, &c., S. R., for John Alde, after Oct. 15; reprinted by Shak. Soc.   On 10th Dec. 1576 Tarlton's *Toys* was entered S. R. for R. Jones; on 5th Feb. 1578, for Hy. Bynneman, his *Tragical Treatises;* on 7th Feb. 1579 his *Device upon this unlooked-for great snow.* These three productions are lost.   Before 1583 he performed a jig at the Curtain (printed by Shak. Soc.), *A horse-load of Fools,* the first being Himself, the Player fool; the second Goose' Son (S. Gosson), the Puritan fool; the fourth a poet ape, a wine-bibber, who makes ballads by the bushel and pastorals for us players to speak—William Elderton, surely; and the sixth a lover fool, who sings " My luck is loss," G. Gascoigne.   In 1583 he was chosen (c. March) out of this Curtain company (Sussex' ?) into the new Queen's company; he was also appointed Groom of the Chamber.   He was a master of Fence from 1587 till his death.   The masters used to play their prizes at the Bel Savage; and Tarlton's *Recantation,* being his last theme on '' Now, or else never," was there sung, S. R. for Henry Kirkham 2nd Aug. 1580.   He died 3rd Sept. 1588, and was buried at St. Leonard's, Shoreditch.   His will, dated that same day, shows that, as I had conjectured, W. Johnson was one of the Queen's men. We have no concern here with books written about him, for which see Halliwell's edition of *Tarlton's Jests* (Shak. Soc.). In this book it is repeatedly asserted that the Queen's men played at the Bull; but that inn-yard was closed before that company was formed.

1. *The Seven Deadly Sins* was "a famous play of Tarlton's. For my identification therewith of *The Five plays in one* and *The Three plays in one* of 1585, Jan. 26, Feb. 21—for *The Seven Sins* was written in two parts—see my *History of the Stage*, p. 67, and *Life of Shakespeare*, pp. 27, 296, 264; but correct the date of revival from c. 1594 to 1593, Mar. 6, for *Three plays in one*, when revived with the Induction, became the *Four plays in one* of that date.

2. *The famous Victories of Henry* 5, acted by the Queen's men (according to the *Jests*, at the Bull; but surely the Bull was closed: if they did act there it must have been surreptitiously), dates c. 1588, not later, for Tarlton acted Derrick the clown in it; and not much earlier, or it would have been forgotten before Nash's well-known allusion to it in *Piers Penniless* Aug. 1592. It was sometimes called *Agincourt;* as, for instance, in the S. R. entry 8th Nov. 1630. I notice it here because Tarlton acted in it, and it is very likely that he wrote the clown part, as was customary at this early time: see *Knack to Know a Knave*. There is, in fact, no other known author of the date to whom I can attribute any part of the play, with its innumerable repetitions and buffooneries.

TATHAM, JOHN. (Plays.)

   1. *Love crowns the End*, T. C. or P., 1640, 1657.

   2. *The Distracted State*, T., 1651.

1. *Love crowns the End*, acted by the scholars of Bingham, in the county of Nottingham, in 1632, was printed in 1640 as a pastoral at the end of *The Fancies' Theatre*,

which had Commendatory Verses by Brome, Nabbes, Chamberlain, Rawlins, &c., but in 1657 as a tragi-comedy.

2. *The Distracted State* was written in 1641. It is very bitter against the Scots, and has Commendatory Verses by J. R. (Rutter), R. D. (Davenport, *not* Daborne), and G. Lynn.

His other plays and pageants are later than my time limit.

TAYLOR, JOHN, the Water Poet. (Pageants.)

1. 1634, Oct, 13, for Henry Gosson. *The Triumphs of Fame and Honor*, 1634.

2. *Ovatio Caroli*, or *England's Comfort and London's Joy*, presented by R. Gurney, Lord Mayor, to Charles I. on his return from Scotland 1641, Nov. 25.

Born 1580 at Gloucester; died 1654. Our chief concern with him in this place is 1. his pageant for the Mayoralty of Henry Parkhurst, cloth-worker. It is one of the entries which proves the ordinary dates assigned to the Mayors 1634–40 to be erroneous.

TOMKI[N]S, JOHN. (University.)

1. 1607, Feb. 23, for Simon Waterson. *Lingua*, C., 1607 [1610], 1617, 1622, 1632, 1657.

2. 1615, April 28, for Nicholas Okes. *Albumazar*, 1615, 1634, 1668.

Son of Thomas Tomkins, organist of His Majesty's Chapel-Royal in Ordinary, and scholar of Trinity, Cambridge, 1594; B.A. 1598.

1. *Lingua*, or *The Combat of the Tongue and the five Senses for Superiority*, had always been attributed to Antony Brewer, on Winstanley's authority, till the appearance of my article in *Shakespeariana*, Mar. 1885, from which I here give an extract. Mr. Furnival in April 1890 discovered definite evidence as to Tomkins' authorship, thus confirming my conjecture.

Lingua was entered in the Stationers' Registers Feb.
23, 1606–7. This play is clearly founded on an Italian
model, and was written by the same hand as *Albumazar*.
The manner of dividing the scenes, the frequent use of the
phrase "What you will," the minute knowledge of games
at cards, the command of technical astrological terms, the
great likeness of style and metre, the turns given to the
epilogues, the knowledge of Marston's plays, and many other
similarities too numerous to be mentioned now, all point to
identity of authorship. Mr. P. A. Daniel, who suggested to
me this attribution of *Lingua* to Tomkis, moreover, has
pointed out to me that in the original Quartos "tiff toff" is
continually used as a sort of stage direction to indicate the
sound of the beating, or, as we should say, "dusting the
jackets" of one personage by another; and "tick tock" in
like manner to indicate knocking at a door. This is taken
directly from the Italian. It is common in *L'Astrologo* and
many other plays, but occurs in no other English ones that
have fallen under my notice. In Hazlitt's *Dodsley* there is
an absurd note (ix. 434) by Collier, telling us that "tiff toff"
expresses Crapula's coughing, and concluding with this significant statement as to these words: "Though it might not
be necessary to insert them, their omission ought to be mentioned." Both he and Hazlitt do, notwithstanding, omit them
in nearly every instance, and *do not mention the omission*.
As to the date of this play, it was certainly not, as Reed says,
in the reign of Elizabeth : the whole plot is one depreciation
of women, and would have been most offensive to Her Majesty;
on the other hand, it must be early, very early, in James'
reign. In iii. 5 Memory remembers "about the year 1602
many used this skew kind of language." The point of the
jest would be lost if the play were several years later than
1602. I place it very early in 1603, almost immediately

after James' accession, at the time when he was expressing his disparaging opinions about his predecessors. (See Aikin's *Memoirs of James I.*, vol. i. ch. 5.) I will even venture to conjecture that this play was performed at Hinchinbrook before James I., when the heads of the University came to meet the King on his entrance-journey to London 27th–29th April 1603: note that 1602 had ended 24th March. " The matchless entertainment " then given to him by Master Oliver Cromwell included speeches and poems (among others one by P. Fletcher) from these University men, and it is hardly likely, considering James' proclivities, that plays should be omitted. Still further: there is an old tradition traceable to S. Miller, who published an edition of this play in 1657, that Oliver Cromwell, the Protector, had taken a part in it. Winstanley's exaggeration of this tradition to the effect that the part was that of Tactus, and that his ambition was swollen thereby, is (as this kind of moral falsehood usually is) as contemptible as absurd. But S. Miller's statement is not so easily disposed of. It is usually explained as referring to some hypothetical performance of *Lingua* at Cambridge of uncertain date on an unknown occasion, because Cromwell, born in 1599, would be too young to take part in the original performance—certainly too young for the part of Tactus, but not, I think, too young for another part. There is one of two words only, which he may have taken. In iv. 7 Appetitus says, " How now; what small, thin fellow are you here ? Ha ? " and Small Beer replies, " Beer, forsooth ! Beer, forsooth ! " The boy to represent Small Beer would be, of course, the youngest procurable; the opportunity of introducing any member of the family to the new King's notice was not to be neglected. Why should not Oliver Cromwell, then about three years old, have taken this part in a play performed at his uncle's house ? Of course, on Winstanley's principles, it would have led to his taking "small beer" parts ever after, but this argument does not greatly affect me.

2. *Albumazar*, by Thomas Tomkis. This play was acted by the gentlemen of Trinity College, before King James I., on Mar. 9, 1614–15, on the occasion of his first visit to the University of Cambridge, in his Progress of that year. Besides Latin plays, which were performed, the *Piscatory* of Phineas Fletcher was to have been acted if the King could have tarried another night. *Albumazar* is founded on *L'Astrologo* of Giam Battista della Porta, printed at Venice in 1606. [The Fortune and Red Bull are mentioned ii. 1 ; also yellow starch as fashionable. Mrs. Turner was executed 1615, Nov. 29.]

TOURNEUR, or TURNER, CYRIL. (Plays.)

2. 1607, Oct. 7, for George Elde. *The Revenger's Tragedy*, T., 1607, 1608.

1. 1611, Sept. 14, for John Stepneth. *The tragedy of the Atheist*, 1611.

In 1600 Cyril Turner published his *Transformed Metamorphosis;* on 14th Oct. 1609, S. R., his *funeral poem on Sir Francis Vere;* in 1613 his *grief on the death of Prince Henry,* one of three elegies, of which Webster and Heywood wrote the other two. He adopted the spelling Tourneur in 1611. The *Elegy on Sir F. Vere* was published anonymously, and Mr. Churton Collins in his elaborate edition gives no evidence of its being Turner's ; nor do Hazlitt or Lowndes, who also assume his authorship.

1. *The Atheist's Tragedy*, or *The Honest Man's Revenge,* founded on Boccaccio's *Decameron*, vii. 6, was acted "in divers places." From a passage in ii. 1 it appears to have been wrttten before the siege of Ostend (1601–Aug. 1604) had ended. I conjecture, therefore, that this play was acted

during the plague of 1603 (June–Dec.) when the players
"travelled." The "great man who went to the war" in
ii. 1 was, I suppose, Sir Francis Vere, who had resigned his
government of Ostend Mar. 1602. In ii. 4 the title of
Dekker's *Fortune's Tennis* seems to be alluded to. The play
is one of the "Revenge for a father" group of the *Hamlet*
time. The metrical system is quite different from that of
The Revenger's Tragedy.

2. *The Revenger's Tragedy* was acted by the King's servants. It was entered S. R. along with Middleton's *Trick
to catch the old one*. Elde also published *Northward Ho*, by
Dekker and Webster, to the latter of whom I should have
attributed *The Revenger's Tragedy*, were it not for the uni-
versal concensus of the authorities, founded on some evidence
unknown to me. The play was published anonymously, and
seems to me far superior to anything Turner (judging from
his known writings) could have produced.

3. *The Nobleman*, T. C., was entered S. R. for Edward
Blunt 15th Feb. 1612, and was acted at Court by the King's
men 23rd Feb. in the same year, and again in 1612–13.
The M.S. was destroyed by Warburton's servant.

4. In 1613, June 5, Daborne writes to Henslow that he
has given Tourneur an act in *The Arraignment of London* to
write (for the L. Elizabeth's men). Tourneur had then left
writing for the King's company.

TOWNSEND, AURELIAN. (Masks.)

　　1. *Albion's Triumph*, 1631.

　　2. *Tempe Restored*, 1631.

1. 1632, Jan. 8. *Albion's Triumph* was presented by the
King and his Lords, 1631–2, Sunday after Twelfth Night.
Inigo Jones contrived the mask and procured the appoint-
ment of Townsend (who had been Lord Salisbury's steward)
to write the words. The names of the performers are given.

2. 1632, Feb. 13, Shrove Tuesday. *Tempe Restored*, by the Queen and fourteen ladies, also by Jones and Townsend. It had been delayed because the Queen had an inflamed eye. The story is that of Circe.

UDAL, NICHOLAS. (Plays and University.)

1. 1566–7, for Thomas Hackett. *Rafe Royster Doyster*, 1566.

Born in Hampshire 1506; scholar of Corpus Christi, Oxford, 13th Jan. 1520; B.A. 3rd Sept. 1524; Master of Eton; M.A. 1534; Canon at Windsor. Died 1564.

1*. *De Papatu*, C., was written early; probably at Eton 1526.

1. [1562–3]. *Ralph Roister Doister*. See my *History of the Stage*, p. 59.

2. 1564, Aug. 8. *Ezechias*, an English play, was acted at Cambridge before the Queen by King's College men [Udal's former pupils at Eton].

VENNARD, or VENNAR, RICHARD. (Play.)

1. *England's Joy*. The plot, " to be played at the Swan this 6th Nov. 1602," is preserved in a broadside in the library of the Society of Antiquaries. Reprinted *Harl. Misc.* Alluded to in Saville's *Entertainment of King James at Theobald's*, 1603, and in Taylor's *Cast over the Water to Fennor* (who is not identical with Vennard), 1614. See also the text of Jonson's *Love Restored* and *Augurs*. It was a Dumb Show of chief events in Elizabeth's reign, and produced before Dekker's *Whore of Babylon* (*q.v.*), but after his *Truth's Supplication*, from which it was probably imitated.

VERE, EDWARD, EARL OF OXFORD, is mentioned by Meres in his *Wit's Treasury*, 1598, as one of our best for Comedy.

VINCENT, THOMAS. (Latin.)

1. *Paria*, 1648.

This was acted before Charles I., Mar. 1627, at Trinity, Cambridge, of which college Vincent was a Fellow.

W., L. (Play.)

1. *Orgula,* or *The Fatal Error,* T., 1658. Scene, Segusia, East Gaul. Preface on poetry and plays.

W., M. (Play.)

The Marriage Broker, or *The Pander,* C., by M. W., 1662.

Scene, London. Time, the reign of Sebert, King of the West Saxons.

W., T. (Play.)

Thorney Abbey, or *The London Maid,* T., by T. W., 1662.

Scene, London. Plot, an imitation of *Macbeth.*

These two plays were published with *Grim the Collier of Croydon,* or *The Devil and his Dame,* "with the Devil and St. Dunstan," C., by I. T., as *Gratiæ Theatrales,* or " A choice Ternary of English plays, composed upon especial occasions by several ingenious persons." The substitution of I. T. for Haughton as the author of *Grim* throws a doubt on the authenticity of M. W. and T. W.

W., J. (Play.)

1. 1637, April 26, for J. Waterson. *The Valiant Scot,* T., 1637, " by J. W., gent." On Sir William Wallace. The Dedication to the Marquis of Hamilton is signed William Bowyer. Was the play written by the publisher?

WADESON, ANTONY. (Plays.)

2. *Look about you* [Anonymous], for William Ferbrand, 1600.

1. 1601, June 13, July [24]. Henslow paid him £1, 10s. od. as part-payment for *The honorable life of the humorous Earl of Gloster and his conquest of Portingal,* acted by the Admiral's men at the Fortune. This humorous Earl of Gloucester is a character in *Look about you,* published 1600, in the last scene of which he promises to fire the

Saracens, &c., from Portingal. I have no hesitation in ascribing *Look about you* to Wadeson.

2. *Look about you*, C., was published 1600, as lately played by the Admiral's men [at the Rose]. It must, therefore, have been mentioned in Henslow's *Diary*. The entry is not there now, but the entries, 1599, April 17–May 26, have been cut out (a practice not unknown elsewhere among the Shakespeare Society), and at that date no doubt this play was written.

WAGER, LEWIS. (Early Play.)

1. 1566–7, for John Charlewood. *The Repentance of Mary Magdalen,* by the learned clerk, Lewis Wager, 1567. Four could play this interlude.

WAGER, W. (Early Plays.)

1. 1565–6, for Thomas Colwell. *The cruel Debtor* [Query the Shylock story].

2. 1571–6. *The longer thou livest the more fool thou art,* n.d. The characters are given in *Biog. Dram.* Four may play it.

3. *'Tis good sleeping in a whole skin,* MS., destroyed by Warburton's servant [Query the same as *The Cruel Debtor*].

WAPUL, GEORGE. (Early Play.)

1. 1576, Oct. 22. *The tide tarrieth no man,* C., 1576. Four may play this.

WATSON, JOHN. (Latin.)

Born at Bengeworth, Worcestershire, 1520; member of All Souls; Master of the Hospital of St. Cross 1559; prebendary; dean; Bishop of Winchester 18th Sept. 1580. Died 1583.

1. *Absalon,* T., in MS. at Penshurst, is mentioned by Meres in his *Palladis Tamia* with George Buchanan's *Jephtha* as "amongst all modern tragedies able to abide the touch of Aristotle's precepts and Euripides' examples."

WÈBSTER, JOHN. (Plays and Pageant.)

7. 1605, Mar. 2, for Henry Rockett. *Westward Ho,*
C., 1607.

8. 1607, Aug. 6, for George Elde. *Northward Ho,*
C., 1607.

3, 4. *Sir Thomas Wyatt,* H., 1607, 1612, for Thomas
Archer.

9. *The White Devil,* T., 1612 (by N. O[kes] for
Thomas Archer), 1631, 1665.

11. *The Devil's Law Case,* T. C., 1623 (by A. M. for
John Grismund).

12. *The Duchess of Malfi,* T., 1623 (by N. Okes for
John Waterson.)

14. *Monuments of Honor,* pageant, 1624 (by N.
Okes).

10. *Appius and Virginia,* 1654, 1659, 1679 (*The
Roman Virgin,* or *Unjust Judge*).

Webster was born free of the Merchant Taylors' Company,
perhaps a son of the John Webster, Merchant Taylor, mentioned in *The Alleyn Papers,* p. 14, on 25th July 1591. He
wrote in 1602 or earlier (see MONDAY) Verses Commendatory for *Palmerin of England,* in 1604 for Harrison's
Arches of Triumph, and in 1612 for Heywood's *Apology for
Actors;* also in 1612 (Dec. 25, S. R.) he joined Tourneur
and Heywood in *Three Elegies to the memory of Prince
Henry:* Webster's, the second of these, called *A Monumental
Column,* was dedicated to Carr, Viscount Rochester; in
1623 verses for Cockeram's *English Dictionary.* He was
probably the John Webster, cloth-worker, who made his will
5th Aug. 1625; proved 7th Oct. At any rate nothing else
is known of him after 1624.

1. 1602, May 22. *Cesar's Fall* (with Drayton, Middleton,
Monday, and "the rest:" Query Dekker). This was his

first play. "Webster" in the *Guise* entry in Henslow's *Diary*, 3rd Nov. 1601, is connected with properties for the revival of an old play (Marlow's, of course), not with writing a new one: it is not the name of the tailor, which was Radford, but a forged "interlineation."

2. 1602, May 29. "*Too Harpes*" (with Dekker, Drayton, Middleton, Monday). The foregoing were written for the Admiral's men at the Fortune; the next two for Worcester's at the Rose.

3, 4. 1602, Oct. 15, 21. 1, 2 *Lady Jane* (with Chettle, Dekker, Heywood, Smith). The parts written by Dekker and Webster were cobbled into a play called *The famous history of Sir Thomas Wyatt*, and published in 1607, "with the coronation of Queen Mary and the coming in of King Philip, as it was played by the Queen's servants" (formerly Worcester's). Queen Anne had been crowned, James had come in, and the Cobham plot had been detected in the meanwhile. Another name for this play in the *Diary* is *The overthrow of Rebels*, for which properties were bought 1602, Nov. 6, 12. The fall of Cromwell (in the *Wolsey* play of the Admiral's men June 1602, not the *Cromwell* of the King's men) is alluded to in Sc. 15. I think Webster wrote Sc. 1–9, Dekker Sc. 11–17, the change of *Dram. Pers.* being very marked in Sc. 10.

5. 1602, Nov. 2, 23, 26. *Christmas comes but once a year* (with Chettle, Dekker, Heywood).

6. The Induction to *The Malcontent* was written by Webster for the King's men in 1604. See MARSTON.

7. *Westward Ho*, by Dekker and Webster, was acted by the children of Paul's. Acts i., ii., iii., and iv. 2*a* are by Webster, written in the summer of 1603, while "the sickness was hot," iii. 4; Ostend holding out, i. 1; the term lying of Winchester (in the days of Henry III.), iii. 3. Compare

"August 10" in i. 1, and "Midsummer night" in ii. 3. The last two acts are nearly all Dekker's in Dec. 1604. "The book of Ostend" is out, iv. 4*b*; the time of action is 1st Nov., a fortnight after St. Luke's Day, *i.e.*, 18th Oct., in iv. 1; and St. Thomas' Day, 21st Dec., in v. 4. In *Northward Ho* we are told that *Westward Ho* was acted "before Christmas," but it was only just before. Webster calls Mrs. Justiniano Moll; Dekker calls her Clare. Dekker's part is personally satiric. Sir Gosling (Query the same as Sir Giles Goosecap) is a new version of Tucca in v. 3, quite unlike the rest of the play; Mrs. Birdlime in the same scene is, I think, the Madge Owlet of *Histriomastix*, *i.e.*, Worcester's company, formerly Pembroke's. The allusion in v. 1 is probably to Dekker's play, not to Shakespeare's; but "mad Hamlet" in v. 4 is, of course, the Shakespeare *Hamlet. Westward for Smelts* is several times alluded to, but this is not the extant pamphlet which was entered S. R. 15th June 1620. Master Parenthesis, Justiniano's assumed name, means "horns," cuckold. See DAY.

8. *Northward Ho*, also acted by the Paul's children, dates 1605 c. Feb., *Eastward Ho* having come between the two plays we are here concerned with. See i. 3. Dekker certainly wrote the Doll scenes, i. 2, ii. 1, iii. 1, iv. 1, and Webster, I think, the rest. In i. 1 a passage of *Hamlet* is imitated. The Dekker part is personally satirical, Bellamont being, I think, Chapman. He is represented as an "old" poet and playwright. Chapman at this time was forty-eight. In iii. 1 Bellamont has made fools of 500 people, *i.e.*, in the last line of *All Fools* addressed to his audience. In iv. 1 he writes of Cesar and Pompey as Chapman did in his play of that name. The marriage of "Chatillion, the Admiral of France," looks like an allusion to *Chabot, Admiral of France,* long after altered and revived by Shirley. The Duke of

Biron and his execution surely alludes to Chapman's tragedy, which was prohibited in 1608, after having been acted we know not how long : it is true that the quoted lines are not in the extant version, but that has been expurgated and altered, and these lines are very like Chapman in style. The "worthy to be one of your privy chamber or laureat" is still more definite in allusion ; it means worthy to succeed Daniel, now in disgrace for *Eastward Ho* and *Philotas,* but gentleman of the Queen's privy chamber and laureate notwithstanding this. Captain Jenkins, though with far less certainty, I would identify with Drayton. If Drayton's college at Oxford were known it would help us to decide the question. Jenkins was of Jesus College, iv. 1. Belch is a name that occurs also in *Twelfth Night* and *Histriomastix ;* Greenshield in *The London Prodigal. Northward Ho* preceded Day's *Isle of Gulls* and Sharpham's *Fleire,* both of which allude to it.

9. *The White Devil,* or *The tragedy of Paulo Giordano Ursini, Duke of Brachiano,* "with the life and death of Vittoria Corombona, the famous Venetian Curtizan," was Webster's first work without a coadjutor, and acted by the Queen Anne's servants in a dull time of winter, in a black (dark) open theatre, to an auditory neither full nor understanding, *i.e.,* at the Curtain, probably in the cold winter 1607–8. This play afterwards, in 1622, passed to Queen Henrietta's servants, who acted it at the Phœnix. Dyce has confused these two Queen's companies, and made Queen Anne's men act at the Phœnix many years before it was built. R. Perkins pronounced the Epilogue. In Sc. 6 is an allusion (evidently topical) to a French Ambassador who tilted with a staff little bigger than a candle "at last tilting : " this was Monsieur Goterant, and the tilt was on 24th Mar. 1607. No other Frenchman's name occurs in the tilt-lists.

The extreme likeness of this play to *The Revenger's Tragedy* (attributed by common consent to Tourneur, on I know not what authority) is remarkable. The manner of poisoning, Sc. 4; the "discovery" of Lodovico and Gasparo, Sc. 13; the "behind and before," Sc. 14 (compare *R. T.*, ii. 2); the treading on him, Sc. 16 (compare *R. T.*, iii. 5, "stamping on him") in the stage directions; and the procuring a brother to debauch a sister (compare the mother in *R. T.* and the father in *The Usurping Tyrant*), are all salient to understanding eyes. Still more so is the metre of *R. T.*, which is purely Websterian, and quite unlike that of *The Atheist's Tragedy.* When Webster published this play in 1612 he had clearly left the Queen's men. Of the playwrights whom he praises in his Address—Chapman, Jonson, Beaumont, Fletcher, Shakespeare, Dekker, Heywood—only two had written for that company, and these he puts last. In the forged enlargement of the *Elegy on Burbadge*, that actor, who never left the one company then called the King's, is made to act Brachiano as a Queen's man.

10. *Appius and Virginia*, from its allusion at the end to *Lucrece* (Heywood's play of 1608), would seem to date c. 1609. It was undoubtedly a play acted by Queen Anne's men, and passed with *The White Devil* to Queen Henrietta's. It is one of the plays in Beeston's 1639 list.

11. *The Devil's Law Case*, or *When women go to law the Devil is full of business*, was also acted by Queen Anne's servants, and therefore before 1619. Mr. Dyce asserts that it was acted not earlier than 1622, on the strength of a supposed allusion to the Amboyna massacre in Feb. of that year; but, unfortunately for this hypothesis, the play was printed in 1623, and the news of the massacre did not reach England till 1624. This fact relieves Webster, notoriously a slow writer, from the imputation of having written a hurried

play. The true date of the play is 1610 : see ii. 4, where Romelio is thirty-eight, and he was born in 1572, the year after the battle of Lepanto. Compare with this Winifred's recollection of two great frosts, 1564, 1598, (but not 1607), and three great plagues, 1563, 1593, 1603, and the loss of Calais, 1556, which would make her true age about fifty-six, as it should be. The enclosure of common lands was just beginning, i. 2.

12. *The Duchess of Malfy* was played by the King's men at the Blackfriars and the Globe. It has a list of actors. Its date of production (as to which Malone is right and Dyce utterly wrong) was c. 1612, when *The White Devil*, with the praise of the King's men's poets, was published. It was revived after Burbadge's death, c. 1620–1622. This play was published 1623, with verses by Ford, Middleton, and Heywood.

13. 1624, Sept. *A late murder of the Son upon the Mother*, "A new tragedy. Written by Ford and Webster," was licensed. It is not likely that Webster returned to his old business in play-writing. Probably Ford altered some old play of his, as he did those of Dekker, about this time.

14. 1624, Oct. 31. *Monuments of Honor*. This was the City pageant for the Mayoralty of John Gore, Merchant Taylor. Middleton, the regular City poet, was in trouble about *The Game of Chess*, and Webster, for this occasion only, being a Merchant Taylor, filled his place.

15. *A cure for a Cuckold* and 16. *The Thracian Wonder* were attributed to Webster and W. Rowley by Kirkman in 1661, quite wrongly. See under these titles.

17. *Guise*. Mentioned in the Dedication of *The Devil's Law Case*, 1623. Note that in the "Guise" entry in Henslow's *Diary*, 1601 Nov., "Webster" is a forged insertion.

WHETSTONE, GEORGE. (Play.)

    1. 1578, July 31, for Richard Jones. *The Famous History of Promos and Cassandra*, "divided into two Comical Discourses," c. 1578.

Courtier, soldier, farmer; went in the unsuccessful expedition for Newfoundland with Sir Humphrey Gilbert; published many books from 1576 to 1587.

    1. *Promos and Cassandra* was dedicated to his kinsman, William Fleetwood, Recorder of London. It is dated 29th July 1578. This Dedication contains an interesting notice of the plays of that time: the Italian, French and Spanish as too lascivious; the German too holy and pulpiteering. The English "grounds his work on impossibilities, marries, gets children, makes children men, men to conquer kingdoms, murder masters, and bringeth Gods from Heaven and fetcheth Devils from Hell." He complains also of their using "one order of speech for all persons: a gross *indecorum.*" This play was the prototype of Shakespeare's *Measure for Measure;* contains a scene, v. 5 (in First Part), utilised in Chapman's *Mayday*, and the name Grimball, for which see Dekker's *If it be not good*, &c. In i. 9 (Second Part) the singers are "near unto the Music, on some stage erected from the ground."

WHITE, ROBERT. (Mask.)

    1. 1617, May 4. *Cupid's banishment* was presented to Queen Anne (by young gentlewomen of the Ladies' Hall in Deptford) at Greenwich. Printed in Nichols' *James*, iii. 283. Halliwell says in Nichols' *Elizabeth !*

WIBURNE, D. (Latin.)

    1. *Machiavellus*, acted at Cambridge 1597. MS. (dating 1600) Douce, 234, Bodleian.

WILDE, GEORGE. (University and Latin.)

Son of Henry Wilde of London. Born in Middlesex

1609; educated at Merchant Taylors' School; scholar of St. John's, Oxford, 1628; B.LL. 1634; chaplain to Archbishop Laud; LL.D.; turned out of his Fellowship by the parliamentary visitors 1648; Bishop of Londonderry after the Restoration.

1. *Hermophus,* or *Kermophus,* L. C. Several times acted, but never printed.

2. *Euphormus sive Cupido adultus.* Acted at St. John's 5th Feb. 1635. Brit. Mus., *MS. Addit.,* 14,047.

3. *The Hospital of Lovers,* or *Love's Hospital,* C. Acted before the King and Queen by the students of St. John Baptist's College in Oxon. 29th Aug. 1636. Brit. Mus., *MS. Addit.,* 14,047.

4. *The Converted Robber,* P. Acted at St. John's 1637. *MS. Addit.,* 14,047. Scene, Salisbury Plain.

WILKINS, GEORGE. (Plays.)

    2. 1607, June 29, for John Wright. *The Travels of the three English Brothers,* H., 1607.

    1. 1607, July 31, for George Vincent. *The Miseries of Enforced Marriage,* C., 1607, 1611, 1629, 1637.

1. *The Miseries of Enforced Marriage,* " as it is now played by His Majesty's servants," is founded (as Mr. P. A. Daniel first pointed out) on the story of the Calverley Murder, but only includes Calverley's (Scarborough's) life up to 1604. The story was completed in *The Yorkshire Tragedy* (*q.v.*). The date of this play as published cannot be earlier than 1605 : in iii. 2, " Now am I armed to fight with a windmill" must allude to *Don Quixote,* written in 1605, and known in England in that year, though not translated till 1612. The action of the play comprises five years. Scarborough is eighteen at its commencement, ii. 2, " next Pentecost," and twenty-three at the end, v. 2. According to the prose tract S. R. 12th June 1605, William, the eldest of Cal-

verley's sons, was about four years old at the time of the murder, April 1605. But the youngest son, not mentioned in the play, "was out at nurse." The second son, Walter, we know from the parish register of Calverley, was baptized Oct. 1603. Both William and Walter are brought on the stage in v. 2. It was certainly intended that the thin disguise of Scarborough for Calverley should be seen through, and we may expect the utmost attention to local accuracy in the play. The children were probably, then, born in 1601 (William), 1603 Oct. (Walter), and 1605 c. Jan. (the one at nurse): the action of the play will then be 1600–1604; and it was on the stage 1605–1607.

The Clown Robin was, of course, acted by Robert Armin: the Antony Nownow of i. 1 is the minstrel, and *not* Antony Munday: in iii. 2 the two sons are, by inadvertence I suppose, described as twins. In several places the King is mentioned, showing that the date of production is later than Mar. 1603. The reason for the Chamberlain's men enlarging on Scarborow's career in two plays, and not simply representing the murder, as in *The Warning for Fair Women*, is to be looked for in the fact that Calverley's wife was Phillippa Brooke, daughter of Sir John Brooke, son of Lord Cobham, with which family they had been at enmity from the time of Shakespeare's *Henry 4*, 1597; cf. *Merry Wives of Windsor*, 1600. The tract of S. R. June 12 contains also the account of the murder of one Browne by his wife; but this 1605 murder must not be mistaken for the 1573 murder on which *The Warning for Fair Women* was founded. Other tracts on the Calverley Murder are entered S. R. 1605, July 3, Aug. 24.

2. *Pericles.* For Wilkins' share in this play see my *Life of Shakespeare* (*Index*).

3. *The Travels of the Three English Brothers*, Sir Thomas,

Sir Anthony, and Mr. Robert Shirley, as it is now (29th June 1607) played by Her Majesty's servants at the Curtain, was a hurried production by Day, Wilkins, and W. Rowley, founded on Nixon's tract (8th June 1607). The most interesting thing in the play is Scene 9, where Kempe is called "jesting Will," which confirms my identification of him with Lord Leicester's player of 1586, and says he is "hard of study," but will venture to act with the Italians in "any extemporal merriment," which confirms me in referring to Kempe the *Hamlet* allusion to clowns that speak more than is set down for them, iii. 2. In this scene Kempe mentions *England's Joy*, played 6th Nov. 1602; but Kempe had returned to England before then. It is hardly worth the trouble to discriminate the authorship of this play; but as I have tried to do this, I give my results. Rowley, whose metre is easy to distinguish, wrote Sc. 1, 7, 10, 13*b*, and the Prologue; Day wrote Sc. 3 (4, 5, probably), 9, 11, 13*a*; Wilkins, Sc. 2, 6, 8, 12. Wentworth Smith's play of *The Three Brothers* may have been on the same subject. Day was the only one of the three writers who had been employed by the same company as Kempe.

In 1607 Wilkins joined Dekker in writing *Jests of Cock Watt*. See DEKKER.

In 1608 Wilkins published his *Painful Adventures of Pericles, Prince of Tyre*, in which he claims the origination of that play. See my *Life of Shakespeare* (*Index*).

Mr. W. C. Hazlitt is quite wrong in his invention of two dramatists named George Wilkins.

WILMOT, ROBERT. (Early Play.)

1. *Tancred and Gismund*, T., 1591, 1592.

Wilmot was member of the Inner Temple 1568; Rector of North Okeham, Essex, from 28th Nov. 1582; Vicar of Horndon-on-the-Hill, Essex, from 2nd Dec. 1585.

1. *Tancred and Gismund.* See my *History of the Stage,* p. 17.
Wilmot was not the R. W. of *The three Lords of London,*
as Hazlitt guesses.

WILLAN, LEONARD.   (Play).

    1. *Astræa,* or *True Love's Mirror,* P., 1651.

WILSON, ARTHUR.   (Plays.)

    3. 1653, Sept. 9.   *The Inconstant Lady.*   (MS. said
       to have been destroyed by Warburton's servant,
       but printed 1814.)

Son of Richard Wilson, Yarmouth, Norfolk.   Born 1595;
in France 1604–1611; then clerk in the Exchequer Office,
but discharged for quarrelling; robbed his father; became
secretary to the Earl of Essex; was again discharged at the
instigation of Essex' second Countess.   Entered at Trinity,
Oxford; became M.A.; entered the service of Robert Earl
of Warwick.   Died at Felstead, Essex, Oct. 1652.

    1. 1633, Jan. 14.   *The Corporal* was licensed for acting
at Blackfriars by the King's men; a fragment exists in MS.
Scene, Lorraine.   Entered S. R. 1646, Sept. 4, with

    2. *The Switzer* [of about the same date].

    3. *The Inconstant Lady;* cf. *supra.*   This play was also
called *Better Late than Never.*   MS.   Quoted by Halliwell,
Marriage of Wit and Wisdom, p. 85.

WILSON, ROBERT, Senior.   (Actor and Playwright.)

    1. *The 3 Ladies of London,* C.   By Roger Warde,
       1584, 1592 (by R. W.).

    2. *The 3 Lords and Ladies of London,* Moral.   By R.
       Jones, 1590 (by R. W.).

    4. 1594, May 13, for Thomas Creede.   *The Pedlar's*
       Prophecy, C., 1595 (anonymous).

    5. 1594, June 8, for Cuthbert Burby.   *The Cobbler's*
       Prophecy, C., 1594 (by Robert Wilson).

    3. *Fair Em,* 1631 (anonymous).

Robert Wilson was one of the Earl of Leicester's company 1574, May 7, and the only author among them; of the Queen's c. Mar. 1583. As he and Tarlton were the only two Queen's men known to have written plays, and Tarlton, for many reasons, cannot be intended, there can be small doubt that he was the player who introduced Greene to this company after he came to London, 1585–6. The introduction was probably in 1587. This player had been a stroller, and played *Delphrygus, The King of Fairies, The Labours of Hercules,* and *The Highway to Heaven;* but now he has £200 worth of playing apparel, " reputed able at my proper cost to build a windmill;" for seven years was absolute interpreter of the puppets and penned morals: *Man's Wit* and *The Devil and Dives.   Man's Wit* is, I think, *Lusty Juventus.* (See the speech of Abominable Living—

"Your *wit* therein I greatly do allow;
For, and if I were a *man,* as you are," &c.)

At any rate it is not *Wit and Science* nor *Wit and Wisdom,* for in these interludes Wit is a boy.   *The Devil and Dives* may be *The Di·obedient Child,* in which the Rich Man and the Devil are prominent characters.   These two are the plays out of which the interlude introduced in *Sir Thomas More* is made up; but they are both old Edward VI. plays, written by Wever and Ingeland, so that the point of Greene's statement seems to be that the player could only cobble old plays and do nothing original.   All this is to be found in *Greene's Groatsworth of Wit,* 1592.   Wilson was before Heywood's time; cf. his *Apology for Actors.*   This distinguishes him from the younger Wilson; he probably died in the plague-year, 1593, as Heywood's stage career began c. 1594.   Other matter on Wilson's life, being conjectural, will be more appropriately placed under the plays which I shall now consider.

1. *The three Ladies of London* (Lucre, Love, and Conscience), by R. W., is undoubtedly rightly assigned to Wilson by Collier (Hazlitt's suggestion of Wilmot is quite out of the question), and it must have been performed by the Queen's men c. 1583. The date in the play, Sc. 1, "not much more than 26 years; it was in Queen Mary's time," would bring it to Christmas 1584; but it does not occur in the 1584–5 list of Queen's men's plays; and that this was the date of publication, not of performance, is shown by the alteration into "33 years" in the 1592 edition. That it was played by the Queen's men is shown under the next play. Wilson must have been alive when this 1592 edition was issued. It appears from a stage direction in the last scene that Love and Lucre were played by one actor, and so were the English Judge and Nemo: he is called "Judge Nemo" in Sc. 16, to distinguish him from "the Judge of Turkey" in Sc. 13. Gerontus is not the same personage as Gernutus, the Jew of Venice, in the old ballad. Love is a "Deformed creature, much like Bifrons, the base daughter of Juno." Dissimulation is a farmer, Simplicity a miller, in Sc. 2 (ii. 1). This play was "publicly played," but no statement is made where.

2. *The three Lords* (Policy, Pomp, and Pleasure) *and three Ladies* (Love, Lucre, and Conscience) *of London* is an amplification of the preceding, still more of a Moral and less of a Comedy: performed shortly after Tarlton's death, *i.e.*, after Sept. 1588; probably 26th Dec.; see Sc. 1. If I rightly understand the allusions, Tarlton had acted in *Wit and Will* [*The Marriage of Wit and Science*] in 1567–8. The allusion to Tarlton's picture shows that *Tarlton's Jests*, in which the picture appeared, had already been published. The statement that Simplicity (probably acted by Wilson himself), Wit, and Will had acted with Tarlton proves that

the present play was acted by the Queen's men. The devices of the Lords, a falcon (merlin), tortoise-shell ("defence"), and lily, seem to be taken from the names Marlow or Marlin, Peele (a fort), and Lyly. The ballad-title, "Mine own sweet Willy is laid in his grave," may allude, like the almost contemporary, "Our own sweet Willy, ah, is dead of late," in Spenser's *Tears of the Muses*, 1590, to the retirement of Lyly from writing for the stage.

3. *Fair Em*, or *The Miller's daughter of Manchester*, "with the Love of William the Conqueror," was acted by Lord Strange's servants c. 1590. In Greene's Introduction to his *Farewell to Folly* (after 2nd Nov. 1590, before 6th Dec. 1591) there is an attack on this play for "abusing of Scripture." Greene reproves the author for distilling out of ballads and borrowing of Theological poets, and calls him the "father of interludes," which goes far towards proving his identity with the seven years' interpreter of the puppets who wrote *Man's Wit* and *The Devil and Dives:* cf. *The Groatsworth of Wit*, 1592. But a comparison of Greene's quotations with passages from Wilson's other plays will remove any outstanding doubt on this matter :—

"A man's conscience is a thousand witnesses" (*Farewell to Folly*).
"Thy conscience is a thousand witnesses" (*Fair Em*, Sc. 17).
"I, Conscience, am a thousand witnesses" (*Three Ladies*, Sc. 16).
"Love covereth the multitude of sins" (*Farewell to Folly*).
"Love, that covers multitude of sins,
    Makes love in parents wink at children's faults" (*Fair Em*, Sc. 17).
"Love doth cover heaps of cumbrous evils,
    And doth forget the faults that were before" (*Three Lords*, &c., Sc. 3).

Wilson had evidently left the Queen's company and Greene, and gone to Strange's in 1590: it was the actor, not the writer, that they missed. Wilson was the Roscius of that time, Alleyn was beginning to be popular, and the union of the two in Strange's company completed their triumph over the Queen's, who practically disappear from London at the end of 1591. It is possible that this play, which has Mandeville for Manvile in its *Dram. Pers.*, may be the *Sir John Mandeville* acted (but not as a new play) at the Rose by Strange's men 1592, Feb. 24. It is still more likely that after Wilson's death the play, having served its temporary satirical purpose, was sold by Alleyn to Sussex' men, who acted *William the Conqueror* at the Rose 1594, Jan. 4. I say satirical purpose, for to any one familiar with the methods of the stage at that time it will be abundantly clear that Greene was satirised in the play as Manvile, Marlow (Marley) being Mounteney, and Peele (a fort) Vallingford (Walling also means a fort). *Fair Em of Manchester* is taken from an old ballad, *The Miller's Daughter of Manchester*, S. R. 2nd Mar. 1580–1 : in the play she is L. Strange's company, who is married to Peele (Vallingford). Manchester was in Lancashire, where L. Strange's chief seat at Knowsley was also situate; while the Chester Earldom, Manvile's place, belonged to the Crown, indicating the Queen's company. The Miller, Sir Thomas Goddard (no doubt from the ballad) is a thin disguise for Sir Edmond Trafford, who in the Norman invasion disguised himself as a miller, on the tradition of which event the Trafford crest was granted c. 1550. Elinor, forsaken by Manvile, is probably the Queen's company ; while Trotter would seem to be Wilson, who may have acted the part himself. This interpretation is, of course, conjectural; but its exact agreement with the careers of every one concerned in it goes far to prove its truth, whatever critics who are unfamiliar with the ways of the early stage may allege against it. The second plot is also personal. William the Conqueror, *alias* Robert of Windsor, was William Kemp, as Mr. Simpson supposed, who went abroad with Leicester in 1586. The English players in that year are traced by Cohn from Denmark to Saxony, and the critics who oppose this part of Simpson's interpretation (which is, however, elsewhere most erroneous, owing to his determination to see Shakespeare in everything) have never offered any explanation how William comes to be Duke of Saxony in Sc. 17. Lubeck is probably Thomas King; Dirot and Demarch, Hemings and Phillips. This second plot is fashioned after Greene's *Tully's Love.* Tully is frequently used by Greene as a pseudonym for himself, and Roscius for Wilson. I believe the Roscius in Nash's epistle before *Menaphon*, 1589, alludes to Wilson, and that Lord Strange's was the "company of taffeta fools with their feathers, whose beauty if our poets had not pieced (peecte) with the supply of their periwigs, they might have antict it until this time up and down the country with *The King of Fairies* and dined every day at the peas-porridge ordinary with *Delphrigus*." Simpson, followed by Arber and other learned Doctors, makes "peecte" mean "pecked," and corrects into "decked"!

4. *The Pedlar's Prophecy* is attributed to Wilson from its likeness to the ensuing play.

5. *The Cobbler's Prophecy* was published as R. Wilson's. Collier says it is similar to *The Three Lords* and to *The Three Ladies.* These were published posthumously. Wilson did not attach his name to any publication overseen by himself.

WILSON, ROBERT, Junior. (Plays.)

1. 1598, Mar. 25, 30. 1 *Earl Godwin and his 3 sons* (with Chettle, Dekker, Drayton).

1*. 1598, Mar. 30. *Piers of Exton* (with Chettle, Dekker, Drayton).

2. 1598, May 22. 1 *Black Batman of the North* (with Chettle, Dekker, Drayton).

3. 1598, May 6, June 6, 10. 2 *Godwin* (with Chettle, Dekker, Drayton).

4. 1598, June 13–26 (seven entries). *Richard Cœur de Lion's funeral* (with Chettle, Drayton, Monday).

5. 1598, June 26, July 8, 13, 14. 2 *Black Batman* (with Chettle).

6. 1598, June 31 [*sic*], July 9, 10. *The Madman's Morris* (with Dekker, Drayton).

7. 1598, July 17, 26, 27, 28. *Hannibal and Hermes:* or 1 *Worse Feared than Hurt* (with Dekker, Drayton).

8. 1598, Aug. 8, 10. *Piers of Winchester* (with Dekker, Drayton).

9. 1598, Aug. 19, 24. *Chance Medley* (with Dekker, Monday).

10. 1598, Aug. 21, 26, 29. *Catiline's Conspiracy* (with Chettle).

11, 12. 1599, Oct. 16. 1, 2 *Sir John Oldcastle* (with Drayton, *q.v.*, Hathway, Monday.

1599, Nov. 1. Borrows 10s. of Henslow. Apparently in difficulties after a year's cessation of writing.

13. 1599, Nov. 8. 2 *Henry Richmond*. No first part known. Mr. Warner, *Dulwich Catalogue*, p. 16, has shown that the plot of Sc. 1–5, assigned by Collier to Richard Crookback, belongs to this play.

14. 1600, Jan. 10. *Owen Tudor* (with Drayton, Hathway, Monday).

Buried at Cripplegate 20th Nov. 1600 as Robert Wilson, yeoman (a player); but his name never appears among the "sharers" in Henslow's *Diary*. There is no evidence that a still younger Robert Wilson (Collier's *Actors*, p. xviii.) had anything to do with the stage, and the attribution to our Wilson of part authorship of *The Shoemaker's Holiday* is founded on a forgery. He, and not the elder Wilson, is the one mentioned by Meres 1598.

WINGFIELD, M. (Latin.)

1. 9th Feb. 1631, for Robert Milborne. *Pedantius*, C., 1631. Mentioned in *Harrington's Apology*, 1591. Ascribed to Wingfield by Nash in his *Strange News*, 1593. Published with two copperplates of scenes.

WOODES, NATHANIEL. (Early Play.)

1. *The Conflict of Conscience*, C., 1581.

See my *History of the Stage*, pp. 65, 71. Woodes was a clergyman in Norwich.

WOTTON, Sir Henry. (Play.)

1. *Tancred.* Written at Queen's College, Oxford, 1586—7. Not extant.

YARRINGTON, ROBERT. (Play.)

1. *Two lamentable Tragedies*, &c., T., 1601, for Matthew Law.

1. *Two tragedies in one.* This singular production is made up of alternate scenes from two stories—1. Merry's murder of Beech, a Thames Street chandler; 2. The murder of an orphan in Italy, the story being the same as that of the ballad of *The Babes in the Wood.* Still more curious is the fact that in Nov. 1599 Chettle began a play for the Admiral's men at the Rose called *The Tragedy of Orphans*, for which in Sept. 1601, when they had removed to the Fortune, he got a further payment on account, but apparently never finished; and that at a very close date, Nov.— Dec. 1599, Haughton and Day got full payment for their *Tragedy of Merry.* This coincidence is sufficiently striking; but when we find that in 1600 the Master of the Revels was paid for licensing *Beech's Tragedy*, which was evidently the same play, the connexion grows stronger; for I have shown in my *History of the Stage* that such payments in

Henslow's *Diary* were for licenses to print, and not to perform. This play was published by Matthew Law, who is only known as a play-publisher from this instance and that of [Heywood's] *How to choose*, &c. I can see no doubt that this play was the publication paid for, made up out of the two by Chettle, Day, and Haughton ; that Yarrington was a fictitious name ; and that the 10s. paid in 1601 was for alterations, perhaps for Chettle's pains in consolidating the two plays. Moreover, on 10th Jan. 1600 Day got paid £2 for his *Italian Tragedy*, which may have been the same as *The Tragedy of Orphans*. There is a queer Induction to the play, palpably in imitation of *The Warning for Fair Women*, which tells us that Beech had been lately murdered.

ZOUCH, R. (University.)

2. 1638, Nov. 7, for Humpnrey Moseley. *The Sophister*, C. Dr. Zouch belonged to New College, Oxford, where this play was no doubt acted.

1. *Fallacy*, or *The troubles of great Hermenia*, an allegorical play, "written by "R. Z.," is almost certainly by Zouch. Brit. Mus., *MS. Harl.*, 6869, dated 16th Aug. 1631.

ANONYMOUS PLAYS.

I. 1559–1583. NON-EXTANT PLAYS.

A. *Court Performances.*

a. Paul's Choir Boys.

1. *Effiginia* (*Iphigenia*), T., 1571, Dec. 28. [Translation from Euripides.]

2. *Alcmeon*, 1573, Dec. 27. [Euripides restored.]

3. *Error*, H., 1577, Jan. 1. [Query from Plautus' *Menœchmi.*]

4. *Titus and Gisippus*, H., 1577, Feb. 17. [Query Ralph Radcliff's *Friendship of Titus and Gysippus*, revived from Edward VI.' time.]

5. *The Marriage of Mind and Measure*, Moral, 1579, Jan. 4. [Is this a mistake for *The Marriage of Wit and Wisdom*, which in the MS. transcript made for printing is dated 1579? It was written in Edward VI.' time: see "King," p. 43, in the Sh. Soc. reprint. The colophon is "Amen quod Fra Merbury." It is the same as *Hit the nail o' the head*, mentioned in *Sir T. More*. See the concluding lines.]

6. *Scipio Africanus*, H., 1580, Jan. 3.

7. *Pompey*, a story, 1581, Jan. 6. [Alluded to by Gosson in his *School of Abuse.*]

b. Chapel Choir Boys.

8. *Narcissus*, 1572, Jan. 6. Cf. Heywood, *Apology for Actors*.

9. *Mutius Scœvola*, H., 1577, Jan. 6. (with the Windsor boys).

10. *Loyalty and Beauty*, H., 1579, Mar. 2.

11. *Alucius*, H., 1579, Dec. 27.

12. *A game of the Cards*, C. or Moral, 1582, Dec. 26.
[Perhaps *The play of Cards* mentioned by Harington in his
Apology of Poetry, 1591 ; but see *Terminus et non*, Nash.]

c. Westminster Schoolboys.

13. *Paris and Vienna*, 1572, Feb. 19.   [These are
characters, not towns.]

14. *Truth, Faithfulness, and Mercy*, 1574, Jan. 1.

d. Merchant Taylors' Schoolboys.

15. *Timoclea, at the Siege of Thebes by Alexander*, 1574,
Feb. 2.

16. *Perseus and Andromeda*, 1574, Feb. 23.

17. *Ariodanto and Geneuora*, 1582, Jan. 12.   [From
Ariosto's *Orlando Furioso*, v.]

e. Windsor Choir Boys.

18. *Ajax and Ulysses*, 1572, Jan. 1.

19. *Quint[us] Fabi[us]*, 1574, Jan. 6.
Mutius Scevola.   See Anon., 9.

f. Unknown Company, 1567--8.

20. *As plain as can be.*

21. *The Painful Pilgrimage.*

22. *Jack and Gill.*

23. *Six Fools.*

24. *Wit and Will.*   [Probably *The Marriage of Wit and
Science*, q.v.]

25. *Prodigality.* [Not *Liberality and Prodigality* of 1602.]

25*. *The King of Scots*, T.

1572-3.

26. *Theagines and Curiclia* [Chariclea].   From Helio-
dorus.

27. *Fortune.* [Query *The Play of Fortune to know each one their conditions,* &c., entered S. R. 1566–7, revived.] Cf. *Common Conditions.*

g. Sir R. Lane's Men.

28. *Lady Barbara,* 1571, Dec. 27.
29. *Cloridon and Radiamanta,* 1572, Feb. 17.

h. Leicester's Men.

30. *Predor and Lucia,* 1573, Dec. 26.
31. *Mamillia,* 1573, Dec. 28.
32. *Philemon and Philecia,* 1574, Feb. 22.
33. *Panecia,* 1575, Jan. 1.
34. *The Collier,* H., 1576, Dec. 30.
35. *The Greek Maid,* P. or H., 1579, Jan. 4.
36. *The Rape of the Second Helen,* H., 1579, Jan. 6.
37. *Delight,* C., 1580, Dec. 26.   See *Play of Plays.*
38. *Telomo,* H., 1583, Feb. 10.   [The *Ptolemy* mentioned in Gosson's *School of Abuse* as performed at the Bull.]

i. Warwick's Men.

39. *The Painter's Daughter,* 1576, Dec. 26.
40. *The Irish Knight,* 1577, Feb. 18; also called *Cutwell.*
41. *The Three Sisters of Mantua,* 1578, Dec. 26.
42. *The Knight in the Burning Rock,* H., 1579, Mar. 1.
43. *The Four Sons of Fabius,* H., 1580, Jan. 1. [Alluded to by Gosson in *The School of Abuse.*]

k. L. Clinton's Men.

44. *Herpetulus the Blue Knight and Perobia,* 1574, Jan. 3.

45. *Pretestus*, 1575, Jan. 2.

l. Lord Charles Howard's Men.

46, 47, 48. *The History of Phedrastus; and Phigon and Lucia;* together, 1574, Dec. 28.

49. *Toolie*, 1576, Dec. 27.

50. *The Solitary Knight*, H., 1577, Feb. 17.

m. Sussex' Men.

51. *The Ccno[ce]fals*, H., 1577, Feb. 2.

52. *The Cruelty of a Stepmother*, H., 1578, Dec. 28.

53. *Murderous Michael*, H., 1579, Mar. 3.

53*. *The Duke of Milan and the Marquis of Mantua*, H., 1579, Dec. 26.

54. *Portio and Demorantes*, H., 1580, Feb. 2.

55. *Sarpedon*, H., 1580, Feb. 16.

56. *Ferrar*, H., 1583, Jan. 6. [Query Ferrara or written by Ferrars?]

n. Derby's Men.

57. *The Soldan and the Duke of . . .*, H., 1580, Feb. 14.

o. L. Hunsdon's Men.

58. *Beauty and Huswifery*, C., 1582, Dec. 27 [but see *Calisto and Melibœa*, or *Beauty and Good Properties of Women*, printed by Rastell, and republished in Hazlitt's *Dodsley*]. *(S)celestina*, T. C., on the same subject, was entered S. R. for W. Aspley 1598, Oct. 5.

B. *Plays only Known by Mention.*

59. *The Blacksmith's daughter*, containing "the treachery of Turks, the honorable bounty of a noble mind, and the

shining of virtue in distress," Gosson, *School of Abuse*, 1579. Acted at the Theater.

60. *Cupid and Psyche. Ibid.* Acted at Paul's.

61. *Cæsar and Pompey. Ibid.*

Ptolemy; acted at the Bull. See *Telomo*, Anon., 38.

62. *The Jew*, containing "the greediness of worldly choosers and the bloody minds of usurers;" acted at the Bull. *Ibid.*

63. *The Cradle of Security*, mentioned in *Sir T. More* and in *Patient Grissel;* acted at Gloucester c. 1570, and described in *Mount Tabor* by R. Willis 1639, written in his seventy-fifth year. Willis stood between his father's legs to see this moral, and was at the date I have given about five years old. Mr. Halliwell gives between 1560 and 1570; but Willis, born in 1564–5, could hardly have been present in 1560, even in embryo. The description of the play is quoted in *Biog. Dram.;* the characters are a Prince (the wicked of the world), Pride, Covetousness, and Luxury (three ladies), the End of the World and the Last Judgment (two old men), &c. The ladies cradle and transform the Prince with "a vizard like a swine's snout;" End of the World strikes the cradle with his mace, courtiers, ladies, and vizard vanish; the Prince is judged, and carried away by wicked spirits.

64. *Mingo;* acted at Bristol Oct. 1577 by Leicester's men; quoted by Collier from City accounts in note to *Northbrooke's Treatise*, p. viii.

65. *What Mischief worketh in the mind of Man;* acted at Bristol July 1578 by L. Barkeley's players. *Ibid.*

66. *The Queen of Ethiopia* [*Theagines and Chariclea;* see Anon., 26]; at Bristol, by L. Howard's men Sept. 1578. *Ibid.*

67. *The Court of Comfort;* at Bristol by L. Sheffield's men Sept. 1578. *Ibid.*

68. *The Red Knight;* at Bristol by the Chamberlain's [Sussex'] men Aug. 1576. *Ibid.*, p. xi.

69. *Delphrygus* (Del Phrygio); mentioned in *Greene's Groatsworth of Wit*, 1592, and Nash's Address in Greene's *Menaphon*, 1589.

70. *The King of Fairies. Ibid.*

71. *The Twelve Labors of Hercules;* mentioned in the *Groatsworth of Wit* only.

72. *The Highway to Heaven. Ibid.* In these four Roscius, the player of Greene's book, acted.

73. *Man's Wit*, a moral. *Ibid.*

74. *Dives*, a dialogue moral. *Ibid.* These two Roscius wrote. [But was this one a revival of Ingeland's *Disobedient Child?* or of Radcliffe's *Dives and the Devil*, temp. Edward VI.?] *Dives and Lazarus* is mentioned in *Sir T. More* along with *The Cradle of Security* (already treated of), *Hit Nail o' th' Head* (*Marriage of Wit and Wisdom;* extant), *Impatient Poverty*, S. R. 1560, *The Play of Four P's* (by John Heywood; extant), *Lusty Juventus* (by R. Wever; extant), and *The Marriage of Wit and Wisdom* (1579, extant; cf. *The Marriage of Mind and Measure*). The play in *Sir T. More* is from *The Disobedient Child*, by T. Ingeland, and *Lusty Juventus;* it has nothing in common with *The Marriage of Wit and Wisdom*, though called by that name. See also Lupton's *All for Money*.

75. *The Prodigal Child* in *Histriomastix* is not, I think, taken from a specific interlude; it rather satirises them as a class, and is only noticeable here as introducing, contrary to the general custom, the Vice and Iniquity as distinct personages.

75*. The *Play of Cards* is mentioned in Harrington's *Apology*, 1591. Was this *Terminus et non?*

C. *Plays Known only from S. R. Entries.*

76. *Witless,* 1560–1, for T. Hackett. Probably an old Edward 6 moral revived, like *Titus and Gisippus.*

77. *The Two Sins of King David,* 1561–2, for T. Hackett. "A new interlude;" but query Bale's *David and Absalom* (extant in MS.) revived.

78. *Far fetcht and dear bought is good for ladies,* 1566–7, for T. Hackett.

79. *The College of Canonical Clerks,* 1566–7, for J. Charlewood.

D. *Miscellaneous.*

80. *Egio.* "An interlude written about the year 1560," Halliwell. I know nothing of it. Is it extant?

81. *Æsop's Crow.* A Court play, in which the actors were dressed as birds. Mentioned in *Beware the Cat,* 1584.

81*. *Hock Tuesday.* The Coventry men's Hock-tide show, representing in a tilting-match the defeat of the Danes by the English A.D. 1002, was presented to Queen Elizabeth at Kenilworth 1575. I do not reckon this as a play.

II. Extant Plays.

82. *Wealth and Health;* 83. *Youth* (for J. Walley, S. R. 1557–8); and 84. *Lusty Juventus* (for J. King, S. R. 1560, Aug. 14), though published in Elizabeth's time, are Edward 6 plays, and beyond my purview.

85. *Calisto and Melibœa,* to which I often have to refer, is still older, and was printed by Rastell.

A. *Court Plays.*

86. *The Nice Wanton,* an Edward 6 play, altered for performance before Elizabeth, was entered S. R. 1560,

June 10, for John King.   See my *History of the Stage*, p. 57.

87. *Impatient Poverty* (which required four players) I have not seen, but as it was entered S. R. with the preceding, I anticipate that the same remarks will apply to it. See Anon., 74.

88. *King Darius*, 1562–3.   See my *History of the Stage*, p. 59.

89. *New Custom*, a Court play (1573, for A. Veale), is another Edward 6 play altered about 1563–4.   See my *History of the Stage*, p. 64.   There is a play mentioned in Captain Cox's library (Nichols, i. 454), called *Nugizee*, i.e., *New Guise* (90), which must not be confused with this play; it is very old, and is undoubtedly the play to which Mr. Collier gave the name *Mankind* (90), in which New Guise is a chief character.   The mischief of this system of name-making in such hands as Mr. Collier and his imitators is considerable.

91. *The Marriage of Wit and Science* was, in my opinion, the same as *Wit and Will*, acted at Court 1567–8.   See my *History of the Stage*, p. 64.   The practice of giving new names to plays when acted at Court lasted at least till 1613.   *Vide* the Court list for that year, *ibid.*, p. 175. This is a most important factor in determining the identity of twice-named plays which has been hitherto unrecognised.

92. *The Marriage of Wit and Wisdom* is an old play of Edward 6' time.   The transcript MS. extant is dated 1579, the date of *The Marriage of Mind and Measure*, as acted at Court by the Paul's boys, with which it was probably identical.   But in .both these "marriage" plays the extant copies are those, not of Court, but of public performance.

B. *Plays not Known to have been Acted at Court.*

93. *Albion Knight*, c. 1560. See my *History of the Stage*, p. 66.

94. *Godly Queen Hester*, 1561; *ibid.*, p. 66. I believe this was written by the author of *Misogonus* [R. Edwards]; but I do not like to speak positively, having only seen the extracts in Collier. Perhaps some more favoured person may be allowed by the Duke of Devonshire to publish a fuller account of it, or even to reprint the play. At any rate, it is most noticeable that *Misogonus* and *Hester* are the only two early plays in which the Vice is replaced by a domestic Fool. The style of both is very similar; so is the metre.

95. *Tom Tiler and his wife*, c. 1560–1, *ibid.*, p. 66, was acted either by the Paul's boys or more likely by those of the Chapel.

96. *The Trial of Treasure, ibid.*, p. 66, is simply a morality, c. 1564.

97. *Common Conditions* is one of the plays describing "the adventures of amorous knights passing from country to country for the love of their ladies" (Stubbes *apud* Gosson, *Plays Confuted*, quoted by Collier). It is called a "pleasant comedy" in the title. Shift, Thrift, and Unthrift are characters in it: Conditions is the Vice. It is very alliterative. It was entered S. R. for John Hunter 26th July 1576. If my interpretation of the words "after the manner of" (*History of the Stage*, p. 70) is erroneous, as it possibly may be, in that case I regret that I had unjustly blamed Halliwell in this instance for inaccuracy.

98. The history of the two valiant knights, *Sir Clyomon, Knight of the Golden Shield,* son to the King of Denmark, and (*Sir*) *Clamydes, the White Knight,* son to the King of

Suavia, was acted by the Queen's players, but is evidently an older play than any originally produced by that company. From them it passed probably through L. Strange's company, and was published by T. Creede 1599 (see *History of the Stage*, p. 107). As this is the only play published at that date with four kings in it, I identify it with *The Four Kings* of Henslow's *Diary*. In this very alliterative play Subtle Shift is the Vice: in Sc. 6 he says he must play the Ambidexter. The Vice in *Cambyses* is Ambidexter, and that was revived 27th Dec. 1578. I think the present play was produced contemporaneously with that revival at latest; it may have been earlier, for *Cambyses* originally appeared 6th Jan. 1570. The authorship has been attributed by Dyce, &c., to Peele, on the evidence of an early MS. inscription in a copy; but the value of such inscriptions is very small when uncorroborated. Compare the well-known triply contradictory instance of *The Usurping Tyrant* (*Second Maiden's Tragedy*). I promised in my previous work to show reason for my then opinion that Wilson wrote these two plays; but later investigations lead me to reject that plausible hypothesis, and to claim them for R. B. (Query Richard Bower), the author of *Appius and Virginia*. The style and metre are very like in all three plays; the alliteration in all three is excessive far beyond any other plays of this period that I know. Shift is a character in *Conditions* and in *Clyomon:* Rumour enters in exactly the same way in *Appius* and in *Clyomon* (in one scene only); "Our author" is mentioned in the Prologues of *Appius* and of *Clyomon*, and, above all, they all contain many singular grammatical inversions which I have seldom found elsewhere, and never in such overwhelming abundance. Any one who can bear the tediousness of reading these long-winded folk-lore romances (for such they are, all three) consecutively will, I think, confirm my present opinion.

99. *Robin Conscience* (which is not connected with the theatre at all) has been sufficiently noticed in my *History of the Stage*, p. 65.

100. *Mind, Will, and Understanding* is an ancient miracle-play outside of my purview.

Plays at Court.
By the Queen's Men, 1584–5.

101*. *Phyllida and Corin*, 1584, Dec. 26.

102*. *Felix and Felismena*, 1585, Jan. 3. The probable foundation of *The Two Gentlemen of Verona*.

103*. *Five plays in one*, 1585, Jan. 6. See *Seven Deadly Sins*.

104*. *Three plays in one*, 1585, Feb. 21. Prepared, but not shown. See *Seven Deadly Sins*.

105*. *Antic Play, and Comedy*, 1585, Feb. 23.

By the Earl of Oxford's Boys.

106*. *Agamemnon and Ulysses*, 1584, Dec. 27.

———

107*. A comedy [*Sylla Dictator* would be a much better name than *Catiline*, as given by Collier] was played before Lord Burghley at Gray's Inn by the members 1588, Jan. 16. See my *History of the Stage*, p. 92.

Anonymous Plays in Henslow's Diary.
i. Performed by L. Strange's Men.
a. Old Plays.

101. *Sir John Mandevile*, 24th Feb. 1592.

102. *Harry of Cornwall*, 25th Feb.

103. *Clorys and Orgasto*, 28th Feb.

104. *Pope Joan*, 1st Mar.

105. *Machiavel*, 2nd Mar. [Query foundation of Daborne's *Machiavel and the Devil*.]

106. *Bendo and Ricardo*, 4th Mar.

107. *Four plays in one*, 6th Mar. [but see *Seven Deadly Sins*].

108. *Zenobia*, 9th Mar.

109. *Constantine*, 21st Mar.

110. *Jerusalem*, 22nd Mar. [but see Legge and Heywood.]

111. *Brandymer*, 6th April.

112. *Cosmo*, 12th Jan. 1593.

b. New Plays.

113. 1 *Henry 6* (with Talbot additions), 3rd Mar. 1592. See my *Life of Shakespeare*.

114. *Titus and Vespasian*, 11th April [but see German plays, *ibid.*].

115. 2 *Tamar Cam*, 28th April [but for extant plot of the First Part see further on, Oct. 1602].

116. *The Taner of Denmark*, 23rd May.

117. *The Knack to Know a Knave*, 10th June. Extant. See Anon., 229*.

118. *The Jealious Comedy*, 5th Jan. 1593 [but see *Merry Wives of Windsor* in my *Life of Shakespeare*].

ii. By the Earl of Sussex' Men : Old Non-extant Plays.

119. *God speed the plough*, 27th Dec. 1593. S. R. 1 Mar. 1601 for J. Harrison, junior.

120. *Huon of Bordeaux*, 28th Dec.

121. *Buckingham*, 30th Dec.

121*. *Richard the Confessor*, 31st Dec. [Query *Alphonsus, Emperor of Germany*.]

122. *William the Conqueror*, 4th Jan. 1594. [Query

Fair Em, retained from L. Strange's men, like *The Jew of Malta.*

123. *Friar Francis*, 7th Jan. Referred to in Heywood's *Apology for Actors*, 1612 : the same story as Heywood's, but without the name of the company, is told in the German *Hamlet*, Sc. 7, and in *A Warning for Fair Women*, ii. 2.

124. *Abram and Lot*, 9th Jan.

125. *The fair maid of Italy*, 12th Jan.; and again 4th April, when they acted [on alternate days] with the Queen's men.

126. *King Lud*, 18th Jan.

127. *The Rangers*, C., 2nd April. Evidently bought by Henslow, for subsequent acting by the Admiral's men.

One New Play Extant.

128. *Titus Andronicus*, 23rd Jan. 1594. See *Life of Shakespeare*. The authorship of this play will, I fear, long remain a puzzle to critics. How such a play came to be produced by Sussex' men, who have left us no other play whatever (except *George a Greene*, and that was probably not originally theirs), is a mystery. I cannot believe that either Kyd or Marlow would have written for these strollers, who only appear in London between 27th Dec. 1593 and 4th April 1594, in consequence, probably, of their one Court play of 2nd Jan. 1592 (the theatres were closed, remember, from June to December 1593). The more likely view is that the author was dead, and they got the play cheap in some exceptional fashion. Again, the absence of any trace of allegorical personages or Induction militates against its being Kyd's work. I fear it is Marlow's. But the most puzzling thing of all is, that it is so close a reproduction of the *Titus and Vespasian* of 1592 in plot and treatment, for this is the first instance I can find of any such use of a preceding play. Shakespeare often did this,

notably in his *John, Henry 4, Henry 5, Hamlet, Taming of the Shrew*, &c., but never while the play thus used as a foundation for his new one was in possession of a rival company. This consideration persuades me that this play was such a re-fashioning of the *Titus and Vespasian* written for L. Strange's men; and if so, probably by Marlow, who was writing for them up to the closing of the theatres in January 1593. At his death in September the MS. might easily stray to Sussex' men, but we know that Derby's (who had been L. Strange's) took care to get it before 16th April. Sussex' had it in February; sold it to Pembroke's (probably soon after breaking on Feb. 8); and about two months after Pembroke's parted with it to Derby's, who, having become the Chamberlain's men, acted it 5th June, as well as other plays, viz., the following:—

iii. Plays Acted by the Chamberlain's Men: all Old Plays.

129. *Hester and Ahasuerus*, 3rd June 1596. [Query *Godly Queen Hester*, q.v.]

130. *Hamlet*, 9th June. See KYD.

131. *The taming of a Shrew*, 11th June. See KYD.

iv. Play Acted by the Queen's Men.

132. *Leir*, 6th April 1594. See LODGE.

v. Plays Acted by the Admiral's Men.

a. Old Plays.

133. *Cutlack*, 16th May 1594. Alleyn played Cutlack. "With Alleyn's Cutlack's gait," Guilpin's *Skialetheia*, 1598.

134. *Philippo and Hypolito*, 9th July. Probably the *Philenzo and Hypolita* which Massinger altered [from Dekker], *q.v.*, and which was entered S. R. 9th Sept. 1653. One MS. was destroyed by Warburton's servant,

but another is said by Collier to exist in the Conway papers.

135. *Mahomet,* 14th Aug.; but see PEELE. Bought from Alleyn 2nd Aug. 1601.

136. *The Love of a Grecian Lady (The Grecian Comedy),* 4th Oct.

137. *The French Doctor,* 18th Oct. Probably Dekker's *Jew of Venice,* q.v. See also *Jew of Venice* (German plays). Bought from Alleyn 18th Jan. 1602.

138. *Dioclesian,* 16th Nov. Probably Dekker's; altered by Massinger to *The Virgin Martyr,* q.v. See also *The Martyr Dorothea* (German plays in my *Life of Shakespeare*).

139. *Warlam Chester,* 30th Nov.

140. *The Siege of London,* 26th Dec. See *Edward* 4.

141. [*Galfrido and Bernardo,* 18th May 1595, is a forged entry.]

142. *Antonio and Vallia,* 20th June. Probably Dekker's; altered by Massinger, *q.v.* S. R. 29th June 1660. MS. destroyed by Warburton's servant; but a MS. with Antonio of Ragusa as a character is in the Bodleian, MSS. Rawl., Poet, 93.

143. *Olimpio and Hengenyo,* 4th Sept.

144. *The Welshman,* 29th Nov.

145. *Fortunatus* ("the first part" only), 3rd Feb. 1596. See DEKKER.

146. *Phocas,* T., 19th May. Bought by Henslow of Slaughter 1598.

147. *Osric,* 3rd Feb. 1597. An Osric is an important character in *A Knack to Know a Knave.*

148. *Time's Triumph,* 13th April. Probably Heywood's *Timon* or *Misanthropos,* from Lucian. See HEYWOOD and FLETCHER, 3.

149. *The Witch of Islington,* 14th July.

All these old plays must have belonged to the Admiral's men on 3rd June 1594, and as the theatres were closed May–Dec. 1593 and June–Dec. 1592, they must nearly all (allowing for a few written Jan.–April 1593 and Jan.– May 1594) have been originally produced before June 1592. The comparison instituted with the lists of early English plays in Germany in my *Life of Shakespeare* fully bears out this conclusion. Some additions to these will be noticed in the list now given.

b. New Plays.

150. *Belin Dun*, 8th June 1594; S. R. for William Blackwall 24th Nov. 1595, as "The true tragical history of King Rufus I., with the life and death of Belin Dun, the first thief that was ever hanged in England." The prose story on which this was founded was entered S. R. 17th May 1594 for T. Gosson, and in that entry the King named is Henry I. See also Henslow's Inventory, 1598, in my *History of the Stage*, p. 114.

151. *Galiaso*, 26th June.

152. 2 *Godfrey of Bulloigne*, 19th July. But see Heywood, *Four Prentices*. *Godfrey of Bulloigne, with the Conquest of Jerusalem*, was entered S. R. 19th June 1594 for John Danter. This must have been the First Part, which may have been the *Jerusalem* of 22nd Mar. 1592 retained by Henslow from L. Strange's men. "With the Conquest of Jerusalem" is kept in the title-page of Heywood's play, the title of which has evidently been altered.

153. *The Merchant of Emden*, 30th July.

154. *Tasso's Melancholy*, 11th Aug. This was altered by Dekker 16th Jan. 1602, and still further 3rd Nov., 4th Dec. (Query for the Court at Christmas). He was probably the original writer of it. See also Henslow's

Inventory, 1598, in my *History of the Stage*, p. 114. Tasso died 25th April 1595.

155. *Venetian Comedy*, 25th Aug.

156. *Palamon and Arcite*, 17th Sept. Same subject as *Two Noble Kinsmen*.

157. *The Love of an English Lady*, 24th Sept.

158. *A knack (how) to know an honest man*, 22nd Oct. Extant. "A pleasant conceited comedy, several times played about the City of London." It was played at the Rose as well as in the City. Entered S. R. 26th Nov. 1595 for C. Burby as a "most rare and pleasant history." The scene is at Venice, but it cannot be *The Venetian Comedy*, as that was previously performed as a new interlude.

159. 1 *Cesar and Pompey*, 8th Nov. Compare Chapman, *Cesar and Pompey*.

160. *The Wise Man of West Chester*, 2nd Dec. See MONDAY, *John a Kent and John a Cumber*. Bought from Alleyn 19th Sept. 1601.

161. *The Set at Maw*, 14th Dec. See DEKKER.

162. *The French Comedy*, 11th Feb. 1595.

163. *Long Meg of Westminster*, 14th Feb. Acted as late as Field's *Amends for Ladies*, which alludes to it c. 1616.

164. *The Mack*, 21st Feb. See DEKKER.

165. *Seleo et Olympo*, 5th Mar. See HEYWOOD, *Golden Age*, and Henlow's Inventory, 1598.

166. 1 *Hercules*, 7th May. Bought May–July 1598 of Martin Slaughter for the Admiral's men. Slaughter left them 18th July 1597, and it seems that he had been a sharer with Alleyn in the properties and plays of those men up to that time. We shall find more instances of his being in possession of the right to plays acted before then, but he was certainly not the author of them. This play was pro-

bably Heywood's *Silver Age*, q.v. See also Henslow's Inventory, 1598.

167. 2. *Hercules*, 23rd May. Bought with the preceding by Henslow 1598. Probably Heywood's *Brazen Age*, q.v. See also Henslow's Inventory, 1598.

168. [1] *The Seven Days of the Week*, 3rd June. "See *The Christmas Prince*, 1607," Halliwell.

169. 2 *Cæsar*, 18th June. See *Cæsar's Revenge*, 1607.

170. *Longshank*, 29th Aug. Probably a "mended" version of Peele's "*Edward 1, surnamed Longshanks*," q.v. See also Henslow's Inventory, 1598. Bought from Alleyn 8th Aug. 1602.

170*. *Crack me this nut*, 5th Sept. Alluded to in Dekker's *Fortunatus*. Bought from Alleyn 18th Jan. 1602.

171. *The New World's Tragedy*, 17th Sept.

172. *The Disguises*, 2nd Oct. Probably the original version of Chapman's *Mayday*, q.v.

173. *The Wonder of a Woman*, 15th Oct.

174. *Barnardo and Fiametta*, 28th Oct.

175. *A Toy to Please my Lady (Chaste Ladies)*, 14th Nov. A play called *The Toy* was acted at Dublin c. 1638. See SHIRLEY.

176. *Harry 5*, 28th Nov. Probably a mended version of *The Famous Victories of Henry 5*, which had been published S. R. 14th May 1594 as "acted by the Queen's servants." *Biog. Dram.* (of course followed by the trustful Halliwell) reads "King's" for "Queen's," which in my early books led me into serious mistakes. See also Henslow's Inventory, 1598.

177. *Chinon of England*, 3rd Jan. 1596. S. R. 20th Jan. 1596, for T. Gosson and J. Danter, as *The first part of the famous History of Chinan of England;* but not extant.

178. *Pythagoras,* 16th Jan. Sold to Henslow by
Slaughter 1598.

179. 2 [*Seven days of the*] *Week,* 22nd Jan.

180. *Julian Apostata,* 29th April.

181. [1] *Tamar Cham,* 6th May. For the Second Part
see 28th April 1592. It was this First Part, of which the
plot is extant, which was revived in 1602. Henslow bought
it of Alleyn 2nd Oct. 1602, and charged it to Worcester's
men, as well as to the Admiral's, who performed it at the
Fortune. See my *History of the Stage,* pp. 112, 113, 141.

182. *Troy,* 23rd June. Probably Heywood's *Iron Age,*
q.v.

183. *The Paradox,* 1st July.

184. *The Tinker of Totness,* 18th July.

185. *Valteger* (Vortiger), 4th Dec. The same play as
Hengist, 22nd June 1597, which was not a new play;
beyond doubt Middleton's *Mayor of Quinborough,* q.v., for
that is called *Hengist* in an extant MS. See also Henslow's
Inventory, 1598. Bought from Alleyn 20th Nov. 1601.

186. *Stewtley* (*Stukely*), 11th Dec. (by Dekker, Peele,
&c.). See DEKKER.

187. *Nabuchodonozer,* 19th Dec.

188. *That will be shall be,* 30th Dec.

189. *Alexander and Lodowick,* 14th Jan. 1597. Bought
by Henslow of Slaughter, 1598.

190. *Woman hard to please,* 27th Jan. Compare HEY-
WOOD, *Challenge for Beauty.*

191. *Guido,* 19th Mar. See Henslow's Inventory, 1598.

192. *Five Plays in One,* 7th April. Probably by Heywood, *q.v.*

193. *Uter Pendragon,* 29th April. For subject compare
Merlin, under MIDDLETON. See also Henslow's Inventory,
1598.

194. *Comedy of Humors*, 11th May; *i.e.*, Chapman's *Humorous Day's Mirth*, q.v. See also Henslow's Inventory, 1598.

195. *The life and death of Harry* 1, 26th May.

196. *Frederick and Basilea*, 3rd June. For the extant plot see my *History of the Stage*, p. 141.

197. *The life and death of Martin Swart*, 30th June.

vi. Plays Acted by Pembroke's Men.

198. *Hardicanute*, Oct. 1597. *Knewtus* is probably only another name for this play.

199. *Friar Spendleton* (*Pendleton*), 31st Oct.

200. *Burbon* (*Borbonne*), 2nd Nov. Not the same play as *Berowne*.

Some of Pembroke's plays were acquired by the Admiral's men Oct.–Dec. 1597.

201. *Black Joan.* See also Henslow's Inventory, 1598.

202. *Sturg flattery* (Stark flattery.)

203. *Branhowlte*, or *Brunhowlte* (Brunhalt; see *Thierry and Theodoret*). See also Henslow's Inventory, 1598.

204. *The Cobler of Queenhithe.*

205. *Alice Pierce.* See also Henslow's Inventory, 1598.

No entry of payment for the former two occurs under the head of Admiral's men, and they may have been retained ultimately by Pembroke's; the latter three were certainly purchased for the Admiral's.

vii. Plays Written for the Admiral's Men.

206. *Dido and Æneas*, 5th Jan. 1598. This has always been supposed to be a revival of Marlow's play; but if so, how did it get from the Chapel boys to the Admiral's men? I find no parallel instance on record, nor any note, however slight, of the acquisition of the play at all. But on 3rd

Dec. 1597 there is an entry of a plot of a play by Jonson to be delivered at Christmas, and this *Dido* apparently was delivered at Christmas; certainly no other play by Jonson was so. Moreover, in Shakespeare's *Hamlet*, ii. 2, there is a long extract from " Æneas' tale to Dido," taken from a play which was " caviare to the general " and " never acted above once." Was not this the play ? and was it not Jonson's ? and is not this Shakespeare's way of showing that Jonson had been reconciled to the Chamberlain's company in 1601, after the three years' stage war ? For the style of the *Hamlet* extract compare Jonson's 1602 additions to *The Spanish Tragedy*. 1 am rather diffident about putting forth this conjecture, because my former ephemeral hypothesis published in a magazine many years since, and not very absurd in our then state of knowledge, was raked out of its congenial dust-heap by my friend Mr. A. H. Bullen. This poor little butterfly was impaled by him with the ticket, " Titanic absurdity, gross as a mountain, open, palpable." Shade of Mrs. Malaprop, what a derangement of epitaphs !

206*. 1598, Feb. 22, *The Miller :* bought of, not written by, R. Lee for 20s.

207. *The Welshman's prize.* Probably the same as *The Welshman, or The Famous Wars of Henry* 1 *and the Prince of Wales.*

207*. *Vayvode,* 21st Aug., and again 21st Jan. 1599; bought of Alleyn by Henslow : but there appears no notice of it among the plays when Alleyn was connected directly with the company. Halliwell gives this as " *Vayoode*, by Henry Chettle," from Collier's index, I suppose. He did not see that this was a preparation for an " interlineation " in the *Diary*.

208. *Brute,* 12th Dec. Licensed as *Brute Greenshield*

Mar. 1599.　Not in.S. R.; probably an old Queen's men's play.　Brutus was Locrine's father.

209. *Friar Fox and Gillian of Brentford*, 10th Feb. 1599.　Author's name omitted by accident, but certainly not written by Dowton and Redley, who were the purchaser's agents.

210. *Tristram de Lyons*, 4th Oct. : bought of Downton.

vii. Plays Acted by Pembroke's Men at the Rose.

211. *Like unto Like*, 28th Oct. 1600.　Probably the foundation of Collier's forged entry of *Like quits Like* [*Hoffman*], as if rewritten by Chettle and Heywood Aug. 1602— Jan. 1603, *q.v.*

212. *Roderick*, 29th Oct.　Probably a play on the death of Hoffman's father; possibly the foundation of Chettle's *Danish Tragedy*, 7th July 1602; but this may have been only another name for *Hoffman*.

viii. Plays Acted by the Admiral's Men at the Fortune.

213. *The Spanish Fig*, 6th Jan. 1602.　Probably *The Noble Spanish Soldier*, q.v.

214. *Malcolm, King of Scots*, 18th April.　Bought of C. Massey.　Query same subject as *Macbeth*.

215. *Samson*, 19th July.　Author's name accidentally omitted.　Bought for £6.

216. *Philip of Spain*, 8th Aug.　Bought of Alleyn.

217. *Mortimere*, 10th Sept.　Jonson's *Mortimer*.　See 23rd Oct. 1598 and JONSON.

218. The new play of *The Earl of Harford*, Sept.　Not elsewhere mentioned.

219. *The Four Sons of Aymon*, 10th Dec. [but query 10th Feb. 1603].　Bought of Shaw for £2.　"If it be

not played by the company of the Fortune, nor no other company by my leave " [*i.e.*, by Worcester's men], " I bind myself to repay the said sum on the delivery of my book at Christmas next, which shall be in the year of our Lord God 1603, and in the 46th year of the Reign of the Queen," *Diary*, p. 233. This must have been of a date after 25th Dec. 1602. It was retained by the Admiral's company; for 6th Jan. 1624 it was relicensed by Herbert for the Prince's [Charles] company as " an old play, and not of a legible hand."

220. *The Siege of Dunkirk, with Alleyn the Pirate,* 7th Mar. 1603, was bought of Massey.

ix. Plays Acted by Worcester's Men at the Rose.

221. *Burone,* or *Berowne,* 21st Sept. 1602. Berowne was the English representation of the French pronunciation of Biron. See *Love's Labor's Lost.* But this was not Chapman's play; he did not write for Worcester's men. Possibly a play on the same subject belonging to these men before they came to the Rose ; but see Anon., 249.

" Pulleys to hang Absalom," 3rd Oct. Whence it seems that Peele's *David and Bethsabe* had passed to them.

222. *The Overthrow of Rebels,* 6th Nov. Query another name for 1, 2 *Lady Jane,* q.v. under WEBSTER.

PLAYS NOT EXTANT, BUT ENTERED S. R. 1582–1603.

223. *The famous history of John of Gaunt,* son to King Edward 3, *with his conquest of Spain,* and marriage of his two daughters to the Kings of Castile and Portugal, &c., 14th May 1594, for Edward White. Probably the foundation of *The Conquest of Spain by John of Gaunt,* by Hathway and Rankens, *q.v.*

223*. A Pastoral pleasant Comedy of *Robin Hood and Little John,* for E. White (with 223), 1594, May 14.

224. *The life and death of Heliogabalus,* 19th June 1594, for John Danter.

225. *The tragedy of Ninus and Semiramis, the first monarchs of the world,* 10th May 1595, for John Hardy. Alluded to in Heywood's *Apology for Actors,* 1610.

226. *Valentine and Orson,* played by Her Majesty's players. An interlude, 23rd May 1595, for Thomas Gosson and Raphe Hancock; and re-entered 31st Mar. 1600 for W. White.

227. A moral of *Cloth Breeches and Velvet Hose,* as it is acted by my Lord Chamberlain's 27th May 1600, "provided he is not to put it in print without further and better authority" than the Wardens'. Probably not printed.

228. *Give a man luck and throw him into the sea,* 24th July 1600, for R. Oliff (with *The Maid's Metamorphosis*). One of the old plays, I think, revived by the Paul's boys in 1600.

ANONYMOUS PLAYS ACTED BY L. STRANGE'S MEN.

229. *Fair Em.* See WILSON.

229*. A most pleasant and merry new Comedy entitled *A [merry] Knack [how] to Know a Knave,* with Kemp's applauded merriments of the men of Goteham in receiving the King into Goteham, 1594, was acted as a new play at the Rose 10th June 1592 by "Edward Allen and his company," and entered S. R. 7th Jan. 1594 for Richard Jones. Kemp's part is Sc. 12, in which he no doubt acted the Cobbler. The original story of Edgar and Alfrida appears to me to have been written by Peele. This part includes Sc. 1*b,* 3, 5, 7, 9, 11, 13, 15 (part). The remainder is quite in the style of R. Wilson. It includes

Sc. 1*a*, 2, 4, 6, 8, 10, 14, 15 (part), and is independent in plot. No character in this part has a proper name; allegorical personages such as Honesty, or generalised representations of classes such as the Bailiff, make up the *Dram. Pers.* There are also many Euphuistic bits inserted by this second hand in caricature of Greene's style, "the ape of Euphues." The character of the Clerk of the Assize occurs, I think, only in this play and in *The Three Ladies of London.* The "abuses" satirised are the same as in Wilson's recognised works. The continual references to the *Titus and Vespasian* play in the Peele part are very noticeable. This play was performed at Court. See prayer at the end.

230. *The Deadman's Fortune.* Plot only extant, from which we find that Burbadge acted as messenger; Darlowe (query Marlowe), R. Lee, and b[oy] Sam [Gilburne] as attendants. As this plot belonged to Alleyn, it must date when he was connected with Burbadge, *i.e.*, as members of L. Strange's company, 1592–3. See my *History of the Stage,* p. 85.

ANONYMOUS PLAYS ACTED BY THE CHAMBERLAIN'S MEN.

231. *Mucedorus.* See LODGE.

232. *Alphonsus, Emperor of Germany,* T., 1654, for Humphrey Moseley, was acted by the King's men at Blackfriars; but is evidently an old play. The date of the Blackfriars revival was 5th May 1636; it was there acted before Queen Henrietta and the Prince Elector. The attribution of its authorship by Moseley to Chapman in 1654 has not the slightest value. See the list of Moseley's entries in my *Life of Shakespeare,* p. 358. Wood and Winstanley, with much greater probability, assign it to Peele. It is a Machiavelian revenge-play, and has much German in it. The principal character is Richard "the conqueror,"

v. 1, Duke of Cornwall, and I have no doubt is the person alluded to in *The Taming of the Shrew*, Ind. 1. 5, who has so much perplexed the commentators. This Richard Conqueror and Sly came to L. Strange's men together., *i.e.*, in Feb. 1592. May not, then, this be the play called by Henslow *Harry of Cornwell*? No Harry of Cornwall is known in history.

233. *Sir Thomas More* was printed from MS. by Dyce for the Shakespeare Society, and dated by him c. 1590. The company by which it was acted is fixed as the Chamberlain's by the name T. Goedal, which is the same as the T. Goodall of *The Seven Deadly Sins*. The date is 1595–6, as appears from the passages deleted by Tylney, evidently because they too closely represented in Sc. 1–8 the prentice riots of 29th June 1595 (see Maitland, *London*, p. 278, *Stow*, p. 769*b*), and in Sc. 11 the imprisonment of Hertford for contempt Oct. 1595 (see Aikin, *Elizabeth*, chap. 25). All disparaging allusions to the French were also cut out. The many mentions of "abuses" in the early scenes, and the fact that this play consists of "a tragedy and a comedy," identify it with the play acted by the Paul's boys 30th July 1606 before the Kings of England and Denmark. They had probably bought it off the Chamberlain's men after it had been put down by the Master of the Revels, and revived it under a new name. On the actors' Christian names see my *Life of Shakespeare*, p. 266. Dyce's muddled text is neither the original version nor the altered. but a farrago of the two. The most interesting thing in the play is the list of pieces performed by the strollers (Sc. 10): *The Cradle of Security* (which see); *Hit Nail o' th' Head* (*The Marriage of Wit and Wisdom*); *Impatient Poverty* (extant; Dyce denies this, but wrongly); *The Play of Four P.s* (by John Heywood; extant); *Dives and Lazarus*

(by Ralph Radcliff; not extant); *Lusty Juventus* (by R.
Wever; extant); *The Marriage of Wit and Wisdom*, the
play acted by the "Cardinal's players" [not the extant play
of that name, but made up from *The Disobedient Child* and
Lusty Juventus]. What Dyce means by "no such drama
ever existed" I cannot tell. Why this editor has sophis-
ticated his text by such alterations as "mountanish" for
"momtanish," *i.e.*, Mahometanish, mawmtanish, must remain
an enigma which I care not to solve. In my opinion T.
Lodge wrote this play and acted Justice Suresby in it; but
this depends on the correctness of my identification of Lodge
with Philomusus in *The Return from Parnassus*, q.v.

234. *The Larum for London.* See LODGE.

235. *A warning for Fair Women.* See LODGE.

236. *The Merry Devil of Edmonton*, C., 1608, 1617,
1626, 1655. Acted by the King's men at the Globe
before 22nd Oct. 1607. S. R. for A. Johnson. All previous
authorities wrongly assume that the S. R. entry for Hunt
and Archer, 5th April 1608, of the prose story by T.[homas]
B[rewer] refers to the play. Coxeter saw an old MS. with
the inscription "by Michael Drayton," against the accuracy
of which no tittle of evidence has been adduced. Moseley
entered it 9th Sept. 1653, S. R., as Shakespeare's. Readers
of this book will know the value of any statement by
Moseley. The copy published is evidently much abridged
(perhaps to make it one of *The Four plays in one*, c. 1605):
there is no conclusion to the Induction; and the part of
Smug, as St. George, alluded to in the last scene, has been
cut out, and the allusion without the fuller prose story
would be unintelligible. Moreover, the priest Sir John was
originally called Oldcastle. Howell in his *Letters* speaks of
the ale "that Sir John Oldcastle and Smug the Smith was
used to drink," and allusions to Oldcastle's carbuncled nose

occur in Gayton's *Festivous Notes to Don Quixote* and in *Hey for Honesty*. As both these allude to Falstaff as a separate character, it cannot be that Shakespeare's Oldcastle is intended. Moreover, *Sir John Oldcastle* was acted 8th Mar. 1600 by the Chamberlain's men before Hunsdon and Vereiken, the ambassador from the Low Countries, and this certainly could not be *Henry* 4. I have also found a trace of the name Oldcastle in the unexplained passage in the last scene, in which no entrance of Sir John is marked. The Host says, "How now, my old Jenerts' Bank, my horse, my castle!" I conjecture that the MS. from which this was printed stood thus :—

> "Old   J. enter | *Host.* How now, my, my, my horse !"
> castle Banks |

The Host is astounded at the trick played with his sign. The printer, not seeing this, thrust the marginal direction into the text, whence the astounding reading of the editions.

I believe, then, that this play was originally called *Sir John Oldcastle*, and was written by Drayton for the Chamberlain's men before Dec. 1597, when we find him writing for the Rose, *i.e.*, contemporaneously with *Henry* 4. Allusions to it will be found in *Sir Giles Goosecap*, 1601, and *Grim the Collier of Croydon*, 1600. I may just mention that *The Merry Pranks of Fabel*, confused by W. C. Hazlitt with *Fabyll's Ghost*, 1533, is Brewer's prose tract of *The Merry Devil . . . with the pleasant Pranks . . . &c.*, 1631. I cannot help thinking that the "merry devil" of *The Merchant of Venice*, ii. 3, alludes to this play, which would date both plays in 1597.

PLAYS ACTED BY QUEEN ELIZABETH'S MEN.

237. *The Famous Victories of Henry* 5. See TARLTON.
238. *Jack Straw*. See PEELE.

239. *The reign of King John.* See LODGE.

239*. *The true chronicle history of King Leir.* See LODGE.

240. *The First Part of the Tragical reign of Selimus* (with his wars against his father Bajazet, and the murthering of his two brethren Crocut and Acamat), 1594, by T. Creede; 1638, "by T. G.," was played by the Queen's players. The Second Part, like that of *Orlando*, was not produced. This play has been assigned to Greene by Dr. Grosart, who has for some ten years kept his subscribers waiting for the completion of his edition of Greene's works: when he issues his promised justification of this assumed authorship I shall examine its value. Meanwhile it is enough to say that, while the most cursory reading shows that Greene had a hand in *Selimus*, his worst enemy would not, I think, assert that he wrote the whole of this wretched production. The date is c. 1588, soon after *Tamberlane*, but probably before *Alphonsus of Arragon*. The Prologue calls it a true "lamentable history." The greater part of the play seems to me to be by Lodge. Greene certainly wrote Sc. 24; probably Sc. 9, 11, and other scenes. I have not looked far into the question. The apocryphal T. G. of the 1638 edition was no doubt meant to indicate T. Goffe.

241. *Arden of Feversham.* See KYD.

242. *The true tragedy of Richard 3,* (Wherein is shown the death of Edward 4, with the smothering of the young princes in the Tower. With a lamentable end of Shore's wife, an example for all wicked women; and lastly, the conjunction and joining of the two noble houses Lancaster and York,) 1594. S. R. 19th June 1594, for T. Creede. "Played by the Queen's Majesty's players." It was played at Court (see prayer at the end), and therefore cannot date later than 1591; but as it was evidently meant as a con-

tinuation of the series 1 *Henry* 6 and *The Contention of York
and Lancaster*, it cannot be much earlier. All these were
Queen's men's plays. The "true tragedy" in the title is
from that of *Richard Duke of York*, a rival continuation by
Pembroke's men. One of the actors in it, Sc. 11, is called
Will Slaughter, "yet the most part calls him Black Will,"
i.e., the Black Will of *Arden of Faversham*, q.v., which had
no doubt been acted by the same man. Another actor is
called Jack Donton (Dutton) or Denten, an accommodation
of the Dighton of history to the actor's real name. Lodge,
who seems to me certainly to be one of the authors, left
England 6th Aug. 1591. Lodowick, Sc. 10, who in this
passage is certainly the Lodowick of *Edward* 3, is going to
write the Shore story in "heroical verse," as "the shameful
end of a King's Concubine, which is no doubt as wonderful
as the desolation of a kingdom." *Shore's wife* was written
in verse by A. Chute, S. R. 16th June 1593, and in Drayton's *Heroical Epistles*, which were certainly written years
before their publication in 1597 : see Spenser's allusion to
him as Aetion in *Colin Clout's come home again*, 1595, where
this "Heroical" work is distinctly indicated. As other of these
Epistles relate to the story of Edward the Black Prince and
the Countess of Salisbury, which story is also connected
with Lodowick in *Edward* 3 (although the Black Prince is
there transformed into the King), I have no doubt that
Drayton is meant in both plays. As to the authorship, I
doubt not that the Induction is by Lodge; Sc. 1, 3, 4, 8,
11, 12, including the death of Edward IV., and the smothering of the Princes, seem to be Peele's; Sc. 2 (with its
"looking-glass" bit), 6 (with its "cooling card" and ballad
metre), 7 (which, like 6, contradicts 8 as to the whereabouts of Earl Rivers), 9, 13 (with "Catesby" instead of
the "Casbie" of Sc. 3), 10 (which, like 2, belongs to the

Shore story), and 14–20 (on the conjunction of the houses)
I attribute, as also the Epilogue (with "kneel upon thy hairy
knee"), to Lodge.   Compare the "Marques" of Sc. 20 with
the "Marcus" of the earlier scenes.   But the play was
printed from a playhouse copy, with the metre corrupted
into prose, [note the introduction of the cue word "confusion" into the text in Sc. 1, and the double reading in
Sc. 13—

    "Cat. Prythee tell us is it concluded?
    Page. How says thou, is it concluded?"]

and requires careful editing before minute points can be
profitably discussed.   I may, however, say that indications
are not wanting that it is founded on an earlier play in
which Kyd had a hand.   Note especially in Sc. 9 the
phrase, "Blood is a threatener and will have revenge."
Nash, when twitting Kyd with his Seneca phrases in the
Address before *Menaphon,* quotes as one of them "Blood is
a beggar."

PLAYS ACTED BY PEMBROKE'S MEN.

242*. Hamlet.   See my *Life of Shakespeare,* and KYD
and Anon., 130.

243. *Hester and Ahasuerus.*   See *Godly Queen Hester* and
Anon., 129.

244. *Edward* 3.   See MARLOW.

245. *The taming of a Shrew.*   See KYD.

PLAY ACTED BY OXFORD'S COMPANY.

246. *The weakest goeth to the Wall,* 1600, 1618.   S. R.
23rd Oct. 1600, for R. Oliffes.   This has been attributed to
Webster without a particle of evidence.   It is founded on
Sappho, Duke of Mantona, the first story in B. Rich's *Fare-*

well to Military Profession, 1581. Now, c. 1586–8 Oxford's players were acting in London. This company is sometimes called "Oxford's boys," and as such in ii. 1 they are alluded to as "pigmies." The only authors known to me who wrote for this company are Monday and the Earl of Oxford. I do not say either of them wrote this play. If the allusions to the title, which are very frequent, were collected, they might aid in determining author and date.

247. *The true history of George Scanderbage* was entered S. R. for E. Allde 3rd July 1601 as "lately played." This looks as if both these plays were acted c. 1600; but if so, where? Possibly at the Swan or Curtain. The *George Granderburye* alleged by Halliwell as a distinct play on the authority of Malone's *Supplement*, i. 78, is only a mistaken reading of George Scanderbagge. The titles are in all else exactly alike.

PLAYS ACTED BY DERBY'S MEN.

248. *Histriomastix.* See MARSTON.

249. The history of *The Trial of Chivalry*, with the life and death of Cavaliero Dick Bowyer, 1605, was entered S. R. 4th Dec. 1604, for N. Butter, as "The life and death of Cavaliero Dick Boyer," and published as "lately acted." The chief tragic character in the play is Burbon, which would seem to identify it with the *Burbon* (also spelled Borbonne) acted at the Rose by Pembroke's men in 1597 Oct. There are certainly two hands in this play: cf. the spellings Sentronell, Sentinel; mordu, mort dew; &c.: for that of Sarlabois compare Sarlebois in *The Captives*, and Sarlois in *Hoffman*. In Henslow's *Diary*, Sept. 1602, a play called *Burone* or *Berowne* is mentioned as revived by Worcester's men at the Rose. This name looks more like Biron than Bourbon, but as it is not quoted by Malone I cannot

tell how far Collier's transcript is trustworthy. The "scaffold and bar" purchased for *Burone* would suit iv. 1 (but see *Royal King and Loyal Subject*). Immediately preceding this Henslow enters "additions of Cutting Dick" by Heywood, which I think must refer to this play, if to any now extant. If so, the Pembroke play of 1597 (by Chettle?) may have passed with Heywood to Derby's men in 1599, and to Worcester's in 1602. In any case the extant copy is that performed by Derby's, without the Heywood 1602 additions. They probably contained the "death of Dick Bowyer," which are not in the printed edition. The "copy" was a stage exemplar: a marginal direction for "pen, ink, and paper" in v. 1 has got into the text, where Mr. Bullen's "own" repetition of it is quite unneeded.

PLAYS ACTED BY THE ADMIRAL'S MEN.

250. *Charlimayne* (printed from, Egerton MS. 1994 by Mr. A. H. Bullen, and misnamed by him *The Distracted Emperor*) is, I have little doubt, the play referred to by Peele in 1589 along with *Mahomet's pow* (*Alphonsus*, by Greene), *Tamburlaine* (by Marlow), and *Tom Stukely* (*Alcazar* by Peele), as then on the stage. Peele seems to have tried to give one play by each author then writing, and this one, I imagine, was by Dekker, then a playwright for the Admiral's men. My suggestion that it was by Field was made before the play was published, and founded on Mr. Bullen's assumption that one of the mottoes at the end was an anagram. The other motto, which he did not then disclose, is the same that Dekker uses at the end of *Dr. Faustus*. "Baw waw," iv. 3 (Dekker's spelling for Bow-wow), and "Fate's tennis ball," iv. 2, are minor confirmations of authorship. The cancelled passage in iii. 1 shows revision by the Master of the Revels.

251. *A Knack how to know an honest man*, 1596. Cf. Anon., 158.

252. *Stukeley*. See DEKKER, and Anon., 186.

253. *Look about you*. See WADESON.

PLAYS ACTED BY UNCERTAIN COMPANIES.

254. A pleasant comedy wherein is merrily shown *The Wit of a Woman*. 1604, for Edward White. Not in S. R. I have not seen this play. The date seems very late for a publication by E. White. Chapman wrote *The Will of a Woman*, May–June 1598, for the Admiral's men at the Rose.

255. *Richard 2.* Egerton MS. 1994. Mr. Halliwell printed eleven copies. On the early part of the reign, with the death of Gloucester. Query c. 1591 for the Queen's men.

256. *Wily Beguiled.* See PEELE, 17.

257. The lamentable tragedy of *Locrine*, the eldest son of King Brutus, discoursing the wars of the Britains and Huns, with their discomfiture; the Britains' victory, with their accidents; and the death of Albanact. No less pleasant than profitable. Newly set forth, overseen, and corrected by W. S., 1595. S. R. 20th July 1594, for T. Creede. Creede's other publications are plays by the Queen's men. The date in the concluding lines, "eight-and-thirty years the sceptre swayed," must refer to publication, not production on the scene, and cannot be placed earlier than 17th Nov. 1595, when the 38th Eliz. began. There must have been a delay in the printing from 1594 July to 1595 Nov. Doubtless the original copy read "eight-and-twenty years," *i.e.*, 1585–6. In ii. 3 the burning of Mary Breame, 3rd Feb. 1583 (*Stow*, p. 696), is alluded to; in ii. 2 the press-

ing for soldiers, 23rd July 1585 (*Stow*, p. 709); in the
Epilogue the woman (Mary Queen of Scots) that sets her
" broils abroach " for her " private amours " (with the Earl of
Shrewsbury) is warned. This must be anterior to Mary's
execution in 1587, and applies to the Babington conspiracy,
1586. The conspirators were taken in July, executed in
September. I should date the writing of the play c. July.
Mr. Simpson says it was written " by " Charles Tilney, one
of the conspirators; but surely " by " here means " concern-
ing." I assign the authorship to Peele. The expression
" Vindicta " ridiculed in *The Poetaster* occurs in this play,
Alcazar, and the Induction to the old *Richard* 3, all by
Peele; the " 38 years " of the Epilogue is exactly paralleled
in the title of his *Anglorum Feriæ* (38 Eliz.). One line
and a half-line are repeated from the play in the *Tale of
Troy*, 1589; it has some Devonshire dialect in it, and
Peele was a Devonshire man; and the " not only, but also "
ridiculed by Nash as a character of Harvey's style in his
Have with you, &c., is put in Signior Strumbo's letter, i. 2.
Peele caricatured Harvey in his *Old Wife's Tale*. If the
Dumb Shows, bombast, and pedantry be thought to indicate
an inferior writer, it must be remembered that this would
be Peele's earliest attempt at tragedy, and would date before
he had Marlow's example to guide him. I have faith in
the view that W. S., who saw this play through the press
between 1595 Nov. and 1596 Mar., was W. Shakespeare,
and that he did this from charity to his old coadjutor, " long
sick and in necessity," 17th Jan. 1596, when he sent his
Tale of Troy to L. Burleigh, which is the latest fact we
know of him. *Locrine* was evidently presented at Court;
most probably on 13th Feb. 1586.

258. *Every Woman in her Humor*, 1609, by E. A[llde]
for Thomas Archer. This play was evidently an answer to

Jonson's Comical Satires. The date of production was, I think, 1602. Acutus, who looks as he were changing his religion, i. 1; and whose imprisonment is alluded to, seems to be Jonson: but the play was not written till after *The Poetaster;* cf. the "vomit" in i. 1, and the plain allusion to Marston's *What you Will* in iii. 1. The acting company was probably Pembroke's (just before they became Worcester's men), and the fat Host was most likely performed by Duke, "the fat fool;" in iv. 2 he says he has been called a politician, and these were the "politician players." See *Histriomastix* and *The Poetaster.* The plot is founded on Greene's *Tully's Love.* There are allusions to Nash's *Isle of Dogs,* v. 1 (compare the passage in Meres' *Palladis Tamia* almost in the same words); Dekker's *Triplicity of Cuckolds,* ii. 2 and last scene; the Globe, iv. 1; Sybil in *The Shoemaker's Holiday,* i. 1; &c. Tully, in ii. 1, can tell the ladies tales of Venus and Adonis. The whole thing is one of the comical-satirical-humourist series, and bears marks of Dekker's influence. I do not pretend to guess at the authorship.

PLAYS ACTED BY THE CHAPEL CHILDREN.

259. *The Wars of Cyrus, King of Persia,* against Antiochus, King of Assyria, with the tragical end of Panthea, 1594, by E. A[llde] for William Blackwell. Possibly the play alluded to in *Summer's Last Will* as acted at Croydon (? at the Archbishop's) in 1591.

260. *Sir Giles Goosecap, Knight,* 1606, 1636. S. R. 10th Jan. 1606, for E. Blount. "Provided that it be printed according to the copy whereat Master Wilson's hand is at." This entry shows that the play had been revised by authority, evidently on account of its personal satire. Goosecap of Essex, with his endless "tickle" and "mortal" (for which

compare *Merry Devil of Edmonton, passim ;* 2 *Henry* 4, ii. 1 ;
Cromwell, i. 1)'; Rudesby, the Northern or Western man,
"two parts soldier;" Foulweather, the Southern man, the
"emphatic" Captain of the Low Countries, with his "com-
mendations;" Tales of Kent, and Kingcob, the Western man,
are certainly personal caricatures; while Clarence is, I think,
meant for the author himself: who is said in the 1636
edition to be then dead.   The only authors known to be in
connexion with this Children's company c. 1601 and dead
before 1636 are Marston, Middleton, and Chapman; and
the only one of the three who could have written such a
comedy is Chapman.   He was a friend and coadjutor of
Jonson, and this play bears manifest marks of Jonson's influence.   For its likeness in style to Chapman see especially
iii. 1 for serious writing; and the letter dictated in iv. 1 for
comic effect.   Compare *Gentleman Usher*, iii. 1, and *M. D'Olive*,
iv. 1.   See also my letter in *The Athenæum* 9th June 1883.
I think Drayton is aimed at as Goosecap.   The date is late
in 1601, after Biron's visit, 5th–14th Sept., to which allusion is made iii. 1, "Your greatest Gallants for men in
France were here lately."   It is possible, however, that "the
French gallants" mentioned by Chamberlain 26th April
1602, who came after Biron's leaving (*Nichols*, iii. 577), are
the persons intended.

260*. *The Contention between Liberality and Prodigality*,
C., 1602, by S. Stafford for G. Vincent (not in S. R.), was
"a pleasant comedy played before her Majesty," 1601, Feb.
22, "in the three and forty year of Elizabeth," v. 5, evidently by the Chapel children, whose "childish years" (and
not the author's) are alluded to in the Prologue.   The "Feb.
4" in v. 5 seems to be the date of the revision; for it is an
old *Edward* 6 play revived, the "prince," not the "queen,"
having been left by accident by the reviser in iii. 5, v. 4.   It

may, therefore, be a revision of the interlude of *Prodigality*, Anon., 25, *q.v.* "Rip rap" in the stage directions points to an Italian original. See *Lingua*.

PLAYS ACTED BY THE PAUL'S BOYS.

261. *Katherine and Pasquil.* See MARSTON, *Jack Drum's Entertainment.*

262. *The Wisdom of Doctor Doddypol.* See PEELE.

Give a man luck and throw him into the sea. See ANON., 228.

263. *The Maid's Metamorphosis*, 1600. S. R. 24th July 1600, with the preceding play. Some Paul's plays of this year were published immediately after they were produced (e.g., *Katherine and Pasquil*). This play was acted in a Leap-year—iv. 1 ; in a time of dearth, ii. 1 ; at a marriage—

"when their wedding chanced
Phœbus gave music and the Muses danced " (last lines).

This fixes the date. On 16th June 1600 Lord Harbert married Lady Anne Russel at Lord Cobham's house, Black-friars. Eight ladies (Muses evidently) danced to Apollo's music, and invited the Queen to make up the Nine, which she did (*Nichols*, iii. 499, where the names of the eight Maskers are given). The Prologue is quite suitable to this occasion, but by no means for a public audience : moreover, it contains one line which is taken from Daniel's first Sonnet—

"Then to the boundless ocean of your worth."

Daniel had, at the death of Spenser, 1599, become the Court poet, and the style of most of the play is just that of his earlier dramatic work. The fondness of rhyme, the intro-

duction of Juno, Iris, and Somnus in ii. 1 (some of the very
words in which are repeated in his *Vision of the Twelve
Goddesses*, 1604), the fall of the metre, and the pastoral plot
all point to Daniel as the main author; but the prose bits,
which are clearly insertions by a second hand, the pages
Mopso and Frisco, ii. 2, iii. 2, and especially the Fairies in
ii. 2, are almost certainly by Lyly. Mr. Bullen indulges in
the commonplace sneer at those who judge by thumb and
not by ear (probably meaning the critic who announced
Barnaveldt as a play of Chapman's, and *Captain Underwit*
as Shirley's), and attributes the play to Day; but not even
Mr. E. Gosse's authority can make me allow that a playwright of the Admiral's men would have been employed to
write for the Paul's boys in a Court performance

Tempore JAMES I.

Plays not Extant, but Entered S. R. 1603–1625.

264. *The history of Richard Whittington, his low birth,
his great fortunes*, as it was played by the Prince's servants,
8th Feb. 1605, for T. Pavyer.

265. *Bonos Nochios*, an interlude 27th Jan. 1609, for J.
Charlton; and with it

266. *Craft upon Subtilty's back.* Both evidently very old.

Plays in the Revels Licenses, 1623–4.

267. *The Black Lady*, 10th May 1623, new, for L. Elizabeth's men at the Cockpit.

268. *The Witch Traveller* [10th May], new, for the
Revels' men [at the Bull]: called *The Welsh traveller* by
Halliwell, and dated 1623.

269. *The Valiant Scholar*, 3rd June, for L. Elizabeth's
men.

270. *The Dutch Painter and the French Branke* [Brinch], new, for the Prince's men at the Curtain; but see *The Wisdom of Doctor Doddypol.*

271. *The Plantation of Virginia,* Aug., for [the Prince's] company at the Curtain. The profaneness to be left out. Probably, therefore, an old play.

272. *The Peaceable King, or the Lord Mendall,* 19th Aug., old, for the Prince's men at the Bull. Formerly allowed by Sir George Buck.

273. *The Whore in grain,* T., 26th Jan. 1624, for the [Palsgrave's men at the] Fortune. Revampt for the Red Bull [Prince's men] 29th Sept. 1639. The poet, actors, and licenser were then ordered to be punished for introducing libellous matter. See my *History of the Stage,* p. 358.

274. A play called *Humour in the End,* 21st May, for the Palsgrave's men [at the Fortune]. It was advertised as in the press in *Wit and Drollery,* 1661; but the title is there given as *Honor in the End.*

275. *The Parracide,* c. 27th May, for the Princes' men [at the Red Bull]; entered S. R. 29th Nov. 1653 by R. Marriott as Glapthorne's, with title *The Parricide, or Revenge for Honor,* and issued by him 1654 as *Revenge for Honour,* "by G. Chapman." How any one can attach the slightest value to such attributions of authorship is a puzzle to me. This was one of the only two plays of which Marriott gave an author's name in his numerous entries at this date; and it is the only one of the plays then entered that remains to us. The change of theatre (from the Curtain to the Bull) is alluded to in the Prologue. The known authors connected with the Prince's men 1623–4 are Middleton, Rowley, Ford, Broome, Barnes, and Sampson. Yet Mr. Swinburne says, "That it is the work of Chapman I see no definite reason to disbelieve, and not a little room to suppose that

it may be." But Chapman's writing for the stage had ceased in 1608. It is certainly not by Broome, Barnes, or Sampson. The date excludes Ford, as he was not yet writing without a coadjutor. Rowley is shut out by the metre, which is in every way unlike his. Again, Rowley and Middleton had before this date joined the King's men, but the Prologue shows that the author of this play was still with the Prince's. Weak endings are frequent. On the whole, I can only say that there is no author known to me to whom I can assign it, and that I dare not imitate the rashness of those who set value on Marriott's statement. When Mr. Swinburne (for whose judgment I have the greatest respect) shall think fit to disclose his reason for thinking it Chapman's I may possibly change my opinion.

276. *The Fair Star of Antwerp*, T., 15th Sept., for the Palsgrave's men [at the Fortune].

277. *The Angel King*, 15th Oct., new, for the same. The story of Robert, King of Sicily, I suppose.

The Masque, 29th Dec., new, for the same. The book (*i.e.*, copy) was brought by Mr. Jon., and was licensed for the press. See under JONSON, 56, where this Mask is proved to be *The Fortunate Isles and their Union*.

Plays Non-extant Presented at Court.

278. *Abuses*, " containing both a Comedy and a Tragedy," was presented to the Kings of Great Britain and Denmark 30th July 1606 by the Paul's boys. See *Sir T. More*.

279. *The Spanish Maz*, 12th Feb. 1605, occurs in the forged document published by F. Cunningham, *Revels*, p. 203, on which see my *History of the Stage*, p. 177. Presented by the King's men. Possibly *The Spanish Muz*[*idarus*]. See *Mucedorus*.

280. *The Almanac*, according to a similar list, was presented by the Prince's men 29th Dec. 1612.

281. *The Proud Maid*, T. [not *The Maid's Tragedy*, which was the King's men's], was, according to this same list, presented by the Lady Elizabeth's men 25th Feb. 1613.

282. *Cockle de moy* was presented [20th Feb.] 1613 before the Palatine and the Lady Elizabeth by the L. Elizabeth's men. Undoubtedly Marston's *Dutch Courtesan*, q.v.

283. *Raymond Duke of Lyons*, [1st Mar.] 1613. *Ibid.*

284. *Cardenna*, or *Cardenno*, was presented by the King's men 1612–13. See FLETCHER, *Love's Pilgrimage* (Cardenas).

285. *The Knot of Fools*. *Ibid.*

286. *A bad beginning makes a good ending*. *Ibid.* S. R. 29th June 1660 as *An Ill beginning has a good end, and* [or] *A bad beginning may have a good end*, by John Ford. The MS. was destroyed by Warburton's servant. But it was probably the same as *The London Prodigal*, q.v

287. *Benedict and Bettris*. *Ibid.* Undoubtedly Shakespeare's *Much Ado about Nothing*.

288. *Tom Bedlam the tinker*. Acted before the King at Theobald's 9th Jan. 1618 by " Sir T. Dutton, Sir T. Badger, Sir G. Goring, Sir T. Tyringham, Sir E. Zouch, Sir R. Yaxeley, and the like."

289. *The Woman's too hard for him*, C. " Acted at Court 1621," *Biog. Dram.* Query Fletcher's *Wildgoose Chase*.

290. *A vow and a good one*, by the Prince's players 6th Jan. 1623. Query Middleton and Rowley's *Fair Quarrel*, q.v.

291. *The Buck is a thief*, by the King's men 28th Dec. 1623. Query Fletcher's *Wit at several weapons*, q.v.

Other Non-extant Plays.

291*. *Torrismount* [*Torismond*, the King of France, in Lodge's *Rosalynde*] belonged to the King's Revels boys in Mar. 1607–8, and was specially reserved from publication for a full twelvemonth. It must, therefore, have been popular. See Mr. James Greenstreet's valuable paper on the White-friars Theatre, read 1888, Nov. 9, to the New Shak. Soc., but not published till after my *History of the Stage*.

292. *Gowry*, T., played by the King's men twice, " with exceeding concourse of all sorts of people : but whether the matter or manner be not well handled ; or that it be thought unfit that princes should be played on the stage in their lifetime, I hear that some great councillors are much dis-pleased with it, and so 'tis thought it shall be forbidden " (Chamberlain to Winwood, 18th Dec. 1604).

292*. *The Noble Grandchild.* Alleyn's *Memo. Book*, 1614. See Warner's *Dulwich Catalogue*, p. 48. This must have been played by the Lady Elizabeth's men.

Extant Plays.

293. *The Fair Maid of Bristow*, C. S. R. 8th Feb. 1605. Played at Hampton by His Majesty's players before the King and Queen. The King was at Hampton early in Oct. 1604.

294. *Nobody and Somebody*, printed 1606. See HEY-WOOD.

295. *The Puritan*, printed 1607. See MIDDLETON.

295*. *The Fair Maid of the Exchange*, " with the pleasant Humors of the Cripple of Fenchurch. Very delectable and full of mirth." S. R. for H. Rockitt 1607, April 24 editions 1607, 1625, 1634, 1637. Attributed, by guess apparently, to Heywood (? because he wrote *The Fair Maid*

of the West), but published without name of author. It has
an arrangement of characters showing how "Eleven may
easily act this Comedy," and a Sonnet Prologue, in which
the "tender pamping twig" certainly indicates a young
author, not one of Heywood's standing. Nor is the play in
any respect like his other productions. It is filled with
allusions to Shakespeare's plays, among which the most important are Sc. 5, "The night hath played the swift foot
runaway:" a passage which ought to settle the interpretation
of *Romeo and Juliet*, iii. 2, 6, a line on which so much nonsense has been written by New Shaksperians, and which
the Cambridge editors obelised as unintelligible; Sc. 9, the
Ovid imitator (Drayton), who writes letters, ditties, and
sonnets; the dead modern writer (Nash), biting, bitter, and
sharp-witted; the collector of humours in taverns (Jonson),
who puts them into plays, fix the earliest possible date of
production to 1602; and Sc. 6, which confirms the date by
its imitation of *Twelfth Night*, iii. 1, in the money-multiply-
ing method of begging. This is the latest play of Shakespeare's to which I have traced allusion. But beyond all
these, in Sc. 6 there is a broken quotation from *Venus and
Adonis*, so exactly like that in Machin's part of *The Dumb
Knight*, iii. 4, that I cannot help believing it to be written
by the same author. Exactly the same stanzas are quoted
from, and (which is the decisive point) the same erroneous
version, "sit thee down," instead of "come and sit," is
adopted. I have little doubt that the play was written by
Machin for the Paul's boys c. 1602, and published, like so
many others, on their breaking in 1607. If so, it was acted
at Whitefriars. In any case, I am sure it is not Heywood's.

296. *The Usurping Tyrant*, T., commonly called *The
Second Maiden's Tragedy*. Printed from one of the Warburton MSS. now in the Lansdowne collection. The MS.

has no title-page. "The Second Maiden's Tragedy" is prefixed in a different hand from that of the play. I think the Master of the Revels objected to the true title, *The Usurping Tyrant* (compare *Dram. Pers.*), and substituted this because he had just licensed *The* (first) *Maid's Tragedy*, by Beaumont and Fletcher. The license endorsement dates " 31st Oct. 1611 : G. Buc." At the back it is said to be first by Thomas Goughe (nearly obliterated); then by George Chapman (scored through); finally by William Shakespeare. This inscription has evidently no authority whatever. The original attribution to T. Goffe no doubt arose from the fact that Mr. [Robert] Gough was known from the MS. itself to have acted the Tyrant. The play has been reformed by Buc, especially where King James might be supposed to be alluded to. Even the innocent expression, "Your King's poisoned," v. 2, was altered into "I am poisoned," for fear, I take it, that the reported assassination of James in 1606 should be called to mind. The subordinate plot is, as in several other plays, taken from *The Curious Impertinent* in *Don Quixote*. I have little doubt that this play was by the author of *The Revenger's Tragedy*. It could not be by Middleton, *q.v.*, who did not attain a connexion with the King's men (who performed it) until 1622. The "bay windows," i. 1 ; the poisonous painting of the corpse, v. 2 ; the temptation scene, ii. 1 ; the "stealing through the house," ii. 2 ; the "cards," iii. 1 ; and the whole conduct of the plot remind one of that play. Compare *Rev. Trag.*, i. 2, iii. 5, ii. 1, &c. The regularity of the metre is accounted for by our having access to the original MS.

297. The Faithful Friends. Entered S. R. 29th June 1660 as by Beaumont and Fletcher, but not printed till 1812, from a stage MS. The date of production I take to be c. 1614. The description of the "Hymeneal sports," i. 1,

seems to fit very closely with those at Carr's wedding, 26th
Dec. 1613. The lines—

> "Alexander the Great had his Hephæstion,
> Philip of Spain his Lerma," i. 1,

may seem to indicate a later date; but if it be thought
necessary, we may read "has Lerma," not a very violent
alteration. The different handwritings show that the play
was altered, iv. 5 being inserted, and large pieces omitted
in ii. 1, 2; but whether the reviser was the original author
I have not cared to investigate. I guess Daborne, whose
liking for the expression "faithful friend" is shown in *The
Honest Man's Fortune*, as possibly the author. But it is useless to multiply hypotheses on so poor a production.

298. *Swetnam the Woman-hater arraigned by Women*,
C., 1620; S. R. 17th Oct. 1619, for Richard Meighen,
was acted at the Red Bull by Queen Anne's men. The plot
is from a Spanish book, *Historia da Aurelia y Isabella hija
del Rey de Escotia*, &c. Swetnam's *Arraignment of Women*
was printed 1615. The Queen died 2nd Mar. 1619. The
play must date between these.

299. *The Thracian Wonder*, C. H., 1661. Published
by F. Kirkman as "by John Webster and William Rowley,"
which certainly is incorrect. He put the same inscription
on *A cure for a Cuckold*, q.v., published just before; and
although the statement as to authorship is palpably untrue,
I think I may fairly conclude that he acquired both MSS.
from one company. The probable date of production is c.
1617, and the company Prince Charles'. The plot is from
Curan and Argentile, William Webster's poem, 1617, which
was an enlargement of Warner's story in his *Albion's
England*, 1586. Kirkman may have confused the two
Websters.

300. *Barnaveldt.* See FLETCHER.

301. *Two Wise men and all the rest Fools,* "A comical moral censuring the follies of the age, Anno 1619," was "divers times acted" before "a right noble and worthy assembly," but evidently not royal. I believe that Signor Antonio, the "Imp (graft) unfortunately fostered up to this day," at whom this "Dialogue" was "specially pointing," may have been Antony Monday. Antonio is an Englishman, born seventy miles N.W. of London, whose name is plain Antony, but is called Signor Antonio on account of his travels in Italy: he is a covetous ten in the hundred man, who has lawsuits of very dubious character with his tenants, &c., many of whose names are given (mostly spelled backwards)—Cole, Sir Walter, his son-in-law, Bishop Piller, Susanna Richardson, Farmer Thompson: he was nicknamed Judas ; had been, and still was, secretly a Papist ; has some acquaintance with the grooms at Court, and "20 years since," *i.e.*, in 1599, was "at the point of death by rigor of law," but pardoned by the Court at Proberio's intercession, who then lent him money in his poverty. A whole scene ii. 3*b*, is taken up with ridicule of the polysyllabic title of "historiographer," and this scene has no bearing on the rest of the play.

Now, Monday was of a family which probably came from a Midland county (the place of his birth is unknown). He was called Antonio by Jonson in *The case is altered ;* gave up writing for the stage in 1602, so that he must have had other means of subsistence ; and in 1599 was away from Henslow's company, probably with a strolling company, and possibly in hiding for some offence against the Court ; was nicknamed Judas and accused of papistry, having been a member of the Seminary at Rome. He had travelled in Italy, &c., and had been a messenger of Her Majesty's chamber until 1592. In 1618 he was the City "historio-grapher," for he then published his edition of *Stow's London*, and he had been their pageant poet, &c., from 1592 onward. The one difficulty is that Antonio had been "beyond seas 11 or 12 years;" but Monday, for all we know, may have been so, and only visited England at intervals.

This play is interesting apart from the Antonio question. It was privately acted, and doubtless privately printed (it has no printer's name on title-page), on account of its personal satire; is arranged in seven acts, which should be five, for iii. and iv., vi. and vii., of the editions palpably form but one act each; and contains allusions to Sir R. Shirley, iii. 2, and yellow starch, vii. 1.

302. *The Two Noble Ladies*, or *The Converted Conjuror*, Eg. MS. 1994, was acted at the Red Bull by the company of the Revels, and therefore dates 1619–22. It is founded on Calderon's *Magico Prodigioso*.

303. *The Welsh Ambassador* is extant in MS. "in private hands" (Halliwell); date 1623, "in the reign of this King here, 1621, 22, and 23," says the play. Among the characters are Athelstan, King; Edmond and Eldred, his brothers; the Duke of Cornwall, the Earls of Kent and Chester, the Baron of Winchester, a Clown, and Captain Voltimar.

304. *The stately* (but this word is omitted in most copies) *Tragedy of Claudius Tiberius Nero*, Rome's greatest Tyrant, truly represented out of the purest records of those times, 1607. S. R. 10th April 1607, for F. Burton, as "The tragical life and death" of C. T. N., was dedicated to Sir Arthur Mannering. Whether acted or not I know not.

305. *The tragedy of Nero*, newly written, 1624, by A. Matthews and J. Norton for T. Jones, was licensed for the press 15th May 1624 by the Master of the Revels. Ap-

parently a closet play; not publicly acted.   Reprinted with collections from Eg. MS. 1994 by Mr. A. H. Bullen.

Tempore CHARLES I.

Plays not Extant, but Entered S. R. 1653–1660.

306. *The Countryman*, 9th Sept. 1653.

307. *The King's Mistress*, 9th Sept. 1653.

308. *The Politic Bankrupt*, or *Which is the best Girl?* 9th Sept. 1653.

309. *The Bondwoman*, 23rd Sept. 1653.

310. *The Soldiered Citizen*, 29th June 1660.   One of the plays destroyed by Warburton's servant; and in his list it has the additional title of *The Crafty Merchant*, by S. Marmion.   But *The Cra[fty] Merchant*, or *Come to my Country House*, was licensed as by W. Bonen, *q.v.*, 12th Sept. 1623.   *The Merchant's Sacrifice*, a title in Warburton's list, but afterwards cancelled, was probably a jumble of *The Crafty Merchant* and *Minerva's Sacrifice*.

311. *Iphis and Ianthe*, or *A Marriage without a man*, 29th June 1660, and absurdly ascribed to W. Shakespeare.

312. *Duke Humphry.   Ibid.* in all respects.

313. *The History of King Stephen.   Ibid.* in all respects.

314. *The History of Madoc, King of Britain*, 29th June 1660, and ascribed absurdly to Beaumont.

All these entries are for H. Moseley.   But in Warburton's list, which seems to have consisted of unprinted MSS. formerly belonging to this publisher, we find the following additions :—

315. *The City Shuffler.*   Acted at Salisbury Court by the Revels company Oct. 1633, and stayed by Herbert. See my *History of the Stage*, p. 337.

316. *The Fairy Queen.*

317. *The Great Man.*

318. *The Lovers of Ludgate.*

319. *Orpheus.* A fragment is extant in the British Museum.

320. *The Spanish Puecas* [Purchase, wrongly, in *Biog Dram.* and Halliwell].

There are also entries for R. Marriott, 29th Nov. 1654, viz. :—

321. *The Black Wedding.*

322. *Castara,* or *Cruelty without Lust.*

323. *The Conceits.*

324. *The Divorce.*

325. *The Florentine Friend.*

326. *A Fool and her Maidenhead soon parted.* This play occurs between two plays by Davenport in the 1639 Cockpit list, and had, therefore, belonged to the Queen's men before the 1636 closure of the theatres. It probably is by Davenport, *q.v.*

327. *The Law Case:* probably *The Devil's Law Case,* by Webster, which also belonged to Queen Henrietta's men.

328. *The Noble Ravishers.*

329. *Pity the Maid.*

330. *The Proxy,* or *Love's Aftergame.* Played " at Salisbury Court 24th Nov. 1634," Halliwell : who, as usual, conceals his authority for the statement.

331. *Salisbury Plain.*

332. *The Supposed Inconstancy.*

333. *The Woman's Law.*

334. *The Woman's Masterpiece.*

335. *The Younger Brother.* Played at the Red Bull 3rd Oct. 1617 by Queen Anne's men, from whom it probably passed to Queen Henrietta's. See Collier's *Alleyn,*

p. 107. Alleyn received for this performance (no doubt a first one) " but £3, 6s. 4d."

---

336. *The Conceited Duke*, mentioned in the 1639 Cockpit list, is not Fletcher's *Noble Gentleman*, which was a King's men's play. It, like *A Fool* &c., *supra*, belonged to the Queen's men.

Plays extant in MS., of which I, not having seen them, can give no further account.

337. *Battle of the Vices against the Virtues.* Moral. MS., *temp.* Charles I, in Thorpe's *Catalogue*, 1835, p. 11.

338. *Demetrius and Marsina*, or *The Imperial Impostor and The unhappy heroine*, T. One of Warburton's MSS. not destroyed.

339. *Diana's Grove*, or *The Faithful Genius*, T. C. In private hands.

340. *The Fatal Marriage*, or *A second Lucretia*. Galeas, Jacomo, and Jovanni are characters in it. Eg. MS. 1994.

341. *Grobiana's Nuptials.* MS. Bodl. 30.

342. *Love's changelings changed.* Founded on Sidney's *Arcadia*. Eg. MSS. 1994.

343. *Pelopidarum Secunda*, T. MS. Harl. 5110. Acted at Winchester School.

344. *Sight and Search*, dated 1643. *Ibid.*

345. *The Tell Tale.* Dulwich MSS. Advertised 1658 in *The New World*, &c., and 1661 in *Wit and Drollery*. See Warner's excellent *Dulwich Catalogue*, p. 342.

346. *The Whimsies of Senor Hidalgo*, or *The Masculine Bride*, C. MS. Harl. 5152.

347. *The Wizard*, C. Brit. Mus., *MSS. Addit.* 10,306. Belonged to Cartwright the actor.

Plays Known only by Advertisement.

348. *The Chaste Woman against her Will*, C., 1658. "In the press and ready for printing." At the end of *The New World of English Words*, for N. Brook; 1661, at the end of *Wit and Drollery*.

349. *The Comical History of Don Quixote*, or *The Knight of the ill-favoured face*, C. *Ibid.*, 1658, 1661.

350. *The Fair Spanish Captive*, T. C. *Ibid.*, 1658, 1661.

351. *The Fool Transformed*, C. *Ibid.*, 1658, 1661. Query Cockain's *Trappolin supposed a Prince*, 1658.

352. *The history of Lewis* 11, *King of France*, T. C. *Ibid.*, 1558, 1661.

353. *The Tooth-drawer*, C. *Ibid.*, 1658, 1661.

354. *Fulgius and Lucrelle.* Kirkman's *Catalogue*, 1661.

355. *The French Schoolmaster*, 1662. At the end of *The Wits*, for H. Marsh.

356. *Nineveh's Repentance*, T. C. Catalogue at the end of *The Careless Shepherdess*, 1656. Query Greene and Lodge's *Looking-Glass for London*.

357. *Edmund Ironside, the English King*, or *A true Chronicle History called War hath made all friends.* Eg. MS. 1994.

Plays only Known by Mention in other Works.

358. *The Greeks and Trojans.* See Gayton's *Notes on Don Quixote*, 1654. Query Heywood's *Iron Age*.

359. *The Invisible Knight.* See Shirley's *Bird in a Cage*, 1633.

360. *A Projector lately dead*, C. Noy being dissected in his lawyer's robes, they find 100 proclamations in his head:

moth-eaten records in his maw, &c. See *A collection of judgements upon Sabbath-breakers*, 1636.

361. *The Roaring Girl*, or *The Catchpoll*, C. See Jordan's *Walks of Islington and Hogsden*, iii. 3, 1641. Probably *Moll Cutpurse*, q.v.

362. *The Whisperer*, or *What you please*. Acted at the Red Bull. See Tatham's Prologue to it in *Ostella*, 1650.

363. *The Toy*. Acted at Dublin. See *Toy to please chaste ladies*. Shirley wrote the Dublin Prologue.

364. *The Guelphs and Ghibellines*. See Gayton's *Notes on Don Quixote*, 1654.

EXTANT ANONYMOUS PLAYS. *Temp.* CHARLES I.

364. *Pathomachia*, or *The Battle of the Affections. Shadowed by a feigned Siege of the City Pathopolis.* Written some years since, and first published by a friend of the deceased author. Running title, *Love's Lodestone.* S. R. 16th April 1630 for F. Constable. 1630.

365. *Wine, Beer, Ale, and Tobacco*, &c., "A dialogue," 1629, has no proper connexion with the subject of the present work.

366. *The Costly Whore*, C. H., was acted by the Revels company [at Salisbury Court 1629–31, at the Fortune 1632]. S. R. 2nd Nov. 1632 for W. Sheares. 1633. The date is fixed to 1631–2 by the allusion to the use of coals instead of wood for glass and iron furnaces :—

"I'll make them search the earth to find new fire," i. 2.

Mr. A. H. Bullen, who republished this play, quotes this as an evidence that the play was produced in 1613; but there was no "company of the Revels" till 1619. But this is only one of many allusions to the time c. 1631. I have only space to mention the famine and exportation of corn.

367. *The General*, T. C., has been printed from MS. which may be the play performed at Dublin c. 1638 under Shirley's management.

368. *The Ghost*, or *The Woman wears the Breeches*, C., was written 1640; printed 1653.

369. *The Cruel War*, T., was printed 1643.

370. *News out of the West*, or *The Character of a Mountebank*, was printed 1647. It is a kind of interlude.

371. *Marcus Tullius Cicero, that famous Roman Orator, his Tragedy*, was printed 1651, but probably never acted.

372. *The Queen*, or *The Excellency of her Sex*, T. C., printed 1653, was edited by Alexander Gough, as discovered by a " person of Honor." Founded on Belleforest's *Histoires Tragiques*, Nov. 13. This play ought to be reprinted.

373. *The Bastard*, T., printed 1652. Founded on *Schiarra and Florelia*, or *The English Lovers, and Roberto and Isidaura*, in *Gerardo the Unfortunate Spaniard*, p. 87.

374. *The Unfortunate Usurper* (Andronicus Comnenus) was printed 1663.

375. *The London Chanticleers*, A witty Comedy, full of various and delightful mirth, 1659, for Simon Miller, was "often acted," but not in London. See Prologue. I judge from the plays alluded to in it, *The Changeling*, *Love Tricks*, *The Vestal*, &c., that it was acted by Queen Henrietta's men when travelling, very likely in the plague-time, 1636–7. Cf. also "the whole royal progeny," Sc. 5, which implies a late date, when they were numerous. There are many allusions to ballads, chap-books, &c., in this play worthy of further investigation.

376. *The Cyprian Conqueror*, or *The Faithless Relict*. Brit. Mus., *MS. Sloane*, 3709. Scene, Ephesus.

MASKS BY ANONYMOUS AUTHORS.

1. 1572, June 15–18. [*Peace and Discord*], a mask at Whitehall before the Queen and Montmerency, the French Ambassador, in which Apollo, the Muses, Peace, Argus, and Discord were characters. Prepared, but not shown, May 1562.

2. 1573, Jan. 1. The mask of *Janus*. A "double mask."

3. 1573, c. Nov. A mask of *wild men* was shown at Greenwich after the marriage of William Drury, Esq.

4. 1573, Dec. 27. A mask of 6 *Lance Knights*.

5. 1574, Jan. 1. A mask of 6 *Foresters* or *Hunters*.

6. 1574, Jan. 6. A mask of 6 *Sages*. Halliwell (*Dicty.*) omits this and the *Lance Knights*, and makes the *Foresters* and *Hunters* two masks. He follows the Index to Cunningham's *Revels*, not the documents.

7. 1574, Feb. 2. A mask of 6 *Virtues*. Prepared, not shown.

8. 1574, Feb. 22, 23. Masks of 7 *Ladies* and 7 *Warriors*.

9. 1575, Jan. 6. The *Pedlar's* mask.

10. 1577, Feb. 19. A mask of *Boys*.

11. 1579, Jan 11. Masks of *Amazons* and *Knights*.

12. 1583, Jan. 5. A mask of *Ladies*.

13. 1583, Feb. 12. A mask of 6 *Seamen*. Prepared, but not used.

All these are from the Revels accounts.

14. 1594, Dec. 12–1595, Mar. 4. i. *Gesta Graiorum*, Gray's Inn Revels, containing a mask performed at Court

4th Mar. 1595, Shrove Tuesday. Printed in *Nichols*, iii. 262 *seq.*

1604, Mar. 15. There were several accounts of the passage of King James from the Tower to Whitehall. See under JONSON and DEKKER. Also the following:—

15. *The Royal entertainment into London* of our Royal King James with our Renowned Queen, together with their eldest son, Henry Frederick, Prince of Wales. S. R. 1604, Mar. 21, for Thomas Pavier.

16. *The Time Triumphant*, or the true model, as well of the King's Majesty's first coming into England, as also his Royal progress from the Tower through the City, 15th Mar. 1603, to his highness' Manor of Whitehall. S. R. 1604, Mar. 27, for Ralph Blore.

17. *The Arches of Triumph*, &c., invented and published by Stephen Harrison, joiner and architect, and graven by William Kip. See *Nichols*, i. 328 *seq.*

18. 1606, July 16–Aug. 11. *The King of Denmark's Entertainment at Tilbury Hope by the King*, &c., 1606. S. R. 1606, July, for Henry Roberts, who wrote the description. See *Nichols*, ii. 54 *seq.*

19. *The King of Denmark's Welcome into England*, &c. S. R. 1606, Aug. 8, for Edward Allde.

20. *England's Farewell to Christian 4, famous King of Denmark*, &c., written by H. Roberts, 1606. See *Nichols*, ii. 75 *seq.* S. R. 1604, Aug. 19, for William Welby. See also JONSON.

21. 1610, May 31. *London's Love to the Royal Prince Henry*, meeting him on the River of Thames at his return from Richmond, &c.; with a brief report of the water-fight and fireworks. Printed by Edward Allde for Nathaniel Fosbrooke, 1610.

Thus far we meet with anonymous shows only in James'

time. The following are masks proper. The names are
from Brit. Mus., *MS. Addit.* 10,444, a book of tunes:
they are most likely only duplicate titles for masks otherwise known, but not yet identified. 22. *Adson's mask;*
23. *Bateman's m.;* 24. *The Blackfriars m.,* see JONSON, 51;
25. *The Broxbournbury m.;* 26. *The Bull m.;* 27. *The
Hampton Court m.* This last was published as

27. *The true description of a royal Mask at Hampton
Court,* 1604 (Lowndes). It was Daniel's *Vision of the* 12
Goddesses, q.v.

28. c. 1610, April. *The Mask of the Twelve Months.*
Printed from MS. by the Shak. Soc. Evidently performed
before Prince Henry. Possibly the date may be 1st May
1611.

1613, Dec. *The Gentlemen's mask.* Merely another
name for Jonson's *Love Restored,* q.v.

30. 1614, Jan. 6. *The Mask of Flowers* was presented
by the gentlemen of Gray's Inn at the Banqueting House,
Whitehall, at the marriage of the Earl of Somerset, 1614,
by N. Okes for Robert Wilson, for whom it was entered
S. R. 1614, Jan. 21. J. G., W. D., T. B., who sign the
address to Bacon, were probably the authors: not Campion,
as, by a printer's error, is stated in my *History of the Stage,*
p. 182. Campion's mask for this occasion is sometimes
called *The Squires' mask.*

31. 1618, Jan. 3. *The Mask of Amazons,* of *Ladies,* or
of *Disappointed Ladies,* was prepared by nine ladies at their
own cost, but disallowed by both King and Queen, *Nichols,*
iii. 453. The ladies were—

1. Lady Hay, Queen of the Amazons, *née* Lucy Percy.
2. L. Dorothy Percy, afterwards L. Robert Sidney's
   lady.
3. Sir Robert Rich's lady, *née* Frances Hatton.

4. Sir Henry Rich's lady, *née* Isabella Cope.
5. Isabella Rich, afterwards Mrs. Richard Rogers.
6. Jane West, daughter of Lord De la War.
7. Barbara Sidney, afterwards married Thomas, Viscount Strangford.
8. Sir Humfrey May's lady.
9. Lady Cave, daughter to Sir Herbert Croftes.

32. 1617, Feb. 2. ii. *Gesta Graiorum.* This revel, printed in *Nichols* (Eliz.), iii. 342, as acted at Gray's Inn, contains *The Mask of Mountebanks.* *MS. Addit.*, Brit. Mus., 5956, gives the mask as performed afterwards at Court 16th Feb. 1618, with a song in place of the final paradoxes. Collier printed this version from the Duke of Devonshire's MS. for the Shak. Soc., without any knowledge of its connexion with Gray's Inn. It was partly written by Campion.

33. 1618, April 23. *Chester's Triumph in Honor of her Prince, Henry Prince of Wales, Earl of Chester,* 1610. S. R. 1610, June 12. Performed at Chester on St. George's Day. Reprinted *Nichols*, ii. 291. Richard Davies drew up the Relation: Robert Amery, late sheriff, partly at least composed it: he calls himself "the author of the Show."

34. 1620, Feb. 12. Chamberlain, in a letter to Carleton, mentions a "*running*" or travelling mask as ranging "all over the country," *Nichols*, iii. 587.

c. 1620. 35. *The Fairy mask;* 36. *The Fools' mask;* 37. *The Sailors' mask;* and 38. *The Essex antic mask*, are said in Halliwell's *Dict.* to have been presented c. 1620; but I cannot find on what authority the statement is made. There was a mask at Essex House 1621, Jan. 8, *Nichols*, iii. 647. In like manner Halliwell gives 39. *The Haymakers' m.,* c. 1623; and 40. *The Furies' m.,* c. 1624; and 41. *The Shepherds' m., temp.* Jac. 1. This last I take to be another name for Jonson's *Pan's Anniversary,* and I believe the others are only duplicate names for other masks taken from the character of the dancers therein.

42. *The mask of the Four Seasons, temp.* James I, was printed from MS. for the Shak. Soc. 1848.

----

43. 1625, c. Mar. *The Theater of Apollo,* where Fires of Joy are raised sacred to the ever-happy and eternal memory of our Sovereign the Great Apollo and his most royal Offspring, before prepared to be offered to the Sacred Majesty of our deceased Sovereign King James, and now presented to the royal hands of our gracious Lord King Charles, heir of the Kingdoms, virtues, and glories of his Father. Brit. Mus., *MS. Bibl. Reg.,* 18A. lxx.   Scene, Parnassus.

44 c. 1625, May 11. *Virtue and Beauty reconciled.* In honor of the marriage of the King and Queen; n.d.

45. *The Cuckolds' mask;* and 46. *The mask of Durance,* are given by Halliwell as *temp.* Car. I.

47. 1634, Sept. 12. *The King and Queen's entertainment at Richmond* after their departure from Oxford, in a mask presented by Prince Charles. 1634, 1636. The Prince danced in it; so did Lord Buckhurst and Mr. Edward Sackville as a Captain and a Druid. Simon Hopper composed the dances, Charles Colman the music. The Prince "was not then above *six* years old," *Biog. Dram.,* followed verbatim, as usual, by Halliwell, *Dict.* He was born 1630, May 29.

48. 1635, Dec. 21. *Florimene,* P., presented by the Queen's commandment before the King at Whitehall. 1635. Written in French. The argument, in English, was allowed to be printed 14th Dec. by Herbert. *MS. Lansd.* 1171, contains Inigo Jones' "profile of the stage for the proportioning the shortening sides of scenes with triangular frames

when there is but one standing scene:" also a ground plot.

49. 1636, Feb. 27. *Corona Minervæ*, 1635, presented before Prince Charles, the Duke of York, and the Lady Mary at the Museum Minervæ, Whitehall being closed for painting.

50. 1638, Feb, 6, Shrove Tuesday. *Luminalia*, or *The Festival of Light*, 1637. Presented by the Queen and her Ladies. With Inigo Jones' machinery, by "her Majesty's command." Night presented the anti-mask.

FULL LIST OF UNIVERSITY PLAYS IN ENGLISH.

A. At Cambridge.

i. *Tempore* Elizabeth.

Acted at King's.

1564. *Ezechias.* See Udall.

Acted at Christ's.

1566. *Gammer Gurton's Needle.* See Still.

Acted at St. John's.

1577. *The Destruction of Jerusalem.* See Legge.

Anon. 1. *The Pilgrimage to Parnassus.* Acted at St. John's, Cambridge. The MS. of this play was discovered by the Rev. W. D. Macray, and published by him in 1886. He assigns to it a date of 1597 in the title, which is palpably wrong. In Act ii. the following books are mentioned: Kinsader's *Satyrs* (Marston's *Scourge of Villany*, entered S. R. 1598, Sept. 8.); Lodge's *Fig for Momus*, 1595; Bastard's *Epigrams*, S. R. 1598, April 3; and Lichfield's *Trimming of Nash*, S. R. 1597, Oct. 11. This "Christmas toy," written in three days, was evidently performed in the Christmas of 1598. This mistake sets all Macray's dates wrong. In i. Colin (Spenser) is mentioned. In ii. Madido translates Horace' *Satires*. Can he be meant for T. Drant? The pun on *Dialectica est Ars* is the same as that so often repeated by Heywood. I cannot identify Stupido the Martinist: of Amoretto more hereafter; but these are all, I am certain, personal caricatures. In v. Ingenioso the pamphleteer, who is certainly Nash, is "schoolfellow" with the pilgrims Philomusus and Studioso, but I take it in the University Schools, not at a Grammar School. Kempe is mentioned; and the pilgrimage at the end has, at Christmas 1598, lasted four years.

ANON. 2. *The Return from Parnassus*, Part i., also discovered by Mr. Macray, and by the same author, was acted at St. John's. In i. 1 the pilgrimage has lasted seven years, which brings us to 1601 Dec. for the date of performance. It appears from the Prologue that, having, in consequence of the former play, been refused a B.A. degree, the author had taken one in Germany. He must have been about twenty-one years of age in 1598; also his name was probably Cheshire, Chester, or something of that sort :—

"Though Cheshire seem to priviledge his name ;"

but may not this refer to the Ashton foundation of fellowships at St. John's, limited to natives of the diocese of Chester? There are allusions to Greene's mottoes, i. 1 ; Tarleton dead, i. 1 ; Harington's *Metamorphosis of Ajax*, i. 1 ; Nash's pamphleteering in London, i. 1 (which fixes the date of the events in the play to 1589); to Elderton dead, i. 1 : Gullio the plagiarist (who imitates every one, Gascoigne, Shakespeare, Daniel, &c.; has been at Padua, and is like to die in the Low Countries) awaits identification, iii. 1. Weever's *Epigrams*, 1599, are alluded to iii. 1 ; "acorn" (ackhorns) is curiously interpreted "Acheron's" by the editor. "M. Mingo," in Ingenioso's speech v. 1, confirms my view that Ingenioso is Nash.

Before passing to the next play I must note that Mr. Macray edited that play also, with valuable various readings from a MS. in the possession of Mr. Halliwell Phillipps.

This MS. appears to be the origin of numerous emendations set forth in the last edition of *Dodsley* as made by Mr. W. C. Hazlitt. It was evidently a copy of the play as acted; and the "four year" in the Prologue fixes the date of acting to Christmas 1602, as I had previously assigned it, and shows that Mr. Arber's guess, 1601, is erroneous. Both parts were meant to be presented in 1601, but only the First Part was then acted; the second lay neglected "this twelve-month in a coal-house." The MS. refers to the 1601 play, "unless ye have heard the former," where the editions (from a copy altered for the press) have "unless you know the subject well." That the Recorder in the Second Part of the play is meant for Francis Brackyn, Recorder of Cambridge, I learn from Mr. Macray's preface. Amoretto seems identical with Gullio in the First Part. The reference in the Prologue to the son-finding in the end of a play is probably to *Patient Grisel*, acted 1599 Dec. Malone, referring to the published title-page, says 1603: this instance (one of scores) shows the need of a book like the present with the plays arranged in order of performance, not of publication. I leave my notice of Part ii. of this play, as I had written it before I heard of Mr. Macray's discovery or saw his excellent and scholarly edition.

ANON. 3. 1602, Dec. *The Return from Parnassus*, Part ii., S. R., for J. Wright, Oct. 16, 1605. There is abundance of evidence in this play that fixes the date to 1601 or thereabouts; but before entering on this I may point out that it was "publicly acted by the students of St. John's College," and not merely presented to the King or other great personage, like many preceding plays. It was, most likely, written by a member of St John's.

The play opens with a Prologue, of which more hereafter. Then Ingenioso, the satirist, enters with *Juvenal* in his hand.

He is manifestly Nash, "young Juvenal." For proof of this read the first speech, especially the line,

> "O suffer me among so many men
> To tread aright the traces of thy pen."

Then comes in Judicio, a "corrector[1] for the press," who criticises the numerous Anthologies or *Flores Poetarum* recently published, among them specially *Belvedere*, or *The Garden of the Muses*, entered S. R. Aug. 11, 1600, and again Nov. 3—both times for H. Astley. He then gives the following list of poets from that book, and Ingenioso proposes to "censure" them :—

1. Edmund Spenser . dead . Cantab., ——
2. Henry Constable . living . Cantab., Academico.
3. Samuel Daniel . . living . Oxon., ——
4. Thomas Lodge . . living . $\begin{cases} \text{Oxon.} \\ \text{?Cantab.,} \end{cases}$ Philomusus.
5. Thomas Watson . dead . Oxon., ——
6. Michael Drayton . living . Cantab., Studioso.
7. John Davis . . . living . Oxon., Phantasma.
8. John Marston . . living . Oxon., Furor.
9. Christopher Marlowe dead . Cantab., ——

They censure them accordingly. But between Davis and Marston in the play as it stands comes a censure in prose on Locke and Hudson, which is clearly an interpolation, made probably when the play, which had been thrown aside, was revised and publicly acted. In like manner in another interpolation after Marlowe we find censures on Jonson, Shakespeare, Churchyard (the latter two not University men), and Nash—this last one as deceased. Now, as the

---

[1] This is important as showing the existence of such an avocation in 1601. It is constantly decried by many critics of our time, and I have been blamed for maintaining it, just as I have for asserting the existence of short-hand at the same date by those who ought to know better.

original production of this play was on some Christmas (see Prologue, " a Christmas toy "), and Nash was certainly alive when he published his *Summer's Last Will*, Oct. 2, 1600, and Elizabeth died in Mar. 1602–3, the " censure " of that poet must have been inserted at some date not earlier than Christmas 1600, nor later than Christmas 1602. With regard to the original list of nine poets, it will be noticed that three poets mentioned in them were dead, and I shall try to show that those still living correspond to characters in the play itself.   Of these more by-and-by.

We next have Danter, the printer, entering and bargaining with Ingenioso (Nash) for a satire on Cambridge.   This scene is meant, I think, to distinctly point out that Ingenioso and his friends are no fictions, but representations of real living men.

But if they be such, if the whole play be, as I believe, one continuous personal satire, we ought to be able to identify some of the characters.   It will to this end be convenient to leave further consideration of the course of the plot and to examine each personage separately.   The *dramatis personœ* fall into groups, the first of which is that of the satirists Ingenioso, Furor, Phantasma.

1. INGENIOSO, " young Juvenal," who carries the vinegar-bottle, sells Danter a libel on Cambridge, is " an inventor of slight prose " (i. 6), satirises the Recorder, takes refuge in the Isle of Dogs, is too clearly Thomas Nash to need further comment.   Note specially the allusion to his expulsion from Cambridge for his satire, *Terminus et non Terminus*, in v. 4—

> " For had not Cambridge been to me unkind,
>   I had not turn'd to gall a milky mind,"

and the opening censure of Nash in i. 3, which was clearly inserted after Nash's death.

2. FUROR, of "the roaring Muse" and "high, tiptoe, strutting poesy" (iii. 4), who satirises Sir Roderick, is no less clearly Marston. He is distinctly identified by the phrase used by Furor in iv. 2, "lift his leg;" compare the opening censure on Marston, "What, Mr. Kinsayder, lifting your leg?" &c. He, too, retires to the Isle of Dogs, that is, goes to live among the lawyers, as we are told in the play itself. Marston was a member of the Temple. His style is admirably parodied in the character of Furor.

3. PHANTASMA, who satirises Amoretto, and also retires to the Isle of Dogs, is harder to identify. He must have been a member of one of the Inns of Court, and probably one of the list censured by Ingenioso and Judicio. The only satirist in that list available to us is Sir John Davies, among whose *Epigrams* is one on Publius, whom I shall presently try to identify with Amoretto. He had also been expelled from the Middle Temple for quarrelling with Richard Martin, who is not however the Recorder of this play. The indications are slight, but, I think, taken in conjunction with the other characters, sufficient.

A second group consists of Philomusus and Studioso.

4. PHILOMUSUS, who is disguised as Theodore, the French doctor, who has travelled in Italy and France, who has pursuivants out against him, who is engaged by Kempe to play the "foolish justice," afterward turns fiddler, and finally Arcadian shepherd or poet, and who while he acts as a French doctor lives in Shoe Lane, can hardly be mistaken. Thomas Lodge was a French doctor, M.D. of Avignon, had travelled in Italy and France, was frequently in danger of imprisonment for debt, was connected with the Chamberlain's Company of players, and relinquished the stage for poetry and other writings. He lived in Warwick Lane, which is close by and parallel to Shoe Lane. It is possible that

"When shall our souls their wearied *lodge* forego?" (i. 4.)
may contain an allusion to Lodge's name. It is doubtful
whether Lodge was a member of Cambridge University.
Langbaine says he was, and although we know that he
belonged to Trinity College, Oxford, it does not follow that
he did not afterward go to Cambridge. Such migrations
were much more frequent at that time than now.

5. STUDIOSO appears as Jacques, Theodore's man; he too
has travelled in France, &c.; the pursuivants are out for
him; Burbadge sets him to play Jeronymo and Richard 3.
—in fact, he follows Philomusus in all his fortunes. It is
noticeable that Kempe persists in calling him Otioso, not
Studioso. The only writers for the Chamberlain's men
known to us of this date are Shakespeare, Drayton, and
Jonson. Shakespeare and Jonson were not then University
men, although Jonson became so afterward. Drayton no
doubt did write for the Chamberlain's men about 1597.
The commencement of his dramatic career was *The Merry
Devil of Edmonton*, acted by that company. He was also
at that time very intimate with Lodge and Shakespeare,
although the general reader will find no evidence of this in
his published works: he cut out all allusions to them in his
later editions, although, like Jonson, he praised Shakespeare
highly after his death. Drayton is reckoned a tragedian
by Meres in 1598, but Lodge as a comic writer, which
agrees with the parts they play in the scene with Kempe.
Drayton was a Cantab., like Studioso. In v. 1, "The
World and Fortune hath played on us too long," seems to
allude to Drayton's writing for the Fortune company after
he left the Globe. He and Philomusus finally retired from
the stage to "the downs of Kent," *i.e.*, to seek the patronage
of the Countess of Pembroke. Compare Drayton's eighth
Eclogue in his *Pastorals*.

6. ACADEMICO is very hard to decipher: he is a Cantab. who seeks to obtain a living because gratitude is due to him from Amoretto, for whom he had written a speech for the Queen's birthday at Cambridge. Amoretto sells the living to an undeserving ignoramus. Academico hates the Popish tongue of Latin. Constable would answer in other respects, but he was a Roman Catholic—unless, indeed, this hatred of Popish Latin be a sort of ironical apology for him. This, however, is the only character of whose identification I feel any doubt.

The next point to determine is the date of the acting of the play. Doubtless the original conception and most of the composition was completed soon after the appearance of *Belvedere* in Nash's lifetime, but there are unmistakable evidences of later revision. The siege of Ostend had commenced, Nash was deceased, &c.,—but the conclusive datum lies in the examination of Immerito, from which we learn that the Dominical letter was C, and that the last quarter of the moon was on the fifth day at 2h. 38m. in the morning. This fixes the date as January 1602–3, and if confirmation be needed we find it in what Momus says in the Prologue, "What is here presented is an old, musty show that hath lain this twelvemonth in the bottom of a coal-house."

The intent of the play is to set forth the ill fortunes of University poets, exemplified by Nash, Marston, Davis, Constable, Lodge, and Drayton, the only living one quoted on the other side being Daniel. There is, however, one more character worth examining, Amoretto. He is a Cambridge man, a plagiarist, for whom Academico writes a speech on the Queen's Accession-day, Nov. 17th; he forms his style on Ovid's *Art of Love*, uses technical hunting and other sporting phrases in his conversation, is a member of the Temple, son of Sir Roderic, knows no languages, is satirised

by Phantasma (? Davies), is a " carpenter of Sonnets,"
writes of his mistress' sweetness in a most equivocal manner,
has been in Italy, is a friend of the Recorder (Brachyn),
has a living in his gift, but is not in holy orders himself.
Does all this point to Daniel? We know too little of his
life to answer definitely " yes," but the point is worth noting.

One point more and we may dismiss the play. Kempe
says: " Few of the University men play well. Why here's
our fellow, Shakespeare, puts them all down, ay, and Ben
Jonson too. Oh! that Ben Jonson is a pestilent fellow; he
brought up Horace giving the poets a pill; but our fellow,
Shakespeare, hath given him a purge that made him bewray
his credit." Jonson's representation of himself as Horace
in the *Poetaster* and of Marston as Crispinus has been more
than sufficiently commented on; but the fact here proved,
that Shakespeare satirised Jonson, has been neglected. It
must have been, I think, *Troylus and Cressida*, q.v., that
contained the purge referred to.

Acted at Queen's.

c. 1587. *Tancred.* See Wotton.

Acted at Clare Hall.

1598. *Club Law.* See Ruggle.
? 1598. *Re Vera,* or *Verily.* See Ruggle.

Acted at some place unknown.

Anon. 4, c. 1601. *Timon.* Obscure; topical; printed
from MS. by Dyce. 1842. Not connected with Shakespeare's *Timon.*

ii. *Tempore* James I.

Acted at Trinity.

1603. *Lingua.* See Tomkis.

1615. *Albumazar.* See TOMKIS.
1613. *Sciros.* See BROOKES.

Acted at Clare Hall.

1615. *Club Law.* See RUGGLE.

Acted at some College unknown.

ANON. 5, c. 1615. *Work for Cutlers,* or a Merry Dialogue between *Sword, Rapier, and Dagger.* "Acted in a Show in the famous University of Cambridge." Printed by T. Creede, 1615. Reprinted, *Harl. Misc.,* x. S. R., for Richard Meighen, 1615, July 4.

ANON. 6, c. 1615. *Exchange Ware at the Second Hand;* viz., *Band, Ruff, and Cuff,* "lately out, and now newly darned up; or a Dialogue acted in a Show in the famous University of Cambridge." Second edition, 1615. S. R., for Miles Patrich, 1615, Feb. 10.

iii. *Tempore* CHARLES I.

At Trinity.

1630–3. For *The Pedlar, Aristippus, The Jealous Lovers,* and *Hey for Honesty,* see RANDOLPH.
1641. *The Guardian.* See COWLEY.

B. AT OXFORD.

i. *Tempore* ELIZABETH.

Acted at Christ Church.

1566. *Palamon and Arcite.* See EDWARDS.

Not Acted.

1586–7. *Tancredo.* See WOTTON.

ii. *Tempore* JAMES I.

Acted at Christ Church.

1605. *The Queen's Arcadia.* See DANIEL.

c. 1614. For *The Courageous Turk* (Amurath), *Orestes*, *The Raging Turk* (Bajazet), *The Careless Shepherdess*, see GOFFE.

1618. *Technogamia.* See HOLLIDAY.

Acted at Trinity.

ANON. 7, 1606. *Cæsar and Pompey*, or *Cæsar's Revenge*, T., 1607. S. R. 1606, June 5, for John Wright and Nathaniel Fossbrook, "*Julius Cæsar's Revenge.*" The Duke of Devonshire has a copy without date or mention of Trin. Coll.

Acted at Oxford.

ANON. 8, 1607. An account of the *Christmas Prince*, as it was exhibited in the University of Oxford in the year 1607. *Misc. Antiq. Angl.*, from the MS. in St. John's Library. 1816.

iii. *Tempore* CHARLES I.

Acted at Magdalen.

c. 1633. *Fuimus Troes.* See FISHER.

Acted at St. John's.

1636. *Stonehenge.* See SPEED.

1636. *Love's Hospital.* See WILDE.

1637. *The Converted Robber.* See WILDE.

Acted at Christ Church.

1635. *The Combat of Love and Friendship.* See MEAD.

1636. *The [Settling of the] Floating Island[s].* See STRODE. Also called *Passions Calmed.*

1636. *The Royal Slave.*   See CARTWRIGHT.

Acted at Gloucester Hull.

c. 1636. *The Scholar.*   See LOVELACE.

Acted near Eastgate.

ANON. 8, 1636. *Moore's Mask.*   Mr. Moore was one of the six Moors in the Anti-Mask.   MS.   Exhibited twice in public; once in private for gentlewomen.

? Acted at Oxford.

1637, Sept. *The Ward.*   See NEALE.

? Acted at New College.

1638. *The Sophister.*   See ZOUCH.

UNIVERSITY PLAYS IN LATIN.

A. At Oxford.

i. *Tempore* Elizabeth.

Performed at Christ Church.

ANON. 1, 1566, Sept. 1, Sunday. *Marcus Geminus.* The Queen was absent, but the Spanish Ambassador highly commended it to her, and she said she would "lose no more sport hereafter," Nichols, *Eliz.*, i. 210.

1566, Sept. 5. *Progne.* See CALFHILL.

Before 1578. *Absalon.* See WATSON. No place of production is given in the MS., but if acted at all at the University, which is very doubtful, it would be at Christ Church. No other College at Oxford acted plays in Elizabeth's time. But Watson was of All Souls.

c. 1579. *Œdipus.*
1580. *Ulysses Redux.*
1581. *Meleager.*   } See GAGER.
1583, June. *Rivales.*
1583, June. *Dido.*

1582. *Julius Cæsar.* See GEDDES.

1582. *Nectar et Ambrosia.* See CAMPION, E.

Before 1591. *Bellum Grammaticali.* See SPENSE.

ii. *Tempore* JAMES I.

At Christ Church.

1603. *Nero.*
1606, Aug. 29. *Vertum-*
nus.   } See GWYNNE. These plays were acted by Johnians, who joined Christ Church in acting as early as 1583. See *Rivales.*

ANON. 2, 1605, Aug. 27. *Alba*, P. (also called *Vertumnus*, but not Gwynne's play), performed before the King. Much like one at King's, Cambridge. Five or six men in it were nearly naked, which was much disliked by the Queen and her ladies. The rustical songs and dances were tedious. The King would have left before half were finished, *i.e.*, about 11 P.M., had not the Chancellors of both Universities entreated him earnestly. Nichols *James*, i. 549. See I. JONES.

At Magdalen.

ANON. 3, 1605, Aug. 28. *Ajax Flagellifer*, in goodly antique apparel, and in which "the stage varied three times." But not so well acted as at Cambridge, *q.v.*, 1564. Very tedious to all, especially the King. See I. JONES.

1618. *Theomachia.* See HEYLIN.

At Hart Hall

614. *Spurius.* See HEYLIN.

iii. *Tempore* CHARLES I.

At St. John's.

1630. *Hermophus.*
1635, Feb. 5. *Euphormus.* } See WILDE.

At some College unknown, and of uncertain date.

ANON. 4. *Fucus sive Histriomastix*, MS.
ANON. 5. *Antoninus Bassianus Caracalla*, T., MS. Rawl., C., 590.   } Bodleian.
ANON. 6. *Perfidus Hetruscus*, T.   MS. Rawl., C., 787.
ANON. 7. *Thibaldus sive Vindictæ ingenium*, T., 1640. Oxford. Scene, Iberia or Arragon.

B. University, Unknown.

i. *Tempore* Elizabeth.

1570. *Byrsa Basilica.*   See Rickets.

Anon. 8, 1581, Mar. *Solyman.*   Brit. Mus., *MS. Lansd.,*
723.   *Mustapha filius Solymanni regis* is a chief character.

1596. *Amores Perinthi et Tyantes.*   See Burton.

Anon. 9. *Sapientia Salamonis*, T. C.   *MS.* Bright sale,
225.

ii. *Tempore* James I.

Anon. 10, 1620. *Sophomorus*, C.   *Bliss MSS.*

1619. *Aluredus.* ⎫
1619. *Mars.*   ⎬ See Drury.
1619. *Reparatus.*⎭

iii. *Tempore* Charles I.

Anon 11, 1635. *Senilis Amor.*   *MS. Rawl.*, Poet, 9.
Query by Peter Hausted, who wrote *Senile Odium*, q.v.

Silvia.   See Kynder.

Mercurius Britannicus.   See Braithwaite.

iv. Of Unknown Date.

Adrasta parentans.   See Mease.

Anon. 12. *Fatum Vortigerni.*   Brit. Mus., *MS. Lansd.,*
723.

Anon. 13. *Fraus pia. MS. Sloane*, 1855.   Scene, London.

Anon. 14. *Lusiuncula.*   Plot from the Macbeth story.

Anon. 15. *Nottola.   Douce MSS.*, 47.   Scene, Ferrara.

Anon. 16. *Sanctus Edwardus Confessor.*   See *Bibl. Heber,*
xi. 113.   Query *temp.* James I (as Halliwell thinks); and
if so, at which University was it presented to him?   I take
it to be a Latin play from the title.   I know nothing more
of it.

Tomumbeius.   See SALTERNE.

C. AT CAMBRIDGE.

i. *Tempore* ELIZABETH.

At King's.

1564. *Dido.*   See HALLIWELL.
1598, 1602. *Leander.*   See JOHNSON.

At Trinity.

1586. *Ricardus* 3.   See LACEY.
Before 1591. *Pedantius.*   See WINGFIELD.

At St. John's.

1579. *Richardus* 3.   See LEGGE.
1588. *Terminus et Non.*   See NASH.

Microcosmus. ⎫
Mundus Plumbeus. ⎭ See ARTHUR.

At Clare Hall.

ANON. 17, c. 1590. *Tararantantara.*   See under NASH.

At Peterhouse.

ANON. 18, c. 1590. *Duns Furens,* Dick Harvey in a
frenzy.   See NASH.

At Queen's.

ANON. 18*, 1590. *Lælia. MS. Lambeth,* 838.   Acted
1598, after Aug. 4, when the Earl of Essex was chosen
Chancellor of Cambridge.   Fuller, *History of the University
of Cambridge,* p. 156.

At some College unknown.

ANON. 3, 1564, Aug. 9.   *Ajax Flagellifer.*   Intended to
be presented to Elizabeth, but she was too tired.   This was

merely a translation from Sophocles, and is inserted here solely to avoid the reader's being misled by Halliwell's inaccurate statements. See also *supra*, Oxford, 1605.

After 1567. *Herodes.* See GOLDINGHAM.

1596. *Hispanus.* See MORRELL.

1596. *Silvaney.* See ROLLINSON.

1597. *Machiavellus.* See WIBURNE.

1598. *Leander* was acted, and again in 1602. MS. copies in Univ. and Emanuel Libraries; Brit. Mus., *MS. Sloane*, 1762; Bodl., *MS. Rawl. Misc.*, 341. The name William Johnson on this last is probably that of its owner, W. J., of King's, *q.v.* This play, I think, was acted at Trinity, as "*Leander, Labyrinth,* and *Loiala*" are united in the Prologue, quoted Nichols (*James*), iii. 836.

ii. *Tempore* JAMES I.

At Sidney Sussex?

1616. *Julius Cæsar.* See MAY.

At St. John's.

1612. *Homo.* See ATKINSON.

1612. *Atalanta.* See PARSONS.

1615, Mar. 7. *Æmilia.* See CECIL.

At Trinity.

ANON. 19, 1613, Mar. *Adelphe,* C., before Prince Charles and the Count Palatine. It lasted six hours, and the Court slept. MS. Trin. Coll., Camb.

1613, Mar. 3. *Sciros.* } See BROOKES.
1615, Mar. 10. *Melanthe.* }

After Feb. 1616. *Fraus Honesta.* See STUBBE.

1623, Shrovetide. *Labyrinthus.* See HAWKESWORTH.

1623, Feb. 28. *Loyola.* See HACKETT.

At Clare Hall.

1615, Mar. 8. *Ignoramus.*   See RUGGLE.

iii. *Tempore* CHARLES I.

At St John's.

ANON. 20 [1627]. *Stoicus Vapulans,* c. 1648. "An allegory of the passions." My reason for the conjectural date is that it was published with *Paria, Loiola,* and *Cancer.* *"Typis,* R. C. *Impensis,* Andr. Crooke," 1648.

At Trinity.

1627, Mar. *Paria.*   See VINCENT.
1632. *Roxana.*   See ALABASTER.
1638, Feb. *Naufragium joculare.*   See COWLEY.

At King's.

1638. *Valetudinarium.*   See JOHNSON.

At Queen's.

1633. *Senile Odium.*   See HAUSTED.

At some College unknown.

ANON. 21 [1627]. *Cancer,* 1648.   For date see *Stoicus Vapulans.*
1631. *Versipelles.*   See PESTELL.
1631. *Zeno.*   See SIMON.
Cornelianum Dolium.   See RANDOLPH.

OF UNKNOWN DATE.

At King's.

ANON. 22. *Pastor Fidus.*   Univ. MS., Ff. ii. 9.

At some unknown College.

ANON. 23. *Hymenæus*, C.   MS. in St. John's Library.

Pseudomasia.   See MEWE.

Clitophon.   See AINSWORTH.

Euribates.   See CROUSE.

ANON. 24. *Catilina Triumphans*, C.   MS. in Trinity Library.   Seventeenth century.

ANON. 25. *Leo Armenus* sive Ludit in humanis divina potentia rebus, T.   MS. in the University Library.

ANON. 26. *Parthenia*, P.   MS. in Emanuel Library.

ANON. 27. *Zelotypus*, C.   MS. in Emanuel Library.   It has a list of the student actors.

TRANSLATORS.

I HAVE taken no note of translators, who wrote no original plays, in the body of this work; but the following list, which does not pretend to completeness, may have some use :—

BRISTOWE, FRANCIS. *King Freewill,* T., 1635. MS. From the French, *Roy Franc Arbitre*, T., 1558, translated from the Italian.

CODDRINGTON, ROBERT. *Ignoramus,* C., 1662. See RUGGLE.

D. D[YMOCK]. *The Faithful Shepherd*, T. C., 1602, 1633. From Guarini, *Il Pastor Fido*.

ELIZABETH, QUEEN. A *play* of Euripides'.

FRAUNCE, ABRAHAM. *Amyntas*, P., 1591. From Tasso, *Aminta*.

GOLDING, ARTHUR. *Abraham's Sacrifice*, T., 1577. From Beza.

GOLDSMITH, FRANCIS. *Sophompaneas,* or *Joseph*, T., n.d. [c. 1630]. From Grotius.

HERBERT, MARY, Countess of Pembroke. *Antonius*, T., 1592. From the French. Query, Beliard's *Les Delicieux Amours de Marc Antoine et de Cleopatre*. Called *Antonie* 1595. Written 1590, Nov. 26. See DANIEL.

HEYWOOD, JASPER. *Thyestes*, T., 1561. *Hercules Furens*, T., 1561. *Troas*, T., 1559. From Seneca. Much altered.

KYFFIN, MAURICE. *Andria*, C., 1588. From Terence.

MABBE, JAMES. See p. 57, vol. ii.

NEVILL, ALEXANDER. *Œdipus*, T., 1581. Written 1560. From Seneca.

NEWMAN, THOMAS. *Andria*, C., 1627. From Terence.
Eunuch, C., 1627. From Terence.

NEWTON, THOMAS. *Thebais*, T., 1581. From Seneca.

NICHOLAS, HARRY. The Enterlude of *Minds*, n.d. [1574, *Biog. Dram.*]. From the Low Dutch.

NUCE, THOMAS. *Octavia*, T., 1581. From Seneca.

R., T. *The Extravagant Shepherd*, P. C., 1654. From Corneille.

S., J. *Filli di Sciro*, P., 1655 (written c. 1635). From Bonarelli. This J. S. (who is not James Shirley) I take to be the same man as the author of *Andromana* and *The Prince of Priggs' Revels*, C., 1651.

SANDYS, GEORGE. *Christ's Passion*, T., 1640. From Grotius.

STANLEY, THOMAS. *The Clouds*, C., 1656. From Aristophanes.

STUDLY, JOHN. *Medea*, T., 1563. *Agamemnon*, T., 1581. *Hercules Œtæus*, T., 1581. *Hippolytus*, T., 1581. All from Seneca.

WARNER, WILLIAM. *Menœchmi*, C., 1595. From Plautus.

ADDENDA

BARKER, THOMAS.

To this author (who wrote on angling, 1651–7) some catalogues attribute *The Bloody Banquet*.   See DRUE.

BEARD, Dr. THOMAS.

Oliver Cromwell's schoolmaster.   To him has been attributed *Pedantius*.   See WINGFIELD.

BOURNE, WILLIAM.

1*. 1601, Dec. 20–24.   *Judas*, with S. Rowley.

BURTON, WILLIAM, *q.v.*

Brother of Robert Burton, author of *The Anatomy of Melancholy*.   He was born at Lindley, Leicestershire, 1575, Aug. 24.   His autobiography was printed by Nichols, 1811, in his *History of Leicestershire*.

CAMPION, EDMOND, *q.v.*

Born in London 1540 Jan.   Educated at Christ's Hospital; scholar of St. John's, Oxford, at its foundation, 1557; M.A. 1564; Junior Proctor 1568; went to Ireland and wrote its history; became Jesuit at Rome 1573; was sent to Vienna; wrote his *Nectar et Ambrosia;* returned to England; in 1581 printed his *Rationes decem* at Henley, Oxfordshire (privately); was executed at Tyburn for treason 1581, Dec. 1.   Compare MONDAY, ANTONY.

CAREY, HENRY: VISCOUNT FALKLAND.   (Play.)

1. *The Marriage Night*, T., 1664.

Not acted; reprinted in *Dodsley*.

Carey was born 1610; killed in the battle of Newbury 1643, Sept. 20.   Said in Dodsley's preface to have written the Epilogue to Rochester's *Valentinian*, *i.e.*, in 1685!

DAVENPORT, ROBERT.

The Pirate. Not printed (Malone, *Attempt to ascertain the dates of Shakespeare's plays*, p. 331).

GARFIELD, BENJAMIN. (Play).

Robert Baron, in *Pocula Castalia*, 1650, p. 112, addressed verses to his friend Garfield on the under-mentioned play.

1. *The Unfortunate Fortunate*, T. C.

GOVELL, R. (Mask.)

This untitled mask was destroyed by Warburton's servant.

GREVILLE and GREENE should be transposed, p. 250.

HEYWOOD, THOMAS. (*Addendum.*)

Halliwell, blindly following *Biog. Dram.* as usual, says *Fast bind [and] fast find* is "a play by Heywood, mentioned in Gabriel Harvey's *Pierce's Supererogation*, 1593." I should be only too glad to have proof that T. Heywood had written a play at this date, but Harvey's words, "Epicharmus' incredulity, Dion's apistie, or Heywood's Fast bind and fast find" certainly do not justify the assumption that anything more than phrases are intended. Did Epicharmus write a play called *Incredulity*, or Dion one called *Apistie?* Halliwell probably would have answered, Yes; I say, No: nor do I know which Heywood Harvey referred to, although *Biog. Dram.* puts its *addendum* under Thomas Heywood.

HUNNIS, WILLIAM. (Devices and (?) Plays.)

Gentleman of the Chapel-Royal under Edward 6 and Mary; succeeded R. Edwards at his death, 1566, Nov. 15, as Master of the Chapel children; obtained a grant of arms (*armes parlantes*, as usual) from Dethick 1568, Feb. 14: "Bendy of six, Or and Azure, a Unicorn [Hunni-corn] rampant Vert, armed Argent. Crest; on a wreath, between two honeysuckles [Hunni-suckles] proper, a Unicorn's head couped, Or, charged with two bendlets azure." Wrote poems, for which see Lowndes, Warton, &c. Died 1597, June 6, and was succeeded by Nathanael Giles.

He was one of the device-makers for *The Princely Plea-sures of Kenilworth,* q.v., and I have little doubt one of the authors of the plays performed by the Chapel children 1570–82. The fact that the inhibition of the Chapel boys was removed at his death points to some offence given by them at their last performance, 1582, Dec. 26, in *The Game of Cards.* They were then restrained, and do not appear again *at Court* till 1601, though they certainly performed elsewhere. See my *History of the Stage.*

J., B.

1. Massinger's *Bashful Lover* is in some old catalogues ascribed to B. J. or Ben Jonson; in my opinion, through some confusion with *The City Madam,* q.v.

2. *Guy, Earl of Warwick,* q.v., was published 1661 as "by B. J.," evidently intended for Ben Jonson, and no doubt fraudulently.

LATEWARE, Dr. RICHARD.   (University.)

Born in London 1560; educated at Merchant Taylors School; entered at St. John's, Oxford, 1580; M.A. 1588; Rector of Hopton, Suffolk; Proctor 1593; Rector of Finch-ley, Middlesex; D.D.; chaplain to Lord Montjoy; was shot at Benburb 16th July 1601; died 17th July, and was buried at Armagh.

Daniel, in his *Apology for Philotas,* mentions his play on the same argument presented at St. John's, Oxford, "above eight years since;" *i.e.,* before 1599; probably c. 1588. The play is not now known.

LEE, ROBERT.   (Actor.)

This actor *may* have been the author of *The Miller,* q.v.

MARLOW, CHRISTOPHER.

10. *The Massacre of France* [Paris] was bought of Allen by Henslow for the Admiral's men 18th Jan. 1602.

MIDDLETON, THOMAS.   (*Addendum.*)

This notice was written before Mr. A. H. Bullen's edition appeared, and printed before I had an opportunity of examining it. It would be most unfair to him to omit the additions he has made to Dyce.   These are:—

The travels of Sir Robert Shirley, entered S. R. 1609, May 30, for John Budge, with the note, "He saith it is authorised by master Etkins," and issued 1609 with a long-tailed title, *Sir Robert Shirley sent ambassador*, &c.; reprinted 1810 in *Harl. Misc.*, vol. v.   Mr. Bullen does not give the S. R. entry.   The dedication to Sir T. Shirley is signed Thomas Midleton.

The Peacemaker, or Great Britain's blessing, printed by T. Purfoot, 1618 : some copies have 1619.   "The sole printing and publishing" was licensed to William Alley 1618, July 19 (*Calendar of Domestic State Papers*), as of a book by T. Middleton, but the book seems from its contents to be meant to be taken by the public as of royal authorship. The name of Alley I do not find anywhere in S. R.   Purfoot at this time occurs in many entries as printer and publisher of *Briefs of letters patents for losses by sea and land*, and was, therefore, probably employed by the Court.   Mr. Bullen does not notice this discrepancy between the licensed and the actual publishers.

Annales of London, beginning 1620; MS.; mentioned by Oldys.   See Bullen, p. li.

46*. *An Invention for the Service of the Rt. Hon. Edward Barkham, Lord Mayor*, at his entertainment of the Aldermen, &c., at his house in the Easter holidays 1623. Printed from MS. in the Conway papers (*State Papers, Domestic*, cxxix.).   But Barkham was Mayor 1621–2, Proby 1622–3, according to the lists.   There is either a mistake of date, 1623 for 1622, or Barkham's Mayoralty extended over one year, and Proby was elected at his vacating office (? by death) in 1623, after Easter. This difficulty (apparently not known to Mr. Bullen) is worth notice, because no pageant is extant for Proby's Mayoralty.

Middleton's Farrago, c. 1625–7 ; MS. ; mentioned by Oldys. See Bullen, p. li.

In my article on Middleton, 39* is inadvertently placed among the shows and 47 among the plays. Please correct.

48. *A Game at Chess (addendum)*. Mr. Bullen most cleverly identifies the Black Duke with Olivarez, the Black Bishop's Pawn with Father John Floyd, the White King's Pawn with Sir Toby Matthew, the White Bishop with Archbishop[1] Abbot, the Black Bishop with the Archbishop of Toledo. With all these successful identifications he might have credited me with those of the White Duke and the White Knight, and with drawing his attention to Dyce's deficiency in this matter. But a still more important service to the student than any of these identifications has been rendered by Mr. Bullen by his fixing the tracts which were used by Middleton as materials for this play, viz. :—

1. *Vox Populi*, by T. Scott, 1620.

1622, May 11. *The Anatomy of the English Nunnery at Lisbon*, by T. Robinson.

2. *Vox Populi*, by T. Scott, 1624.

1624, May 1 (cf. entry of Mar. 20). *The foot out of the snare*, by J. Gee.

1624, May 24. *New shreds of the old snare*, by J. Gee.

To these I would add—

---

[1] In p. 106 there is a bad *lapsus* of mine. I wrote this Middleton notice next to that on Jonson, and having my head full of Bishop Williams, wrote Archbishop Williams for Archbishop Abbot. Williams, of course, was never Archbishop. I may add that pp. 97–160 of this volume had to be sent to press when I was away from home, and from all books of reference. This was not through any fault of negligence on my part.

1622. Sept. 20. *The Friar's Chronicle . . . enlarging far more . . . than 'the Anatomy of the Nunnery at Lisbon' . . .*

For all these S. R. dates I am responsible: Mr. Bullen does not notice them. It is with the deepest regret that, after noting such valuable additions to our knowledge of Middleton, I feel bound to record that Mr. Bullen has, in this same book, p. xc., stated that "Mr. Fleay injures his own credit by his habit of jumbling fact and fiction[1] to-

---

[1] I have this day, 31st Aug. 1891, accidentally come across an instance of the way in which accusations of mingling "fact with fiction" are manufactured against me in certain "Societies," and as I hope never to return to the subject again, I trust the reader will pardon the insertion of this note. I trust also, since the Præpositus of these numerous Societies (for they, like the Jesuit seminaries, are all subject to one General) has a special liking for abbreviated appellations, such as Hell.-P. for Halliwell Phillips, and Pigsbrook for Swinburne, that I may be allowed to shorten his fuller title of Præpositus Imperio Generalis into P. G., and be spared the unpleasantness of having to designate him more particularly.

Sir H. Nicolas, in his *Life of Chaucer*, mentions two missions concerning a proposed marriage of Richard 2—one when he was Prince of Wales, in Feb. 1377, "with Mary, daughter of the King of France," who died in that year; the other, when he was king, "with a daughter of the French monarch," in Jan. 1378. In my *Guide to Chaucer*, p. 38, I, alluding to this other daughter, used the words "date 1378, as it refers to the Embassy concerning the marriage of Richard 2 to the French King's daughter," which were historically correct and exact. In the *Chaucer Society's publications*, Series ii., No. 12, p. 105 (no date, but in the issue for 1878), the P. G. writes : "The latest is Mr. Fleay's, of the corpse of the infant princess Mary of France ! Mr. Fleay dates the *Parlament* 1578, and makes its heroine the Princess Mary (*Guide to Chaucer and Spenser*, p. 38), not having taken the trouble to ascertain that she died, aged seven, in 1377." Having never mentioned or alluded to the Princess Mary, and being desirous of ascertaining the origin of this astonishing untruth, I, after some trouble, have just discovered that in *Trial Forewords*, p. 22, 1871, the P. G. himself had written : "1378, Jan. 16, Chaucer perhaps goes with the Embassy to France to negotiate a marriage with the French King's daughter Mary." I have not been able to find any other writer so ignorant as to mention Mary in this connexion, and this historical blunder will henceforth stand in literary history only to be paralleled by the well-known instance in which the dead Johnson was made to write the Preface for Dr. Latham's edition of his own *Dictionary*. On p. 407, two pages after his notice of Mary's corpse, the P. G. writes thus of Princess Isabella's daughter : 'Philippa, born in 1367, was betrothd [*sic*] in 1371 to Robert de Vere, Earl of Oxford,' and the 'marriage was effected in 2 Ric. ii.,' June 1379 to June 1380. . . . Their five children were, 1. *Roger*, . . . born 1374 . . . . 4. *Eliza-*

gether." This is a libellous attack on my moral character which neither deserves nor will receive refutation or retaliation. If gratitude has no influence on the heart of this New Shaksperian, surely respect for "his own credit" in every sense should restrain his effeminately facile pen. These personalities are out of place in books addressed to serious students, and ultimately come home to roost as surely as curses. I am thankful that I have never wittingly yielded to the temptation of making an unprovoked attack on any contemporary, and if any words of mine can be twisted into any semblance thereof, I will withdraw them with an apology. I have no space here to refute Mr. Bullen's further statements about me in this Introduction, but I may note that others fare no better at his hands. Mr. W. C. Hazlitt, p. 24, is accused of depriving Middleton of *The Black Book* and *Father Hubbard's Tale* without adducing "a grain of evidence." The only grain of evidence for his authorship is that they are by T. M., and no instance of Middleton's signing himself "T. M." has ever been adduced. Hazlitt pointed out that he invariably signs in full "Thomas Middleton," and this is evidence of a most weighty kind. Again, in p. lviii., he accuses Mr. Aldis Wright of "temerity" in assigning "some of the finest passages in *Macbeth*" to Middleton. I have always understood that Mr. W. G. Clark was responsible for this matter. It was purely through confidence in his judgment, which I had learned to value when he was my composition tutor at Cambridge in 1851, that I adopted his views in 1874; but immediately

---

beth, born . . . 1371." So that Philippa, according to the P. G., had a child by her husband at four years old, and five years before the marriage was effected. O Princess Mary,

"Make of your wifehood no comparison !
Philippa cometh, that all this may distain."

Of course these were really children of Philippa, daughter of Prince Lionel.

on reading Middleton, c. 1879, I withdrew my assent. Of this fact Mr. Bullen was informed by me before he published his edition. The parts of *Macbeth* which I assign to Middleton are the Hecate bits, iii. 5, iv. 1, 39–43 (forty lines in all), not the "finest passages." Finally, I am again indebted to Mr. Bullen's industry for the following *addenda* to Middleton's life: they should be inserted p. 89 :—

Middleton was admitted City Chronologer 1620, Sept. 6, at a salary of £6, 13s. 4d.; Nov. 10 this was raised to £10. On 17th April 1621 a Freedom was granted him towards his expenses, and on 7th May 1622 another for his better encouragement. On 17th Sept. 1622 he had a gift of £15 for his further encouragement, and of £20 on 6th Feb 1623. On 24th April 1623 another Freedom, and on 2nd Sept. £13, 13s. 4d. for his services at the shooting at Bunhill and the Conduit Head before the Lord Mayor. If the personalities were expunged and the views of apocryphal authorship revised, this edition of Mr. Bullen's would be his masterpiece.

P., R. See *Appius and Virginia*.

RANDOLPH, THOMAS.

The Prodigal Scholar. Entered S. R. 29th June, 1660.

SHAKESPEARE, WILLIAM.

Some reference numbers are accidentally duplicated; but as they are not used outside this article, it will lead to no inconvenience.

THOMPSON, THOMAS. (Plays.)

I do not know (not having seen the play) whether I am right in including *Mother Shipton*, by T. T. (*q.v.*), in the present work; but as Thompson's other play, *The English Rogue*, C., was acted (privately, I suppose) "before persons of honor," and not published till 1668, I ought probably to have omitted any notice of T. T.

ERRATA.

Vol. i. p. 16, line 6, insert "so" before "continually."

  ,,   ii. p. 149, line 6 (from bottom), read "acted *by the King's men.*"

  ,,   ii. p. 251, line 6, read "two masks *were also presented.*"

INDEX.

I. PLAYS, 1559–1583.

II. PLAYS, 1584–1642.

III. MASKS AND ENTERTAINMENTS.

IV. UNIVERSITY PLAYS. ENGLISH.

V. UNIVERSITY PLAYS. LATIN.

VI. MAYORS' PAGEANTS, 1585–1640.

VII. LIST OF AUTHORS CHRONOLOGICALLY ARRANGED UNDER THEIR COMPANIES.

1 Group.—*The Admiral's men*, 1587–1603 ; *Prince Henry's*, 1603–12 ; *Palsgrave's*, 1613–24 ; *Fortune*, 1625–31 ; *Prince Charles'*, 1632–42.
Porter, 1598–9 ; Wilson, junior, 1598–1600 ; Haughton, 1597–1602 ; Rankin, 1601 ; Wadeson, 1601 ; S. Rowley, 1601–24 ; Bird (Bourne), 1600–2 ; Robinson, 1599 ; Boyle, (?) 1600 ; Pett, (?) 1600 ; Singer, (?) 1602 ; Gunnel, 1623–4 ; Drue, 1624 ; Randolph, 1633 ; Heming, 1633.

2 Group.—*Paul's boys*, 1560–90 ; *Sussex'*, 1592–3 ; *Derby's*, 1599 ; *Paul's*, 1600–7 ; *King's Revels boys*, 1607–9 ; *Duke of York's*, 1610–12 ; *Prince Charles'*, 1613–25 ; *Outsiders*, 1625–36 [but from 1637 to 1642 the *Outsiders* seem to have incorporated with the *King's Revels*].
Ingeland, 1561 ; Fulwell, 1562 ; Percy, 1601–2 ; Barry, 1608 ; Machin, 1607 ; Mason, 1608 ; Jonson, junior, 1623 ; Richards, 1637 ; Rawlins, 1639 ; Jordan, 1641.

3 Group. — *Oxford's*, 1584–8 ; *Pembroke's*, 1589–97, 1600 ; *Worcester's* 1602–3 ; *Queen Anne's*, 1603–18 ; *Revels men*, 1619–23 ; *King's Revels*, 1629–36 ; *King's and Queen's* (*Beeston's boys*), 1637–42 ; Cooke, 1611 ; S. S., 1615 ; J. C., 1619 ; Tatham, 1641 ; Jordan, 1641.

4 Group.—*Chapel boys*, 1559–83 ; *Queen's*, 1583–91 ; *Chapel*, 1592–1603 ; *Queen's Revels*, 1603–13 ; *Lady Elizabeth's*, 1613–25 ; *Queen Henrietta's*, 1625–42.
Edwards, 1559–66 ; Still, 1562–3 ; R. B[ower], 1563 ; Preston, 1570, 1578 ; Gosson, c. 1576 ; Tarleton, 1583–8 ; Greene, 1587–91 ; Nash, 1592–7 ; Daniel, 1604–5 ; Sharpham, 1607 ; Daborne, 1610–13 ; H. Shirley, (?) 1616 ; May, 1620 ; Davenport, 1624 ; Rutter, 1635 ; A. Brome, c. 1635 ; Sharp, published 1640 ; Lovelace, 1637 ; Chamberlain, published 1640 ; Kirke, 1636.

5 Group.—*Leicester's*, 1586–8 ; *Strange's*, 1589–94 ; *Derby's*, 1594 ; *Chamberlain's*, 1594–6 ; *Hunsdon's*, 1596–7 ; *Chamberlain's*, 1597–1603 ; *King's*, 1603–42.
Shakespeare, 1589–1610 ; Kempe, 1592 ; Nicolls, 1611 ; Shank, 1623 ; Carlell, 1629–42 ; Cartwright, 1636 ; A. Wilson, 1633 ; H. Killigrew, 1634 ; Suckling, 1638 ; Mayne, 1639 ; Cavendish, 1640 ; Habington, 1640 ; T. Killigrew, 1041 ; Denham, 1641.

6 Group.—*Authors for other or unknown companies.*
Garter, 1560 ; Udal, 1561 ; Bale, 1563 ; Bower (Westminster), 1563 ; L. Wager, 1566 ; Pickering, 1567 ; Wilmot, 1568 ; W. Wager, 1566–71 ; Elderton (Westminster boys), 1572 ; Wapul, 1576 ; Lupton, 1577 ; Whetston, 1578 ; Woodes, 1581 ; Puttenham, 1588 ; Philip, 1599 ; Brandon, 1598 ; Yarrington, 1601 ; Vennard, 1602 ; Alexander, 1603–5 ; Brewer, 1604 ; Greville, 1608 ; E. Carew, 1612 ; Stephens, 1603 ; Tailor (Prentices), 1613 ; W. S., 1619 ; Le Grys, 1629 ; Cokain, 1631–3 ; Gomersal, 1628 ; Rider, 1630 ; Formido, 1633 ; M. W., 1633 ; Jones, 1635 ; Lovelace, 1636 ; J. D., 1639 ; Freeman, 1639 ; Lower, 1639 ; G. Cartwright, 1640 ; T. Ford, 1640 ; J. Gough, 1640 ; Harding, 1640 ; Manuche, 1640 ; Sharpe, before 1640 ; Stapylton, 1640 ; Witham, 1640 ; Swinhoe, 1640 ; L. W., T. W., M. W., 1640 ; J. W., 1639 ; T. T., n.d. ; Barclay, 1638 ; Burnell (Dublin), 1641 ; Jaques, 1642 ; Peaps! (published), 1649 ; Quarles (published), 1649 ; Burroughs (S. R.), 1646.

Beside the preceding authors who wrote for one company only, there are many who frequently changed their companies : these are given in the following table. The grouping is the same, and the dates sufficiently indicate the particular company intended in each case. Note that of all the authors of considerable importance Shakespeare is ·the only one who adhered to one company throughout his career :—

	I.	II.	III.	IV.	V.
Lilly . . .	—	1587-9	—	1580-3	—
Peele . . {	1594-7	—	—	1582 1588-90	1590
Wilson, sen. .	—	—	—	1583-9	1590
Lodge . . .	1587	—	--	1587-91	1595-9
Kyd . . .	—	—	1589	1587-8	—
Marlow . .	1587-8	—	1589-92	1588-9	1593
Dekker . .	1587-1604	1601, 1623	1602-10: 1623	1622	1601
Monday . .	1599-1600	—	1588	—	—
Heywood . .	1594-1603	—	1602-9	1622-1634	1634-5
Chapman . .	1594-9	1604	—	1603-8	—
Hathway . .	1598-1601	—	1602-3	—	—
Chettle . .	1598-1603	—	1602-3	—	—
Drayton . .	1598-1602	—	—	—	1597: 1602-5
Jonson . . {	1597:1602	—	—	1598: 1600-1 1605, 1609 1614, 1633	1598-9: 1603-5 1610-11: 1617-32
Marston . .	1599	1600-1	—	1602-5	—
Day	1599-1603	1608: 1623	1607: 1623	1606	—
Smith, Went.	1601-2	—	1602-3	—	—
Webster . .	1601-2	1602-5	1605-10	—	1612
Middleton {	1602, 1610	1600: 1608 1617-21	1602-3	1604-7: 1622-3	1623-7
Armin . . .	—	1608	—	—	1599-1610
Barkstead .	—	1608?: 1616	—	1609-13	—
Wilkins . .	—	—	1607	—	1604-7
Tourneur . .	—	—	—	1613	1605-11
Barnes . . .	—	1624	—	—	1605
Rowley, W. .	—	1617-21	1607	1607: 1617-23	1623-27
Beaumont .	—	1607	—	1608-10	1611-13
Fletcher . .	--	—	—	1608-10: 1613-16	1611-13: 1616-25
Field . . .	—	—	—	1610-16	1616-19
Massinger . .	—	—	1620	1613-16: 1626-7	1617-22: 1627-39
Markham . .	—	1608	—.	1620	—
Smith, Will	—	—	1612: 1623	—	1614
Sampson . .	—	1625	1620	—	—
Bonen . . .	1623	—	—	1623	—
Brome . . .	—	1623: 1640-1	1635	1636-8	1629-34
Ford . . .	1624	—	1638	1621-7	1628: 1633
Shirley. . .	—	—	1632	1625-36	1640-2
Davenant . .	—	1641-2	—	—	1627-39
Nabbes . .	—	1638	1633-4	1632: 1635	—
Marmion . .	1631-2	—	—	1639	—
Glapthorne .	—	1637-39	1635	—	1639
Killigrew, T.	—	—	—	1637	1641
Kirke . . .	1637	—	—	1636	—

AFTERWORD

DURING the revision of the proofs of this book I have noted two points that demand notice, if not apology, from me: 1. The fragmentary appearance of some of the notes on plays, which could have been easily avoided by expansion, but at the expense of making the book three volumes instead of two: this, I think, the student will forgive me. 2. The apparent contradiction in some as yet doubtful questions, such as the identification of the play called *Abuses*, or the " second pen," mentioned in Shakespeare's *Sonnets*; this is, however, intentional; I thought it better to send forth the arguments for rival hypotheses, and leave the decision to the reader, than to espouse one of them where doubt is at present unavoidable, and to advance my own opinion too decidedly, and so expose myself to a renewed charge of claiming infallibility. I am fully conscious of the limits of the weakness, of all human intellectual effort, and the only claim I make is that I have spared no pains in what must be to me an unremunerative but yet a grateful task, because it has been self-imposed.

I have also to gratefully acknowledge the receipt of corrections for my former book (mostly errata in printing) from Mr. H. A. Evans of Westward Ho, and Mr. W. Young, one of the Governors of Dulwich College, and author of a very valuable history of that institution. My obligations to Mr. J. Greenstreet I have already noticed. Finally, I must express my fear that the Index, in spite of long-continuous labour, is not perfect. Although the book has been in the printer's hands since April last, it is not till September that I get proofs of this Index, and the exigencies of the publishing season do not allow me time for a thorough revision. I do not, however, anticipate either numerous or serious mistakes, as I took great pains in drawing it up.